Development, Markets, and Institutions

Collected Papers in Theoretical Economics

Volume I

Development, Markets, and Institutions

KAUSHIK BASU

UNIVERSITY PRESS

OXFORD
UNIVERSITY PRESS

YMCA Library Building, Jai Singh Road, New Delhi 110001

Oxford University Press is a department of the University of Oxford.
It furthers the University's objective of excellence in research, scholarship,
and education by publishing worldwide in

Oxford New York

Auckland Cape Town Dar es Salaam Hong Kong Karachi Kuala Lumpur
Madrid Melbourne Mexico City Nairobi New Delhi Shanghai Taipei Toronto

With offices in

Argentina Austria Brazil Chile Czech Republic France Greece
Guatemala Hungary Italy Japan South Korea Poland Portugal
Singapore Switzerland Thailand Turkey Ukraine Vietnam

Oxford is a registered trade mark of Oxford University Press
in the UK and in certain other countries

Published in India
By Oxford University Press, New Delhi

© Oxford University Press 2005

The moral rights of the author have been asserted
Database right Oxford University Press (maker)

ISBN 019 566761 1

Typeset in Adobe Garamond 10.5/12 by Jojy Philip, New Delhi, 110 027
Printed by Pauls Press, New Delhi 110 020
Published by Manzar Khan, Oxford University Press
YMCA Library Building, Jai Singh Road, New Delhi 110 001

Contents

1 Introduction

1.1. BY WAY OF PREFACE

One subject that would certainly figure among the sub-disciplines of economics that have witnessed dramatic change over the last few decades is development. Its concerns were always large, but the early studies in development were long-winded and unstructured, stemming no doubt from the frustration of having to deal with a very hard and important subject with hardly any instruments of analysis. Hence many precious ideas lay tucked away in long essays and books and failed to attract the attention they deserved.

All this has changed in recent decades. Economists working on development have discovered ways to modify the tools of economic theory and econometrics to the needs of their discipline. And, equally, advances in economic theory, especially the rise of game-theoretic methods and strategic analysis, and the availability of new data sets have made it easy for the researcher to find the instruments and statistics needed for the task at hand. But despite this greater ease, the subject is now emerging as one of the most challenging sub-disciplines of economics. It makes use of the latest techniques of analysis available but, at the same time, the subject matter pertaining to some of the most interesting questions is so amorphous that one cannot get away by simply being a good technician. The intellectual challenge of the discipline will hopefully attract some of the best minds in economics and that will be fortunate because development economics deals with some of the most compelling questions of our times, namely, how to provide minimal prosperity and a decent standard of living to the deprived and dispossessed, most of whom live in poor countries, often euphemistically called developing nations.

I was lucky to have come into the field at such an interesting juncture. It would not be too far from the truth to describe my development economics as 'picked up from the streets'. As a graduate student at the London School of Economics I had not taken any course in development and had only a tangential interest in the subject. My PhD was on rational choice and welfare economics, and my main interests were those of an economic theorist. I use the term 'economic theorist' in its original sense, to describe someone interested in the analytical foundations of economics and the general principles which apply to economies irrespective of their location in time and place, and not in the sense in which it is nowadays often used, to describe someone with moderate competence in mathematics and a demonstrable lack of interest in economics.

My serious engagement with development economics arose on my return to India. And this was not so much from reading journals and scholarly texts as from talking to people in the streets, straining my ears to catch other people's conversations in buses and trains, chatting with shopkeepers and workers, and from everyday events and news. My main interest was in trying to fit in the bits and pieces of information thus gathered into some coherent form, and also to check them out against the body of mainstream theory that I had been taught in London and, before that, in Delhi.

In the early 1980s I also began reading extensively and exploring the development literature, starting with the classics of the post World War II period, such as the writings of Ragnar Nurkse, Paul Rosenstein-Rodan, Tibor Scitovsky, Albert Hirschman and Arthur Lewis. Out of this theorist's effort to find coherence between what I was reading and what I was seeing emerged my book *The Less Developed Economy: A Critique of Contemporary Theory* (Blackwell, 1984). It was well received and spurred me on to invest more time on development economics and to write papers on it, a fair selection of which appears in this book.

In putting together a book of previously published papers, it is customary to justify one's decision by shelving the laws of arithmetic and asserting that a collection of papers somehow adds up to more than the total of each paper counted separately. In my case it must be admitted that Oxford University Press's interest in publishing such a collection seemed reason enough. But even though that is a sufficient reason, there is, fortunately, another more respectable one. Despite the march of information technology, for a vast majority of people, especially for students in developing countries, it remains notoriously hard to access journals. I hope that this collection of my main papers in development economics, previously published in many disparate fora, will make the task of access easier for the reader. A companion volume, *Collected Theoretical Papers, Volume 2: Rationality, Games and Strategic Behaviour* (Oxford University Press) collates another set of my papers in another field, in which I got interested a little later but which has since been of abiding interest.

1.2. MEASURING DEVELOPMENT

Thanks to my early training in social choice theory and axiomatic methods, I have always had an interest in what is at times called 'evaluative statistics', namely the problem of developing indices to capture different aspects of performance of a developing economy. This work, thanks to its methodology, sits somewhat uncomfortably in development economics but is at the same time quite germane to it.

Policy makers, journalists, and politicians keep referring to different indices to praise or castigate economies and sectors. Because of this, the specific indices used make an enormous difference to policy. If the index of choice for measuring a nation's overall development is per capita GNP, then over time this becomes the index that policy makers and even the people strive to enhance. This can shift our attention away from the special problems of the poor and deprived who may need help more than anybody else. The works of Anthony Atkinson, Amartya Sen, and many others, including the now well-known effort of the UNDP to develop a 'human development index' were efforts to correct for precisely this bias. Chapter 2 in this volume is a contribution along the same route.

This chapter, some of the main ideas of which I had originally developed in a report I wrote for the United Nations Development Programme (UNDP) and then developed further when Gerald Meier and Joseph Stiglitz invited me to contribute to a volume they were editing, argues that instead of per capita income, we should evaluate the economic well-being of a nation using the per capita income of the poorest 20 per cent of the nation or the 'quintile income'. And likewise, growth rate should be measured by the growth rate of the per capita income of the poorest 20 per cent people. This has at times been misread as a suggestion to ignore other indicators of well-being such as literacy, mortality, and morbidity. But that was not the idea behind my case for looking at the quintile income. My suggestion was that in most places where we used per capita incomes to evaluate performance, it would be better to use quintile incomes instead. This paper, which also examines other problems of development policy making, such as the much-neglected problem of interdependence of morality ('If everybody takes a bribe so will I'; 'If others paid their taxes, I would happily do so') and, relatedly, the interdependence of international labour standards policy, is analytically straight-forward to the point of being what is often pejoratively called journalistic. The reason for including it here and that too as an opening chapter is my belief that it addresses policy issues that can actually influence human welfare. Hence this is an effort to thrust it under the nose of those who actually make policy.

Chapters 3 and 4 are axiomatic exercises that take a tradition developed in the area of measuring poverty and inequality to newer domains, namely those of measuring a population's aging and a society's effective literacy. Consider two countries that have a 50 per cent literacy rate, but with one country having 50 per cent of each household literate and another having 50 per cent of households fully literate and 50 per cent of households with no literate members. It is easy to agree that the second country is much more severely disadvantaged than the first, where each person, in principle, has access to a household member who is literate. Pamphlets distributed by extension workers, prescriptions written down by doctors are likely to be much more effective in the first country. It is this concern for how literates are distributed across households that led James Foster and me to investigate the possibility of developing new measures of *effective literacy*. The paper that emerged from this, 'On Measuring Literacy' (Chapter 3 in this book), develops a new measure and characterizes it by a set of axioms and checks out its implications with the 1981 Indian census data. Subsequent work by other economists has tended to confirm *effective literacy* to be a better determinant of human welfare than the standard literacy rate, but it has also suggested ways of modifying and extending the measure we had suggested.

The aging of populations has been of concern primarily to industrialized nations but now, increasingly, even to poor countries like China and India. Demographers usually measure a nation's aging in terms of the percentage of people aged above 65 years. Such measures of course miss out on the fact that in recent times, not only has the above-65 population increased in many countries, but the average age of the people above the age of 65 has also gone up. The problem is akin to the one faced by the head-count index of poverty, which ignores the depth of poverty of those who are poor. The paper 'The Greying of Populations: Concepts and Measurement' (Chapter 4 in this book), written jointly with Alaka Basu, exploits this analogy and develops more sophisticated measures of population aging.

1.3. INSTITUTIONS, NORMS, AND POWER

One of the most exciting areas of theoretical research in economics—and indeed the implications of this go well beyond development—is the analysis of institutions, social norms, and power. The demands here are, at one level, minimal. There is hardly any scope for the use of standard techniques; and, as a consequence, there is little by way of a well-developed body of systematic work that one needs to master to get into this field. Yet, and perhaps for some of these same reasons, this is a hard area, where one has to use careful observation and combine it with deductive reasoning to inch forward. Indeed, one of the reasons traditional economics has been so silent on these important topics is the difficulty of using standard research methods in this field. The absence of writings on them (at least till very recent times) has had the unfortunate effect of making many well-trained economists forget that these are important topics in the real world. Fortunately, there is now a surge of interest in this field, which forms a meeting ground for economics with other social sciences.

Power and influence, we all know, are extremely important in life. They are also closely related to the world of money. Power often arises from wealth and can, in turn, contribute to a person's ability to muster up wealth. Power and influence can help commerce and trade and, at the same time, give rise to oppression and inequality. But what is power and what is its mainspring? My papers, 'One Kind of Power' and 'A Theory of Association: Social Status, Prices and Markets' (especially the former), written in the mid-1980s and reproduced here as Chapters 5 and 6, deal with these questions. I use the term 'deal with' deliberately, for I really do not manage to give any definitive answers. Drawing on the earlier works of Vaclav Havel and George Akerlof, Chapter 5 argues that a crucial element of understanding an important and pervasive form of power is to recognize that relations between two trading or contracting parties can often be influenced in fairly direct ways by each of their relations with uninvolved 'third parties'. Inspired by the work of the sociologist Georg Simmel this chapter argues that, whereas much of standard economics is 'dyadic', to understand certain social phenomena, such as power and influence, it is important to construct 'triadic models' of human interaction, where a third party (or, for that matter, fourth and fifth …) can influence the relation between the two directly involved in trade or exchange.

In Chapter 6, institutional matters come in in a somewhat different way. It is arguable that there are certain goods and services for which the value depends on the mechanism by which the product is distributed. Consider a prize or a driving licence. A prize is meant to go to the most deserving by some criterion and a licence is supposed to go to someone who passes a driving test. The prize and the driving licence of course have market value and people have been known to 'buy' them, but if they are routinely sold to the highest bidder, they will cease to be valuable. This is because their value depends on their being distributed by non-market mechanisms. The recognition that there are goods and services like this has important implications for understanding the functioning of the economy and crafting policy. The popular prescription from market fundamentalists that all products should be sold through the market, that is, to the highest bidder, now rings hollow. It can also help us understand important social phenomena, such as 'Sanskritization', the quest for social status, and the sustenance of caste norms.

My paper, 'Civil Institutions and Evolution: Concepts, Critique, and Models' (reproduced here as Chapter 7), written much later than the other two papers in this section, is concerned with similar issues but uses very different methods of analysis. The aim of this paper was to understand why certain norms persist and others die out and the method that I used was that of evolutionary game theory. I have had a certain ambivalence about this method. Evolution is, undoubtedly, extremely important for understanding social and economic phenomena; my doubts have been about whether evolutionary game theory, the way this has gone, is the right way to understand social evolution. In this chapter I present some of the rudiments of evolutionary game theory, closely scrutinize its assumptions, and then try to suggest new methodological directions to explore. In making these latter suggestions I do not think I have been successful; nevertheless the paper tried to grapple with some potentially important ideas and that is what prompted me to include it in this collection.

A society that is secluded from external aggressors or migrants over a certain period of time may develop norms which make it vulnerable when exposed to outsiders, who may not be endowed with those norms, occurs. If one society learns to respect queues and that becomes an accepted social norm, it may cease to be vigilant against queue-breakers. The entry of queue-breakers into such a society can cause havoc. I called this concept a 'normative loophole', to capture the idea of a society's vulnerability that arises from its having acquired a certain social norm. Though its modelling leaves room for improvement, it can shed light on important events like why imperialist nations so often overran large, densely-populated nations so effortlessly. The kind of aggression used by the conquering nations as well as the motivation for their behaviour were often so novel to the defending nations that they did not know the art of appropriate response, just as a person who habitually never breaks a queue may not realize until it is too late that the person edging in is about to break into the queue in front of him.

1.4. AGRARIAN ORGANIZATION

From the late 1980s my work on development acquired a somewhat unusual, empirical twist. This came from a series of informal field trips that some of my colleagues at the Delhi School of Economics and I organized with different batches of Master's students of the School to a village called Nawadih in the state of Jharkhand (then Bihar). These were typically four-day trips during which students collected data from the villagers on a variety of different aspects of agrarian economic relations.

The celebrated Indian anthropologist, M.N. Srinivas, after collecting meticulous data from a village over a long period of time, had the tragedy of losing all his field notes in a fire at Stanford. This forced him to write from memory. *The Remembered Village*, written without the appendage of scholarly footnotes and data, turned out to be one of the great classics of anthropology. Being aware of this history and an admirer of that book, I had toyed with the idea of holding our Nawadih data, once they were all collected, close to open flames in the hope that a spark would fly their way. But no such strategy was necessary. My main reason for organizing these field trips was not the data but to give my students and myself some experience of direct interaction with the tillers, traders, moneylenders, and borrowers who were the subject of so much of our textbook theorizing. The data collection was partly meant to be a pretext for such interaction and indeed the data that were collected turned out to be patchy and insufficient for statistical analysis. But fortunately, while the students went around with their pads and pens, some of my colleagues and I spent a disproportionate amount of time sipping tea and chatting with the villagers. The anthropology-style information that I picked up from these conversations and the day's-end interchange of information that we (the professors and the students) had every evening turned out to be extremely useful to me for my subsequent research on agrarian organization.

I owe several of my papers in this area to this experience. The paper, 'Limited Liability and the Existence of Share Tenancy' (reproduced as Chapter 13 in this volume) was a direct product of Nawadih and, in particular, conversations with a very poor 'landlord', Sukur Mian, who was blind and, thanks to this handicap, had no option but to lease out his little land to others.

My interest in agrarian organization often led me to issues very close to the concerns of modern industrial organization. Indeed I owe my subsequent interest and research in industrial organization to some problems of strategic decision making and moral hazard that I encountered in my development work. The paper, 'Technological Stagnation, Tenurial Laws, and Adverse Selection' (Chapter 8 here) and the one written with Clive Bell—'Fragmented Duopoly: Theory and Applications to Backward Agriculture' (Chapter 11 here)—certainly belong to this category. The latter paper tries to give a definition and build a formal model to interpret the oft-heard claim that markets in backward rural areas are 'fragmented'.

In the literature, fragmentation was then equated with little 'monopolistic islands'. So in formally capturing the idea of fragmentation, each moneylender, for instance, would be thought of as having his exclusive set of clients. This gave him monopoly power and allowed different moneylenders to charge different interest rates.

It seemed to us much more reasonable to assume that while some borrowers may have access to exactly one moneylender, there may also exist some who have access to more than one moneylender. Such a market structure was not one of separate monopolies, nor one of an oligopoly. We called this hybrid market structure a fragmented market and analysed its implications for the formation of prices and interest rates. The formation of interest rates is also the subject of the paper 'Disneyland Monopoly, Interlinkage, and Usurious Interest Rates' (Chapter 10 here). This was a model of conventional monopoly, but with the added feature that the monopolist could charge non-linear prices. It shed some interesting light on interlinkage and on the welfare properties of interlinked markets.

The paper, 'Market for Land: An Analysis of Interim Transactions' (Chapter 9 here), though it was written before the Nawadih fieldwork, is focused on a very real question that rural researchers in India had observed and puzzled about. This had to do with the fact that land sales are few and far between in India. Land sales are often associated with 'distress selling', an act of last resort when bad times come. The paper is an attempt to understand why this may be so. I believe that modern search models may give us better insights into this question now, but this was a model rooted in reality and, viewed as a stylized description of land markets in rural India, it may be of some interest.

Another enduring puzzle in the field of agrarian organization concerns 'surplus labour'. It has frequently been maintained that in backward agrarian economies, even when everyone seems to be employed, there is hidden unemployment, in the sense that removing some workers would leave total output unchanged. That is, some of the seemingly employed workers constituted 'surplus labour'. In case this was empirically true, as some studies had claimed, how was one to explain it? One route was to treat workers or their employers as irrational, which would explain why people with zero marginal productivity would still be working. In the mid-1960s there was some important research that explained surplus labour without abandoning the rationality assumption, but this usually made use of very special assumptions. My paper. 'The Broth and the Cooks: A Theory of Surplus Labour' (Chapter 12 here), is an attempt to understand surplus labour based on more general assumptions, by making use of the axiom that a worker's productivity, in a poor country, rises with his or her wage, since a higher wage leads to better nutrition.

1.5. INTERNATIONAL LABOUR STANDARDS AND CHILD LABOUR

Since the mid-1990s I have been engaged in a very different area of development economics—one that is contentious and, of considerable policy significance. This is the field of international labour standards and global policy, with particular focus on the problem of child labour. My involvement in this research is a matter of accident.

In 1994, when I moved from India to Cornell University, one of the bills that the US Congress was considering was the so-called Harkin's Bill, which would allow the US to stop the import of all goods that had a child-labour input. This was meant to be a bill to help end child labour; but also was viewed by many as Northern protectionism behind the façade of a noble cause. Having just moved from India, where I had seen child labour, I felt upset about the bill. It seemed to be founded on the assumption that child labour was caused by entrepreneurial greed and parental sloth. It was the parental-sloth assumption that I contested in an op ed essay in *The New York Times*, arguing that child labour was, typically, caused by the parents striving to give themselves and their children subsistence consumption. And once this was recognized, it would be clear that to try to control child labour by legislatively banning it was not the correct way to go. We must try to end child labour, but the policy interventions for achieving this have to be much more sophisticated and founded on a proper understanding of why child labour exists in the first place. A legal ban or an import blockade on products made by children may not be the right strategy.

I was completely taken aback by the reaction to the article. Senator Harkin wrote a long letter to the editor and a host of people wrote letters directly to me, some in support, but mostly challenging my argument. I was in trouble, for the article was written based on my experience in India and a reading of some versions of Harkin's Bill. I knew none of the scholarly literature on the subject and had no idea of the statistics of child labour. So I decided that, now that I had written on the subject, it was time to read.

I began reading as in a crash course and out of the reading some ideas began to strike me about how to model and understand child labour. At that time I had a very talented PhD student, Pham Hoang Van. Together we wrote the paper, 'The Economics of Child Labour', which is reproduced here as Chapter 15. In this we argued that a labour market in which children are potential workers is prone to exhibiting 'multiple equilibria'. And even though legislative bans were, in general, not a good idea, if it was found that an economy had multiple equilibria and was caught in an equilibrium with high child labour, then there would be a case for using a state-imposed ban.

This paper gave rise to two spin-off theoretical questions. First, can there be multiple equilibria of the kind we had described in the paper 'Economics of Child Labour', in a general equilibrium? In other words, was our multiple-equilibria result in an artefact of partial-equilibrium analysis? Second, could the use of minimum-wage legislation achieve the same result as a ban on child labour? The first question was answered in the affirmative in the paper 'A Note on Multiple General Equilibria with Child Labour', which is reprinted here as Chapter 16. The second question turned out to have a more complex answer caused by the fact that a minimum-wage legislation may give rise, ex post, to two kinds of households— those where the adult breadwinner finds a job at the new higher wage and those where the adult breadwinner is unemployed. These two kinds of households may well take different decisions about their children's work. In particular, the former households are likely to keep the children out of work, whereas the latter households may find it necessary to send the children to work. The analysis of the net affect of minimum-wage legislation was done in my paper, 'The Intriguing Relation between Adult Minimum Wage and Child Labour' (Chapter 17 here).

The debate on possible global action on child labour is part of a larger controversy on how much and how international organizations should intervene to uphold minimum international labour standards. This is a difficult subject, where it is easy to pronounce on what should be done in distant, poor countries without a proper understanding of their ground realities, and to be supercilious about Third World governments and bureaucrats. International labour standards is also a concern that can become an alibi for protectionism on the part of industrialized nations. To avoid these pitfalls we need to understand the economics of international labour-market interventions and also to understand the existing structure of global legislation and policy making through international organizations. My papers, 'Compacts, Conventions and Codes: Initiatives for Higher International Labour Standards' (Chapter 14 here) and 'Child Labour: Cause, Consequence, and Cure, with Remarks on International Labour Standards' (Chapter 18 here), are meant to be contributions towards precisely such an understanding.

The latter paper also opened up some general questions of law and economics. If a poor worker is willing to take on huge health hazards in order to earn a subsistence income, should he be stopped from doing such a job? Suppose a nation runs an export processing zone (EPZ) to work in which a labourer has to forgo some basic rights (for instance, the right to be part of a trade union). Given that workers are free not to work in an EPZ, is there reason to disallow such an EPZ? Suppose a firm makes it clear to its workers that, while it will give a high salary, it reserves the right to sexually harass its workers, should a nation's sexual-harassment law ban such a practice? The way we answer these questions can have important implications for economic efficiency and well-being.

These questions and the contents of the chapters in this collection form a tiny fraction of the scope of development economics. There are vast areas of the subject on which I have no knowledge and even more on which I have written nothing. So before venturing to read this book the reader will be well advised to keep in mind that this book is no more than an idiosyncratic collection of a small segment of a large discipline. And so if this collection disappoints the reader (I hope it will not) or its concerns seem too constraining, this should not be taken as a reflection of what development economics is all about.

If the principle objective of economics is to enable people to live better and more prosperous lives, then development economics deals with what is germane to economics. After a slow start some half a century ago, the subject has moved more and more to the centrestage of economics. And that is as it should be, for not only does development economics have its share of deep intellectual puzzles and scientific conundrums to occupy the best minds, how those puzzles are solved can have significant implications for well-being in the poorest regions of the world.

PART I
Measuring Development

2 On the Goals of Development

The development debate appears to be, at last, coasting towards a consensus: developing nations must not focus their energies on the growth rates of their gross domestic product (GDP), net national product (NNP), gross national product (GNP), and the like but should instead try to achieve 'human development' or 'comprehensive development'. A remarkable feature of these new goals is that everyone seems to be supporting them, although few know what the terms mean. This is in some sense understandable. First, the terms 'human' and 'comprehensive' are so enticing that no one can proclaim being against them without sounding absurd and boorish. And given that the aim of these new objectives is to go beyond narrow economic objectives to larger social and political goals, some vagueness in the target is inevitable. Attempts to give these goals sharper focus, as in the United Nations Development Programme's (UNDP's) construction of the Human Development index, have inevitably been criticized for arbitrariness. Even on this, however, one may argue that it is better to be somewhat arbitrary but have your broad objective right than to have a sharply defined but morally indefensible objective.

In this chapter, I join the debate somewhat idiosyncratically. After a discussion of the concept of development as it has evolved over time, I propose and evaluate some particular goals that countries should adopt. I then suggest some perspectives on measuring and evaluating the progress of nations, without claiming that these measures should be the end-all of what nations strive to achieve; rather, they should be a part of the larger goal of human development. Next, I discuss a relatively ignored subject: the interdependence of the goals of different nations. Even if all nations were to agree on the ultimate aims, there is enough interdependence in the global economy for the journey towards these goals to be marred by skirmishes, as each nation wants others to make certain moves first before it does so (if at all).

Previously published in Gerald M. Meier and Joseph E. Stiglitz (eds), *Frontiers of Development Economics: The Future in Perspective*. The World Bank and Oxford University Press, 2001: 61–101.

The strategic interaction between the goals of different nations has received little attention, the presumption being that strategic problems arise when agents act selfishly and vanish when we put on our normative hats and try to advance general human well-being. But this presumption is wrong. Some of the most serious problems of development—for instance, those related to labour standards and the environment—have remained unresolved because of strategic problems or morality. The final sections of this chapter discuss the problem of the interdependence of nations' goals and supply an illustrative example on international labour standards.

2.1. THE IDEA OF DEVELOPMENT

By leafing through Forbes magazine and some recent *World Development Reports*, it is easy to compile the following facts. The total income, in 1998, of Hollywood's richest fifty individuals exceeds the total income of Burundi's entire population of seven million. If Bill Gates decided to encash and consume the *increase* in the value of his total assets that occurred over the past year, he would be able to consume more than the total annual consumption of the sixty million people of Ethiopia. These numbers reflect both the phenomenal scope for wealth and economic well-being that the modern world makes possible and also how easy it is for this enormous potential to bypass large masses of humanity. That even today, in this unbelievably rich world, large numbers of children have to work 12 to 14 hours a day to enable their families to barely survive; that in many countries more than 100 babies die in the first year of their lives for each 1000 live births; and that in many countries more than half the population does not have access to electricity or safe drinking water—all this shows a massive failure not in our scientific achievements (because technically we can provide for all) but in our social and political institutions. Have we had our goals right? Have we striven too hard for narrow economic amassment without paying adequate attention to basic human well-being and equity?

For long stretches of history, a nation's achievement was measured by its territorial control, and progress was equated with sending out armies and armadas. Although there was always trade, which could create value simply by altering the ownership of goods and services, a large part of the global game was viewed as a zero-sum competition. As a consequence, development, which connotes advance and progress, was not an important part of the human agenda. The aim of a state or a kingdom was to have peace and general prosperity; expansion meant encroachment into what belonged to others. One can see this in one of the earliest books on economics, *The Arthashastra*, written by Kautilya around 300 BC. Despite its attempt to be a comprehensive treatise on statecraft and the economic management of a nation (*arthashastra* literally means 'the doctrine of wealth'), its obsession is with order and static efficiency and on how the king should have a well-defined set of laws and punish anybody who disrupts the functioning of society. There are long tracts on the management of state finances, on how profligacy must be avoided, on fiscal discipline, and on effective tax collection.

The concern about budgetary discipline is so great that in times of financial shortage the *Arthashastra* (272) permits the king to exploit the gullibility of the masses and raise funds by 'building overnight, as if it happened by a miracle, a temple or a sanctuary and promoting the holding of fairs and festivals in honour of the miraculous deity' and (273) to use 'secret agents to frighten people into making offerings to drive away an evil spirit'. Despite such attention to detail and its range of concerns, which trespasses the boundaries of economics, politics and sociology (not to mention morality), what is surprising about this classic work, viewed at the beginning of the twenty-first century, is how little it dwells on *progress* or growth of aggregate material well-being. This was, in general, true of the early view of the good life.

With the growth in trade and breakthroughs in science and technology, of which in theory there need be no end, this has changed. Our goals have moved away from purely tangible wealth such as land and gold and also away from static well-being. One can have a large income despite having little control over not just land but anything tangible. By sending one's capital to distant lands, one can partake in the success of faraway places without the aid of soldiers and guns. The discovery of a new technology in one laboratory in one city can spread to faraway lands. In principle, prosperity can extend to all, and greater income over time can accrue to all.

Yet that has not happened. China's per capita income grew at the astonishing rate of 6.7 per cent a year for thirty years beginning in 1965; during the same period Sierra Leone's per capita income fell 1.4 per cent a year. Chile's per capita income grew at the more sober rate o 1.6 per cent a year over the same thirty years, while Ghana's declined at an annual rate of 0.9 per cent. Negative average growth rates over the past thirty years were also observed in Bolivia, El Salvador, Madagascar, Senegal, and several other nations.[1] These anomalies raise a host of new questions concerning development and distribution. What policies should developing countries follow? What policies should global organizations such as the World Bank and the World Trade Organization (WTO) follow or advocate?

With the rise in the popularity of measuring and monitoring national incomes (clearly a phenomenon of this century), progress and development also came to be measured in terms of GNP or the per capita income of a nation. This intellectual tradition, with its limited objective, helped nations focus their energies narrowly and must have played a role in the rapid growth of national incomes that this century has witnessed. But it also brought in its wake dissension and disappointments. To maximize income growth, environmental considerations were left to languish on the sidelines; the standard of living was often allowed to slide; large inequalities between classes, regions, and genders were ignored; and poverty was tolerated more than it should have been in the rush to generate maximum growth.

Fortunately, that has been changing. A large number of economists have argued the need for moving beyond this narrow goal.[2] This is precisely the line along which Stiglitz (1998a: 31), for instance, has contested the 'Washington consensus'. 'The Washington consensus advocated use of a small set of instruments ... to achieve a relatively narrow goal (economic growth). The post-Washington consensus recognizes both that a broader set of instruments are necessary and our goals are also much broader'. Stiglitz goes on to emphasize, rightly, the need to focus attention on improvements in income distribution, environment, health, and education.

In a series of influential publications, Sen (1983, 1985, 1999) has contributed to the broadening of the goals of development. He has argued the need to move away from the commodity fetishism of the earlier approaches and toward the evaluation of development and progress in terms of functioning and capability. A functioning is what a person manages to do or be. A good can enable a functioning but is distinct from it. For example, a bicycle is a good, whereas being able to transport oneself rapidly to work is a functioning. Several persons, each owning a bicycle, may be able to achieve different kinds of functioning depending on their other attributes—how well fed they are, their morbidity statistics, and so on. As Sen has pointed out, this approach has its roots in an intellectual heritage that goes back to Adam Smith and Karl Marx (see the discussion in Basu and Lopez-Calva 1999), but it was lost in the increasing fervour of measuring the progress of nations by their incomes that we have seen in this century.

This broader approach to the concept of well-being and progress has generated two kinds of literature: one that formalizes this still somewhat nebulous idea (see, for instance, Atkinson 1995; Herrero 1996; Romer 1999; Suzumura 1999), and one that tries to put it into operation. Dasgupta and Weale (1992), Brandolini and D'Alessio (1998) and the UNDP'S *Human Development Reports* are examples of the latter. Since I am concerned here with some of the more practical and policy-oriented issues of development goals, and the modifications I suggest are based on the latter approach, the next section begins with a statement of the method used by the UNDP.

2.2. QUINTILE INCOME AND QUINTILE GROWTH

The UNDP, beginning with its *Human Development Report 1990*, has argued strongly for an indicator of a nation's progress that is a weighted average of the nation's literacy and educational achievement, the citizen's life expectancy, and the nation's per capita income. Recently, the World Bank has argued for widening our goals beyond the traditional macroeconomic objectives, such as national income, fiscal health, and stability in the balance of payments, to encompass 'societal development' including basic human rights, access to a just legal system, literacy, and good health (see Stiglitz 1998a; Wolfensohn 1999). Streeten (1994) has tried to bring order into these expanding objectives by classifying them into two categories, resource development and humanitarian progress, and by giving six reasons why we should be interested in human development. These reasons are, briefly, as follows:

- Human development is desirable as an end in itself.
- It can promote higher productivity and so enhance human command over goods and services.

- It reduces human reproduction, an outcome that is generally considered desirable.
- It is good for the environment.
- It can contribute to a healthy civil society and democracy.
- It can promote political stability.

Most of these objectives are related to the objective of equity and poverty reduction—of including people in the development process rather than excluding or abandoning them. Streeten points out that the poor are not just victims of environmental degradation but often its cause and shows how human development promotes a healthy civil society by improving the lot of the poorest people and making them feel included.

This suggests a natural correction for the way we evaluate different economies. Essentially, it says that in evaluating an economy's state or progress, we must focus primarily on how the poorest people are faring. A first cut at doing this—and the criterion that I want to advocate in this section—is to look at the economic condition of the poorest 20 per cent of the population. In other words, instead of bothering about the per capita income of the nation as a whole, we should be concerned about the per capita income of the bottom quintile. Instead of equating a country's progress with the growth rate of per capita income in general, we should look at the growth rate of the per capita income of the poorest 20 per cent of the population.

In recommending the use of these measures and commending them as goals of development, I am not taking issue with the advocacy of non-economic goals, which has gathered strength in recent years with the publication of the UNDP'S annual *Human Development Reports* and the World Bank's new interest in 'comprehensive development'. My suggestion is not meant to deny the larger aims of trying to achieve political stability, environmental goodness, and a higher general quality of human life. In understanding this recommendation, two factors have to be kept in mind. First, to the extent that we do look at income and income growth, I am suggesting that we should focus on the per capita income of the poorest 20 per cent of the population ('quintile income') and the growth rate of the per capita income of that poorest 20 per cent ('quintile growth rate'). Second, these quintile objectives are likely to correlate better with other non-economic indicators, such as environmental conditions and social stability, for the reasons Streeten (1994) has suggested.[3] (See also Aturupane, Glewwe, and Isenman 1994.)[4] Thus, even when we decide to play the dismal scientist and focus on income, if the focus is on *quintile* income we will automatically capture some of the social indicators emphasized in broader notions of human development.

Before proceeding further, it is useful to specify some definitions formally. Let us define the *income profile* of a country with n persons as vector, $x = (x_1, x_2, \ldots x_n)$, of non-negative numbers such that x denotes the income of person i. Without loss of generality, it will be assumed that if x is an income profile, then $x_1 \leq x_2 \leq \ldots \leq x_n$. This simply entails renaming the citizens so that the poorest person is named person 1, the second poorest person is named person 2, and so on, with ties being broken arbitrarily. Since populations can vary, we will, for explicitness, use $n(x)$ to denote the number of elements in x. Now, let $t(x)$ be the largest integer r such that $r/n(x) \leq 1/5$.

Given a country with an income profile x, the quintile income of the country is denoted by $q(x)$, which is defined as follows:

$$q(x) = [x_1 + \ldots + x_{t(x)}]/t(x).$$

Suppose a country's income profile changes from x^t in period t to x^{t+1} in period $t + 1$. Then the quintile growth rate (call it g) of this country between years t and $t + 1$ is defined as:

$$g = 100[q(x^{t+1}) - q(x^t)]/q(x^t).$$

2.2.1. Balancing Equality and Growth

This criterion for assessing the economic performance of an economy stems from a combination of normative and pragmatic considerations Suppose one looks at the gross inequalities of income that prevail in the world, as suggested by the few striking examples cited at the start of the preceding section. A question that the lay person often asks, even though it may not arise in discussions among professional economists is whether there is a case for limiting the incomes of the richest people. It seems to me that the answer should depend crucially on what such a policy would do to the poorest people. It is indeed a shame that Bill Gates earns so much more than the average person in Burundi and, for that matter, in the United States. But if trying to curb Bill Gates's income would cause poor people to be worse off, there would be no case for such a curb. Not only in distributional questions such as this but in deciding on any economic policy, it seems morally appealing to check what the policy change will do to the poorest people.[5] This is the normative consideration.

One may legitimately ask whether it is reasonable to hold up the progress of the better-off segment of a society's population for the sake of the bottom quintile, which may contain a disproportionate amount of dysfunctional individuals. There are several possible responses. First, thanks to a variety of market failures, a society's bottom quintile is likely to contain not just dysfunctional individuals but also many talented people whose talents are not realized or nurtured because of limited access to education and credit. Second, even for the dysfunctional people, there is a moral case for directly supporting them by taxing the rich. Of course, if the tax becomes too large and, therefore, inefficient, the society in question will do badly in the long run, and so, by the criterion of the long-run interest of the bottom quintile itself, such a policy will turn out to be undesirable. This criterion is thus attractive because it sets limits to how much the government should try to redistribute wealth and income to the poor through a self-referential calculation that looks at the long-run interests of the poor.

Although Rawls (1971), in his abstract models, could focus attention on *the* worst-off person, in reality we seldom know who the worst off is. Indeed, thanks to earnings from the informal sector, income data for the poorest persons are very difficult to collect. However, most nations do provide information on the income or expenditure share that goes to the poorest 20 per cent of the population. So the suggestion that we concentrate on the poorest 20 per cent is the pragmatic part of the recommendation.

An advantage of designing policy by focusing attention on the poorest 20 per cent is that one cannot totally ignore the effect on people outside this group. If others fare too badly, they will become part of the poorest 20 per cent and so will automatically come into focus. For this same reason, raising the quintile growth rate can never mean totally ignoring the overall growth rate of the country. For certain periods of time, a positive quintile growth rate can occur together with a negative per capita income growth rate. But if that happens for too long, there will be perfect equality of income in the country, and at that point the per capita growth rate will coincide with the quintile growth rate. For this reason, the criterion suggested here is distinct from that of mere poverty reduction. The objective of reducing poverty satisfies the property of satiation. That is, it is a self-liquidating objective: once poverty is removed, there is nothing more to strive for. The aim of improving the lot of the poorest 20 per cent can never be satiated. It gives us a moving target.

The relation between this criterion and inequality reduction is more compli-cated. If a society is locked in a zero-sum game, to improve the condition of the bottom quintile of society is also to reduce inequality (for reasonable definitions of inequality), since in a zero-sum society one has to take from Peter to give to Paul. As discussed above, however, allowing some people to become richer may be essential to enable the bottom quintile of society to do better. In such situations my criterion will tend to exacerbate inequality. One may, of course, bring in a special consciousness of inequality by requiring that inequality reduction be a lexicographically secondary objective. That is, if there are two policies that leave the quintile income the same but one of them lowers inequality, we should choose the latter. In general, the principle worth upholding is that equality is a desirable objective as long as it does not occur at the expense of the poorest people. If some aggregate welfare has to be sacrificed for greater equality, that is worthwhile, but if poverty has to be increased in order to have greater equality, the greater equality is not worth it.

Measuring welfare in terms of the welfare of the bottom quintile of society also has the advantage of satisfying the criterion of anonymity and the weak Pareto principle. In other words, if two societies were such that one could be made to look just like the other through a permutation of the individuals, then under my criterion the two societies would be judged equally good. If everybody's income rises in a society, this will be considered a better society according to this criterion of evaluation.

There are, however, some desirable axioms that the quintile measure does not satisfy. One is what I will call the weak transfer axiom. This says that when a fixed sum of money is transferred from a rich person to a poorer person who also happens to be in the bottom quintile of society, such that the income ranking of people remains unchanged, the new income profile thus created should be considered socially superior to the old one. It is easy to see that when money is transferred from a person above the bottom 20 per cent to someone in the bottom quintile, the quintile income will rise. When the transfer takes place from a person in the bottom quintile to someone poorer, the quintile income remains unchanged. Hence, the quintile income as a measure of welfare violates the weak transfer axiom.

This weakness may be rectified by using an index that I shall call the rank-weighted quintile income. This is essentially an ordinal index that penalizes a country if, within the poorest 20 per cent, income is distributed in favour of the relatively rich. Let x be an income profile. Then the rank-weighted quintile income (RQI) is denoted by $\hat{q}(x)$ and is defined as follows:

$$\hat{q}(x) = \sum_{i=1}^{t(x)} [t(x) + 1 - i] x_i / \sum_{i=1}^{t(x)} [t(x) + 1 - i]$$

where $\hat{q}(x)$ is the weighted average of the incomes of the poorest 20 per cent and the weight for the poorest ith person's income is given by $t(x) + 1 - i$. Hence the poorest person gets the highest weight, $t(x)$, and the richest person in the bottom quintile is assigned the lowest weight, 1.

By rearranging terms, the above equation can be rewritten as:

$$\hat{q}(x) = 2q(x) - \frac{2\Sigma ix_i}{t(x)\,[1 + t(x)]}$$

One can proceed in this vein and create variants that are more complex. These more nuanced measures may be pursued in the future to yield more sophisticated measurements of welfare based on the general idea that the welfare of a society ought to be equated with the welfare of the poorest people. To spend more time on these variants here would distract us from our present objective. I will, therefore, focus on quintile income and quintile growth.

2.2.2. A Practical Illustration: Country Rankings

Some changes in welfare criteria may be important notionally but make very little actual difference when put into practice. This possibility prompts me to ask, if international organizations displaying comparative income and growth information, as in the World Bank's *World Development Reports*, instead gave data on quintile income and quintile growth, would this result in important changes in rankings? If not, the whole exercise outlined here would be academic and of little consequence from the practitioner's point of view. It is, however, easy to see that the changes in rankings could be quite sharp.

Table 2.1 shows the relative performance of a group of nations using the criteria of income and quintile income. The forty countries selected include the world's ten richest and ten poorest nations. A handicap in doing the calculation was that for most nations, the share of income going to the bottom 20 per cent is not available on an annual basis. I, therefore, use the latest available data on income shares.

Subject to this caveat, it is interesting to see how large a difference the shift from per capita income to quintile income makes. Switzerland, which was the richest nation in per capita income, drops below Norway and Denmark. The United

Table 2.1: Per Capita Income and Quintile Income, 40 Countries, 1997

Country	Percentage share of income of poorest 20 per cent (various years)[a]		GNP per capita 1997 (US dollars)	Per capita income of poorest 20 per cent or quintile income 1997 (US dollars)
Ethiopia	7.1	(1995)	110	39
Sierra Leone	1.1	(1989)	160	9
Niger	2.6	(1995)	200	26
Rwanda	9.7	(1983–5)	210	102
Tanzania	6.8	(1993)	210	71
Nepal	7.6	(1995–6)	220	84
Guinea-Bissau	2.1	(1991)	230	24
Burkina Faso	5.5	(1994)	250	69
Madagascar	5.1	(1993)	250	69
Mali	4.6	(1994)	260	60
Vietnam	7.8	(1993)	310	121
Bangladesh	9.4	(1992)	360	169
India	9.2	(1994)	370	170
Pakistan	9.4	(1996)	500	235
China	5.5	(1995)	860	237
Ukraine	4.3	(1995)	1040	224
Indonesia	8.0	(1996)	1110	444
Egypt, Arab Rep.	8.7	(1991)	1200	522
Romania	8.9	(1994)	1410	627
Russian Federation	4.2	(1996)	2680	563
Thailand	5.6	(1992)	2740	767
South Africa	2.9	(1993–4)	3210	465
Venezuela	4.3	(1995)	3480	748
Poland	9.3	(1992)	3590	1669
Mexico	3.6	(1995)	3700	666
Hungary	9.7	(1993)	4510	2187
Malaysia	4.6	(1989)	4530	1042
Brazil	2.5	(1995)	4790	599
Chile	3.5	(1994)	4820	844
Israel	6.9	(1992)	16,180	5582
Netherlands	8.0	(1991)	25,830	10,332
Sweden	9.6	(1992)	26,210	12,581
France	7.2	(1989)	26,300	9468
Belgium	9.5	(1992)	26,730	12,697
Austria	10.4	(1987)	27,920	14,518
Germany	9.0	(1989)	28,280	12,726
United States	4.8	(1994)	29,080	6979
Denmark	9.6	(1992)	34,890	16,747
Norway	10.0	(1991)	36,100	18,050
Switzerland	7.4	(1982)	43,060	15,932

[a] Figures in parentheses are the years for which the share data were obtained.
Source: World Bank (1998).

States, which was the fourth richest country, drops to tenth place. Among poor nations, Sierra Leone's per capita income of US$160 is already low, but its quintile income is a shocking US$9. The South Asian countries are very poor, but they do relatively better viewed through the lens of quintile income.

2.2.3. Recapturing Past Insights

It is one thing to present data and information on the bottom quintile of societies (as urged in this section) and another actually to design policy and set development goals. When we move to designing policy, there are two issues that I want to address: the trade-off between economic well-being and other indicators of welfare, and conflicts between global goals and the goals of nations. The latter takes us into new analytical territory concerning strategic issues in policy making and conditional morality. I will first briefly take up the matter of trade-offs between different goals.

Given the recent effort to make economists, international bureaucrats, and policy makers aware that 'there are things in life that matter, apart from income and wealth', one might be led to think that the focus on income had always been the principal focus of nations. But, as mentioned above, that is not so. Classical writers had considered the significance of a good quality of life, and their definitions typically went beyond material plentitude. Adam Smith, in a letter to Lord Carlisle written on 8 November 1779, wrote about how Ireland could make greater progress: 'It wants order, police and a regular administration of justice both to protect and to restrain the inferior ranks of people, articles more essential to the progress of industry than both coal and wood put together' (Smith 1987: 243). In discussing the alienation of labour, Karl Marx (1844) stressed how a life in which only one's material wants are met is animalistic—freedom to choose being an essential constituent of good human life. These traditions, via modern formalizations, have influenced the construction of the Human Development Index.

2.2.4. The Relevance of Indexes for Policy Makers

Before proceeding further, one question worth asking is this: even though the need to broaden our goals of development, as suggested in the *Human Development Reports*, has great normative appeal, is there a case for constructing a single index from a composite of varied indexes? While it is true that such an index can have (and indeed has had) the desirable effect of mobilizing popular opinion, its conceptual underpinnings are questionable. Ray (1998) has rightly questioned the method of aggregating diverse indicators of the quality of life, as is done in the *Human Development Reports*.

Another problem with the use of such aggregate measures has not always been noted. Let us suppose that we take all the variables that are worthwhile and construct a strictly concave welfare function in which these variables enter as arguments. For simplicity, we often use a linear aggregator, such as the Human Development Index, but clearly, as we have too much of one variable, we would expect the weight on that variable to decrease. Hence the strict concavity is natural. What I am arguing is that if we use such an aggregate notion of welfare and do cost–benefit analysis to determine which projects are desirable, we are likely to run into important flaws in our decision making.

Note that in standard treatments of cost–benefit analysis or project evaluation, the content of the project is considered unimportant. Whether it be a school or a dam, the same method of analysis is supposed to apply. This would be fine if all projects were fully specified, alternative courses of action open to a nation. But in reality, projects do not come in that form. Separate projects come up one at a time, and each is typically evaluated separately. And therein lies the problem of evaluating all projects against one aggregate measure of welfare.

Suppose that welfare depends on only two variables, income and literacy, and that the welfare function is strictly convex. Hence the indifference curves (or, more precisely, the superior sets) in the income–literacy space are strictly concave. Suppose there are two projects: a school and a dam. The former generates two units of literacy and causes a drop of one unit of income, whereas the latter causes a rise of two units of income and a drop of one unit of literacy. It is entirely possible that if each project is evaluated individually (as is usually done in reality) by the yardstick of this all-embracing welfare function, each will be rejected, although the combination of the two projects is clearly desirable.

What this suggests is that either projects have to be bunched together and evaluated all at once, or we must evaluate different projects against different yardsticks. Since it is virtually impossible to conceive of all projects at once, we are forced to rely on the latter course. In other words, we must evaluate a school for what it does for schooling and literacy. If it contributes greatly to literacy without 'too much' damage to other things, it must be considered desirable. Similarly, a dam may have to be evaluated in terms of what it does mainly for income. This is not a well-defined rule for project analysis (since the worth of a project depends on what other projects are *likely* to come up in the future, and there may be no hard information on that at the moment), but it is close to what policy planners, through their intuition, tend to do. I argue that the policy planners may in this case be right.

To reject the use of an aggregated index is, however, no reason to reject the importance of the components of an index. One way of capturing this importance is to look at a vector of a nation's achievements, leaving the exact trade-offs one considers reasonable to be determined at the time of specific decisions and perhaps varied depending on the context. This section has argued that an important component of this *vector* should be quintile income. International organizations such as the World Bank and the UNDP should make data on quintile income widely available.

In addition, one can take the spirit of this proposal further and focus on the performance of the bottom 20 per cent in various dimensions of well-being, such as life expectancy and sundry health indicators. Concerning literacy, one has to be more innovative because whenever a country has a literacy rate of less than 80 per cent, the least literate quintile will be completely illiterate, and there will be little to distinguish among most developing nations on this score.

In a recent paper, James Foster and I argue that there are two kinds of illiterate persons: an 'isolated literate' who lives in a household consisting of all illiterates, and a 'proximate illiterate' who lives in a household that has at least one literate person (Basu and Foster 1998). We argue that a proximate illiterate's access to a literate person can relieve the darkness of illiteracy non-negligibly.[6] Thus, a nation in which the literacy rate is 50 per cent, with half the members of each household being literate, is much better off than one in which 50 per cent of the people are literate and 50 per cent are isolated illiterates (that is all those who are illiterate live in households with no literate members). An implication is that if we were to start bottom up, as the quintile approach would require us to do, in devising literacy programmes, we would first start with the isolated illiterates.

One reason why individual nations do not give adequate attention to quintile incomes, the environment, education, and minimal labour standards is that in the rough and tumble of international competition, they find little room for such soft targets. Just as, according to one theory, firms that do not maximize profit risk getting wiped out by the process of evolution, nations fear that to keep afloat in the global economy, they must try to achieve higher growth. Thus, a part of the problem is not so much to persuade leaders that quintile income matters, the environment matters, and so on (since not many national leaders will disagree *in principle*) but, rather, to create global institutions that make it possible for countries to pursue these goals. This requires us to understand why, even when each country wants to pursue a certain goal, in the strategic environment of the global economy countries may fail to do so. That is the subject matter of the next section.

2.3. CONDITIONAL MORALITY

Economists usually give advice on and write about the goals of development without specifying who the recipient of the advice is. This may be satisfactory for some very broad kinds of advice, but not for all. It seems eminently reasonable to give different advice to different agents, even when these pieces of advice are mutually inconsistent.

Consider the following example. Suppose you are a 'good adviser' in the sense that you give advice in the best interests of the particular advisee, without allowing it to be distorted by your self-interest. If you are a doctor and a patient comes to you complaining of an ailment, 'good advice' consists of recommending a medicine that, to the best of your knowledge, will cure the ailment, disregarding, for instance, the fact that the patient happens to be your tenant who is refusing to quit your apartment![7]

Now suppose that there are *n* nations in the world and that each of them seeks your advice individually. It is not unreasonable for you to advise each nation to aim for the highest possible growth rate of per capita income. If you know that each nation's aim is to achieve overall economic prosperity or to be the most powerful country in the world, then such advice is quite reasonable. Now assume that a truly international organization, one that represents global interests or the interests of all nations—in brief, an international organization of a kind that does not exist in today's world—seeks your advice on what each of the nations should do. It is entirely reasonable for you to advise it that the aim should be for countries not to grow too fast, since that may cause a deterioration in the global environment and create political and social tensions, and since you know that if every country tries to be the most powerful nation in the world, that can only make the world a worse place.[8] In other words, it may be reasonable for you to advise each nation to do what you would not advise all nations to do.

To see this even more transparently, consider two nations playing at prisoners' dilemma. Let the player choosing between rows be country 1 and the player choosing between columns be country 2.

Game 1

	C	D
C	5, 5	0, 6
D	6, 0	2, 2

Assume that the players know that they have to choose between C and D but do not know the pay-offs. Country 1 contacts an expert (by definition, someone who does know the pay-offs) for advice on what it should do. Clearly (since a good adviser gives the advice that is in the advisee's best interests), the correct advice is for the country to play D. This is the advice that the expert would give if he were called upon by each nation individually. If his advice were followed, the global economy would reach the outcome (D, D) in which both would be worse off than if they had chosen C. Now suppose the World Bank, trying to devise an outcome that serves the interests of the global economy, asks the expert what both countries should do. It is quite reasonable to respond by saying that both nations should choose C. Hence, the outcome, if the advice were followed, would be (C, C).

At one level, the three pieces of advice given—1 and 2, 'choose D' and to the global organization, choose (C, C)—are contradictory, but this is exactly what a good adviser should do. Moreover, strictly speaking, there is no contradiction, since the advice given is a function not only of the question asked but also of who asked the question.

One can add flesh to this story by thinking of different accounts of what C and D represent. In one story, D could represent 'go nuclear' and C, 'shun nuclear'. In that case the game describes the realistic possibility that each country stands to gain by having nuclear weapons but that both are better off if neither has nuclear weapons. In another story, D could be the strategy of rapid growth and C the strategy of moderate growth. Suppose that fast growth causes the environment to deteriorate but that a part of this environmental cost is borne by the other nation. It is now very possible to think of a case in which no matter what the other country does, it is better for each country to choose D, but the outcome if both choose D is worse than if both choose C, since the total environmental degradation causes an overall deterioration in living conditions.

In both these stories, knowing that you are advising both countries, you may be tempted to be moral and advise each nation to choose C and so create a better world. If, however, you want to carry out your job as adviser honestly and each nation has asked you, 'Keeping only my interest in mind, tell me whether I should do C or D?' the correct answer is 'D'. Of course, in reality, you may decide to go beyond what you are asked and tell both nations that there is much to be gained by sitting down at a round table and trying to play co-operatively. But such options are not always available, and so there is an unavoidable moral conundrum here for the adviser.

In prisoners' dilemma type games, the prospect of getting nations to co-operate seems hopeless at first sight. But the situation is not as bad as it seems because most nations, like most individuals do adhere to some basic norms and morality. Now, conditional behaviour is typically taken to be the domain of self-interested decision making: 'It is in my interest to confess if the other agent confesses'. However, in reality, we often express even our morals in this form: 'I believe in paying taxes because it is every citizen's duty to do so; however, I believe that this ceases to be a duty on my part, and indeed I would not pay taxes, if others did not'. Similarly, nations may be willing to control environmental pollution as long as other nations also do so. This, of course, gives rise to a free-rider problem, but it is very different from the usual free-rider problem with self-interested agents because here even the co-operative outcome is not one that is in each agent's self interest. I may be better-off not paying taxes even if everybody does. A small nation may not benefit by controlling pollution even if other nations do.

Much of our morality, especially morality that translates into action, is conditional. 'I will behave like a good utilitarian as long as others do, or I would be happy to play like a Rawlsian, but only as long as I know that others are not violating the Rawlsian norm for selfish gain.' Such conditional morality stems from two urges, as basic to human nature as the propensity to maximize utility (and perhaps even more so): the urge to adhere to *some* morality, and the urge not to be a sucker. Unfortunately, the strategic aspects of moral behaviour have not been discussed much in the literature—certainly not as much as the strategic problems of selfish behaviour.[9]

Let us, for purposes of illustration, assume that the moral system that people adhere to is utilitarianism but that they do so conditionally. To keep the analysis tractable, let us assume that the conditionality works in the following way: agents take the view that they will behave according to utilitarian norms if and only if others behave like utilitarians;[10] if others do not do so, they will revert to selfish utility maximization. It is interesting to check what happens in Game 1 when it is played by two conditional utilitarians.[11] Place yourself in the shoes of agent 1. If the other person chooses D, clearly violating utilitarianism, you will behave selfishly and choose D. If the other person chooses C, behaving as a utilitarian, you will be a utilitarian and will choose C, since (C, C) generates a total utility of 10, while (C, D) gives a total of 6 utils.[12]

Let me now define a pair of strategies (or an *n*-tuple of strategies, in an *n*-player game) to be a behavioural Nash equilibrium if, given the other player's strategy, each player chooses not to alter his or her strategy. It follows that this game (with the conditional morality and consequent behaviour that we have defined) has two behavioural Nash equilibria: (C, C) and (D, D), although (D, D) is the unique (conventional) Nash equilibrium. Given that human beings, across cultures and nations, do frequently subscribe to conditional morality, what the example illustrates is that an outcome that conventional game theory would not declare sustainable as an equilibrium may actually turn out to be an equilibrium.

I see illustrations of this abstract idea quite regularly in the town of Ithaca, New York. On Forest Home Drive there is a bridge so narrow that cars can travel on it in only one direction at any given time. The convention that has been established is that a convoy of three or four cars travels in one direction and the next car then stops and allows a convoy of three or four cars to come from the other side. There is no one to police the norm, but it seems to work well, with an occasional breakdown at the start of the academic year—no doubt because new students and faculty are unaware of the norm.

The fourth or fifth car that stops to allow cars to start up from the other side clearly makes a small sacrifice in self-interest in the larger interest of society. So what we have in Ithaca is a behavioural Nash equilibrium that leaves the whole society better off. What sustains this outcome is conditional morality; it seems unlikely that a driver would voluntarily stop to let oncoming cars pass if he believed that no one else in town adhered to this rule. In other words, what one is exercising is the norm that one will make small sacrifices for society as long as others are also willing to make such sacrifices.

I have not seen an equilibrium like this work in many other places, and I used to wonder whether it showed some innate differences in preferences or social norms between the citizens of Ithaca and those elsewhere. But I now believe that it is much more likely that people are at an innate level similar (at least more similar than their behaviour taken at face value, would lead us to believe) and that all human beings adhere to conditional morality. Once they do so, games like the bridge-crossing one and the prisoners' dilemma described above acquire multiple equilibria, and it becomes possible to think of different communities being caught in different equilibria even though the game being played and the preferences and values of the people may be identical.

International relations are riddled with conditional morality. Nations are often willing to make small sacrifices for the larger global good, but they do not want to do this alone. This is reason for hope because certain desirable outcomes that do not occur may nevertheless be potential equilibria, by this argument. Consider, for instance, the goal of limiting environmental pollution. Because of externalities, it is not always in a nation's self-interest to curtail pollution adequately (Repetto 1995). Similarly, any country trying to raise its labour standards risks losing capital to some other country with laxer standards. For these reasons, nations left to themselves are more likely to strive for faster growth to the neglect of these other objectives. This makes it difficult for countries to strive to improve the lot of their poorest people or to raise living standards generally. Yet, as the above argument clarifies, there is scope for co-ordinated behaviour—in fact even behaviour that does not constitute an equilibrium in a conventional sense but that is a *behavioural* equilibrium and would lead to the global optimum.[13]

2.4. AN EXAMPLE: INTERNATIONAL LABOUR STANDARDS

This section presents a small model on the pursuit of international labour standards to illustrate the problem of interdependence of moral goals. The subject is of some importance in its own right in this age of globalization and multinational action. I begin with a brief statement of the issues involved.

International labour standards (ILSs) are meant to be policy measures aimed at helping poor nations achieve certain minimal living standards. What is remarkable about these measures is that the most consistent opposition to them has come from the alleged beneficiaries. The fear of the poor nations is that labour standards are a Trojan horse which conceals the true agenda of industrial nations—protectionism. The fear is partly justified: the demand for labour standards, as it stands today, comes overwhelmingly from protectionist lobbies in industrial countries. Developing countries fear that once an international organization is empowered to enforce standards, it will use this power in the interest of the richer and more powerful nations. Indeed, we know that at the level of the nation, a government empowered to tax people often intervenes in practice in favour of the rich while using the rhetoric of helping the poor. Subtle systems of taxation and subsidy are often used to redistribute in favour of those who need the redistribution the least (see Stiglitz 1989: 46–8 for a discussion). This is a general problem, and there is no reason to expect that it will not make its appearance at the level of multinational organizations.

I have argued elsewhere that although labour standards as they are currently conceived ought to be rejected, there is nevertheless scope for a minimal and differently conceived set of international labour standards. But the construction of this argument requires us to recognize the strategic problems that arise *among* the developing nations.

As a general principle, hardly anyone can oppose the goal of international labour standards. Workers are among the poorest people in most developing economies, and a policy to raise their standard of living can be justified as a step to raise the quintile income of a nation. One important component of ILSs is the goal of putting an end to child labour. Given that it is the poorest households that send their children out to work, if the conditions of these households can be improved so that they do not have to do so, this can again be justified as a step toward raising the quintile income. The reason why poor countries have nevertheless resisted ILSs is that setting standards has been posed in most industrial nations as a tussle between developing and industrial countries, and the latter group has tried to use it as an instrument of protection (Bhagwati 1995; Srinivasan 1996).

I will illustrate my argument with the case of international child labour standards. A myth that has fuelled support for protectionism among the uninitiated of the North is that the low labour standards in developing countries rob adults in industrial countries of their jobs. What is overlooked is that the products that are manufactured in the worst conditions in developing countries, often using child labour, are not those that involve any serious competition between industrial and developing countries.

A nice natural experiment actually occurred in the carpet industry. Hand-knotted carpets are a classic example of labour-intensive production. For historical reasons, Iran was the largest exporter of hand-knotted carpets to the United States. Then, in the late 1980s, the United States placed an embargo on imports from Iran. Did that boost production in industrial countries? The answer, not surprisingly, is no. China, India, Nepal, and other poor countries stepped in. India, which used to be a small exporter of carpets, suddenly became a big player. In 1996 the United States, which does not make any hand-knotted carpets, imported US$316 million worth of this product. The five biggest suppliers were India (45 per cent), China (25 per cent), Pakistan (16 per cent), Turkey (6.5 per cent), and Nepal (2.9 per cent). The competition is clearly much more acute among developing countries than between developing and industrial countries.[14]

A natural consequence of this, often overlooked by the countries of the North, is that labour standards are of great concern *within* the developing countries. This concern is combined with a fear that any action on this front by any one country will cause a shift in production to some other developing country.[15] In today's world of mobile capital, each of these countries is aware of how easily capital can leave its territory and go elsewhere if its cost of labour goes up. If co-ordinated action is possible regarding certain kinds of labour standards (not necessarily the ones that industrial nations are campaigning for), this may be to the benefit of all nations. It is conceivable that if this happens, then—and this is my central argument here—even if there is scope for free-riding, each nation will be willing to forgo it as long as other nations do the same, in a manner reminiscent of traffic on the bridge on Forest Home Drive in Ithaca.

To illustrate this formally in a very simple model, assume that the developing world consists of T nations and N households. Each household has one adult and m children. Each adult produces 1 unit of labour, and each child produces $\gamma\ (< 1)$ unit of labour.

Let each household's utility function be represented by:

(2.1) $u = u\ (c, e),\ u_c \geq 0,\ u_e \leq 0$

where $c\ (\geq 0)$ denotes total consumption in the household and e is the amount of work done by each child. We assume that $e \in [0,1]$ and, for algebraic simplicity, that all children work the same amount and that adults always work; that is, adults' labour supply is perfectly inelastic. It is easy to think of the utility function as having the property that if the wage drops too low—in particular below ω—households will choose $e = 1$. This turns out to be a critical assumption in modelling child labour (Basu and Van 1998; Basu 1999).

Suppose that there are n firms operating in the developing world and that there is perfect capital mobility, so that firms will go wherever the most profit is to be made. Each firm's demand for labour is a function of the wage rate. Using w to denote the wage (for each unit of labour) and d for the demand for labour from each firm, we have:

(2.2) $d = d(w), d'(w) < 0$

First, consider a free-market equilibrium, that is an equilibrium in which there is no law against the use of child labour. Let us suppose that the free-market equilibrium occurs at a wage below ω. Hence the *free-market equilibrium* wage, w^*, is given by:

(2.3) $nd(w^*) = N + \gamma m N.$

Note that since w^* is less than ω, all children supply their labour. Hence, the total supply of labour is the total amount of adult labour (N) plus the total amount of child labour in the developing world ($\gamma m N$). An equilibrium wage is one at which total labour supply equals total labour demand

Next, consider the case in which ILSs are imposed, so that no child is allowed to supply labour. Let us call the equilibrium that prevails an *ILS equilibrium*. Clearly, in an *ILS* equilibrium, the wage, w^I, is given by:

(2.4) $nd (w^I) = N.$

Finally, consider the case in which only one country bans child labour, so that the labour standards are imposed only within the nation's boundary. Call this an NLS *equilibrium*. Evidently, in an NLS equilibrium, the wage, w^N, is given by:

(2.5) $nd(w^N) = N + \gamma m(T - 1)N/T.$

Note that (2.4) and (2.5) may be alternatively written as:

(2.4') $nd(w^I) = [N + \gamma m N] - \gamma m N$

and

(2.5') $nd(w^N) = [N + \gamma m N] - \gamma m N/T.$

It follows from (2.3), (2.4'), and (2.5') that

(2.6) $nd(w^*) > nd(w^N) > nd(w^I).$

Hence:

(2.7) $w^* < w^N < w^I.$

Let the utility levels of worker households in the three equilibria be denoted as follows. Let u^* and u^I be utilities in the free-market equilibrium and the NLS equilibrium. In an NLS equilibrium, let u^N and u^{-N} be the utilities of households in, respectively, nations that adopt the standard and nations that do not. There is much that one can do with this model, but for our present purpose it is enough to take note of two results that are easy to prove.

RESULT 2.1: Workers in a nation that imposes labour standards alone are worse-off than workers in a world in which all countries impose labour standards; that is $u^I > u^N$.

RESULT 2.2: If all developing countries impose labour standards, it is possible that all workers in these countries will be better-off. But this is not necessarily so; it is possible that

(2.8) $$u^I > u^*$$

but it is also possible that

(2.9) $$u^I < u^*.$$

Now think of the developing world as consisting of only two nations ($T=2$). Suppose that each nation has the policy option of banning child labour (strategy B) or not banning child labour (strategy N) and that each nation's own interest is to promote the welfare of its workers. Then, plainly, these two nations will be locked in the following game, in which nation 1 chooses between rows and nation 2 chooses between columns:

Game 2

	B	N
B	U^I, u^N	u^N, u^{-N}
N	U^{-N}, u^N	u^*, u^*

If (2.9) were true—which, by Result 2.2, we know is possible—ILSs would not be worthwhile from the point of view of the developing world, and so they should not be considered, assuming that the aim of ILSs is to help poor workers in poor countries and not to support small, special-interest groups. Since (2.9) and Result 2.1 imply $u^* > u^N$, (N, N) is a Nash equilibrium. It is easy to check that (B, B) is not a Nash equilibrium.

If, however, (2.8) happens to hold, it is in both nations' interest to reach the outcome (B, B). Given the parameters of this model, (B, B) may or may not be a Nash equilibrium, but (B, B) will be a behavioural Nash equilibrium whenever it is a Nash equilibrium, and it may be a behavioural Nash equilibrium even when it is not Nash. It is easy to check that a Nash equilibrium is always a behavioural Nash equilibrium (see note 11); hence, if (B, B) is a Nash equilibrium, it is also a behavioural Nash equilibrium. Next, consider the case in which (B, B) is not a Nash equilibrium but $u^{-N} + u^N < 2u^I$ and $u^N < u^*$. It is easy to check, using the above model, that these inequalities are feasible. Since (B, B) is not a Nash equilibrium, it must be that $u^{-N} > u^I$. Hence, if a player plays B, it will be taken to be a utilitarian act by the other player, and so the other player will be willing to play B.

Once again we have reached the kind of impasse that we discussed in the preceding section: no nation will individually adopt labour standards, yet all nations as a whole may be interested in such a goal.

The contentious manner in which the debate on international labour standards has been conducted illustrates many of the issues discussed in this chapter. If only national income or even per capita income is at issue, there may not be any reason to be especially concerned about labour standards. As soon, however, as we begin to show special solicitude for the standard of living of the poorest people in a society, there arises reason to be concerned about labour standards. The debate on labour standards has been so contentious that one may be led to wonder whether all nations share this concern. The above discussion suggests that even if they did share these goals, this may not be manifested in their behaviour because of conditional morality, leading to a refusal to partake in the programme unless each country perceives that others are doing their share.

2.5. CONCLUSION

This discussion began by recounting the evolution of the goals of development and the management of the national economy. I argued that the recent and growing emphasis on goals that go beyond income and economic growth to broader objectives—a better quality of life, increased education, and a more equitable distribution of goods and services—actually represents a revival of objectives that were emphasized by classical writers but had fallen into disrepute during this century. This broadening of objectives, it was argued, is desirable, but it would be helpful to have some meaningful summary measures that capture some of these multiple objectives. I proposed that in evaluating an economy's performance we should pay much greater attention to the per capita income of the poorest 20 per cent of the population and the growth rate of the per capita income of these poorest people. I did not suggest that we ignore all other indicators of the quality of life but, rather, that we use these measures in place of per capita income and the overall growth rate of an economy. The quintile income was shown to have many attractive properties, among them the fact that it probably correlates more strongly with other indicators of well-being, such as greater life expectancy and higher literacy, than does per capita income. I raised the question of why many national goals, even when they are generally recognized as important, get ignored in practice. I argued that even in our normative pursuits, there are strategic considerations that come into play because most agents have an innate sense of conditional morality. To recognize this is important because it can enable the design of co-ordinated action on the part of nations for achieving developmental objectives that go beyond national income and income growth. The problem of conditional morality was illustrated with a simple example concerning international labour standards, where desirable actions are often thwarted for reasons of strategic disadvantage. It was argued that recognizing this problem can lead to a conception of minimal international labour standards that are different from those currently being demanded by many industrial nations and that, if pursued, could make a significant contribution to improving the quality of life in developing countries.

NOTES

1. The statistics cited in this paragraph are from World Bank (1998).
2. For a lucid and comprehensive account of the changing objectives of development over the past fifty years, see Thorbecke (1999).

3. For certain kinds of social problems, such as crime, the crucial variable may be the *gap* between the per capita incomes of the richest and the poorest people in a society.
4. A similar exercise that broadens the idea of human well-being to take account more explicitly of political and civil liberties was undertaken by Dasgupta and Weale (1992).
5. Answering an interviewer's question about what is a 'successful' economy, Amartya Sen (*Chicago Tribune*, 28 March 1999) pointed out, 'This concerns how the worst-off members of society share in that society. Neglect of people at the bottom of the ladder would indicate a failed economy'.
6. An empirical study by Basu, Narayan, and Ravallion (1999) based on individual income and literacy data from Bangladesh confirms the enormous externalities of having a literate person at home. Illiterate people in households with literate members seem to earn systematically more than isolated illiterate persons. Gibson (forthcoming) finds confirmation of this result in his study of nutrition in Papua New Guinea.
7. This somewhat chilling illustration of the problem of conflict between the interests of the adviser and advisee involves the *self*-interest of the adviser. But the same problem can arise even when the adviser distorts his advice because of some *moral* interest of his that happens to conflict with the interest of the advisee. These problems are addressed at length in Basu (1997) and O'Flaherty and Bhagwati (1997). In the present exercise I stay away totally from the problem of conflict of interest between the adviser and the advisee, whether it be self-centered or moral. My focus here is on the conflict of interest between various advisees and the dilemma that this creates for the adviser who happens to be advising several advisees.
8. I have often wondered about the merit of those popular books that tell people how to become leaders. For a single individual, the advice of such a book can indeed be valuable, but if everybody follows the advice in such a book, the world can only be a worse place.
9. An exception is Hardin (1988: ch. 2), although the particular problem that I am about to discuss is not a matter that he dwells on.
10. In a more sophisticated approach, we may want to add the proviso 'as long as the personal loss from behaving like a utilitarian is not too large'.
11. Singh (1995) has presented a related analysis in which one player plays entirely to maximize aggregate utility.
12. I have not defined precisely what 'being a utilitarian' means, and indeed this is open to different interpretations. I shall here define a person choosing a certain action as being a utilitarian if that action cannot be justified in terms of his self-interest, no matter what the other person chooses, and it can be explained in utilitarian terms for some choice of action by the other person. By varying what we take to be evidence of utilitarian behaviour, alternative definitions of equilibrium play are easy to create.
13. Frank (1999) makes a similar point at the level of individuals. Conspicuous consumption and materialist zeal in modern industrial societies reach the point at which the people who practice them are worse-off in terms of their own preferences. Yet, short of some policy aimed at co-ordinated behaviour, or taxes that create the right incentives, society cannot break out of this equilibrium once it is trapped in it.
14. All statistics quoted in this paragraph are from US Department of Labor (1997).
15. This point has been made by several commentators, for instance Grimsrud and Stokke (1997) and Harvey, Collingsworth, and Athreya (1998).

34 ▪▪ DEVELOPMENT, MARKETS, AND INSTITUTIONS

REFERENCES

Atkinson, A. 1995. 'Capabilities, Exclusion and the Supply of Goods'. In K. Basu, P. Pattanaik, and K. Suzumura, eds. *Choice, Welfare and Development*. Oxford: Oxford University Press.

Aturupane, H., P. Glewwe, and P. Isenman. 1994. 'Poverty, Human Development and Growth: An Emerging Consensus?' *American Economic Review* 84 (May): 244–9.

Basu, K. 1997. 'On Misunderstanding Government: An Analysis of the Art of Policy Advice'. *Economics and Politics* 9 (3, November): 231–50.

—— 1999. 'Child labor: Cause, Consequence and Cure, with Remarks on International Labor Standards'. *Journal of Economic Literature* 37: 1083–1119.

Basu, K. and J. Foster. 1998. 'On Measuring Literacy'. *Economic Journal* 108: 1733–49.

Basu, K. and L. Lopez-Calva. 1999. 'Functionings and Capabilities'. In K. Arrow, A. K. Sen, and K. Suzumura, eds, *Handbook of Social Choice and Welfare*. Amsterdam: North-Holland.

Basu, K. and P. H. Van. 1998. 'The Economics of Child Labor'. *American Economic Review* 88 (3, June): 412–27.

Basu, K., A. Narayanan, and M. Ravallion. 1999. 'Is Knowledge Shared within Households?' Policy Research Working Paper 2261. Office of the Chief Economist, Development Economics, and Poverty and Human Resources, Development Resource Group, World Bank, Washington, DC.

Bhagwati, J. 1995. 'Trade Liberalization and Fair Trade Demands: Addressing the Environment and Labor Standards Issues'. *World Economy* 18: 745–59.

Brandolini, A. and G. D'Alessio. 1998. 'Measuring Well-Being in the Functioning Space'. Banca d'Italia. Processed.

Dasgupta, P. and M. Weale. 1992. 'On Measuring the Quality of Life'. *World Development* 20 (1, January): 119-31.

Frank, R.H. 1999. *Luxury Fever: Why Money Fails to Satisfy in an Era of Success*. New York: Free Press.

Gibson, J. Forthcoming. 'Literacy and Intrahousehold Externalities'. *World Development*.

Grimsrud, B. and L.J. Stokke. 1997. *Child Labour in Africa: Poverty or Institutional Failures?* Fafo Report 223. Oslo: Fafo Institute for Applied Social Science.

Hardin, R. 1988. *Morality within the Limits of Reason*. Chicago, Ill: University of Chicago Press.

Harvey, P. J., T. Collingsworth, and B. Athreya. 1998. 'Developing Effective Mechanisms for Implementing Labor Rights in the Global Economy'. International Labor Rights Fund, Washington, DC. Available at <http://www.laborights.org/ilrf.html>.

Herrero, C. 1996. 'Capabilities and Utilities'. *Economic Design* 2: 69–88.

Kautilya. 1992. *The Arthashastra*. Edited by L. N. Rangarajan. New Delhi: Penguin.

Marx, K. 1844. *The Economic and Philosophic Manuscripts*, trans. London: Lawrence and Wishart.

O'Flaherty, B. and J. Bhagwati. 1997. 'Will Free Trade with Political Science put Normative Economists out of Work?' *Economics and Politics* 9 (3, November): 207–19.

Rawls, J. 1971. *A Theory of Justice*. Oxford: Oxford University Press.

Ray, D. 1998. *Development Economics*. Princeton, NJ: Princeton University Press.

Repetto, R. 1995. 'Trade and Sustainable Development'. In M. G. Quibria, ed., *Critical Issues in Asian Development*. Hong Kong: Oxford University Press.

Romer, J. 1999. 'What We Owe Our Children, They Their Children, and ...'. University of California at Davis. Processed.

Sen, A. 1983. 'Development: Which Way Now?' *Economic Journal* 93 (December): 745–62.

—— 1985. *Commodities and Capabilities*. Amsterdam: North-Holland.

—— 1999. *Development as Freedom*. New York: Knopf.

Singh, N. 1995. 'Unilateral Altruism May Be Beneficial: A Game-Theoretic Illustration'. *Economics Letters* 47 (March): 275–81.

Smith, A. 1987. *The Correspondence of Adam Smith*. Edited by Ernest Mossner and Ian Ross Indianapolis, Ind.: Liberty Fund.

Srinivasan, T.N. 1996. 'International Trade and Labor Standards from an Economic Perspective'. In P. van Dyck and G. Faber, eds, *Challenges to the New World Trade Organization*. Boston, Mass.: Kluwer Law International.

Stiglitz, J. 1989. *The Economic Role of the State*. Oxford: Basil Blackwell.

—— 1998a. 'More Instruments and Broader Goals: Moving Towards the Post-Washington Consensus'. WIDER Annual Lecture, Helsinki, 7 January. Available at <http://www.worldbank.org/html/extdr/extme/js-010798/wider.htm>.

—— 1998b. 'Towards a New Paradigm for Development: Strategies, Policies and Processes'. Prebisch Lecture at the United Nations Conference on Trade and Development, Geneva, 19 October. Available at <http://www.worldbank.org/html/extdr/extme/jssp 101998.htm>.

Streeten, P. 1994. 'Human Development: Means and Ends'. *American Economic Review* 84 (May): 232–7.

Suzumura, K. 1999. 'Consequences, Opportunities and Procedures'. *Social Choice and Welfare* 16: 17–40.

Thorbecke, E. 1999. 'The Evolution of the Development Doctrine and the Role of Foreign Aid, 1950–2000'. Cornell University, Ithaca, N. Y. Processed.

UNDP (United Nations Development Programme). 1990. *Human Development Report 1990*. New York: Oxford University Press.

US Department of Labor. 1997. *By the Sweat and Toil of Children*. Vol. 4: *Consumer Labels and Child Labor*. Washington, DC: Bureau of International Labor Affairs.

Wolfensohn, J. 1999. 'A Proposal for a Comprehensive Development Framework'. Washington, DC: World Bank. Processed.

World Bank. 1998. *World Development Indicators 1998*. Washington, DC.

3 On Measuring Literacy

with James E. Foster

3.1. PROXIMATE ILLITERACY

A country's overall level of literacy is usually measured by taking the number of adults who are literate as a percentage of the total number of adults—the so-called *literacy rate*. Following Sen (1985) there has been increased use of the literacy rate and other social indicators to evaluate the overall standard of living in a country.[1] The present chapter is concerned with a particular deficiency of the literacy rate as an indicator of the aggregate benefit from this important functioning. It draws attention to this inadequacy, develops a new measure, gives it a full axiomatic characterization and offers an illustration of its use.

Suppose we learn that a certain country has a literacy rate of 40 per cent. To be sure, this number is compatible with very different scenarios of the distribution of literate persons across households. In one scenario, the literate population could be highly concentrated and separate from the illiterate population so that, say, every household is either fully literate or fully illiterate; in another, the literate individuals might be 'evenly distributed' with, say, every household containing at least one literate member. In this chapter we argue that, in a well-defined sense, a more even distribution of literacy across households leads to greater *effective* literacy. However, unlike in the similar task of measuring poverty (Sen 1976;

Previously published in *The Economic Journal*, 108 (November), 1998: 1733–49.

The authors would like to thank Kathryn Anderson, J.S. Butler, Jean Dreze, Bhaskar Dutta, Gary Fields, Andrew Foster, Bob Margo, Debraj Ray, Amartya Sen, and S. Subramanian for comments and suggestions. We are also grateful to Tridip Ray for research assistance, and to participants of the 1996 NEUDC Conference at Boston University, the 1996 India and Southeast Asia Meeting of the Econometric Society, the NBER Economic Fluctuations Working Group on Income Distribution, and the Theory Workshop at Cornell University for helpful discussions. This paper was written while Foster was on leave at Cornell; he thanks the department for its hospitality. Foster is also grateful to the John D. and Catherine T. MacArthur Foundation for financial support through its Network on Inequality and Poverty in Broader Perspective.

Clark et al. 1981; Foster et al. 1984), the concern for distribution need not reflect a concern about distribution per se. It is, of course, possible to argue that, as with all good things in life, a more even distribution of literacy is innately, ethically appealing. In the present chapter though, we contend that even if we ignore the inherent appeal of an equitable distribution, there are important *instrumental* reasons for being concerned about a 'better' distribution of literacy.

To see this, consider the following examples that involve the use of literacy skills.[2]

A. A low-skilled job is available which requires the ability to read and write.
B. Agricultural extension workers come with information on how to plant and take care of high-yielding varieties. They leave behind brochures explaining these matters.
C. A medical facility is set up in a neighbouring village. The staff distributes pamphlets on methods of preventing disease and infection, as well as information on the various services offered by the facility.

Observe that while each of these opportunities—the low-skilled job, the agricultural information, and the health facility—is intimately connected to literacy, the connection is not of the same kind. In case A, the person has to be literate himself or herself to take advantage of the opportunity. In cases B and C this may not be necessary. All one really needs is access to a literate person who is willing to provide the requisite literacy services.

It is our contention that having a literate member *in the household* can make a substantial difference for each illiterate member in accessing information and accomplishing tasks that require literacy skills. In other words, literate household members generate a *positive externality* or a kind of *public good* for illiterate members. A wide variety of studies support this intuitive hypothesis. For example, Green et al. (1985) identified family literacy as a key variable in the propensity of Guatemalan peasant farmers to adopt modern farm practices and concluded that in this respect 'an illiterate farmer with a literate family is not at a disadvantage to a farmer who is literate himself'. More recently, Foster and Rosenzweig (1996a) found that the productivity of a household farm is linked to the education level of the most educated member of the household, and that these productivity gains are greatest at the lowest education levels.[3] It is, therefore, important to distinguish between two types of illiterate persons when assessing the distribution of literacy: *a proximate illiterate,* an illiterate person who lives in a household with at least one literate member, and hence has access to the public good; and an *isolated illiterate,* an illiterate person whose household has no literate members.

The key difference between the two motivating scenarios—each having the same 40 per cent literacy rate, but a different pattern of literacy—should now be evident. In both cases, three out of every five persons are illiterate. But in the evenly distributed scenario, all three are proximate illiterates who thus share in some of the benefits of literacy; whereas in the highly concentrated scenario all are isolated illiterates who do not. Our aim in this chapter is to develop a measure of literacy which reflects this important distinction by taking account of the incidence of proximate illiteracy.

Before we proceed to measurement, some caveats are worth mentioning. There are surely cases where close proximity to a literate may be a handicap rather than a help. An illiterate woman married to a man scheming to extort more dowry may well be better off if the husband were illiterate and thereby less proficient in this effort. While we recognize that relative literacy levels can alter power relationships in a household, which in turn may affect the capabilities of household members to function, these issues are beyond the scope of the current chapter and we do not address them here. Second, in certain cases there may be differential externalities to illiterate household members from, say, a father being literate, a mother being literate, or both being literate. Our formal presentation initially abstracts from this possibility. However, in Section 3.5, we extend our measure to account for differential effects that are gender based, an alteration that may be especially important when significant inequalities between the sexes are evident. Third, the household is not the only social unit that matters in questions of literacy. If no one is literate in the household, it could still help if one person in the village were literate or even one person in the *zilla* were literate. These more distant externalities are clearly missed by our household-based measure. However, our general approach easily accommodates larger social units, and this extension is discussed in the concluding section.

3.2. EFFECTIVE LITERACY

We propose in this chapter a simple measure of a society's 'effective literacy' which takes account of the externalities mentioned above. This section provides the framework within which the measure can be defined.

Consider a country in which there are n adults and m households. Each household $h = 1, 2, ..., m$ has a *household literacy profile*, x^h, indicating each adult household member's level of literacy, where $x^h_j = 1$ is interpreted to mean that the jth member of household h is literate and $x^h_j = 0$ means that the member is illiterate.[4] We use the term *society* to refer to the vector of household literacy profiles $x = (x^1, ..., x^m)$. So, for example, x= [(0, 1): (1, 0, 0)] is a society of two households with two and three members respectively, each of which has exactly one literate member. It is important to note that x conveys information on the household structure as well as the literacy levels in the country. The household structure can be ignored by concatenating the household vectors in x to obtain the *literacy profile* $x°$. For example, society x = [(0, 1), (1, 0, 0)] has the literacy profile $x° = (0, 1, 1, 0, 0)$. Since we shall have occasion to vary the population and number of households in the country, we shall often use n_x and m_x to denote the (respective) numbers of adults and households in x. We denote the set of all possible societies (with arbitrary population size and number of households) by Δ.

A measure of literacy (*MOL*) is a mapping

$$\mathcal{L} : \Delta \to \mathfrak{R},$$

from the set of all societies to the real numbers, where $\mathcal{L}(x)$ represents the overall level of literacy associated with society x. The traditional MOL is the literacy rate R defined by

$$R(\mathbf{x}) = \sum_i x_i^o / n_x$$

where $\sum_i x_i^o = \#\{i | x_i^o = 1\}$ is simply the number of literate persons in society **x**. By definition, $R(\mathbf{x})$ is the same for all societies having the same literacy profile x^o and, consequently, the household structure is ignored by R. We now turn to a new MOL whose definition crucially depends on the specific assignment of individuals to households.

We argued in the introduction that having a literate person in a household provides external benefits to illiterate members of the same household. For simplicity, let us assume that the magnitude of these benefits, say α (with $0 < \alpha < 1$), is independent of the characteristics of household members.[5] Then the effective literacy profile for household h, denoted $\tilde{x}^h$, can be defined as follows:

$$\tilde{x}_j^h = \begin{cases} 1 \text{ if } x_j^h = 1 \\ \alpha \text{ if } x_j^h = 0, \text{ and } x_k^h = 1 \text{ for some } k \neq j \\ 0 \text{ if } x_j^h = 0 \text{ for every } k. \end{cases}$$

The overall *effective literacy profile*, which we denote by x^*, is simply the literacy profile obtained from the resulting vector of effective household profiles, that is, $x^* = (\tilde{x}^1, ..., \tilde{x}^m)^o$. So if the society is given by $\mathbf{x} = [(0, 1), (1, 0, 0), (0, 0)]$, then $x^* = (\alpha, 1, 1, \alpha, \alpha, 0, 0)$. This transformation leaves the literacy levels of the literates and isolated illiterates unchanged while assigning every proximate illiterate the 'effective' literacy level α. The magnitude of α reflects the extent to which having a literate member of household augments an illiterate's capabilities in this regard—a kind of effective literacy *equivalence scale*.[6] More generally, x_i^* is an indicator of i's access to literacy functionings.

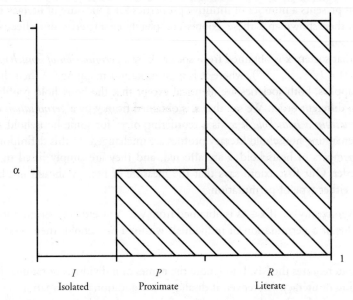

Figure 3.1 Effective Literacy Distribution

Our overall *measure of effective literacy* $\mathscr{L}^*$ is defined by

$$\mathscr{L}^*(x) = \sum_i x_i^* / n_x$$

or the original literacy rate measure applied to the effective literacy profile. Figure 3.1 depicts the ordered profile of effective literacy from lowest to highest levels, with isolated illiterates to the left, literates to the right and proximate illiterates in the middle. It is easy to see that $\mathscr{L}^*$ is the area below this graph or, equivalently,

$$\mathscr{L}^* = R + \alpha P,$$

the sum of the literacy rate R and α times P, the share of the population that is proximate illiterate.

Another related interpretation of $\mathscr{L}^*$ relies on the fraction I of isolated illiterates in the population:

$$\mathscr{L}^* = \alpha(1 - I) + (1 - \alpha)R.$$

The number $1 - I$ represents the fraction of the population with one or more literate persons in the household which may be interpreted as an alternative indicator of literacy.[7] Our measure $\mathscr{L}^*$ is a convex combination of these two literacy indicators with α being the weight on $1 - I$. Note that if the externality indicator α were 0, the measure would reduce to the usual literacy rate R; if α were 1, so that a proximate illiterate were deemed equivalent to a literate, we would obtain the measure $1 - I$. In Section 3.4 we select $\alpha = 1/4$ and $\alpha = 1/2$ for reasons of illustration.

3.3. A Simple Characterization

This section presents a number of intuitive properties for a measure of literacy to satisfy. It is then shown that these axioms completely characterize our effective literacy measure.

We say that society **x** is obtained from society **y** by a *permutation of households* if $(x^1, ..., x^m) = (y^{\pi(1)}, ..., y^{\pi(m)})$, where π is a permutation mapping.[8] When this definition applies, both societies are identical except that the household profiles are listed in different order. We say that **x** is obtained from **y** by a *permutation of individuals within a household* if x^h is a reordering of y^h for some household h, while the remaining household literacy profiles are unchanged. In this definition, only the members of household h are affected, and they are simply listed in a different order. Our first axiom says that the measure of literacy should not be affected by either type of permutation.

AXIOM A (Anonymity):   If $\mathbf{x} \in \Delta$ is obtained from $\mathbf{y} \in \Delta$ by either a permutation of households or a permutation of individuals within a household, then $\mathscr{L}(\mathbf{x}) = \mathscr{L}(\mathbf{y})$.

This axiom requires the MOL to ignore the names of individuals or families in the evaluation of literacy. Moreover, it disallows any additional information on a person to be considered, such as the gender of the person or the gender of fellow household members.

We say that society $\mathbf{x}$ is obtained from society $\mathbf{y}$ by a *simple increment* if $x_j^h = 1$ and $y_j^h = 0$, while $x_j.^{h'} = y_j.^{h'}$ for all $(h', j') \neq (h, j)$. In other words, the only change in this case is that one person goes from being illiterate in $\mathbf{y}$ to being literate in $\mathbf{x}$. The next axiom requires the literacy measure to be consistent with this change.

AXIOM M (Monotonicity): If $\mathbf{x} \in \Delta$ is obtained from $\mathbf{y} \in \Delta$ by a simple increment, then, $\mathscr{L}(\mathbf{x}) > \mathscr{L}(\mathbf{y})$.

If one person's literacy level rises, and the rest of the society stays unchanged, the Monotonicity axiom requires overall literacy to rise.

We say that society $\mathbf{x}$ is obtained from society $\mathbf{y}$ by a *household split* if $\mathbf{y}$ has m households, $\mathbf{x}$ has $m + 1$ households, y^m is the concatenation of x^m and x^{m+1}, and $x^h = y^h$ for all other households $h = 1, ..., m - 1$. In other words, the last household in $\mathbf{y}$ splits into the two final households in $\mathbf{x}$, while the rest of the households remain the same.[9] The split is called *externality-neutral* if either (i) both x^m and x^{m+1} contain a literate person, or (ii) neither of x^m or x^{m+1} contains a literate person. It is called *externality reducing* if exactly one of x^m or x^{m+1} contains a literate person. The next axiom ensures that the MOL reflects the change in externality due to the changing household structure. If the split does not affect anyone's access to a literate household member, then literacy is unchanged. If the split creates isolated illiterates, then literacy must decrease.

AXIOM E (Externality): Suppose that $\mathbf{x} \in \Delta$ is obtained from $\mathbf{y} \in \Delta$ by a household split. If the split is externality-neutral, then $\mathscr{L}(\mathbf{x}) = \mathscr{L}(\mathbf{y})$; and if the split is externality-reducing, then $\mathscr{L}(\mathbf{x}) < \mathscr{L}(\mathbf{y})$.

Clearly this is the central axiom of our effective literacy proposal. In particular, if Axiom E is accepted, then the traditional literacy rate R is no longer viable as it regards all household splits with indifference.

We say that society $\mathbf{x}$ is *completely literate* if $x_j^h = 1$ for all h and all j; $\mathbf{x}$ is *completely illiterate* if $x_j^h = 0$ for all h and all j. The next axiom normalizes the MOL.

AXIOM N (Normalization): If $\mathbf{x} \in \Delta$ is completely literate, then $\mathscr{L}(\mathbf{x}) = 1$; if $\mathbf{x} \in \Delta$ is completely illiterate, then $\mathscr{L}(\mathbf{x}) = 0$.

The final axiom allows the MOL to be calculated from regional data and aggregated to obtain the original level of literacy. We say that society $\mathbf{x}$ is *decomposed* into societies $\mathbf{y}$ and $\mathbf{z}$ if $y^h = x^h$ for all $h = 1, ..., n_y$ and $z^h = x^{n_y + h}$ for all $h = 1, ..., n_z$, where $n_x = n_y + n_z$. Note that this definition requires individual households to remain intact (that is, no splitting) when society $\mathbf{x}$ is broken down into societies $\mathbf{y}$ and $\mathbf{z}$.

AXIOM D (Decomposition): Suppose that $\mathbf{x} \in \Delta$ is decomposed into $\mathbf{y} \in \Delta$ and $\mathbf{z} \in \Delta$. Then $\mathscr{L}(\mathbf{x}) = (n_y/n_x) \mathscr{L}(\mathbf{y}) + (n_z/n_x) \mathscr{L}(\mathbf{z})$.

In other words, overall literacy in $\mathbf{x}$ is a weighted average of the levels of literacy in $\mathbf{y}$ and $\mathbf{z}$, with the weights being the population shares. Repeated application of Axiom D shows that the same relationship holds for any number of constituent societies. So, for example, if we know the effective literacy rates of Bihar, Kerala,

West Bengal, and the remaining states of India, then India's overall level of literacy is the weighted average of these component rates, with the weights being the states' (adult) population shares. Properties of this type have proved to be extremely useful in the measurement of poverty and inequality, particularly when it comes to analyses by region, ethnicity, or other population subgroups.[10]

Note that the traditional measure of literacy, R, satisfies each of Axioms A, M, N, D, and the first part of Axiom E. The second part of Axiom E is violated since R is unaffected by household splits. In addition, the other literacy measure $1 - I$ satisfies Axioms A, E, N, D, but not M, since a simple increment leaves $1 - I$ unchanged if it occurs in a household that already has a literate member. We now show that $\mathscr{L}^*$ is the unique measure satisfying all five of these axioms.

THEOREM 3.1: *A measure of literacy $\mathscr{L}$ satisfies axioms A, M, E, N and D if and only if $\mathscr{L} = \mathscr{L}^*$ for same α satisfying $0 < \alpha < 1$.*

Proof: Let $\mathscr{L}$ be a MOL which satisfies axioms A, M, E, N, and D. Consider any society $\mathbf{x} \in \Delta$. Applying Axiom D repeatedly yields $\mathscr{L}(\mathbf{x}) = \sum_h (n_h/n_x)\mathscr{L}(x^h)$, where n_h is the size of household h and $\mathscr{L}(x^h)$ is the level of literacy of the society containing the single household h. We need only determine the form of $\mathscr{L}$ over single household societies to derive the overall form of $\mathscr{L}$.

Let us define $r(x^h)$ and $s(x^h)$ to be the numbers of literate and illiterate members in x^h. Axiom A ensures that $\mathscr{L}(x^h) = \mathscr{L}(y^h)$ wherever $r(x^h) = r(y^h)$ and $s(x^h) = s(y^h)$. Consequently, if we define f by

$$f(r, s) = n_h \mathscr{L}(x^h),$$

where x^h is any household profile with $r(x^h) = r$ and $s(x^h) = s$, then f is a well-defined function. Moreover, from Axiom N we obtain $f(t, 0) = t$ and $f(0, t) = 0$, while Axioms D and E yield $f(t, t) = tf(1, 1)$, for all integers $t \geq 1$.

Now define $\alpha = f(1, 1) - 1$ and let $t \geq 1 + |r - s|$. Then by Axioms D and E,

$$f(r, s) + f(t, 0) = f(s, s) + f(r - s + t, 0)$$

for all integers r, s, t with $r, t \geq 1$. But then

$$f(r, s) = r + \alpha s \text{ for } r > 1$$

and hence

$$\mathscr{L}(x^h) = \frac{r(x^h) + \alpha s(x^h)}{n_h} \quad \text{for } x^h \text{ with } r(x^h) > 1.$$

In particular, $\alpha = 2\mathscr{L}(0, 1) - 1$, so that by Axioms E and N we have $\alpha > 2\mathscr{L}[(0), (1)] - 1 = 0$. Moreover, by Axioms M and N we have $\alpha < 2\mathscr{L}(1, 1) - 1 = 1$ and so $0 < \alpha < 1$ as desired. We will now show that the measure $\mathscr{L}$ must be the effective literacy measure $\mathscr{L}^*$ for this α.

Consider the effective literacy profile $\bar{x}^h$ for household h. Clearly $\sum_j \bar{x}^h_j = 0$ in the case where h in $\mathbf{x}$ has no literate members (i.e., $r(x^h) = 0$), while if h has at least one literate member (i.e., $r(x^h) \geq 1$), it follows that $\sum_j \bar{x}^h_j = [r(x^h) + \alpha s(x^h)]$ by definition of $\bar{x}^h$. In either case, then, $n_h \mathscr{L}(x^h) = \sum_j \bar{x}^h_j$ by the above derivation. Substituting this into the decomposition $\mathscr{L}(\mathbf{x}) = \sum_b (n_b/n_x)\, \mathscr{L}(x^b)$ and recalling the definition of the effective literacy profile $x^* = (\bar{x}^1 \ldots, \bar{x}^m)^\circ$ yields $\mathscr{L}(\mathbf{x}) = \sum x_i^*/n_x = \mathscr{L}^*(\mathbf{x})$ as we originally set out to prove.

To complete the proof, one can easily check that $\mathscr{L}^*$ satisfies Axioms A, M, E, N, and D.

The above result offers support for our effective literacy measure $\mathscr{L}^*$ as the only MOL satisfying the five axioms. Of course, this is not a particularly noteworthy result if the axioms used to characterize the measure are not justified. The motivation for Axiom E has been rather extensively addressed; but what about the remaining four axioms? Several arguments have been given on their behalf, including the fact that the traditional literacy rate R itself satisfies all four of them. But we can actually take this argument a step further. Consider the following alternative to Axiom E:

Axiom I (*Indifference*): If $\mathbf{x} \in \Delta$ is obtained from $\mathbf{y} \in \Delta$ by a household split, then $\mathscr{L}(\mathbf{x}) = \mathscr{L}(\mathbf{y})$.

Axiom I is the embodiment of the observation that the literacy rate R is indifferent to household structure. It is easy to show the following result:

THEOREM 3.2: *A measure of literacy $\mathscr{L}$ satisfies Axioms A, M, I, N and D if and only if $\mathscr{L} = R$, the traditional literacy rate.*

So the four basic axioms A, M, N, and D, provide a basic framework within which the measures R and $\mathscr{L}^*$ can be compared. If we add a requirement that literacy is indifferent to household structure, this leads to the above characterization of R. But if Axiom I is rejected in favour of Axiom E, our effective literacy measure must be chosen. Whenever proximate illiterates become isolated illiterates as a result of a change in household structure, Axiom E requires acknowledgment of this fact; and this in turn justifies $\mathscr{L}^*$.

3.4. LITERACY IN INDIA: AN ILLUSTRATION

Our previous discussion offered a conceptual basis for our measure of effective literacy. We now turn to an illustrative application of the measure to show how it may be used in practice.

The data we use are from the 1981 Indian Census (Registrar General of India, 1988, 1989) and the literacy tabulations of Sharma and Retherford (1993). Table 3.1 reports on several series drawn from the state-wise, cross-sectional data on adult literacy.[11] The first column is the traditional literacy rate R, where the states have been ordered from highest to lowest beginning with Kerala's 81.6 per cent and finishing with Arunachal Pradesh's 25.6 per cent level. The all-India rate of 43.3 per cent has been calculated from the state-wise figures using the decomposition formula.

The Census also provides information on the number of literate members in households of various sizes, and this has been used to obtain the 'proximate illiteracy rate' P and the 'isolated illiteracy rate' I reported in the next two columns.[12] Our literacy measure $\mathscr{L}^*$ appears in Columns 4 and 5 for two values of α, namely, $\alpha = 1/4$ and $\alpha = 1/2$, while the non-isolated literacy rate $1 - I$ is reported in Column 6. The numbers in parentheses are the state's rankings according to each literacy measure; they indicate the extent to which the ordering by R corresponds to the orderings by $\mathscr{L}^*$ and $1 - I$. The 'gender gap' G between male and female literacy rates is listed in Column 7 for comparison purposes.

Let us first examine the overall picture of literacy as revealed by the all-India figures at the bottom of Table 3.1. The percentages of the population that are literate, proximate illiterate, and isolated illiterate are $R = 43.3$ per cent, $P = 31.7$ per cent and $I = 25.0$ per cent, respectively. The proximate illiterate group comprises almost one-third of the entire population of India and more than half of the illiterates. Clearly a significant subset of the population has immediate access to some portion of the functionings typically associated with literacy—an empirical fact that is overlooked by studies that rely exclusively on the traditional rate R.

The quantitative impact on the assessment of literacy is captured by the extent to which our effective literacy rate $\mathscr{L}^*$ exceeds R. This in turn depends both on the observed P and the assumed magnitude α of the intrahousehold externality. When

Table 3.1: Literacy in Indian States (1981)

State	R	P	I	$\mathscr{L}^*$ $\alpha = 1/4$		$\mathscr{L}^*$ $\alpha = 1/2$		$1 - I$ $\alpha = 1$		G
Kerala	81.6	16.7	1.7	85.7	(1)	89.9	(1)	98.3	(1)	12
Mizoram	74.0	21.8	4.2	79.5	(2)	84.9	(2)	95.8	(2)	11
Goa	65.3	26.4	8.3	71.9	(3)	78.5	(3)	91.7	(3)	21
Maharashtra	55.8	31.4	12.7	63.7	(4)	71.6	(4)	87.3	(5)	29
Tamil Nadu	54.4	29.7	15.9	61.8	(5)	69.2	(6)	84.1	(7)	28
Gujarat	52.2	31.4	16.4	60.0	(7)	67.9	(8)	83.6	(8)	27
Himachal Pradesh	51.2	36.8	12.0	60.4	(6)	69.6	(5)	88.0	(4)	27
Nagaland	50.3	32.2	17.5	58.3	(9)	66.4	(9)	82.5	(11)	18
Tripura	50.1	29.9	20.0	57.6	(10)	65.1	(11)	80.0	(12)	23
Manipur	49.7	36.9	13.4	58.9	(8)	68.1	(7)	86.6	(6)	29
West Bengal	48.6	28.7	22.7	55.8	(12)	63.0	(13)	77.3	(15)	24
Punjab	48.2	34.7	17.1	56.9	(11)	65.5	(10)	82.9	(10)	16
Karnataka	46.2	32.4	21.4	54.3	(13)	62.4	(14)	78.6	(13)	26
Haryana	43.9	39.4	16.7	53.7	(14)	63.6	(12)	83.3	(9)	32
Meghalaya	42.0	28.7	29.3	49.2	(16)	56.4	(17)	70.7	(17)	9
Sikkim	42.0	35.4	22.6	50.8	(15)	59.7	(15)	77.4	(14)	26
Orissa	41.0	32.8	26.2	49.2	(17)	57.4	(16)	73.8	(16)	31
Andhra Pradesh	35.7	28.3	36.0	42.7	(18)	49.8	(20)	64.0	(22)	25
Madhya Pradesh	34.2	33.0	32.8	42.5	(19)	50.7	(19)	67.2	(19)	29
Uttar Pradesh	33.4	35.8	30.9	42.3	(20)	51.2	(18)	69.1	(18)	30
Bihar	32.1	32.0	35.9	40.1	(21)	48.1	(21)	64.1	(21)	30
Rajasthan	30.1	35.1	34.8	38.9	(22)	47.7	(22)	65.2	(20)	31
Arunachal Pradesh	25.6	28.1	46.3	32.6	(23)	39.6	(23)	53.7	(23)	21
India	43.3	31.7	25.0	51.3		59.2		75.0		

α = 1/4, so that a proximate illiterate is 'equivalent' to one-fourth of a literate for purposes of evaluation, we obtain an effective literacy rate that is just above 51 per cent. If α rises to 1/2, the figure rises to about 59 per cent. An upper bound on $\mathcal{L}^*$ is given by $1 - I = 75$ per cent; the remaining fourth of the population are isolated illiterates and make no contribution to $\mathcal{L}^*$.

We should emphasize that although our effective literacy measure $\mathcal{L}^*$ is higher than the traditional rate R, this in itself does not imply greater incidence of literate persons nor increased satisfaction with the status quo. The approach simply offers a way of gauging actual achievement more accurately and differentiates between otherwise indistinguishable societies. Thus $R = 43.3$ per cent and $P = 31.7$ per cent presents a rather different view of literacy achievements in India than $P = 0$ per cent or for that matter $P = 56.7$ per cent. The measure $\mathcal{L}^*$ recognizes and incorporates these distinctions.

Now moving to a state-wise view of literacy in India, we note a wide range of literacy rates R across the states, from 25.6 per cent in Arunachal Pradesh to 81.6 per cent in Kerala. There are also tremendous differences in the isolated illiteracy rate I, from 1.7 per cent in Kerala to 46.3 per cent in Arunachal Pradesh. It is interesting, therefore, to note that the proximate illiteracy rate P stays in a relatively narrow band—from 16.7 per cent in Kerala to 39.4 per cent in Haryana— about the all-India level of 31.7 per cent. As we shall see, though, the state wise variation in P is sufficient to lead to a re-ranking of states using $\mathcal{L}^*$ instead of R.

Before proceeding to this discussion, we should point out an interesting phenomenon: the three states with the highest levels of R have the lowest levels of P. The percentage of the illiterate population that is proximate illiterate (namely $P/(P + I)$) is certainly higher in the most literate states. But the lower absolute number of illiterates restricts the magnitude of P and hence the potential importance of the intrahousehold externality in evaluating literacy in high literacy regions. In this sense, our effective literacy approach may prove to be less important for assessments in developed countries—but is particularly well-suited for evaluating literacy in the developing world.[13]

Returning once again to Table 3.1 we see that apart from the especially low values of P for the top three states, there is no readily discernible relationship between P and R. High and low values of P can be found throughout the remaining distribution. The definition of $\mathcal{L}^*$ ensures that states with higher values tend to move up the distribution as α rises; while especially low values of P will have the opposite effect. For example, Manipur, with a value of $P = 36.9$ per cent rises from the tenth spot to seventh as α goes from 0 to 1/2. West Bengal moves down the distribution from eleventh to thirteenth over the same range of α, owing to its low value of $P = 28.7$ per cent. Table 3.2 focus on the relative rankings of 10 'mid-range' states as α takes on the values 0, 1/4, 1/2, and 1. In line with the above discussion, Himachal Pradesh, Manipur, Punjab, and Haryana all rise at least two ranks as α increases from 0 to 1/2; Gujarat, Tripura, and West Bengal likewise fall due to their lower P values. When the intrahousehold externality is taken into account, the relative ranking of the states, and hence the regional picture of literacy in India, is clearly altered.[14]

Table 3.2: Literacy Rankings of 10 Indian States

R $\alpha = 0$	$\mathscr{L}^*$ $\alpha = 1/4$	$\mathscr{L}^*$ $\alpha = 1/2$	$1 - I$ $\alpha = 1$
Tamil Nadu	Tamil Nadu	Himachal Pradesh	Himachal Pradesh
Gujarat	Himachal Pradesh	Tamil Nadu	Manipur
Himachal Pradesh	Gujarat	Manipur	Tamil Nadu
Nagaland	Manipur	Gujarat	Gujarat
Tripura	Nagaland	Nagaland	Haryana
Manipur	Tripura	Punjab	Punjab
West Bengal	Punjab	Tripura	Nagaland
Punjab	West Bengal	Haryana	Tripura
Karnataka	Karnataka	West Bengal	Karnataka
Haryana	Haryana	Karnataka	West Bengal

This new way of viewing literacy leads us immediately to ask about the *causes* of the statewide variations in P and hence the re-rankings of literacy according to $\mathscr{L}^*$. Why, for example, is P so low in Tamil Nadu and so high in Haryana? While a complete answer is beyond the scope of this chapter, we can at least speculate on the types of factors that may be pertinent. For example, to the extent that literacy is related to the status or caste of the individual, and assuming that most households stay within caste, this would tend to *lower* P. On the other hand, if literacy is associated with the gender of the individual then, assuming that most households have a mixture of genders, this would tend to *raise* P. Returning to the case of Haryana, note that both P and the 'gender gap' G between its male and female literacy rates (the last column of Table 3.1) are the highest in India. This suggests that the second of the two explanations might be applicable here. Tamil Nadu also has a high gender gap, and yet it has a modest level of $P = 29.7$ per cent. This points away from the second scenario and towards the first (or some other) alternative as a possible explanation of its lower ranking under $\mathscr{L}^*$ as α rises.[15] Formal testing of these and other potential hypotheses would, of course, require additional data on the gender, caste, and other characteristics of household members.

3.5. LITERACY AND GENDER

The above illustration has emphasized the potential differences between our new measure $\mathscr{L}^*$ and the traditional literacy rate R. In particular, the large variations in the proximate illiteracy rate P, can lead $\mathscr{L}^*$ to paint a rather different picture of literacy across states. But while the two measures may differ in their sensitivity to the distribution of literacy across households, they are quite similar in their treatment of gender, namely both are *gender neutral*. This section considers situations where a *gender-sensitive* literacy measure might be preferable.

First, following Anand and Sen (1995), one might specifically be 'concerned with inequalities in the opportunities and predicaments of women and men' and consequently regard a higher gender gap—at a given average rate R—as inherently undesirable. In response to this concern, Anand and Sen construct a 'gender-equity-sensitive-indicator' for literacy based on the 'equally distributed equivalent (ede)' of Atkinson (1970). The resulting index is a measure of overall achievement which, unlike R, is sensitive to the distribution of these achievements across the two genders.[16]

The second motivation returns to our original, instrumental reasons for caring about the distribution of literacy. Even when there is no particular concern about gender inequality *per se*, if it so happens that females are more effective than males in generating literacy externalities in the household, then a general concern for greater effective literacy could translate into a *specific* concern for greater female literacy. Indeed, there are many studies which suggest the presence of a gender bias in the technology for creating externalities in the household, and hence that the set of functionings available to an illiterate person by virtue of having access to a literate female is larger than the set available when the only literate in the household is male.[17] The measure of effective literacy can be modified to take this into account.

Distinguish between an *m-proximate illiterate*, who lives in a household with at least one literate male and no literate females; and an *f-proximate illiterate*, whose household contains at least one female literate. Compute an effective literacy profile x^{**} by giving an effective literacy value of α_m to each m-proximate illiterate and α_f to each f-proximate illiterate, while, as before literates and isolated illiterates receive values of 1 and 0, respectively. Given the above discussion, we take $0 < \alpha_m < \alpha_f < 1$. Then the *gender-adjusted measure* of effective literacy is

$$\mathscr{L}^{**} = \sum_i x_i^{**}/n_x = R + \alpha_m P_m + \alpha_f P_f$$

where $P_m(P_f)$ is the share of $m(f)$-proximate illiterates in the population.

The measure $\mathscr{L}^{**}$ is clearly sensitive to the distribution of literacy between the genders. But rather than preferring *equality* in literacy achievements, it favours increases in female literacy because of the differential externality levels (α_f versus α_m) conferred on illiterate household members.[18] Indeed, even if a substantial gender gap in favour of female literacy were to exist, $\mathscr{L}^{**}$ would recommend increasing the gap further by a 'transfer' of literacy from, say, male to female in a two-person household. Note also that while the gender-adjusted measure $\mathscr{L}^{**}$ satisfies Axioms A, M, N, and D (where the definition of a society is suitably altered to include gender information), it violates Axiom E since certain splits that were formerly 'externality neutral' now alter the measured level of literacy.

3.6. CONCLUDING REMARKS

This chapter presented a new approach to evaluating literacy and an effective literacy measure that take into account the intrahousehold externality arising from the presence of a literate member. A simple and natural characterization of the new measure was given, along with an empirical illustration of its use. We also considered a 'gender-adjusted' specification in which the magnitude of the intrahousehold externality is sensitive to the gender of literate members.

Our new measures were constructed to include an important externality in the household—an externality missed by the traditional literacy rate. Consequently, they are likely to be superior to R in predicting or explaining other achievements that depend on literacy. For example, we can expect the rate of diffusion of a new technology for farming to be more closely linked to our effective literacy rate than to the usual literacy rate.[19] Similarly if the presence (or lack) of at least one literate household member influences the likelihood of children to become literate, the effective literacy rate should also be a better predictor of future generations' literacy levels. Of course, whether and to what extent our measures are better indicators of these and other attainments are empirical questions. But we have every reason to expect positive results in this regard.

In addition, changing the way that aggregate literacy is measured is likely to alter the perceived efficacy of actual literacy programmes, which in turn may influence their design. For example, R registers the same improvement when, say, (i) five persons from the same household become literate or (ii) five persons from different isolated illiterate households become literate. In contrast $\mathscr{L}^*$ would see greater benefit from (ii) than from (i), while $\mathscr{L}^{**}$ will emphasize female literacy in its selection of the five persons in (ii). Consequently, we could expect some change in emphasis if these measures were used instead of the traditional literacy rate, namely a shift towards ensuring that at least one person per household is literate (under $\mathscr{L}^*$) or focusing more fervently on the problem of female illiteracy (under $\mathscr{L}^{**}$).[20]

Finally, we should note that while our measure is based on the household as the unit of analysis, our general approach has much broader potential application. For example, suppose that each person in society has an extended 'social network' containing close friends and kin (and presumably the members of one's own household) who can be freely accessed for literacy (and other) needs.[21] Then our framework carries over immediately to this expanded environment. Simply define a proximate illiterate to be an illiterate person who has access to a literate person in his or her social network, and then let the effective literacy measure be the usual literacy rate R augmented by some share $\alpha > 0$ of the resulting proximate illiteracy rate P.

Of course, this kind of evaluation would require extensive information on relationships between people—information that is usually not available in conventional data sets. An alternative approach would be to partition the population into *observable* social units in such a way that most of these beneficial connections are likely to reside *within* a group and few are likely to extend *across* groups. Examples might include culturally defined units like ethnic groups, or geographically defined units like neighbourhoods, villages, and districts.[22] The underlying approach would still apply, but the definition of proximate literacy and the nature of the externality would have to be re-evaluated in this setting. For example, one could argue that as the average 'social distance' among members grows there will be a tendency for the literacy externality to become internalized in a 'market for

literacy'. Literacy skills, like other personal services, can be withheld and, therefore, sold for a price; a literate person can charge a fee for writing a letter or for
explaining the contents of a pamphlet. We have assumed that the groups are
altruistic units with strong social ties, and hence that the full externality α is
realized by illiterate members. But if literate and illiterate members are weakly
linked, fees maybe charged, which can result in lower net benefits from the
externality. The exact form that such a market for literacy might take, and how its
presence might alter α, are interesting topics for future exploration.

We should also note that there may be qualitative changes in the way α is
configured as we shift among the various kinds of social units. For instance, in
certain cases the extent of the externality could depend on the *percentage* of
persons in the group who are literate, rather than on the mere presence of a literate
member. The argument would be that a higher percentage of literate adults may
ensure a more frequent access to literacy skills, and hence conveys a greater
externality. Further work may shed some light on this important question.

NOTES

1. See also Sen (1987) and UNDP (1990).
2. For other examples of the use (and impact) of literacy, see Bhola (1984, 1994), Hayes
   and Valentine (1989), Margo (1990), and Wagner and Puchner (1992).
3. See also the many references given in Green et al. (1985) and the case studies presented
   by Fingeret (1983). Dreze and Saran (1995) discuss a related type of externality in
   which the benefits of education accrue across individuals by 'one person taking
   decisions on behalf of another person'.
4. This makes the usual assumption that individual literacy is a $0 - 1$ variable. Of course,
   the underlying literacy variable is likely continuous and even multivariate (see for
   example Harris and Hodges 1995: 140–1) with arbitrary cut-ff (see for example Peck
   and Kling 1977). We abstract from these potentially important considerations.
5. The framework can be generalized to allow α to depend on characteristics like gender
   and age of household members. One such extension is explored in Section 3.5.
6. This analogy between 'equivalent income' and 'effective literacy' is quite apt. Both
   approaches use information on household structure to transform the raw data—
   which in the case of equivalence scales may include the economies of scale from living
   together in a household unit. See, for example, Deaton and Muellbauer (1980) and
   Coulter et al. (1992a, b)
7. See, for example, Rogers and Herzog (1966) or Sharma and Retherford (1993: 117–
   31), although both report the percentage of *households* that are isolated rather than the
   percentage of isolated illiterates.
8. A permutation mapping π is a function on $\{1, 2, ..., m\}$ that is one-to-one and onto.
   Its effect is to change the order of the indexes.
9. Given Axiom A, this definition is applicable to every household. A paper by Foster and
   Rosenzweig (1996b) develops and estimates a model of household splits to help
   understand how the Green Revolution affected the income distribution. Interestingly,
   their model posits a household education externality that influences an individual's
   decision to leave the household.

10. See the careful analysis of Malaysian inequality and poverty by Anand (1983). A general discussion of decomposition postulates can be found in Foster and Sen (1997).
11. We exclude several states and union territories for ease of presentation. Note that India uses a cut-off of 7+ years of age in defining its 'adult' population for purposes of measuring literacy.
12. Since the 'household size' variable reported in the Census is top-coded (at 6) and includes children, certain simplifying assumptions have been made—namely, (i) for households with six or more members, the mean household size for proximate and isolated households is the same; and (ii) the percentage of illiterates that are children is the same for proximate and isolated households. It turns out that our qualitative results are quite robust to alternative specifications.
13. Indeed if all illiterates are proximate illiterates, then the rankings delivered up by $\mathcal{L}^*$ and R will be identical.
14. The figure also depicts many cases of 'dominance' where the ranking of states is independent of α. For example, Nagaland is ranked lower than Tamil Nadu at both R and $1-I$, and hence at all α between 0 and 1.
15. Other possible explanations for the variations in P include statewise differences in the structure of families (prevalence of joint family households) or in the age structure of literacy (higher literacy in younger cohorts). On the latter possibility, see Margo's (1990: 6–9) related discussion of literacy in the US South. There is a positive correlation between P and G, which suggests that a gender-based explanation may be important for several of the states.
16. Their index is $R_{ede} = (s_F F^{1-\varepsilon} + s_M M^{1-\varepsilon})^{1/(1-\varepsilon)}$, where s_F and F (respectively, s_M and M) are the population shares and literacy rate for females (males), and $\varepsilon \geq 0$ is a parameter reflecting aversion to inequality between the sexes. A similar methodology could be applied in the case of our effective literacy measure by separating out the male and female components and aggregating according to the ede.
17. See, for example, the empirical findings of Murthi et al. (1995) or Nag (1983). This distinction may be even more important if other indirect benefits of female literacy— in particular those received by children—are taken into account. For example, infant mortality is well known to have a strong negative correlation with maternal literacy (Caldwell 1979).
18. We are implicitly assuming that each is the first person to be educated in the household, and hence the relevant comparison is between α_m and α_f. If most literates are males, however, the relevant comparison may be between educating another isolated illiterate who is male or an m-proximate illiterate who is female, in which case the magnitude of α_m versus $\alpha_f - \alpha_m$ becomes relevant.
19. This hypothesis receives some support from the work of Green et al. (1985) and Foster and Rosenzweig (1996a)
20. For example, a literacy programme that educates one female member in each completely illiterate, large household would raise $\mathcal{L}^{**}$ most rapidly. Practical considerations, though, can also affect the optimal design of programmes. For example, there may be significant economies of scale from teaching entire families, or entire villages, at the same time. Also, in many societies there are significant social barriers to female household members becoming literate ahead of male members. See, for example, Gustafsson (1991: 100).

21. Case studies of illiterate adults in the United States reveal intricate networks of social connections constructed by illiterates to help them function in a literate society. See, for example, Fingeret (1983) and Ziegahn (1991).

22. See, for example, Benabou (1994), Borjas (1995) and Durlauf (1994) for discussions of externalities in ethnic groups and neighbourhoods.

REFERENCES

Anand, S. 1983. *Inequality and Poverty in Malaysia: Measurement and Decomposition*. New York: Oxford University Press.

Anand, S. and A. Sen. 1995. 'Gender Inequality in Human Development: Theories and Measurement'. Human Development Report Office Occasional Paper 19. New York: UNDP.

Atkinson, A.B. 1970. 'On the Measurement of Inequality'. *Journal of Economic Theory* 2: 244–63.

Benabou, R. 1994. 'Human Capital, Inequality, and Growth: A Local Perspective'. *European Economic Review* 38: 817-26

Bhola, H.S. 1984. *Campaigning for Literacy*. Paris: UNESCO.

—— 1994. *A Source Book for Literacy Work*. London: UNESCO.

Borjas, G.J. 1995. 'Ethnicity, Neighborhoods, and Human-capital Externalities'. *American Economic Review* 7: 365–90.

Caldwell, J.C. 1979. 'Education as Factor in Mortality Decline', *Population Studies 33*: 395–13.

Clark, S., R. Hemming, and D. Ulph. 1981. 'On Indices for the Measurement of Poverty'. *Economic Journal* 91: 515–26.

Coulter, F.A.E., F.A. Cowell, and S.P. Jenkins. 1992a. 'Difference in Needs and Assessment of Income Distributions'. *Bulletin of Economic Research* 44: 77–124.

—— 1992b. 'Equivalence Scale Relativities and the Extent of Inequality and Poverty'. *Economic Journal* 102: 1067–82.

Deaton, A. and J. Muellbauer. 1980. *Economics and Consumer Behaviour*. Cambridge: Cambridge University Press.

Dreze, J. and M. Saran. 1995. 'Primary Education and Economic Development in China and India: Overview and Two Case Studies'. In K. Basu, P.K. Pattanaik, and K. Suzumura eds. *Choice, Welfare and Development*, Oxford: Clarendon Press.

Durlauf, S.N. 1994. 'Spillovers, Stratification, and Inequality'. *European Economic Review* 38: 836–45.

Fingeret, A. 1983. 'Social Network: A New Perspective on Independence and Literate Adults'. *Adult Education Quarterly* 33: 133–46.

Foster, A.D. and M.R. Rosenzweig. 1996a. 'Technical Change and Human-capital Returns and Investments: Evidence from the Green Revolution'. *American Economic Review* 86: 931–53.

—— 1996b. 'Household Division, Inequality and Rural Economic Growth'. University of Pennsylvania, Philadelphia. Mimeo.

Foster, J.E. and A. Sen. 1997. 'On Economic Inequality after a Quarter Century'. Annexe to the expanded edition of *On Economic Inequality* by A. Sen. Oxford: Clarendon Press.

Foster, J.E., J. Greer, and E. Thorbecke. 1984. 'A Class of Decomposable Poverty Measures'. *Econometrica* 52: 761–76.

Green, S.E., T.A. Rich, and E.G. Nesman. 1985. 'Beyond Individual Literacy: The Role of Shared Literacy for Innovation in Guatemala'. *Human Organization* 44: 313–21.

Gustafsson, U. 1991. *Can Literacy Lead to Development? A Case Study in Literacy, Adult Education, and Economic Development in India*. Arlington: University of Texas.

Guthrie, J.T. 1983. 'Equilibrium of Literacy'. *Journal of Reading* 26: 382–44.

Harris, T.L. and R.E. Hodges, eds. 1995. *The Literacy Dictionary: The Vocabulary of Reading and Writing*. Reading Association.

Hayes, E.R. and T. Valentine. 1989. 'The Functional Literacy Needs of Low-literate Adult Basic Education Students'. *Adult Education Quarterly* 40: 1–14.

Margo, R.A. 1990. *Race and Schooling in the South 1890–1950: An Economic History*. Chicago: University of Chicago Press.

Murthi, M., A.C. Guio, and J. Dreze. 1995. 'Mortality, Fertility and Gender Bias in India'. *Population and Development Review* 21: 745–82.

Nag, M. 1983. 'Impact of Social and Economic Development on Mortality: Comparative Study of Kerala and West Bengal'. *Economic and Political Weekly* 18: 877–900.

Peck, C.V.N. and M. Kling. 1977. 'Adult Literacy in the Seventies: Its Definition and Measurement'. *Journal of Reading* 20: 677–82.

Registrar General of India 1988. *Census of India, 1981: Household Tables*. New Delhi: Controller of Publications, Government of India.

—— 1989. *Census of India, 1981: Social and Cultural Tables*. New Delhi: Controller of Publications, Government of India.

Rogers, E.M. and W. Herzog. 1966. 'Functional Literacy among Colombian Peasants'. *Economic Development and Cultural Change* 14: 190–203.

Sharma, O.P. and R.D. Retherford. 1993. 'Literacy Trends in the 1980s in India'. Occasional Paper No.4. Office of the Registrar General and Census Commissioner of India.

Sen, A. 1976. 'Poverty: An Ordinal Approach to Measurement'. *Econometrica* 44: 219–31.

—— 1985. *Commodities and Capability*. Amsterdam: North-Holland.

—— 1987. *The Standard of Living*. Cambridge: Cambridge University.

UNDP (United Nations Development Programme). 1990. *Human Development Report*. New York: United Nations.

Wagner, D.A. and L.D Puchner. 1992. 'World Literacy in the Year 2000'. *Annals of the American Academy of Political and Social Science 520*.

Ziegahn, L. 1991. 'Beyond Reciprocity: Exchange around Literacy'. *Adult Basic Education* 1: 79–97.

4 The Greying of Populations
Concepts and Measurement

with Alaka Basu

4.1. INTRODUCTION

In recent years, in response to an increasing concern in the developed world with the rapid increase in the aging of populations, there has occurred a great expansion in the literature trying to measure the aging of populations, forecast trends and analyse the socio-economic implications of aging (see, for example, Kuroda and Hauser 1981; Ogawa 1982; and Hauser 1983). Yet, despite this great proliferation, the existing measures of aging continue to be crude. The present chapter is intended to be a contribution to this problem of pure measurement.

In discussing the aging of populations we need to distinguish between the following questions:
(i)   What is the age of a population?
(ii)   What is the extent of 'oldness' in a population?
While each of these questions may be interpreted in many ways and, therefore, have different answers, they are clearly concerned with very distinct aspects of populations. Thus the median age of a population or the average age could be thought of as answers to (i) while the percentage of population aged above 65 or above 75 are answers to (ii). In the existing literature on aging, these two questions have not always been distinguished and, for instance, the median age of a population and the percentage of population aged 65 or above (65+, henceforth) have often been thought of as alternative measures of the same larger concept (see, for example, Hauser 1983). In this chapter we distinguish between the two and focus entirely on (ii). In the ensuing pages, a reference to the 'aging populations' is invariably a reference to the extent of 'oldness' in populations.

First published in *Demography India 16*, 1987: 79–89.

The most commonly used index of aging simply computes the proportion of population aged 65+. For brevity, this index will be referred to as H. Our search for a superior measure is motivated by a dissatisfaction with H. We highlight its weakness by stating two axioms which any reasonable measure ought to satisfy. Then we show that both these axioms are violated by H. We state these axioms informally though they can easily be made mathematically precise:

AXIOM C (Continuity): An aging index should be such that a small change in the ages of the people should not cause a jump in the index.

AXIOM M (Monotonicity): If, with all other peoples' ages remaining the same, one person aged 65+ becomes older, the aging index should register an increase.

The index H is simply concerned with the *number* of people aged 65+. So it obviously violates M. To show that it violates C, suppose we have a population where the people are of exactly the same age and are almost 65. The index H of this population is clearly 0. As these people age a little and cross the 65 mark, the index will jump from 0 to 1, thereby violating Axiom C. Everybody becoming older by a day could change the extent of aging from 0 to the maximum possible!

Two clarifying remarks are in order. First, while we have chosen an extreme example to highlight the problem of discontinuity, a little reflection shows that the problem is quite pervasive and would crop up to a smaller extent in a wide variety of situations. Second, for the sake of brevity and uniformity, we adopt in this chapter the language of inter-temporal changes rather than cross-sectional differences. This at times gives a false impression of 'impossibility'. For example, Axiom M seems to be applicable to a strange world where the aging process of some people can be halted. But that need not be so because, at the cost of greater elaboration, M may be restated as follows: If there are two groups of same population size, A and B, with identical age distributions excepting for one person aged 65+ in B who happens to be older than his counterpart in A who also happens to be 65+, then the aging index of B should be higher than that of A. Similarly, later when we make observations like 'suppose one person becomes younger' the reader may wish to translate this to corresponding cross-sectional comparisons of two societies.

Our aim in this chapter is to suggest measure of aging which satisfy Axioms M and C and capture our underlying notion of aging more accurately. We then apply these briefly by computing the extent of aging in Japan and in India. A lot of work in this area has already been undertaken for Japan by several authors and this enables us to compare our new index with the existing ones.

In pursuing our objective of devising a suitable measure of aging, we do not have to begin from scratch. A highly developed and clearly analogous literature in economics on the problem of measuring the extent of poverty in a society (Sen 1976, 1979; Takayama 1979; Kakwani 1980; Foster et al. 1984; and Basu 1985) vastly simplifies the task at hand. In fact, in exploring the need for more sophisticated measures than H, we have already above made use of the method of Sen (1976). In what follows we draw much upon Foster et al.'s family of poverty measures (see also Foster 1984) which seems to us to have a lot to offer in developing indices of population aging.

The most popular traditional measure of the extent of poverty consists of identifying a critical level of income below which a person would be considered 'poor' and then computing the proportion of population that is poor. This is known as the head-count ratio. The present-day method of computing aging, using 65 years as the cut-off, above which people are considered 'old' and then computing the proportion of old, is an exact analogue of the head-count ratio. The head-count ratio came under criticism from Sen (1976). His paper marked the beginning of a period of search for superior poverty measures. Here we draw considerably from this poverty measurement literature; in fact, much of the next section is an exercise in suitable adaptation of this literature to the problem of aging.

4.2. ALTERNATIVE MEASURES AND AXIOMS

This section presents the formal framework and the new measures along with their axiomatic characterizations.

A *population* will be represented here by a vector $y = (y_1 \dots y_n)$ where n is the number of people in the population and y_i is the age of the ith oldest person, ties being broken arbitrarily. Hence the set of all populations may be defined as:

$$X = \{y \mid y \text{ is a finite vector and } y_1 \geq y_2 \geq \dots \geq y_n\}$$

If ϕ is an index of aging then for each $y \in X$, $\phi(y)$ is a real number which indicates the extent of aging in population y. Hence, using R to denote the set of all real numbers, an aging index is a mapping:

(4.1) $$\phi : X \to R$$

In much of the traditional literature a person is described as 'old' if his age is 65 or more. While we comment on this cut-off age later, for our formal analysis we do not contest this. The traditional index of aging is the proportion of old people in a population. We shall refer to this as the head-count ratio, H. For any $y \in X$, denoting the number of people in y by $n(y)$ and the number of people aged 65+ in y by $q(y)$, we have:

(4.2) $$H(y) = \frac{q(y)}{n(y)}$$

This is an aging index: it is a special case of (4.1).

Another aging index which will form an ingredient in the measure that we develop below may be called the age-gap index. Given a population $y \in X$, its age-gap index, $I(y)$, is given by:

(4.3) $$I(y) = \sum_{i=1}^{q(y)} (y_i - 65)/q(y) \cdot 65$$

This measure is created by analogy with the 'income gap' measure in the literature on poverty measurement. Note that $(y_i - 65)/65$ could be thought of as a measure of the extent to which person i is old. Hence the age-gap index is simply an average of the extent to which old people are old.

We have already discussed the shortcomings of the head-count measure. Among these was the fact that H is concerned simply with the numbers that are old. The extent of their of oldness does not matter. I, on the other hand, is concerned about the extent of oldness among the old but is neutral about the numbers involved. If in one society of a 100 people were only ten are old and their age is 70, then I is 1/13. If instead all 100 people were old and were aged 70, even then I would be 1/13.

Clearly a sophisticated measure ought to take into consideration *both* the numbers of the old and the extent of their oldness. In other words, a good measure should be some kind of a combination of H and I. The remainder of this section is a search for such a measure.

Following the poverty-measurement literature we will begin by narrowing down the aging indices possible under (4.1) to a more limited class comprising of a normalization of a weighted sum of individual age gaps of the old.

$$(4.4) \qquad P(y) = A(n(y)) \sum_{i=1}^{q(y)} (y_i - 65) v_i(y),$$

Where P is the aging index, v_i is the weight attached to i's age gap, and A is the normalization factor. Different specific measures can be derived from (4.4) by specifying particular forms for $v_i(y)$ and $A(n(y))$ or by using axioms to restrict (4.4). We use both methods.

In the poverty literature, $v_i(y)$ is set equal to $q(y) + 1 - i$, that is, the rank of person i (with an older person getting a higher rank). Thus the oldest person ($i = 1$) gets a weight of $g(y)$, the second oldest person gets $g(y) - 1$, and so on. The use of *rank* weights has some justification when talking of incomes—as in the poverty literature. This is because incomes are usually surrogate for utility and, for utility, relative weights may make more sense than absolute ones—particularly if utility is ordinal.

In the context of aging, since absolute age has a clear meaning, it seems more sensible to use 'absolute' weights, that is, to use the age-gap as weights. Hence we set, $v_i(y) = y_i - 65$, for all i, which reduces (4.4) to

$$(4.5) \qquad P(y) = A(n(y)) \sum_{i=1}^{q(y)} (y_i - 65)^2$$

Using a suitably adapted argument from Sen (1976), consider a case where all the old people are of the same age. In that case it seems reasonable to argue that P should depend solely on the number that is old and the extent of their oldness. That is, if all the old are of the same age in y, then

$$(4.6) \qquad P(y) = f(H(y), I(y))$$

Let us go along with Sen and assume (4.6) takes a multiplicative form, but with the reasonable additional feature of P being extra sensitive to I for higher values of I.

AXIOM N (Normalization): If all the old are of the same age, then

$$P(y) = H(y) \, (I(y))^2.$$

Axiom N applied to (4.5) gives us a unique and neat aging index. We denote such an index by $\bar{P}$, and derive it in the following theorem.

THEOREM 4.1. *The only aging index of the class of indices given by (4.5), which satisfies axiom N, is the following:*

$$(4.7) \qquad \bar{P}(y) = \frac{1}{n(y)} \sum_{i=1}^{q(y)} (y_i - 65)^2/(65)^2$$

PROOF: Let $y^* \, \varepsilon \, X$ be such that all the old have the same age. Then (4.5) implies

$$\bar{P}(y^*) = A(n(y^*)) \, q(y^*) \, (y^* - 65)^2$$

On the other hand, by axiom N and (4.3), we get

$$\bar{P}(y^*) = H(y^*) \, [(y^* - 65)/65]^2$$

Hence

$$A(n(y^*)) = \frac{1}{(65)^2 n(y^*)}$$

Since A depends on n alone, hence for all $y \, \varepsilon \, X$,

$$A(n(y)) = \frac{1}{(65)^2 n(y)}$$

Substituting this in (4.5) we get (4.7).

(QED)

Index (4.7) is an exact analogue of the Foster et al. (1984) measure of poverty. Among the many properties of index (4.7) is the fact that it satisfies the following: Suppose, of two people aged 65+, the older person becomes older by 1 year and the other person becomes younger by 1 year, and everybody else's age remains unchanged. Then $\bar{P}$, will register an increase. This property is at times referred to as the transfer axiom. The transfer axiom seems attractive because it suggests the reasonable idea that in one year, an older person ages more than a younger one. This axiom does not, however, specify whether it attaches a greater weight to an older person aging (i) because the older person is old *relative* to others or (ii) because of the sheer fact of his being advanced in age. It is our belief that most people find the transfer axiom attractive because they implicitly associate it with explanation (ii). Suppose everybody else's age remaining the same, person i (who is above 65) becomes older by a year. The aging index will register an increase. Should the magnitude of this increase depend on what *rank i* has (in terms of age) among the old or just i's age? Most people would, we feel, choose the latter.

If we adhere to (i), we get a relative weighting scheme of kind used by Sen. If, on the other hand, we accept (ii)—as we do here—then we have an absolute weighting scheme as in index (4.7).

Index (4.7) captures three aspects of a population: (a) the number of old, (b) the extent of 'oldness' of the old, and (c) the age distribution among the old. There are good reasons why all three ought to be taken into account. (a) and (b) have been discussed above and (c) is discussed in Section 4.4. However, as argued in the concluding section, there may be important practical considerations for using a simplex index. An index which takes account of (a) and (b) but ignores (c) is a simple multiplicative combination of H and I.

$$(4.8) \qquad Q(y) = H(y) \cdot I(y)$$

While here we state index Q directly, it is noteworthy that Q can be derived from more basic axioms. This can be achieved from a set of axioms similar to the ones specified in Basu (1985) and by applying a theorem on affine functions (Basu 1983). Note also that Q is analogous to another measure in the Foster et al. family.

$\bar{P}$ and Q are the two measures that we wish to propose here. In the next section we actually compute these indices for India and Japan and also show how these contrast with the traditional head-count ratio.

4.3. ESTIMATES

Using the population projections prepared by the United Nations (1982) to estimate population aging by the existing standard measures, Hauser (1983) concludes that the next few decades will see major increases in population aging not just in the developed or industrialized countries, but in the hitherto young populations of the developing countries as well. We would like to propose that studies such as Hauser's still underestimate the extent of aging that will occur. This is because the focus in all these studies is on the head-count ratio or some related measure. In other words, they look only at the numbers of the old. But as the numbers of the old increase, presumably their average age will increase as well, a factor which is only taken into account in the few simplistic attempts to include a measure of the 'old' old (that is, 75+) as a proportion of the old (that is, 65+). Once both the numbers of the old and the extent of their aging are taken into account, as is the case with our new indices (4.7) and (4.8), we will find sharper increases in aging than those suggested by the head-count ratio.

To illustrate, we compare the changes in the various indices of aging between 1980 and 2025 for the countries of Japan and India, the former one where the sudden burst in population aging has aroused considerable concern and the latter is an example of a country which has still to achieve its demographic transition but where a rise in population aging is distinctly on its way. Like Hauser, we use the population projections prepared by the United Nations (1982). The relevant population age distributions are set out in Table 4.1.

Since the United Nations data are available by five year age groups we have assumed that all the members in each age group are aged at the mid-point of that interval. This assumption causes a difficulty with the oldest or 80+ age category. To decide on the age at which the members of this category are centred we used a simple rule of thumb. We computed the average age of those aged 80 years and

Table 4.1: Population (in thousands) in Various Age Groups

| | Japan | | India | |
	1980	2025	1980	2025
Total population	116,551	131,451	684,460	123,3790
65–9	3917	6736	9450	39,890
70–4	2963	6774	5951	25,999
75–9	1989	6317	3136	15,806
80 +	1477	5817	2032	10,577
65 +	10,346	25,644	20,569	92,272

Source: UN (1982).

above in the Indian censuses of 1971 and 1981 (Registrar General of India 1976, 1983) as derived from the single year age distributions in these censuses. This turned out to be close to 86 years for both the 1971 and 1981 censuses and we used this parameter for all the populations in our estimates. That is, we assumed that the age of all the groups aged 80+ was 86 years.

Admittedly this is a crude method. Its defence rests on two counts. First, the number of people aged above 80 is very small in any population and a crude approximation for this group is unlikely to have a large effect on the final measure. Second, in most censuses there is a tendency for the ages of the old to be significantly misrecorded, so that there is little to be gained by using very refined methods for this category. For example, in the unsmoothed data of the 1971 Indian census, 19 people were stated to be aged above 160 years; and one individual claimed to be above 190, that is, he was born within a couple of years of American independence!

Once the above adjustments are made to the data, the computation of indices is straightforward. The results are given in Table 4.2

Table 4.2: Aging of Population According to Various Indices

	1980	Japan 2025	% change between 1980 and 2025	1980	India 2025	% change between 1980 and 2025
H	.0888	.1951	119.7	.0301	.0748	148.5
Q	.0116	.0315	171.5	.0034	.0089	161.8
$\bar{P}$	.00234	.00716	206	.00062	.0017	175

Source: Computed from Table 4.1.

Ignoring here questions concerning the cardinality of the measures, not that both our measures, Q and $\bar{P}$, register a sharper increase between 1980 and 2025 than does the traditional head-count ratio, H. This is because our measures take into account the fact that by the year 2025 there will not only be more old people, but the old people will be older. Moreover, $\bar{P}$ makes allowance for the fact that in 2025 the old will probably be more sparsely spread over the various age groups above 65.

In comparing Japan and India one finds that both Q and $\bar{P}$ rise faster for Japan. This probably reflects the fact that India is still at the entrance to rapid population aging, a stage at which the average age of the old can rise relatively slowly. We comment on the sociological implications of different age distributions among the old and on other aspects of aging in the next section.

4.4. IMPLICATIONS AND COMMENTS

The greying of a population can have several socio-economic implications, not all of them in the same direction. The three features of aging which are captured in our measures—the proportion that is old, the average age of the old, and the distribution of the old—have different social implications.

To begin with the simplest notion of aging, that is, the numbers of people above some given cut-off point, generally 65, the social and economic implications of an increase in these numbers have already been discussed in several places (see, for example, UN 1973; Kuroda and Hauser 1981; Furuya and Martin 1981; and Heisel 1984). The economic burdens imposed by a rise in the proportions of old include the increased needs for retirement benefits and specialized health services. However, at least at the earlier stages of this trend towards an older population, the economic resources to meet these new demands may be more easily available because of an unchanged aggregate dependency ratio—as the rise in the proportions of the dependent old is matched by a fall in the proportions of the dependent young with falling fertility. It is only with a stabilization of fertility and a continued increase in longevity that the problem may be more acutely felt. Indeed Preston (1984) has argued that in the United States there has occurred a diversion of resources from children to the old in response to the increasing size and influence of the old-age lobby.

Most of the above implications get accentuated in an obvious way when there is not just a rise in the proportion of the old, but a rise in the average age of the old as well. This has led to attempts to distinguish between the 'young' old and the 'old' old as in Kuroda and Hauser (1981). We feel, however, that both our indices provide a better measure of this concept because they use a continuously greater weighting as a person becomes older.

The social impact of an increase in the age of a population is likely to be further complicated by the simultaneous changes that typically occur in other aspects of society as a consequence of the same modernizing forces that initiate population aging. Of these, the two most important are probably an increase in the propensity of the young to migrate in search of a better life and a consequent or an independent breakdown of the traditional joint family (or, more specifically, multi-generation family). Both these processes have the effect of increasing the numbers of the old left to fend for themselves, at least physically and emotionally, if not economically. That such an effect is taking place is seen vividly in the rapid rise in the proportions of the old that live in single person or nuclear households in Japan (Martin and Culter 1983), which is the first of the non-Euro-American countries to experience significant population aging. The level of single-person households is also affected by sex differentials in mortality, which are accentuated in old age in the currently low-mortality countries.

The problem of loneliness among the old indirectly highlights the importance of age distribution. The existing literature on aging is silent on how age is distributed among the old. But this distribution has implications not just for estimating the social security inputs required from the state but also for the individual psychological welfare of the aged themselves. For example, the more dispersed the age distribution of the old, the lonelier old age is likely to be and a normative index of aging should register an increase. On the other hand, with a greater clustering of the old around the average age, the old person can look forward to a greater likelihood of having his spouse and acquaintances around (Bytheway 1970). Our aging index $\bar{P}$, by taking account of the distribution of age among the old, makes some allowance for this loneliness factor.

4.5. CONCLUSIONS

There are three aspects of the aging of populations: (i) how many people are old? (ii) how old are the old? and (iii) how is the age distribution among the old? An ideal measure of aging should combine all three aspects. H reflects only (i). Q reflects (i) and (ii). Only $\bar{P}$ reflects (i), (ii), and (iii). In this sense, $\bar{P}$ is probably the best measure to use.

There is, however, practical consideration which may favour Q. By squaring the age gap, $\bar{P}$ enhances the weightage of the older people in the population. Therefore, if the age reporting of the very old is poor, the accuracy of $\bar{P}$ can be affected. On the other hand, if we cut off the age distribution at some fixed point—as we have done in this chapter at age 86—then, as the population becomes older, its old age distribution improves *by definition* since the population of the old begins to cluster just below this cut-off age. This introduces a special downward bias in $\bar{P}$. Hence Q might be the most suitable aging index given the existing data limitations. Where more detailed and reliable data are available, $\bar{P}$ is the better measure.

Finally, a suggestion for further research. All the existing aging measures, including ours, have one important shortcoming in that, while looking into the future, they keep unchanged the 65 year cut-off point for defining the old. This would be apt if our increasing longevity was explained solely by our ability to survive up to a lower state of health conditions. In reality however one reason for our increased longevity is the fact that our health (at each corresponding age) is, on average, better. Once this factor is taken into account, it follows that the cut-off age itself should be on a sliding scale, being moved upwards as the expected longevity of a population rises.

REFERENCES

Basu, K. 1983. 'Cardinal Utility, Utilitarianism and a Class of Invariance Axioms in Welfare Economics'. *Journal of Mathematical Economics* 12.

────── 1985. 'Poverty Measurement: A Decomposition of the Normalisation Axiom'. *Econometrica* 53.

Bytheway, W.R. 1970. 'Aspects of Old Age in Age-specific Mortality Rates'. *Journal of Biosocial Science* 2.

Foster, J. 1984. 'On Economic Poverty: A Survey of Aggregate Measures'. *Advances in Econometrics* 3.

Foster, J., J. Greer, and E. Thorbecke. 1984. 'A Class of Decomposable Poverty Measures'. *Econometrica* 52.

Furuya, K. and L.G. Martin. 1981. 'Employment and Retirement of Older Workers in Japan'. Research Paper 8. Nihon University Population Research Institute.

Hauser, P.M. 1983. *Aging of Population and Labour Force for World, More Developed and Less Developed Areas and their Regions: Population Aging 1970–2025*; Labour Force Aging 1970–2000'. Research Paper 15. Nihon University Population Research Institute.

Heisel, M.A. 1984. 'Aging and the Developing World'. *Populi* 11.

Kakwani, N. 1980. *Income Inequality and Poverty*, Delhi: Oxford University Press.

Kuroda T. and P.M. Hauser 1981. 'Aging of the Population of Japan and its Policy Implications'. Research Paper 1. Nihon University Population Research Institute.

Martin, L. and S. Culter 1983. 'Mortality Decline and Japanese Family Structure'. *Population and Development Review* 9.

Ogawa, N. 1982. 'Economic Implications of Japan's Aging Population'. *International Labour Review* 121.

Preston, S.H. 1984. 'Children and the Elderly: Divergent Paths for American's Dependents'. *Demography* 21.

Registrar General of India. 1976. Census of India 1971 Series I, Part (ii)C, *Social and Cultural Tables*, New Delhi: Government of India.

────── 1983. Census of India 1981, Series-I India, Part II-special, *Report and Tables Based on 5 per cent Sample Data*, New Delhi: Government of India.

Sen, A.K. 1976. 'Poverty: An Ordinal Approach to Measurement'. *Econometrica* 44.

────── 1979. 'Issues in the Measurement of Poverty'. *Scandinavian Journal of Economics 81*.

Takayama, N. 1979. 'Poverty, Income Inequality and Their Measures: Professor Sen's Approach Reconsidered'. *Econometrica* 47.

UN (United Nations). 1973. *The Determinants and Consequences of Population Growth— New Summary of Findings on Interaction of Demographic, Economic and Social Factors.* New York: United Nations.

────── 1982. *Demographic Indicators of Countries: Estimates and Projections as Assessed in 1980*. New York: United Nations.

Part II
Institutions, Norms, and Power

5 One Kind of Power

5.1. INTRODUCTION

This chapter is about influence and power—concepts which are treated as periph-
eral in conventional economic theory but which, we know, are important in
reality. This is a vast subject and it has received an enormous amount of attention
from sociologists and political theorists (see Lukes 1974, and references therein),
The objective of the present chapter is, however, a modest one: to enquire into the
nature and consequences of one kind of power—that which works through
'triadic' relationships.

We begin with the standard economist's assumption, that all individuals are
selfish utility maximizers (to the extent that they are so in traditional neoclassical
theory).[1] The idea is not to defend this axiom but to demonstrate that even without
relaxing this axiom we can accommodate in our models concepts and results
which have generally been left to the charge of other social scientists. The point of
departure with standard economic theory lies in permitting the relation between
two agents to be affected by and to affect each of their relations with others.

The significance of going from two-person to three-person relationships, that
is from the 'dyad' to the 'triad',[2] has been discussed in sociological writings—most
emphatically in the works of Georg Simmel (Simmel 1950; Caplow 1968).
Simmel argued that as soon as the direct relation between two individuals is
appended by an indirect one, operating via a third person, there occurs a qualitative change from a formal sociological standpoint. Adapting somewhat to the
context of *economic* analysis, the term 'dyad' will be used here to describe models

From *Oxford Economic Papers* 38, 1986, 259–82.

I owe my broad interest in this subject to conversations with Sukhomoy Chakravarty and Mrinal
Datta Chaudhuri. In writing this chapter I have benefited from the comments of H. Leung, Jean-
Phillipe Platteau, and Nick Stern, and from seminars at the London School of Economics, the
University of Warwick and the Institute for Advanced Study, Princeton. I am indebted to Steven
Lukes for a very stimulating conversation and also for acquainting me with Vaclav Havel's manu-
script. This paper was written while I was a visitor at the University of Warwick.

where whether i agrees to trade with j or not does not affect his relation with k. Hence, a dyad is not a two-person society, but a society where individuals interact *pairwise*. The term 'triad' will be reserved for models which allow triangular and, more generally, multiple relations.

In economics our models are *generally* dyadic. 'In previous models current transactions (so long as they are legal) do not result in changed relations with uninvolved parties in subsequent transactions', argues Akerlof (1976: 609), in setting out to construct his extremely insightful triadic model of caste relations. He goes on: 'On the contrary in a caste society any transaction that breaks the caste taboos changes the subsequent behaviour of uninvolved parties towards the caste-breakers'. Once triadic relations are allowed, we are able to explain many interesting social concepts within the bounds of our models. Caste is one of them. The first model in this chapter (Section 5.2) is based on Akerlof's notion of caste equilibrium (which, as an equilibrium concept, need not have anything to do with caste). The second model (Section 5.3) is of agrarian relations which demonstrates how a labourer may agree to an exchange with a landlord from which he gets negative utility. It is argued that what appears to be a voluntary exchange may be indirectly coercive. The third model (Section 5.4) is an attempt to explain the *modus operandi* of that ubiquitous personality, the so-called man of influence.

5.2. POWER AND LOYALTY

History has seen dictatorships where the rulers and the ruled have been 'two socially defined and separate communities'[3] with the former controlling and, perhaps, even tyrannizing the latter. In such 'classical dictatorships' power is concentrated on one side, on the side of the rulers, who devise methods of rewards and retributions to dominate the majority and sustain the regime. Such a dictator-ship can be tyrannical but it is comprehensible, everyone can see who keeps it going. In some ways more frightening is what the Czeck writer, Václav Havel, calls a 'post-totalitarian system'. It may be more tyrannical or less. That is not its distinguishing mark. Its distinguishing mark is that it is faceless. In it power is diffused through society. The line which divides *society* in a classical dictatorship, 'runs through *each person*' in a post-totalitarian system, in which 'everyone is, in his own way, both a victim and a supporter of the system'.

I will return to the work of Havel later, in Section 5.2.3. I will try to argue that Havel's notion of a diffused dictatorship is a coherent concept which can be interpreted very precisely in terms of equilibrium notions. I give a sketch of this interpretation in this section, develop it formally in Section 5.2.1 and discuss its larger implications in 5.2.2 and particularly, 5.2.3.

Let us begin with a simple case of a 'classical dictatorship'. Consider an unwanted ruler (or a ruling class)[4] who punishes whoever does not co-operate with him. Suppose that the agony of punishment is greater than the benefits a person gets from *individually* not co-operating. Then, even if it were true that *if everybody* chose non-cooperation the ruler would get overthrown and everybody would be happier, no *individual* would choose non-cooperation and the ruler would survive to the misfortune of all. This is the Assurance Game—a variant of the classic Prisoner's Dilemma (Sen 1982)—and this is the popular model of power.[5]

Consider an alternative model in which the direct punishment for disloyalty is small (causing k units of disutility to its recipient) and, in particular, smaller than the benefit an individual gets by non-cooperation (say n units), that is, $k < n$. Then the above straightforward argument can no longer hold. However, given the following definition and two assumptions, the sustenance of the unwanted ruler is guaranteed. (Here, as above, I assume that there is a definite behaviour called 'non-cooperation'. What exactly that entails is not immediately relevant to us and, so, is left unspecified).

Definition: A person is considered *disloyal* to the king or the regime if either he does not co-operate or he maintains relations with someone who is disloyal.

ASSUMPTION 5.1: Everybody believes that no one else would be disloyal.

ASSUMPTION 5.2: $n - k - d < 0$, where d is the cost to an individual of being ostracized.

Consider an individual contemplating non-cooperation. This will give him a joy of n units: a punishment of k units and, given his 'conjecture' about others (embodied in Assumption 5.l), he expects an additional cost of d units. These, given Assumption 5.2, add up to a negative number and so non-cooperation is not worthwhile. Everybody reasons in this manner and the regime persists.

Note that Assumption 5.2 *could* be valid even with $k = 0$. This means that even if the direct punishment meted out by the ruler is non-existent, individuals would co-operate with the regime and thereby help its sustenance. The regime persists because of mutual suspicion between the people. Each person is worried about what the others will do to him and so they co-operate. And, of course, as a moment's contemplation will show, there need not even exist a ruler in the system. 'Co-operation' could merely be the name of a certain mode of behaviour (which no one likes). The power that sustains this regime pervades the entire society. And everyone is—as Havel describes—'both a victim and a supporter of the system'.

This then is the essence of Havel's 'post-totalitarian system' with its 'blind automatism'. No individual is at the helm; it is a 'dictatorship of the ritual'. This is also the model of Akerlof's (1976) caste where everybody complies with the caste rules because not to comply is to risk ostracization. And of course those who do the ostracizing do so only because otherwise they would be risking their own ostracization!

5.2.1. Model

Consider an economy with a set N (# $N = n \geq 2$) of individuals. The number of goods is also n. Every $i \in N$ has an endowment of e (>1) units of good i and no other goods.[6] Every $i \in N$, has the same utility function:

$$(5.1) \qquad U^i = x_1^i x_2^i \dots x_n^i = \prod_{j=1}^{n} x_j^i$$

where x_j^i is the amount of good j consumed by person i.

The general equilibrium of this exchange economy occurs at the price vector $p^* = [1, ..., 1]$. This is easy to check. Given this price vector, the usual consumer maximization yields

$$x_j^i = \frac{e}{n}, \quad \text{for all } i, j.$$

Here, aggregate demand for good j equals e, which is also the aggregate supply of good j. Note that at equilibrium each person gets $(e/n)^n$ utils. This equilibrium will be referred to simply as the *Walras equilibrium*.

Now consider the same economy again, with a wicked king added to it. He does no good for the economy but charges from every individual one unit of his endowment. This the king uses for his own merriment and protection. The two essential elements in this model are a definition and a conjecture. These are as follows:

Definition: In this economy a person is described as *disloyal* (to the king) if (i) he does not give the king one unit or (ii) he trades with someone who is disloyal.[7]

Conjecture: Every $i \in N$ conjectures that no $j \in N \setminus \{i\}$ would be disloyal.[8]

This conjecture may, at first sight, convey the impression that i believes that others would be loyal under *all* circumstances. This need not be. Underlying the conjecture may be i's belief that others would be loyal only under *some* circumstances and that the only circumstances that might prevail are a subset of these. In the light of this, it is possible and more interesting to suppose that behind the formal and brief statement of conjecture above is the following: i conjectures that no j would be disloyal unless assured of general disloyalty and i also conjectures that each j lacks such assurance.

We shall suppose that whoever is disloyal 'incurs the king's displeasure'. This, in turn, could take any form. For instance, it could mean being debarred from the annual royal ball or being whipped. It is not necessary to specify this. We simply need to assume that everybody knows what 'incurring the king's displeasure' entails. Let k_i (≥ 0) be the disutility to person i of incurring such displeasure. In other words, k_i is the direct cost to person i of being disloyal.

In this economy, the same price vector as before (that is, p^*), with everybody paying the king one unit, is an equilibrium, in the sense that, given their conjectures, no one expects to do better by altering his strategy. This equilibrium will be referred to as a *C-equilibrium* (to emphasize that its essence is the same as Akerlof's 'caste equilibrium'). Let us check that this is an equilibrium in this sense. If person i pays the king one unit, his disposable endowment is $e - 1$, and usual consumer utility maximization yields

$$x_j^i = \frac{e-1}{n}, \quad \text{for all } i, j.$$

Hence the aggregate demand for good j is $e - 1$ which is also the aggregate supply to the market.

What remains to be checked is that no individual expects to do better by not giving the king one unit. If i gives the king one unit, he buys $(e-1)/n$ units of each good and so gets a total utility of $[(e-1)/n]^n$. Suppose i does not give the king one unit. Then anybody who trades with him will be considered disloyal to the king. Hence i, given his conjecture, will not expect anybody to trade with him. Therefore, his utility from consumption of goods will be $0 \ldots 0.e.0 \ldots 0 = 0$. In addition, there is the direct cost of the king's displeasure, that is, k_1. So total expected utility from this strategy is $-k_i$. Since

(5.2) $$\left(\frac{e-1}{n}\right) > -k_i, \quad \text{for all } i,$$

it is not worthwhile for any i to deny the king one unit, and this establishes the equilibrium.[9]

What is interesting is that (5.2) would continue to be valid even if $k_i = 0$ for all i. That is, even if individuals did not mind at all incurring the king's displeasure (for instance, because they are bold and hate to curry favour or because the displeasure takes the mild form of a snort from the king), they would continue to show loyalty and thereby help sustain the evil regime. And what is more, there need not even be a king. The act of loyalty could merely be a self-sustaining 'ritual' of wasting one unit of endowment. Individuals are not worried about what the king will do to them but what the others will do to them. And it is this interpersonal suspicion which sustains the sub-optimal equilibrium.[10]

Of late, there has developed quite a substantial body of literature on oligopoly equilibria based on 'conjectures' of agents. An important question which has arisen in this context is whether the conjectures postulated in a model are 'consistent'. or not? There are some game-theoretic difficulties with the concept of consistency and so we shall not delve much into this subject. The only matter of interest to us is to note that if $k > 0$ (no matter how small) and $n \geq 3$, then the C-equilibrium is an equilibrium with *consistent conjectures* (Bresnahan 1981). A consistent conjectures equilibrium is basically an equilibrium where the conjectures of individuals would, *given a chance*, be borne out.

Let us spell out the conjecture in our model. What is relevant at the equilibrium is that i conjectures that if he does not give the king one unit then others will refuse to trade with him. We want to check whether this conjecture would actually be true. Without loss of generality, suppose that person 1 does not give the king his due, let us see what 2 will do. If 2 trades with 1, then given 2's conjecture, he will expect no one else,[11] that is, 3, 4, ..., to trade with him. Hence 2's utility would be $-k$ units. If he does not trade with 1, his utility will be zero. Hence he will not trade with 1 and, therefore, 1's conjecture is valid.[12]

5.2.2. The Caucus and the Coalition

This model raises an interesting ethical question. Normally, we castigate men who, by currying favour with an unwanted leadership, help sustain the regime. This model shows that people who do so may be entirely victims of their 'situation'. This can be elaborated by supposing that the economy has two provinces: the inner and the outer. The inner one is exactly like the economy described above. The outer one has a set M (# $M = m$) of individuals, numbered n

+ 1, n + 2, ..., n + m. Every $i \in M$ has an endowment of e units of good i and his utility function is:

$$U^i = \prod_{j=n+1}^{n+m} x_j^i$$

The only difference between these two provinces is that the people want to consume different kinds of goods. Let *disloyal* be defined in the same way and let the conjecture be the same. But it is more convenient to write it more elaborately, that is, as in note 8. Hence the conjecture is as follows:

Conjecture: Every $i \in N \cup M$ conjectures that no $j \in N \cup M \setminus \{i\}$ who is loyal to the king would be disloyal.

Assume that for all $i \in M$, k_i is such that

(5.3)
$$\left(\frac{e}{m}\right)^m - \left(\frac{e-1}{m}\right)^m > k_i$$

Finally, assume that if no one gives the king one unit, the king would get overthrown, and in the absence of a king the Walras equilibrium would be established.

This economy can now be shown to have a very interesting equilibrium, namely, one in which all prices are equal to one, and every $i \in N$ gives the king one unit and every $i \in M$ does not give the king one unit.[13] Hence at equilibrium every $i \in N$ gets $(e - 1/n)^n$ utils and every $i \in M$ gets $(e/m)^m - k_i$ utils. To show that this is an equilibrium we have to go through the same argument as in Section 5.2.1. The only new thing to check is that no $i \in M$ can gain by giving the king one unit. If he gives the king one unit, given his conjecture, he will expect members of N to be prepared to trade with him (which they earlier would not have been willing). But this is of no consequence because there is nothing that $i \in M$ wants to buy from the members of N. Hence the only advantage of giving the king one unit will be that he will not have to incur the cost, k_i. Hence by giving one unit, gets a net utility of $(e - 1/m)^m$ utils. But this is less than what he was getting earlier, because of (5.3).

At this equilibrium, the set N will soon get to be labelled the 'caucus' around the king, who through their fawning and show of loyalty help sustain the regime, whereas the people of the outer province would allegedly be the courageous ones refusing to comply with the king's unfair demands. But of course what is clear to us from a distance is that the members of the caucus and the members of M could be identical human beings, in terms of their attitude to the king, merely caught in different 'situations'. It is interesting to note that the k_i's for the elements of N could in fact be lower than the k_i's of the members of M. That is, the members of N could be the ones who actually care less for the king's favours!

Finally, a comment on coalitions, which Akerlof (1976) showed, could break out of the grip of caste. Return to the C-equilibrium in Section 5.2.1. Clearly if all n members decided to form a coalition and not to pay the king, they could establish the Pareto superior Walras equilibrium. Why do they not do this? There are, of course, the standard arguments in terms of transactions or organization cost. There is, however, a more natural reason here. It seems reasonable to suppose that the definition of 'disloyal' (Section 5.2.1) should include a third category: (iii) he tries to form a breakaway coalition. Now, if we assume that to have a breakaway coalition somebody has to make the first move and that individuals conjecture that the probability of others joining in is below a certain level, then a breakaway coalition would never get formed.

5.2.3. A Political Analogue

Václav Havel's (1978) scenario is Eastern Europe. He argues that the system there is not a 'classical' dictatorship but a 'faceless' one where society cannot be partitioned between the rulers and the ruled. He labels it a 'post-totalitarian system' where totalitarianism permeates through society. In it, the same people who are strangled by power are the ones who constitute power. Havel's post-totalitarian system is a political analogue of the formal model above. This is brought out sharply in his perceptive account of a typical greengrocer.

'The manager of a fruit and vegetable shop places in his window, among the onions and carrots, the slogan: "workers of the world unite":

'Why does he do it? ... Is he genuinely enthusiastic about the idea of unity among the workers of the world?'

Havel argues that the answer to that is No. The greengrocer does it because everybody does it. The poster was delivered to him 'from the enterprise headquarters along with the onions and the carrots. ... If he were to refuse, there could be trouble ... someone might even accuse him of disloyalty'. He would then be persecuted and 'his superiors will harass him'.

That such things happen, we all know. Where Havel shows his insight is not in his analysis of the greengrocer but in his analysis of the superiors—those who harass the dissenting greengrocers. Why would they harass a greengrocer if he refused to put up the poster? Is it because they are, unlike the grocer, committed to the government? The answer once again is No, for the superiors are, in turn, exactly like the grocer.

Most of those who administer these sanctions, however, will not do so from any authentic inner conviction, but simply under pressure from 'conditions', the same conditions, that had once pressured the greengrocer to display the official slogans ... . The executors, therefore, essentially behave just like everyone else, to a greater or lesser degree: as components of the post-totalitarian system, as agents of its automatism, as petty instruments of the social autototality.

(Václav Havel 1978)

Such is the web of interpersonal conjectures that no individual would try to deviate from the 'rules of the game' if he does not 'want to be excluded' and to 'fall into isolation'.

In Havel's system no individual is to blame. From the head of the state to the greengrocer, everybody is a 'victim' of a situation. There is something almost 'metaphysical' in this kind of power where the enemy cannot be identified. Individuals, innocently going about their daily chores, in their totality give rise to this power which then transcends them and acquires its own *raison d'être*.

The empirical accuracy of Havel's description is not our concern here. What is of interest to us is the prior question of internal consistency. And indeed by recognizing its obvious analogousness to a *C-equilibrium* we see that his post-totalitarian system is entirely plausible. It is possible to have dictatorships with no dictators. And the first step in controlling this latent (or not so latent) power in societies must be to recognize it and demystify it. That is precisely what the model in this section has tried to do.

5.3. POWER AND EXTORTION IN AGRARIAN RELATIONS

In this section we turn to another kind of non-dyadic relation—that which can arise in the 'personalized' rural markets in backward economies but has not been adequately captured in the large and growing literature on agrarian economic relations.

Rural landlords in less developed economies are supposed to be extortionate, and they have generally been modelled as such. Consider a case where the landlord is hiring labour. If we use w to denote wage and l the amount of labour that a labourer gives the landlord, we could think of the landlord as offering a labourer a package, (w, l), that is, 'if you work for me for l hours you will get w rupees per hour'. The labourer can take it or leave it. If the labourer leaves it, let $\bar{U}$ be the utility that he gets, and if he takes it, his level of utility is U^*. Usually $\bar{U}$ is referred to as the 'reservation utility'. It is the utility that the labourer gets from the next best alternative open to him if he does not accept (w, l). Many react to this by pointing out that in backward regions labourers often have no alternatives open to them. What they really mean is that often the only alternative open to labourers is starvation; and put in this way it is clear that there is no attempt in our model to deny this.

In this case, a worker will accept the package if $U^* \geq \bar{U}$. In the existing literature, the *most* extortionate landlords are modelled as ones who offer packages (w, l) such that $U^* = \bar{U}$, that is, the labourers are given no more than the minimum they would accept (Braverman and Srinivasan 1981; Braverman and Stiglitz 1982; Basu 1983a).[14]

This would indeed be valid if all relations were dyadic. But that is not the case in reality, where it is possible that a landlord in offering a package (w, l) gives—along with it—the threat that if he does not accept the package the landlord will ensure that a third person i will refuse to trade with him. If the landlord has the ability to influence i, the threat becomes a 'credible' one and the landlord may be able to offer a package which leaves the labourer with less utility than $\bar{U}$ but which he, nevertheless, accepts.

A transaction which leaves one agent actually worse off can be explained in a model with rational agents only if we allow for triadic relationships. The sentiment that 'It's an awful deal he is offering but I'd better take it because he is a powerful man' captures this idea. Though the deal is bad, you might be willing to take it from a powerful man because being powerful he can hurt you in other ways—usually by affecting your relation with agents uninvolved in this transaction.

Having constructed a formal model along these lines, I shall try to argue that this is a case where the landlord may be described as 'coercive'. 'Coercion' and 'voluntariness' are difficult concepts,[15] though economists often taken them for granted. The model in the next section throws interesting light on the meaning of 'voluntary choice' in economics.

5.3.1. Model

There are three agents: labourer (agent 1), landlord (2), and merchant (3). Each of them has an initial cash endowment, in particular agent i has Y_i units. In addition, the labourer possesses labour and the merchant has an endowment of G units of a homogeneous commodity. The labourer sells labour to the landlord and buys goods from the merchant. The merchant sells goods to both labourer and landlord. The landlord, therefore, buys labour and goods: He buys labour not for production but for consumption, that is, as domestic servants, masseurs, etc. In this sense, the word 'landlord' is a bit of a misnomer, for he is really a member of Veblen's leisure class.

Agent 1 has the following utility function:

(5.4)
$$U = Y_1 + wl - px_1 + \phi_1(x_1) - \phi_2(l),$$
$$\phi_1' > 0, \phi_1'' < 0; \phi_2' > 0, \phi_2'' > 0,$$

where w and p are the prices of labour and good, l the amount of labour sold and x_1 the amount of good bought by agent 1. $\phi_1(\cdot)$ is a function which gives the utility that he gets from consuming goods and $\phi_2(\cdot)$ the disutility from giving labour. Utility is, therefore, measurable in money terms and his utility function is additively separable. This simplifies the algebra but is not—as will soon be intuitively obvious—essential for what the model demonstrates.

Agent 2's utility function is

(5.5)
$$V = Y_2 - wl - px_2 + \Omega_1(x_2) + \Omega_2(l),$$
$$\Omega_1' > 0, \Omega_1'' < 0; \Omega_2' > 0, \Omega_2'' < 0;$$

where x_2 is his consumption of goods, and $\Omega_1(\cdot)$ and $\Omega_2(\cdot)$ are interpreted as in agent 1's case.

Agent 3 has the following utility function:

(5.6)
$$\left.\begin{array}{c} W = Y_3 + px + \psi(G - x), \\ \psi' > 0, \psi'' < 0, \end{array}\right\}$$

where x is the amount of good supplied by him. Hence his consumption is given by $(G - x)$, and $\psi(G - x)$ is the utility from such consumption. Recall the merchant does not buy labour.

Since I want to focus attention on the labour market, it is convenient—though not necessary—to characterize the goods market very simply. In particular, it will be assumed that in the goods market all agents act as price-takers. Given a price p, we can find the labourer's demand for the good by differentiating U with respect to x_1 and setting it equal to zero. And similarly for the landlord's demand and the merchant's supply. Hence we get

(5.7) $\qquad \phi_1'(x_1) = p; \quad \Omega_1'(x_2) = p; \quad \psi'(G - x) = p$

I am assuming the existence of interior solutions. The monotonicity of the partial derivatives allows us to invert these functions and we get our usual demand and supply curves:

(5.8)
$$\left. \begin{array}{ll} x_1 = f(p), & f' < 0 \\ x_2 = g(p), & g' < 0 \\ x = h(p), & h' > 0 \end{array} \right\}$$

That $f' < 0$, $g' < 0$, and $h' > 0$ follow from ϕ_1'', Ω_1'', $\psi'' < 0$.

At equilibrium, price is such that aggregate demand equals aggregate supply, that is,

$$f(p) + g(p) = h(p).$$

Let p^* be the equilibrium price and x_1^*, x_2^*, x^* be the corresponding demands and supply. It will be assumed that

(5.9) $\qquad x_2^* > x_1^* > 0,$

that is both agents consume goods and the landlord consumes more than the labourer.

Assume that equilibrium has been achieved in the goods market, and let us turn to the labour market. In a conventional analysis of a labour market, an agent who neither buys nor sells labour would have no role. The merchant in our model is such an agent. So, to start with, we could banish the merchant from the scene. Of course, he will soon have to be resurrected. That is, in fact, the essence of our model.

A standard notion of power is monopoly or monopsony power. Hence one characterization of a powerful landlord is one who is a *conventional monopsonist*, that is, given the labourer's supply curve, he chooses a price strategy to maximize his welfare. This assumption has been used in some recent works on rural usury (Bottomley 1975; Bhaduri 1977; Borooah 1980; Basu 1984a). In our model 1's supply curve of labour is derived by differentiating U with respect to l and setting it equal to zero. Hence

$$w = \phi_2'(l)$$

Hence, a conventional monopsonist landlord's objective is to

$$\underset{\{w, l\}}{\text{Max } V}$$

subject to $w = \phi_2'(l)$.

The solution in this market, w^*, l^*, in conjunction with the solution already derived in the goods market, therefore, describes a general equilibrium in our model.

What is, however, quite well-known is that the conventional monopsonist, of the kind just described, is not the most extortionate person. He could extract more out of the labourer by making 'all-or-nothing' offers. In a growing literature in agrarian economics this has been the standard assumption (see, for example, Braverman and Stiglitz 1982; Mitra 1983; Basu 1983a; also Basu 1984b, and references therein).[16] The *all-or-nothing monopsonist* is easy to characterize. Consider what would happen if the landlord had no transaction with the labourer, that is, $l = 0$. In that case the labourer gets a total utility of $\tilde{U}$, which is defined as follows:

$$(5.10) \qquad \tilde{U} \equiv Y_1 - p^*x_1^* + \phi_1(x_1^*) - \phi_2(0)$$

Note that the goods market is in equilibrium; hence p and x_1 have fixed values. In keeping with conventional usage, $\tilde{U}$, will be referred to as the labourer's reservation utility vis-à-vis the landlord. Clearly, if the landlord offers a deal (w, l) which gives the labourer less utility than $\tilde{U}$, the labourer will not accept it. Hence the landlord's objective is to

$$\underset{\{w, l\}}{Max\ V}$$

subject to

$$(5.11) \qquad Y_2 + wl - p^*x_1^* + \phi_1(x_1^*) - \phi_2(l) \geq \tilde{U}$$

Let the solution of this be $(\tilde{w}, \tilde{l})$. At equilibrium the landlord will offer the labourer no more than his reservation utility, $\tilde{U}$. This is easily proved by contradiction: Suppose the labourer gets more than $\tilde{U}$ at equilibrium, i.e. (5.11) is a strict inequality. Hence it is possible to lower w so that the labourer will still accept the landlord's offer. But a lower w means [given (5.5)] a greater utility for the landlord. Hence the original situation could not have been an equilibrium. This establishes that in equilibrium (5.11) is a strict equality, and the labourer gets utility equal to $\tilde{U}$.[17] The landlord's utility is given by

$$Y_2 - \tilde{w}\tilde{l} - p^*x_2^* + \Omega_1(x_2^*) + \Omega_2(l^*) \equiv \tilde{V}$$

It is easy to check that the all-or-nothing monopsonist does better than the conventional monopsonist and that under all-or-nothing monopsony the labourer gets a lower utility than he would if the landlord was a conventional monopsonist. Of course, that the labourer can do at least as well under conventional monopsony is obvious from the fact that the all-or-nothing monopsonist offers him the lowest he is willing to accept.[18]

At times, the all-or-nothing monopsonist, as just described, is referred to as von Stackelberg leader in his interaction with the labourer. This is so in the following sense. Note that the landlord offers deals (w, l). The labourer can either take it (1) or leave it (0). Hence, the labourer's *reaction function* is a mapping from the set of all alternative values of (w, l) to the set {0, 1}. In the all-or-nothing monopsony case, we are essentially assuming that the landlord knows the labourer's reaction function; and taking that as given, he chooses (w, l) to maximize his own utility. The analogy with the Stackelberg leader in a duopoly is, therefore, clear.

In the literature on agrarian economic relations, all-or-nothing monopsony is treated as the case of maximum extortion. And since there is a belief that landlords usually extort as much as they can, landlords are increasingly being characterized as all-or-nothing monopsonists or monopolists. What is interesting is that in many situations the landlord can, in fact, exercise even greater power over labour and extort more. I shall label such a landlord an *extortionate monopsonist* and illustrate his behaviour with our model. It is useful to begin by spelling out a bit more what the all-or-nothing monopsonist does. He could be thought of as making an announcement:

(a) If agent 1 does not accept my offer I shall not trade with him at all. If this threat[19] is known and believed, he can offer the labourer a deal (w, l) which gives the labourer $\bar{U}$ utils. It may, however, be possible for the landlord to give a larger threat, namely one in which he assures that not only will *he* not trade with the labourer but neither will the merchant. The credibility of the threat clearly depends on the landlord's power over the merchant. What is interesting is that to give this larger threat the landlord has to do nothing qualitatively different from threat (a). He now has to simply make two announcements: (a) and, in addition,

(b) If agent 1 does not accept my offer and despite that agent 3 trades with 1, then I will not trade with 3 at all.

As before, let us assume that these threats are known and generally believed. This in itself does not change anything unless threat (b) is *effective* on agent 3, that is, unless 3 believes that it is better to comply with 2 rather than incur his threat. This will be true in certain parametric situations; and it is true in our model. In deciding whether to comply or not, agent 3 will compute the utilities that he would get if he traded *only* with 1 and, alternatively, *only* with 2. These are, respectively,

$$Y_3 + p^* x_1^* + \psi (G - x_1^*) \equiv W^1$$
$$Y_3 + p^* x_2^* + \psi (G - x_2^*) \equiv W^2$$

If he trades with both, as in the normal goods-market equilibrium, his utility level is denoted by W^*. That is,

$$Y_3 + p^* x^* + \psi (G - x^*) \equiv W^*$$

Given assumption (5.9), it is easy to show that $W^2 > W^1$. Intuitively, this is easy to see. Ideally the merchant would like to sell x^*. If this is not permitted and he has to choose between x_1^* and x_2^*, both of which are less than x^*, he will obviously choose the larger, that is, x_2^*. In everyday language, this simply means that given a choice between retaining *either* his larger customer *or* the smaller one, a merchant would opt for the former.[20] In the context of our model, this means that if the case of actually having to use threat (b) arises, that is, if 1 *does* turn down the landlord's offer, the merchant will immediately respond by cutting off trading links with 1. And it is the knowledge of this which makes agent 1 realize that if he turns down the landlord's offer, (w, l), he will not only have no trade with the landlord but he will also have no trade with the merchant.[21] In the absence of any trade his utility is given by

(5.12) $$U^0 \equiv Y_1 + \phi_1(0) - \phi_2(0)$$

An extortionate monopsonist is a person who gives out threats (a) *and* (b). Thus if 1 turns down the extortionate monopsonist's offer, (w, l), 1 has to fall back on a utility level of U^0. Hence, as long as this monopsonist offers him a deal, which gives agent 1 as much as U^0, agent 1 will accept it. Hence, the monopsonist's objective is

$$\underset{\{w, l\}}{\text{Max } V}$$

subject to $Y_1 + wl - p^*x_1^* + \phi_1(x_1^*) - \phi_2(l) \geq U^0$

Let the solution of this be w^0, l^0. By the same argument as used in the case of the all-or-nothing monopsonist, it is clear that at equilibrium the labourer will be getting a utility of U^0 and no more. It is obvious that $\bar{U} > U^0$ (intuitively this simply means that agent 1 is better–off if he is not allowed to trade with 2 than if he is not allowed to trade with 2 *and* 3)[22]. Hence what we have established is that extortionate landlords would push the labourers onto a utility level (namely U^0) which is below what the standard model of agrarian economics would suggest.

There are three observations. First, note that the landlord in my model is doing qualitatively nothing different from the standard all-or-nothing landlord. In both cases he simply makes it clear that under certain situations he will exercise his freedom not to trade. In the standard case he tells agent 1 he would not trade with him under certain circumstances (namely, if 1 turns down the particular deal he is offering) and in my model he tells 1 the same and in addition tells 2 that he will not trade with 2 under certain circumstances.

Second, just as in the standard all-or-nothing monopsony case it is not assumed that the threat (a) is actually announced but is simply known, similarly we do not have to assume that (a) and (b) are announced. There are many subtle ways in which a landlord can make (b) well-known. He could, for instance, have a reputation for vindictiveness. In particular, he could have a reputation for cutting off relations with anybody who trades with a person who has slighted the landlord by rejecting his offer.

Third, consider first the utility that the labourer gets if he does not trade with the landlord but trades with the merchant. This is given by $\bar{U}$. Now, suppose he begins to trade with the landlord at the equilibrium level of the extortionate monopsony case, that is, he sells l^0 units of labour to the landlord and earns $w^0 l^0$. His utility level in that case is—as we have already seen—U^0. Since $U^0 - \bar{U} < 0$, it is possible to argue that the transaction with the landlord, that is, selling l^0 labour at wage w^0, gives him a negative utility!

5.3.2. Voluntary Exchange

The last observation above shows the 'exploitative' nature of the exchange between the landlord and the labourer. Not only are the gains from this exchange distributed very asymmetrically, the labourer actually gets a negative utility from the exchange! It is possible to respond at this point that this, however, does not entail a violation of the labourer's freedom because the labourer goes in for this deal voluntarily. This is so because, thanks to the landlord's use of triangular threat, the labourer does not face a choice between (i) trading with the landlord and (ii) not trading with the landlord. His choice is between (i) and (iii) not trading with anyone. And given this choice he *opts* for (i). Hence his choice is 'voluntary' indeed. What I want to argue here is that in an important sense his choice is *not* voluntary.

The exact meaning of 'coercion' is a matter of great controversy (see Nozick 1972, for a discussion). So the strategy I shall use is to construct an example where we would all agree that coercion has occurred and then I shall argue that the labourer's exchange with the landlord is analogous to this example.

A is walking down a dark alley when he comes across *B* who pulls out a revolver and offers: 'Either your watch or I kill you'. Confronted with this easy choice *A* parts with his watch. Is this transaction voluntary or not? It definitely is a utility-maximizing act and if we look at *A's* choice *from after the point he is accosted by B*, it is a voluntary act. But of course if we describe this exchange as voluntary, coercion becomes almost an impossibility. And fortunately almost all social scientists who have examined similar situations agree that this is a case of coercion.[23] One important element which makes this a case of involuntary exchange is that once *A* has met *B* he can no longer return to his normal state. Let us suppose that *A's* normal level of happiness — that is, with his life and watch intact—is 100. Without his watch this would be 90, and, alternatively, without his life this would be zero. As soon as *A* confronts *B*, the possibility of 100 vanishes from his feasible set; he can only choose between 90 and 0.[24] And it is in this sense that a transaction at Marks and Spencers is voluntary: if you wish, you can walk out to your normal state. It is not the case that *once* you enter the shop you are suddenly compelled to pay a fine if you do not make a purchase.

Turn back to the model. Suppose that the three agents live on three different islands and while the merchant trades with both 1 and 2, 1 and 2 have not met each other. In this case 1's utility level is

$$\bar{U} = Y_1 - p^* x_1^* + \phi_1(x_1^*) - \phi_2(0).$$

As soon as 1 (the 'tribal') meets 2 (the 'civilized man'), 1's options change and he emerges in the end with U^0 utils which is less than $\bar{U}$. *After the encounter* he makes a voluntary choice alright but the exchange in its entirety is involuntary in the sense of the example just discussed.

Why we do not immediately recognize the landlord–labour exchange as one of coercion as we do in the watch-mugging case is because in the landlord–labour model, the landlord, in reality, always knows the labourer and to establish the analogy we need to go through the *hypothetical exercise* of what it would have been like if they did not know each other and compare it to what actually happens. (This is an instance of Lukes' third-dimensional power.)

Friedman and Friedman (1980) treat 'acting according to one's self-interest' and 'voluntary exchange' as two sides of the same coin. Our model demonstrates that that need not be because in our model every agent maximizes his own utility but nevertheless there is coercion. Moreover, the concept of 'voluntary action' is by no means an obvious one. Friedman and Friedman (1980: 13) claim that the basic argument for *laissez-faire* is 'misleadingly simple': 'If an exchange between two parties is voluntary, it will not take place unless both believe they will benefit from it'. I have tried to demonstrate that this proposition is not '*misleadingly simple*' but misleading.

5.4. On Men of Influence

Once the axiom of dyadic relations is eschewed and triadic and, more generally, multiple relations are allowed, we are better able to understand the *modus operandi* of the so-called 'man of influence' and also the reasons for his existence.

The concept of 'influence' has been subject to considerable sociological examination—at times as a notion indistinguishable from power (Dahl 1957) and at times as a distinct category (Parsons 1963). I will treat influence as a specific kind of power. For the limited purpose of this chapter, we shall take *a man of influence* to be a person who, if he so wishes, can get people to do him favours, that is, he can get things done out of turn. This will be made more precise as we go along.

In most less-developed economies—and even in many advanced countries—where bureaucratic norms are sluggish, there emerges in society, the man of influence (M). If you need a new telephone connection (which in Delhi, for instance, could take up to six years) and do not want to wait for too long, your best strategy would be to persuade M to do it for you. He can simply phone the chief of the telephone *bhavan* and get it done for you. He can also get you railway tickets out of turn during rush seasons and can get your son admitted to a good school and can get you a gas connection, etc., etc. There are many people who have the reputation for being able to get such things done. They are popularly known as men of influence.

The question that will be briefly examined here is: what is the source of this man's power? Why do bureaucrats agree to do him 'favours'? In the light of the discussions in the earlier sections, the answer is straightforward: every *individual* bureaucrat complies with M's request because he *conjectures* that M is a man of influence and by complying with M's request he will, in the long run, benefit. When every bureaucrat makes this same conjecture, the conjecture becomes a self-fulfilling prophecy.

It is useful to formalize this a little bit before examining the phenomenon more closely.

5.4.1. Model

I will construct here a very specific model to illustrate the main argument. Suppose there are k (≥ 3) bureaucrats in k different ministries. Each one has the authority to dispose of a certain number of licences of a distinct type. In particular, bureaucrat j can dispose of n_j licences of type j. 'Licences' is a general term being used here to denote bureaucratic permissions: permissions to buy train tickets from some special quota, to get telephone connections, to get admissions to schools, etc. Strictly speaking, the bureaucrats are not supposed to trade these licences for their own benefit and it will be assumed that they are honest to the extent that they would not do so 'directly'.

Assume that for all $j \in \{1, \ldots k\}$,[25] bureaucrat j needs one licence of type $j + 1$ from which he gets a utility of ϕ units. He needs no other licence. Every time j gives out a licence of type j to a friend or as a 'favour' to someone (basically, gives it not strictly in accordance with the rules in the government's 'rule book') he feels a little guilty and this amounts to d units of disutility. It will be assumed that

$$3d > \phi > 2d.$$

M gets a positive utility from one licence each of type j belonging to a non-empty set $S \subset \{1, \ldots, k\}$.

'To ask a person for a favour' will be taken to mean 'asking the person to get a licence'. An individual can ask anybody for any favour: he could ask bureaucrat j to get him a licence of type t. It is just that he will be wasting his effort if he asks a person who has no power or wish to comply.

Now suppose individuals $1, \ldots, k$ and M have the following conjectures. Every $j \in \{1, \ldots, k\}$ conjectures that M is a man of influence and M can and will do j any favour j asks for, as long as j gives M what M asks for. M conjectures that every j will give him (or to whoever M tells him to give to) a maximum of two licences as long as M gives j what j asks for.

In this model an equilibrium exists and it is as follows. At equilibrium, every j will ask M to get him a licence of type $j + 1$. M will ask every $j + 1$ to give a licence of type $j + 1$ to person j. In addition, he will ask every j belonging to S to give him a licence of type j. Every j will comply with M's request. It is easy to check that through these exchanges every individual, $1, \ldots, k$, and M, is better off [26] and, more importantly, *given their conjectures*, no one expects to do better by altering his strategy (that is, for example, no j would expect to be better-off by not giving M the licence he asks for). Hence, this is an equilibrium situation.

In reality these exchanges will not occur simultaneously but will be scattered over time. And it is this which allows each individual to believe that he is doing someone else a 'favour', while what he is actually doing is performing an extended exchange. In this model, M is the man of influence. Whenever he asks j to do a 'favour' for i, j complies. It is now easy to see why j complies. Precisely because j believes that M is a man of influence. What is interesting is that though M has no initial endowment (unlike the bureaucrats who can dole out licences), he ends up collecting whatever licence he needs for himself (that is, one of all the types in S). In this model M plays the role of money, he facilitates exchange. And just like money, he succeeds because everybody believes he will succeed.[27]

One should be clear that this is a model which merely describes an equilibrium. How this equilibrium comes about, that is, how a particular person *establishes* himself as a man of influence, is a much more complex question, for which this chapter offers no answer.

Some interesting insights can be gained by studying the conditions in which the man of influence would have no scope and, therefore, would not exist.

First, consider the case where there are no rules or social reasons not to dispose of licences as the bureaucrat wishes. In this case the licences would come to have prices and would be traded against money, like any other good. Money having entered, its surrogate—the man of influence—would have no role. Note that money, unlike the man of influence, does not in the process of exchange pocket some of the gains from trade. Hence, if both money and the influential man are there to perform a role, there would be a tendency for the former to displace the latter.

This has two corollaries. (1) Suppose there are rules (licences for school admission should go to the poor, licences to buy train tickets during rush periods are meant for the scheduled castes, etc.) but no proper enforcement machinery, and that bureaucrats are openly unethical. In that case once again the licences will come to have prices; it is just that these will now be called 'bribes'. (2) If there are rules and bureaucrats are meticulously ethical in their behaviour, once again there will be no scope for the man of influence, because who gets the licences is then decided in advance by the rules.[28] The scope for the influential man, therefore, exists in that intermedite situation where individuals are not so unethical as to openly sell what they are not supposed to and not so meticulously ethical that they cannot convince themselves that they are doing a 'favour', and in its guise perform an indirect exchange.

Second, if the demand for licences among the bureaucrats is pairwise compatible, that is i needs what j can give and *vice versa* then, one would expect, over time every pair would develop mutual trust and do each other 'favours', thereby doing away with the need for a go-between.[29]

5.4.2. Social Exchange

A final comment on exchange. What the above model tries to show is that in some situations where all individuals claim to be doing 'favours', the favours can be grouped into pairs which balance out and, therefore, do not constitute favours at all but are really exchanges. Yet it would be wrong to claim that these exchanges are conventional market exchanges. They are indeed more akin to what sociologists refer to as 'social exchanges', that is 'voluntary actions of individuals that are motivated by the returns they are expected to bring and typically do in fact bring' (Blau 1964: 91). At first sight there appears to be no difference between this and economic exchange. If the action is 'motivated by the returns', then that is exactly what economic exchange involves. That part of economic and social exchange is indeed common. The difference lies in the fact that in performing an economic exchange if one party does not fulfil his obligation we could consider it a breach of contract and the offended party could gather people or use the law to either get the other person to pay or recover what he has already paid or given. If on the other hand A gives B a gift and never gets a return gift, he can feel let down but he cannot ask for his gift back. He would simply have to decide not to give B a gift again.[30]

It is precisely for this reason that trust plays a much more important role in social exchange than in economic exchange.[31] And it is for this same reason that the *reputation* of the man of influence as a man of influence is crucial in ensuring that the equilibrium in our model does not break down.

5.5. CONCLUSION

Power and influence are complex concepts, and it is quite likely that these concepts have so many facets and nuances that it will never be possible to capture these in a single definition. As Dahl (1957: 201) observed:

If so many people at so many different times have felt the need to attach the label power, or something like it, to some Thing they believe they have observed, one is tempted to suppose that the Thing must exist ... and [a] more cynical suspicion is that a Thing to which people attach many labels with subtly or grossly different meanings in many different cultures and times is probably not a Thing at all but many Things.

Indeed the difficulty could be even more profound and Lukes (1977: 4) has argued: 'I maintain that power is one of those concepts identified by Gallie as "essentially contested" which "inevitably involve endless disputes about their, proper uses on the part of their users"'.[32]

Even if the concept is inherently contentious, at any point of time the actual contentions could be more than the inherent. Consequently, there is a case for trying to reduce the areas of actual contention. In a sense the large literature on power and influence is an attempt to do so.

The scope of this chapter was limited to examining one kind of power. The focus was on power and influence which work through triadic and, more generally, multiple relations. In each of the three models there was some asymmetry between agents. In the models in Sections 5.2 and 5.4 there is an agent, who, despite having no endowment of his own lives well and perhaps better than the others because of certain mutually reinforcing conjectures in the minds of agents. In Section 5.3 one agent extorts more from another agent than is witnessed in conventional theory because he threatens—explicitly or through a 'reputation' for vindictiveness—to destroy the latter's relation with a third agent if he does not accept his offer. In this model, the labourer, in fact, gets a *negative* utility from his transaction with the landlord. To explain something like this, beginning with standard economic theory, at first sight it seems as if we need to give up the axiom of peasant rationality. What this model tries to show is that that is not necessary. We could get the same result by giving up the much more dubious assumption of economic relations being necessarily dyadic.

I have been content to illustrate the nature of power and influence by constructing some specific examples. No attempt has been made to pursue the popular line of trying to measure power or to give it a general definition. Those who are familiar with the literature that has tried this will have no difficulty in understanding why.

Notes

1. I qualify this because it is becoming increasingly clear that even traditional theory makes implicit use of 'customs' and 'norms' (see, for example, Sen 1983a; Williamson 1983).

2. These are the popular English translations for Simmel's 'zweierverbindung' and 'verbindung zu dreien'.

3. This and the following quotes in this section are from Havel's (1978) manuscript.

4. In his classic essay, Mosca (1939) had argued that power never resides in an individual but in a ruling *class*. He had also argued that nor can it reside in the whole community. Both claims can be and have been contested, the latter—as we shall just see—for an interesting and intricate reason.

5. This is what Crozier (1969) has in mind in his chapter, 'Power through Terror'. Russell (1938) discusses several examples in his Chapter 6.

6. This may, conveniently, be thought of as a *'Parsee* model': The Indian Parsees often have names like Fruitwallah, Topiwallah, ... depending on what they (or their ancestors used to) trade.

7. This definition, though it generally conveys the right meaning, is not quite accurate since we can define arbitrary sets of people who are 'disloyal'. This definition should be treated as a quick reminder of a more precise definition, which is as follows. We first define 'k-disloyalty' recursively:

   A person is k-disloyal if he trades with a $(k - 1)$-disloyal person.
   A person is 1-disloyal if he does not give the king one unit.

   Now we can define disloyalty: A person is *disloyal* if there exists k such that he is k-disloyal.

8. On some occasions we will use a slightly more elaborate conjecture: 'Every $i \in N$ conjectures that no $j \in N \setminus \{i\}$ who is currently loyal would want to be disloyal in other situations'.

9. One question which may be raised is: Could the *king* not do better? What I have implicitly assumed here is that a king is not a 'rational agent', in the conventional sense (an assumption that cannot be faulted for gross unrealism) and that his behaviour is exogenously given. An alternative strategy would be to exploit the fact that, as it stands, there is no *obvious* way for the king to improve his condition. (For instance, if he tried raising the 1 unit demand to 2 units, this could disturb the conjectures that is, some might start believing that given the larger cost of loyalty now, others might not mind being disloyal; and this could end up with no one paying the king anything.) By bringing in some extra assumptions, it may be possible to show that the king in fact cannot improve his welfare.

10. So there is obedience and, at the same time, the people's interest is in opposition to the king. Hence this could be thought of as one formalization of Simmel's (1971) argument that there is, 'an intimate dual relation' (p. 103) between ruler and the ruled. More explicitly, he argued, 'obedience and opposition are merely two sides or links of one human attitude which fundamentally is quite consistent' (p. 104). See also, Goldhamer and Shils (1957: 135).

11. This may be clearer if we think of the conjecture as stated in note 8.

12. What this establishes is a kind of 'first-order' consistency of conjectures, because we are not showing that 2's conjecture (about what others will do to him if he trades with 1 who has refused to pay the king his due) would be true under perturbation. In a more convoluted way, Bresnahan's (1981) argument in the context of duopolies has the same problem. To establish complete consistency would probably require a backward induction argument of the kind used in Basu (1977) and Schick (1977).

13. This equilibrium is, however, not unique.

14. For more explicit discussions of power in the context of agrarian relations see Desai (1984); Rudra (1984); and also Newbery (1975).

15. Nozick (1972) begins by taking a legalistic definition of coercion and proceeds by examining its loopholes and suggesting ways to circumvent these. The paper illustrates well the richness of the concept and the difficulty of a consistent definition.

16. Quite apart from agrarian economics, there are general microeconomic writings on all-or-nothing monopoly: see Burstein (1960); and Oi (1971).

17. Strictly speaking the labourer will get a utility infinitesimally greater than $\bar{U}$. But it is harmless and mathematically neater to assume strict equality. Hence we do so here and in similar situations below.

18. For a comparison of these two kinds of monopoly or monopsony see Basu (1984b: ch. 11).

19. The word 'threat' has been used in a variety of different senses in sociology, philosophy, and game theory (see, for example, Lively 1976; Nozick 1972; Luce and Raiffa 1957). I use it here simply as a statement of commitment by the landlord.

20. Actually the answer depends on what the merchant conjectures will happen if he does not trade with some agent. Since this hypothetical situation does not arise in standard competitive models, there is no set answer to this. There are, however, two obvious strategies. We could assume that the merchant conjectures that if i does not trade with him (A) he will continue to trade with j at the rate and price level that prevailed in the original equilibrium, or (B) a new equilibrium will emerge to clear markets and he will trade at the rate and price level of this new equilibrium. Both strategies could be formalized and used. I have used strategy (A) here.

21. There is, of course, a general difficulty with threats. As Sen (1983b: 17) puts it: 'The person who threatens to harm the other if the bargaining should fail does it at no direct advantage to himself (otherwise it won't be a "threat" but something he may do anyway, and will be thus reflected in the fall-back position). While it is plausible to try to get bargaining advantage out of a threat *during the process* of bargaining, once the bargaining has failed, the threatener has no obvious interest in carrying out the threat. But that recognition on the part of the threatened person would call into question the credibility of the threat itself'. This is a general problem with the Nash equilibrium concept in the context of extensive games. However, given that threats do occur in reality and competing equilibrium concepts, example, subgame perfection, do not allow for real threats, it is probably best to use the Nash equilibrium solution in the present context.

22 A formal proof is as follows:

$$\phi_1(x_1^*) - \phi_1(0) = \int_0^{x_1^*} \phi_1'(x_1) \cdot dx_1$$

Clearly,

$$\int_0^{x_1^*} \phi_1'(x_1) \cdot dx_1 > \int_0^{x_1^*} \phi_1'(x_1^*) \cdot dx_1 = x_1^* \phi_1'(x_1^*)$$

since $\phi_1'' < 0$ Recall that, by definition, $\phi_1'(x_1^*) = p^*$. Hence we have proved that $\phi_1(x_1^*) - \phi_1(0) > p^* x_1^*$, which immediately implies that $\bar{U} > U^0$.

23. Sociologists distinguish between the exercise of physical force and the threat of such an exercise. Thus a large man who ties up a lone walker and then snatches his watch, all without a word, exercises physical force, while our mugger who also ends up with the watch in his pocket merely uses the threat of physical force. However, there seems to be general agreement that both cases engage a person in an involuntary act (see, for example, Simmel 1971: 96–8; Lively 1976; Blau 1964: ch. 5).

24. In game theory, an analogous situation is a game where preplay negotiation far from being advantageous is actually harmful to one player. See Luce and Raiffa (1957: 110–11) for an example.

25. If $j = k$. then $j + 1$ should be treated as equal to 1. In mathematics this would be described by saying that j belongs to a modular number system with mod k.

26. Every $j \in S$ gets a utility of $\phi - 2d$. Every $j \in \{1, ..., k\} \setminus S$ gets $\phi - d$. M gets the total utility of having one of each licence of types belonging to S.

27. In our example if one bureaucrat refuses to comply the whole chain breaks and M loses his influence. In reality, instead of there being one large circle there will generally be several little interconnected ones—like, for example, the symbol eight or the Olympic logo—and if one bureaucrat pulls out, one circle would collapse but not the entire system.

28. It follows from this discussion that the influential man may or may not be socially desirable. In some situations he could be a desirable person activating a sluggish bureaucracy. But he could also in some cases be seen as a surrogate for bribery, diverting licences intended for certain socially disadvantaged groups to the highest 'bidders' instead.

29. There may be rare cases where demands are not pairwise compatible and yet all exchanges take place without a man or influence in the middle. Thus, considering the act of giving gifts within the family, Malinowski (1957: 82) points out that at first sight it appears that here there is no exchange, even indirect, involved. But that, he argues, is an error stemming from 'not taking a sufficiently long view of the chain of transactions'; and once we do so we would discover 'that the system is based on a very complex give and take and that in the long run the mutual services balance'. This kind of exchange is, however, distinct from the economist's model, because individual behaviour cannot be explained in terms of utility maximization, though the group ends up maximizing utility.

30. There can of course be 'real' gifts, but what is being considered here is a gift which is a part of social exchange.

There is a more sophisticated way of reconciling gift-giving with utility-maximization, following Akerlof's (1983) model of honesty. Suppose gift-giving is a habit, which once acquired cannot be easily given up, and that the habit of gift-giving is something that an individual can choose to acquire or not. Then it is possible that individuals acquire the *habit* of gift-giving to maximize utility, though their each act of giving a gift cannot be explained as a utility-maximizing act.

31. This is not to deny that trust has a role even in economic exchange (see Basu 1983b). It ought to be emphasized that while economic and social exchanges are distinct concepts the dividing line between these is probably not a line at all but a hazy boundary.

32. The subquotes are from Gallie (1955–6: 169). It may be worth noting that Gallie's essentially contested concepts are required to be 'appraisive'. Thus it may be questioned as to whether 'power' is essentially contested *in the sense of Gallie*. It is easier to agree that it is essentially contested in a primitive sense.

REFERENCES

Akerlof, G. 1976. 'The Economics of Caste and of the Rat Race and other Woeful Tales'. *Quarterly Journal of Economics* 90.

—— 1983. 'Loyalty Filters'. *American Economic Review* 73.

Basu, K. 1977. 'Information and Strategy in Iterated Prisoner's Dilemma'. *Theory and Decision* 8.

—— 1983a. 'The Emergence of Isolation and Interlinkage in Rural Markets'. *Oxford Economic Papers* 35.

—— 1983b. 'On why we do not try to Walk-off without Paying after a Taxi-ride'. *Economic and Political Weekly* 18.

—— 1984a. 'Implicit Interest Rates, Usury and Isolation in Backward Agriculture'. *Cambridge Journal of Economics* 8.

—— 1984b. *The Less Development Economy: A Critique of Contemporary Theory*. Basil Blackwell.

Bhaduri, A. 1977. 'On the Formation of Usurious Interest Rates in Backward Agriculture'. *Cambridge Journal of Economics* 1.

Blau, P.M. 1964. *Exchange and Power in Social Life*. Wiley.

Borooah, V. 1980. 'High Interest Rates in Backward Agricultural Communities: An Examination of the Default Hypothesis'. *Cambridge Journal of Economics* 4.

Bottomley, A. 1975. 'Interest Rate Determination in Underdeveloped Rural Areas'. *American Journal of Agricultural Economics* 57.

Braverman, A. and T.N. Srinivasan. 1981. 'Credit and Sharecropping in Agrarian Societies'. *Journal of Development Economics* 9.

Braverman, A. and J. Stiglitz. 1982. 'Sharecropping and Interlinking of Factor Markers'. *American Economic Review* 72.

Bresnahan, T.F. 1981. ' Duopoly Models with Consistent Conjectures'. *American Economic Review* 71.

Burstein, M.L. 1960. 'The Economics of Tie-in Sales'. *Review of Economics and Statistics* 42.

Caplow, T. 1968. *Two Against One: Coalitions in Triads*. Prentice-Hall.

Coser, L.A. and B. Rosenberg, eds. 1957. *Sociological Theory*. Macmillan.

Crozier, B. 1969. *The Masters of Power*. Eyre and Spottiswoode.

Dahl. 1957. 'The Concept of Power'. *Behavioural Science* 2.

Desai, M. 1984. 'Power and Agrarian Relations: Some Concepts and Measurements'. In Desai et al. 1984.

Desai, M., S.H. Rudolph and A. Rudra, eds. 1984. *Agrarian Power and Agricultural Productivity in South Asia*. Oxford University Press.

Friedman, M. and R. Friedman. 1980. *Free to choose*. Penguin.

Gallie, W.B. 1955–6. 'Essentially Contested Concepts'. *Proceedings of the Aristotelian Society* 56.

Goldhamer, H. and E.A. Shils. 1957. 'Power and Status'. In Coser and Rosenberg (1957).

Havel, V. 1978. *The Power of the Powerless*. Prague, mimeo.

Lively, J. 1976. 'The Limits of Exchange Theory'. In B. Barry, ed. *Power and Political Theory*. Wiley.

Luce, R.D. and H. Raiffa. 1957. *Games and Decisions*. Wiley.

Lukes, S. 1974. *Power: A Radical View*. Macmillan.

—— 1977. *Essays in Social Theory*. Macmillan.

Malinowski, B. 1957. 'The Principle of Give and Take'. In Coser and Rosenberg (1957).

Mitra, P.K. 1983. 'A Theory of Interlinked Rural Transactions'. *Journal of Public Economics* 20.

Mosca, G. 1939. *The Ruling Class*. McGraw-Hill.

Newbery, D.M.G. 1975. 'Tenurial Obstacles to Innovation'. *Journal of Development Studies* 11.

Nozick, R. 1972. 'Coercion'. In P. Laslett, W.G. Runciman, and Q. Skinner, eds. *Philosophy, Politics and Society*. Fourth Series. Basil Blackwell.

Oi, W. 1971. 'A Disneyland Dilemma: Two-part Tariffs for a Mickey Mouse Monopoly'. *Quarterly Journal of Economics* 85.

Parsons, T. 1963. 'On the Concept of Influence'. *Public Opinion Quarterly* 27.

Rudra, A. 1984. 'Local Power and Farm Level Decision Making'. In Desai *et al.* (1984).

Russell, B. 1938. *Power: A New Social Analysis*. Allen and Unwin.

Schick, F. 1977. 'Some Notes on Thinking Ahead'. *Social Research* 44.

Sen, A. 1982. *Choice, Welfare and Measurement*. Basil Blackwell.

—— 1983a. 'Carrots, Sticks and Economics: Perception Problems in Incentives'. *Indian Economic Review* 18.

—— 1983b. 'Cooperative Conflicts: Technology and the Position of Women'. Oxford. mimeo.

Simmel, G. 1950. *The Sociology of Georg Simmel*. Edited by K.H. Wolff. Free Press.

—— 1971. *On Individuality and Social Forms*. Edited by D.N. Levine. University of Chicago Press.

Williamson, O.E. 1983. 'Credible Commitments: Using Hostages to Support Exchange'. *American Economic Review* 73.

6 A Theory of Association
Social Status, Prices, and Markets

6.1. INTRODUCTION

There are many people who would be glad to pay (on the quiet) large sums of money in order to be knighted. There are persons who would happily give up the Nobel Prize money and even pay some in order to get the Nobel Prize. However, if the ones responsible for giving these awards and honours frequently sold them to the highest bidders, the awards would become devalued. Some government awards which invariably go to 'loyalists' (that is, people who 'pay' the government with their loyalty), instead of the most deserving, get so devalued that even the loyalists are not flattered when they get them.

This shows that the value to an individual of an award or a prize does not depend on merely its inherent value—for example, the gold in an olympic medal, the money in a prize packet, or whatever it is that is used to confer a knighthood. It depends on the *allocation rule* itself which is used to decide who will receive the awards. If the awards are allocated by a rule which picks the 'best' or most talented, they would have a certain value to the recipients. If they are allocated via the price mechanism (that is, they are given to whomever is willing to pay most) they would have another value.

The present chapter looks at a special class of such goods and services. It is a study of commodities (the word 'commodities' being used generally enough to include services, memberships, awards, and, of course, commodities), the utility from which depends on who its other recipients (or consumers) are. By acquiring such a commodity a person tries to gain *association*, in the eyes of fellow human beings, with its other recipients.[1]

From *Oxford Economic Papers* 41, 1989: 653–71.

For helpful suggestions I thank Tariq Banuri, Don Patinkin, Nirvikar Singh, and, especially, Siddiq Osmani. The chapter has also benefited from a seminar at WIDER, Helsinki.

The examples of people seeking association are many. Much of Veblen's (1899) classic work on the leisure class is on this subject. Sociologists even have a name for the process by which members of lesser castes emulate the customs and rites of the *Brahminic* groups in order to impress upon fellow human beings their improving station in life. They call it *Sanskritization*[2] and as a concept we find its counterparts in most societies—backward and advanced. As an essay in the New York Times,[3] entitled 'The Art of Selling to the Very Rich', notes, 'Nobody buys one of Gerry Grinberg's watches to get unbeatably accurate time. Mr. Grinberg admits it. You can get as good time on an $18 watch'. As for the reason why they buy such watches the essay quotes Mr. Grinberg: 'People want to show their station in life'. People also often try to signal their status by pretending to have certain preferences. Thus, among the members of upwardly mobile classes, a larger number eat in ethnic restaurants than enjoy eating ethnic food; a larger number profess to enjoying art than actually do.[4]

The subject of association goods is not new in the sense that it lies at the cross-section of many earlier themes: positional goods,[5] snob effects,[6] the theory of clubs[7] and status goods.[8] Nevertheless, the nature of the equilibrium that arises in the presence of such goods is ill-understood. This chapter illustrates the role of association goods in understanding several real-life phenomena, especially the existence of excess-demand and excess–supply equilibria, through a series of simple models.

6. 2. CLUBS

A classic association good is the membership of clubs and societies which restrict admission to social elites and distinguished persons. Such clubs may have some facilities, like swimming pools and libraries, but the real reason why people toil to become members is that there is status associated with being admitted.[9]

I shall develop a very simple model mainly to illustrate how association goods may exhibit equilibria with excess demand. I consider a club which is run by a profit-maximizing entrepreneur. Before going into a generalized and formal analysis, it may be useful to give an intuitive account. Suppose that there are two kinds of citizens: those who have much status but little money (type 1) and *vice versa* (type 2). Let us now consider the case where the club has many members of type 1 and a few (perhaps none) of type 2. In addition, there are many type 2 people wanting to be admitted as members and willing to pay more than the going membership fee in order to be admitted.

This is an excess-demand situation and at first sight it may appear that this cannot be a profit-maximizing equilibrium from the club entrepreneur's point of view. All he has to do is to take in some of these type 2 people at the higher charge that they are willing to pay (perhaps even replace some type 1 people with type 2) and the club's profit will rise. This, however, need not be so. Since the club membership is an association good, the act of admitting more type 2 people may change the status rating of the club and make everybody willing to pay less membership fee. Thus excess demand may exist in equilibrium with profit-maximizing agents. Any attempt on the part of the club to eliminate the excess demand by taking in more members or changing the composition of members may change the character of the club, make people less eager to join it, and thus lower the club's profits. It should be clear that since my purpose is to explain excess demand, my job would be easier if the club's objective was something other than profits. Thus my assumption that clubs are run by entrepreneurs who maximize *profits* is not made in the belief that this is so in reality, but simply to choose an assumption which is adverse from my point of view. With this, let us proceed to a formal analysis.

Let H be the set of all people and, for all i in H, let $H(i)$ be the set of all subsets of H which have i as an element. For all i in H, let v_i be a real-valued mapping on $H(i)$ such that for all $M \in H(i)$, $v_i(M)$ is the maximum amount that i would be willing to pay to be a member of a club in which M is the set of members.[10]

I shall, to start with, assume that the club cannot charge discriminatory fees from its members, and that admitting additional members does not entail any costs on the part of the club entrepreneur. Hence, a club with a set M of members earns a profit of $(\#M) \min_{i \in M} v_i(M)$, where $\#M$ denotes the number of elements in M. The club's aim is to choose a subset M of H which maximizes profit. More formally, its aim is to:

(6.1)
$$\text{Max}_M \left((\#M) \min_{i \in M} v_i(M) \right)$$

Let M^* be a solution of (6.1). M^* may be described as an *equilibrium* set of members. The equilibrium membership fee is

$$v^* = \min_{i \in M} v_i(M^*)$$

It is easy to show that there may be an excess demand for membership in equilibrium. We shall here say that there is an *excess demand* for membership if there exists a person j who does not belong to M^* and $v_j(M^* \cup \{j\}) > v^*$. In this case j is a person who is willing to pay more than the membership fee to join the club but the club will not admit him.

The possibility of an excess-demand equilibrium may be illustrated with an example. Let $H = \{1, 2, 3\}$, and suppose

$$v_1(H) = v_1(\{1, 3\}) = v_1(\{1, 2\}) = 3$$
$$v_2(\{2, 3\}) = v_3(\{2, 3\}) = 2$$
$$v_2(H) = v_3(H) = v_2(\{2\}) = v_2(\{1, 2\})$$
$$= v_3(\{3\}) = v_3(\{1, 3\}) = v_1(\{1\}) = 0$$

We could think of individuals 2 and 3 as men of status (the old nobility). Person 1 would pay a lot to join a club which has 2 or 3 as member. While 1 (the *nouveau riche*) can pay a lot, he is not quite the coveted person. In fact, his being in a club devalues its membership altogether for 2 and 3.

In the above example, the equilibrium club is one which has 2 and 3 as members and charges a fee of 2. Person 1 is denied membership even though he is willing to pay 3 units, which is more than the membership fee. This is a case of excess-demand equilibrium.

Several existing models of excess-demand or excess-supply equilibria make use of the assumption of non-discriminatory prices, for example, the assumption that a firm cannot pay different wages to its workers. In the above model I also use a similar assumption since it was supposed that all members have to be charged the same fee. However, the excess-demand result is more robust here in that it would survive a relaxation of the non-discrimination assumption.[11]

Let us consider now a club which is allowed to charge discriminatory fees. Its aim is to choose M (subset of H) so as to maximize profit. Profit is now given by the aggregate of the maximum that each member is willing to pay.

In this case there can be different ways of defining excess demand. Consider the following definition which is the most adverse from my point of view: We shall say that *excess demand* exists if there is a person j who is not admitted to the club but who is willing to pay more than the highest-paying club member. That there can be excess demand in this sense in a case where a club can charge differential fees is obvious from the above numerical example. Person 1 would still be kept out even though he would be willing to pay a larger fee than is being paid by either of the two existing members.

Drawing on our knowledge of social psychology, it may be possible to place restrictions on the v_i-functions. For instance, if we wish to characterize a society where wealth or ability to pay is the only thing which gives an individual social status, we would require a condition as follows: for all M subset of H, such that $M \cap \{k, h\} = \Phi$, for all $i \in M$, $v_i(M \cup \{k\}) > v_i(M \cup \{h\}) \leftrightarrow v_k(M \cup \{k\}) > v_h(M \cup \{h\})$.

There may be other ways of formalizing this. It may be interesting to pursue the consequences of different restrictions on v_i-functions. We could also try to isolate conditions under which there is no excess demand in equilibrium or under which the equilibrium is unique.[12]

Finally, it may appear that the club's ability to discriminate in its choice of members is crucial for the existence of excess-demand equilibria. This is, however, not so. Let us assume that a club is required to be non-discriminatory in its selection of members in the sense that its proportions of different types of members must match proportions of different types of people who want to be members.[13] Even in this case it is possible to construct examples to show that there can be excess demand in equilibrium. But instead of dwelling on this I turn presently to the labour market where some related problems can arise.

6.3. JOBS

While people work for money, they also work for the 'recognition' that employment confers. As Sen (1975a: 5) observes, 'Employment can be a factor in self-esteem and indeed in esteem by others'. Taking a cue from this and using a more elaborate version of this basic idea, we could argue that not only do certain kinds of employment give recognition, the amount of recognition may vary with the nature of the employing firm or the job.[14] And, one index of the quality of a firm is the quality of the people employed by it. An important reason why a prestigious university is considered prestigious is the status of its faculty members. Similarly a firm could be prestigious because it employs MBAs of top management schools and the children of the nobility. Now, if i joins such a firm, most people would associate i with the other employees of the firm. Given that individuals do seek this kind of recognition, it is reasonable to expect that an individual would be willing to work for a distinguished firm for a lower salary than what he would demand from a run-of-the-mill employer.[15]

In order to formally analyse the consequence of association effects, consider a 'firm' (this being the generic name for any employer, including universities) employing professional labourers, for example, managers or academics. Assume that there are two kinds of potential employees: (i) those who hold management degrees and are referred to here as prestige workers (type p) and (ii) the rest, who may be called ordinary workers (type o). In this model a worker's type is given exogenously. It is for reasons of simplicity that I desist from modelling the *acquisition* of prestige as a part of the theory. All workers are equally productive. That is, the output, X, produced by the firm depends on the total amount of labour employed by it. If n_i is the number of labourers of type i employed by the firm, then

$$(6.2) \qquad X = X(n_p + n_o), \qquad X' > 0, \qquad X'' < 0$$

The association or status effect is introduced through the assumption that the reservation wages, w_p and w_o (that is, the minimum wages at which workers of types p and o, respectively, would accept the job) depends on what fraction of the firm's employees is prestige labour.[16] In addition, we allow the reservation wages (or supply prices of labour) to depend on the amount of labour of each type employed. Hence,

$$(6.3) \qquad w_p = w_p(q, n_p)$$

$$(6.4) \qquad w_o = w_o(q, n_o),$$

where $q = n_p/(n_p + n_o)$; and we assume (6.3) and (6.4) are continuous and differentiable and satisfy the following:

$$(6.5) \qquad \frac{\partial w_i}{\partial q} < 0, \qquad \frac{\partial w_i}{\partial n_i} \geq 0, \qquad i = o, p.$$

The relation between w_p and n_p (likewise for type-o labourers) is the usual supply-curve relation. The second inequality in (6.5) asserts that supply curves are not downward sloping. The first inequality in (6.5) captures the idea of association effects.

Assuming that wages are specified in real terms and that all workers of the same type have to be paid the same wage, the firm's profit, R, is given by

$$R(n_p, n_o) = X(n_p + n_o) - w_p(q + n_p)n_p - w_o(q, n_o)n_o$$

The firm's aim is to maximize $R(n_p, n_o)$ by choosing (n_p, n_o). Denoting the solution of this by $R(n_p^*, n_o^*)$ (these may be referred to as *equilibrium* values) and assuming that it occurs in the interior, the first-order conditions may be written as:

(6.6)
$$X' - \frac{\partial w_p}{\partial q}\frac{\partial q}{\partial n_p}n_p - \frac{\partial w_p}{\partial n_p}n_p - w_p - \frac{\partial w_o}{\partial q}\frac{\partial q}{\partial n_p}n_o = 0$$

(6.7)
$$X' - \frac{\partial w_p}{\partial q}\frac{\partial q}{\partial n_o}n_p - \frac{\partial w_o}{\partial q}\frac{\partial q}{\partial n_o}n_o - \frac{\partial w_o}{\partial n_o}n_o - w_o = 0$$

It is easy to check that (6.5) and (6.7) imply

(6.8)
$$w_o(q^*, n_o^*) < X'(n_p^* + n_o^*),$$

where $q^* = n_p^*/(n_p^* + n_o^*)$.

This may, at first sight, look like a well-known consequence of the fact that the firm acts like a monopsonist in the labour market (which renders wage to be less than the marginal product of labour). What is interesting and easy to check is that even if, unlike a monopsonist, the firm is unable to vary w_o by varying n_o, that is, $\partial w_o/\partial n_o = 0$, (6.8) would be true. (6.8) here is a consequence of the association effect.

What about the wage earned by type-p labourers? In general we cannot limit this. But as we approach the competitive case we get the proposition that not only does the wage earned by type-p workers exceed the wage of the type-o but it exceeds the marginal product of labour. There are several conditions under which this happens. I state and discuss only one here.

Observe that in the determination of w_p [see (6.3)], n_p operates via two routes: (1) It affects q, which in turn affects w_p. (2) It affects w_p directly. (1) and (2) may be called the association effect and the supply effect. Clearly these two work in opposite directions. As n_p increases, q increases and this results in a fall in w_p. However, since $\partial w_p/\partial n_o > 0$, [see (6.5)], the direct effect of n_p (that is, the supply effect) is a positive one. The case which is of special interest here is one where the association effect dominates the supply effect, that is

(6.9)
$$\frac{\partial w_p}{\partial n_p} < \left|\frac{\partial w_p}{\partial q}\right|\frac{\partial q}{\partial n_p}$$

Since the right-hand side of (6.9) represents the association effect and the left-side, that is, $\partial w_p/\partial n_p$, goes to zero as the labour market becomes competitive (that is, this firm is one among many hiring labour), we shall say that *the association effect is strong or the labour market is near-competitive* if and only if (6.9) is true.

By using (6.5) and (6.6) it is easy to see that if (6.9) holds, then

$$X'(n_p^* + n_o^*) < w_p(q^*, n_p^*)$$

What we have established thus far may be summed up in:

THEOREM 6.1: The wage earned by type-o workers is always less than the marginal product of labour. The wage earned by type-p workers exceeds the marginal product of labour if the association effect is strong or the labour market is near-competitive.

It is claimed by many people that the holders of management degrees from well-known institutions are not as productive as their salaries suggest. The above model shows that this may indeed be so.

The above model also explains involuntary unemployment because the firm employs some prestige workers at $w_p (q^*, n_p^*)$, even though there may be an excess supply of ordinary workers (who are, of course, as productive as type-p workers) offering to work for a smaller wage than this.

Let us now consider a law prohibiting discrimination in wages among labourers of equal productivity which means both types of labourers have to be paid the same wage. In the present model this could have quite unexpected and even adverse affects. Though such a law is a well-meaning intervention, it could have consequences which are undesirable. The next theorem and the discussion that follows capture this phenomenon.

THEOREM 6.2: If the association effect is strong or the labour market is near-competitive, then the prohibition of discriminatory wages would result in either type-p or type-o labour being totally excluded from the labour market.

PROOF: If the firm is forced to pay the same wage to all workers, then its profit function has to be modified from $R\,(\cdot)$ to $\bar{R}\,(\cdot)$, defined as follows:

$\bar{R}\,(n_p, n_o)$

$$
= \begin{cases} X\,(n_p + n_o) - (n_p + n_o)\max\{(w_p(q, n_p), w_o(q, n_o)\}, & \text{if } n_p, n_o > 0 \\ X\,(n_p) - n_p w_p(1\ n_p), & \text{if } n_p, n_o = 0 > 0 \\ X\,(n_o) - n_o w_o\,(0, n_o) & \text{if } n_p =0, n_o > 0 \end{cases}
$$

Assume that in equilibrium $n_p^* > 0$ and $n_o^* > 0$. This implies that the first line of the $\bar{R}$-function is the relevant one. Now, note that if n_p is raised by a small amount, dn_p, then w_p changes by

(6.11) $dw_p = \left[\dfrac{\partial w_p}{\partial q} \cdot \dfrac{\partial q}{\partial n_p} + \dfrac{\partial w_p}{\partial n_p} \right] dn_p$.

This follows directly from (6.3). By (6.5) and (6.9) we see that $dw_p < 0$. Hence if n_p is raised a little and n_o lowered a little, so as to maintain total employment constant, $w_p(q, n_p)$ will fall and [(6.5) implies] so will $w_o(q, n_o)$. It follows from the $\bar{R}$-function that, starting from n_p and n_o^*, if we raise n_p^* and lower n_o^* by the same amount, $\bar{R}$ will rise. This contradicts the fact that (n_p^*, n_o^*) is an equilibrium and thereby establishes that either $n_p^* = 0$ or $n_o^* = 0$.

Whether the firm will employ only type-p workers or only type-o workers will depend on whether the following condition is true or not:

$$\max_{\{n_p\}} X(n_p) - n_p w_p(1, n_p) \geq \max_{\{n_o\}} X(n_o) - n_o w_o(0, n_o).$$

Clearly, depending on the nature of the production function and the w_p- and w_o-functions, the above condition may or may not be true.

The counterpart of Theorem 6.2 in the case of *many* firms is interesting. It asserts that if intra-firm wage discrimination is prohibited, then the labour market will get completely segregated in the sense that each firm will employ only one type of labour.

While I have stated the above non-discrimination provision in terms of the law, it is entirely possible that custom or a system of social sanctions compels a firm to refrain from what society views as discrimination and, in particular, prevents the firm from paying different wages to types o and p. The persistence of such customs can be explained endogenously, though their roots may lie in distant history (Basu et al. 1987; see also Akerlof 1976; Basu 1986). This is what renders simplistic debates on the pros and cons of intervention misleading. What a government intervention achieves may in some societies be achieved through a multitude of rational acts on the parts of individuals.

Finally, a comment on education. In the signalling model (Arrow 1973; Spence 1973), education does not necessarily enhance productivity; but through the working of the general equilibrium, the more educated people turn out to be the more productive (because they are the ones who find it profitable to acquire education) and they command a higher wage. In the present model if we interpret type-p workers as the educated workers, then we find that the link between education and productivity is even weaker than in the signalling model, because everybody's productivity is the same. Nevertheless, in our model there is a positive relation between education and wage, as in the signalling model. And, indeed, it should be possible to have productivity depend on education and to model association effects as an additional feature.

6.4. SCHOOLS

Should schools be allowed to charge students discriminatory fees? In India many schools and institutes (especially engineering and medical) have often charged special fees from some students. 'Capitation fees', as these are usually called, have led to much criticism and, wherever possible, legislation preventing discriminatory fees. The implicit argument has been that this would lead schools to admit only richer students who are able to pay more. This argument ceases to be valid once we recognize that association effects are usually strong in the domain of schooling. In the presence of association effects one can find parametric situations where discriminatory fees may be not just efficient, but ethically desirable.

The intuitive idea is this. Suppose that there are four kinds of potential students: clever and rich (*cr*), clever and poor (*cp*), mediocre and rich (*mr*), and mediocre and poor (*mp*). The term 'clever' is used here simply to denote students who are able to absorb and make good use of education.

The ethical concern here is a limited one: we want to have a system in which *cp* students are not denied education. What I want to argue is that in the presence of association effects (i) there is no reason why allowing discriminatory fees will necessarily lead to *cp* students being denied admission and (ii) there are situations where permitting discriminatory fees may in fact mean more *cp* students will be admitted.

The argument is based on the assumption that school labels help. A student from a college where the average student is brilliant stands a better chance of getting a good job than if the same student had been to an ordinary college. This is because firms and other employers use school labels as indices of quality. It is often too expensive to test each prospective employee and one uses one's knowledge of a school's general standing to judge its alumni.[17]

Now suppose an entrepreneur (a profit maximizer) is setting up a school. If he is allowed to charge any and variable fees, would he admit only the rich at high fees? The answer is 'no' because he will realize that the school's reputation and consequently the fees that the rich are willing to pay depend largely on the average quality of his students. Thus he will always have an eye on taking on good students, if necessary for no fees, because that will enable him to charge a higher fee from the rich. Having a law ensuring non-discriminatory fees may lead him to abandon those who cannot pay altogether.

I construct here a very simple model to illustrate these propositions. Consider a society in which there are $\bar{n}_{cr}$ clever and rich (potential) students. Likewise for $\bar{n}_{cp}$ and $\bar{n}_{mr}$. It is assumed that there are no mediocre and poor students (that is, $\bar{n}_{mp} = 0$). This is because this category plays no role in the present model excepting for the wholly negative one of complicating the algebra.

Consider now a school in which n_{cr} is the number of clever and rich students and likewise for n_{cp} and n_{mr} (recall that n_{mp} has to be zero). The school's reputation depends on what fraction of its students are clever, that is

$$q = \frac{n_{cr} + n_{cp}}{n_{cr} + n_{cp} + n_{mr}}$$

Let s be the (present value of) additional salary that a student would get later on in life by virtue of having been to this school. It is assumed that s depends on the reputation of the school, and thus on q.

(6.12) $\qquad s = s(q)$

Of course, $\partial s/\partial q \geq 0$. If for all q, $\partial s/\partial q = 0$, there is no association effect. Otherwise, there is.

The rich students are willing to pay school fees up to $s(q)$. That is, they would like to join the school as long as the acquisition of education yields a non-negative net life-time income. The poor are not *able* to pay this much. For simplicity, we assume that they are willing and able to pay a fraction, θ ($0 < \theta < 1$) of $s(q)$, that is, up to $\theta s(q)$. This is easily justified. If we assume that the poor have to borrow money at an interest of r to pay their school fees, then we get exactly the above kind of behaviour with $\theta = 1/(1 + r)$. In this sense it is being assumed that the rich have access to money at zero interest rate. All our results would be intact if we assume simply that the rich have access to 'cheaper' money than the poor.

It is supposed that educating students does not entail any cost on the part of the school. There is, however, a maximum number of seats, $\bar{n}$, in the school, so that it cannot admit more students than n. In order to sharpen the conflict between the clever-and-poor and the mediocre-and-rich, we assume

(6.13) $$\bar{n}_{cr} < \bar{n}; \quad \bar{n}_{cr} + \bar{n}_{cp} \geq \bar{n}; \quad \bar{n}_{cr} + \bar{n}_{mr} \geq \bar{n}$$

The school's aim is to maximize profit by deciding on how many students of each category to admit. I shall consider two alternative policy regimes:

CASE 1: The school can charge any student any fee.

CASE 2: The government prohibits discriminatory fees.

I later comment on a third case in which the government actually fixes the school fee or sets an upper bound to it.

In case 1, the profit function is

(6.14) $$\Pi_1(n_{cr}, n_{mr}, n_{cp}) = n_{cr}s(q) + n_{mr}s(q) + n_{cp}\theta s(q)$$

It is quite obvious that before taking students of any other category, the school will admit all cr-students. Since $\bar{n}_{cr} < \bar{n}$, it follows that the profit function may be simply written as

(6.15) $$\Pi_1(n_{mr}, n_{cp}) = \bar{n}_{cr}s(q) + n_{mr}s(q) + n_{cp}\theta s(q)$$

In case 2, since the school cannot charge discriminatory fees it will have to charge all students the fee which the student who is willing to pay the least (among those admitted) is prepared to pay. Hence, the school's profit in case 2, denoted by Π_2, is given by (noting again that n_{cr} will end up equal to $\bar{n}_{cr}$)

(6.16) $$\Pi_2(n_{mr}, n_{cp}) = \begin{cases} \theta s(q)(\bar{n}_{cr} + n_{mr} + n_{cp}), & \text{if } n_{cp} > 0 \\ s(q)(\bar{n}_{cr} + n_{mr}), & \text{if } n_{cp} = 0 \end{cases}$$

In both cases the firm's aim is to maximize profit subject to $\bar{n}_{cr} + n_{mr} + n_{cp} \leq \bar{n}$.

In proving the theorems it is useful to first establish a simple proposition concerning case 2:

LEMMA 6.1: In case 2, either no cp-students will be admitted or no mr-students will be admitted.

PROOF: Using stars to denote the firm's optimal choice, suppose $n_{cp}^* > 0$ and $n_{mr}^* > 0$. Hence, the top line of equation (6.16) is relevant. If the school increases the number of cp-students a little and decreases mr-students by the same amount (by (13), it is possible to do this), then q would rise, and hence $s(q)$ would rise. Since $\bar{n}_{cr} + n_{mr} + n_{cp}$ remains unchanged, the profit would rise by virtue of this adjustment. Hence the original situation could not have been optimal for the firm.

The proof of Lemma 6.1 may give the impression that it is never worthwhile admitting mr-students. This is wrong because there is a discontinuity in profit where $n_{cp} = 0$ and it is easy to check that

$$\max_{n_{mr}} \Pi_2(n_{mr}, 0) > \lim_{n_{cp} \to 0} \max_{n_{mr}} \Pi_2(n_{mr} + n_{cp}).$$

The advantage of Lemma 6.1 is that the profit function (6.16) can now be written simply as

$$\Pi_2(n_{mr}, n_{cp}) = \begin{cases} \theta s(1)(\bar{n}_{cr} + n_{cp}), & \text{if } n_{cp} > 0 \\ s(q)(\bar{n}_{cr} + n_{mr}), & \text{if } n_{cp} = 0 \end{cases}$$

It is quite obvious from the above that if the school decides to admit cp-students, it is best to fill up all seats in the school, that is, admit $\bar{n} - \bar{n}_{cr}$ students of type cp. It follows that Π_2 can be written even more simply as

(6.17) $$\Pi_2(n_{mr}) = \max \left\{ \theta s(1)\bar{n}, \max_{n_{mr} \le \bar{n} - \bar{n}_{cr}} s\left(\frac{\bar{n}_{cr}}{\bar{n}_{cr} + n_{mr}}\right)(\bar{n}_{cr} + n_{mr})\right\}$$

THEOREM 6.3: In case 1 the seats in the school are always filled. In case 2 it is possible to have an equilibrium where seats are left vacant *and* students are denied admission.

PROOF: Consider case 1, and suppose the school has vacant seats. If it admits more cp-students, clearly q will either rise or remain constant. Hence, all terms on the right-hand side of (6.15) will either remain constant or rise and the last term will certainly rise. Hence profit rises. This guarantees that all seats will be filled.

Now consider case 2. From Lemma 6.1 we know that the profit function will be as in (6.17). Clearly if θ is sufficiently small, the right-hand term within the parenthesis in (17) will be relevant. Given that our only restriction on the $s(q)$ function is that $s'(q) \ge 0$, clearly there can be an $s(q)$ function such that

(6.18) $$\hat{n}_{mr} = \underset{n_{mr}}{\text{argmax}}\, s\left(\frac{\bar{n}_{cr}}{\bar{n}_{cr} + n_{mr}}\right)(\bar{n}_{cr} + n_{mr}) < \bar{n} - \bar{n}_{cr}$$

In such a case the school will admit n_{mr} students of type mr, since that maximizes (6.17). By (6.18), the total number of students admitted to the school, $\bar{n}_{cr} + \hat{n}_{mr}$, is less than $\bar{n}$. By (6.13), there are more mr-students in society (that is, $\bar{n}_{mr} - \hat{n}_{mr} > 0$) who would be willing to pay the school fees and be admitted to the school.

Theorem 6.3 shows that with association effects we could have in equilibrium what is usually found only in disequilibrium situations, namely unutilized resources both on the supply and demand sides.

THEOREM 6.4: There is a class of situations where a law requiring that all students be charged the same fees would result in the cp-students being refused admission; and the revocation of such a law would mean that cp-students would be admitted.

PROOF: From Theorem 6.3 we know that in case 2 there are situations where some seats are left vacant; and from the proof of Theorem 6.3 we know that whenever this happens, only mr-students are admitted to the school (that is, of course, after first admitting all cr-students). Consider such a situation. Hence

(6.19) $$\text{argmax}\, \Pi_2(n_{mr}, n_{cp}) = (n_{mr}^*, 0)$$

and

$$n^*_{mr} < \bar{n} - \bar{n}_{cr}$$

(6.15) and (6.16) imply

(6.20) $$\max_{n_{mr}} \Pi_1(n_{mr}, 0) = \max_{n_{mr}} \Pi_2(n_{mr}, 0)$$

Since $n^*_{mr} < \bar{n} - \bar{n}_{cr}$, it follows that if $n_{cp} = 0$, it is best for the school in case 1 to leave vacant seats [see (6.19) and (6.20)]. Starting from this situation if (in case 1) the school admits some cp students, Π_1 must rise since q will rise.

What we have established, therefore, is this. There exists n_{mr}, n_{cp} such that n_{mr} + $n_{cp} \leq \bar{n} - \bar{n}_{cr}$ and $\Pi_1(n_{mr}, n_{cp}) > \max_{n_{mr}} \Pi_1(n_{mr}, 0)$. This, coupled with (6.20), means that the revocation of a law prohibiting discriminatory fees (that is, a switch from case 2 to case 1) would result in cp–students being admitted.

One could utilize the framework of this section to analyse other questions, in particular, the consequence of:

(A) fixing the fees (that is, the case where the government not only prohibits discriminatory fees but actually fixes the fee at some level).

(B) setting an upper limit on the fees (that is, discriminatory fees are allowed but they must not exceed a certain level) .

Instead of analysing these formally, I shall make some brief comments drawing on the intuition already established in this section. Also, I tend to focus on how (A) and (B) *could* have effects which are unexpected and the opposite of what usually motivates the enactment of such laws. It will indeed be a fallacy to treat the could as will.

The adverse effect of (A) on the poorest sections is obvious. In reality, unlike in our model, there are many levels of poverty. So no matter where the fees are fixed the poorest sections would be unable to pay for their education. In our model if, for instance, the fee is above $\theta s(1)$, then none of the poor students (clever or mediocre) would be able join the school.

Indeed, (A) is unrealistic. No government would have such a policy, because presumably no government would prevent schools from giving scholarships and assistance to some chosen students. Now, a system of fixed fees with scholarships to some is effectively system (B), which sets an upper limit on students' fees. So let us turn to analysing the consequence of (B). This is best done in two stages. First consider (A) and then analyse the effect of a switch to (B).

Consider first a case where the school fee was fixed (by law) at a level, $\hat{f}$, which is above $s\theta(1)$. As just discussed, none of the poor will be admitted to school because they are unable to pay the school fees. Now suppose that the law is changed to type (B), with $\hat{f}$ being treated as an upper limit. That is, the government now allows the school to lower the fees for some students if it so wishes. So now the school can, in principle, reach out to the poorer students who were earlier priced out of the market. The question is, will it? Consider the reason why the school may want to lower the fees for some students. This could only be in order to admit some clever-and-poor students which would improve the school's academic rating and thereby allow it (i) to charge higher fees from the rich students, or (ii), in case there were vacant seats in the original equilibrium, to admit more rich students at the ceiling fee. It is immediately obvious that in the case where the seats are full when only one fee is allowed, the option of lowering the fees will not be exercised if the school is not allowed to raise anyone's fee. The maximum fee law, by cutting off the school's option of raising the fees on the rich, cuts off its incentive to make concessions to students who are good but unable to pay their fees for reasons of poverty.

6.5. COMMENTS ON RELATED TOPICS

6.5.1. Prizes

There is now a considerable body of literature in economics on prizes (see, for example, Lazear and Rosen 1981; Nalebuff and Stiglitz 1983; Rosen 1986). In this literature a prize distinguishes itself from other systems of rewards, for example wages, by virtue of the fact that several people toil for it but one (or perhaps few) gets the award in the end on the basis of one's *relative* performance. The others get nothing for their toil. This leads to many interesting questions but those are not my concern here. What this literature does not consider is that a prize usually gives its recipient recognition. To that extent it belongs to the class of association goods, like club membership, jobs, or schools. This immediately means, as is obvious from the models in the earlier sections, that the granting of prizes is a strategic variable in the hands of the prize-giver. The prize-giver can optimize his own profit, utility, or whatever he is trying to maximize by suitably selecting the recipients and extracting payments in kind or as return favours out of them. This objective may not always coincide with that of selecting the most deserving people. However, the prize-giver does have the incentive not to deviate *too far* from selecting deserving people because that may diminish the worth of the prize and once that happens he would no longer be able to 'sell' the prize, that is, exchange it for whatever his objective is.

From the above remarks it is clear that prizes can be modelled much like the theory of clubs in Section 6.2. If we think of the prize-giver as the club entrepreneur and the group of prize recipients as club members, the same kind of theorizing becomes possible. There is one interesting additional literature here, though. Prize-giving is usually a periodic affair (Olympic medals once every four years, Nobel prizes once each year, etc.) which means time is a more pronounced element in the activity of prize giving than in a theory of clubs. This introduces some special elements. For instance, if the prize-giver is myopic in the sense of having a high time discount, then in any particular year he may be more inclined to selling the award to the highest bidder than giving to the most deserving. Of course, this means that the following year's highest bidder win be willing to pay less (because the prize is a little devalued) and the process continues till the prize is totally devalued. The same would have a greater tendency to occur if each year a new selection committee chooses the recipients of the prize. The future value of the prize will be less in its interest than it would be in the case of a more permanent committee.

6.5.2. Sanskritization

Finally, a comment on Sanskritization which is one of the purest manifestations of association activity. This, as already briefly discussed above, refers to rituals, customs, and behaviour which the castes or classes at the lower end of a society's accepted hierarchy adopt in order to signal to others their improving station in life.[18]

Sanskritization cannot be analysed in the same way as we have analysed clubs, jobs, or schools, because an elite group or caste is not an entity whose membership is managed by an agent to achieve some objective. Nevertheless, it raises an interesting question in the light of our models. Clearly for the membership of some group to be an association good, that is, for others to want to join it, there must be costs involved in trying to join the group. If not, then outsiders would continue to rush in as long as there is value in joining the group. Its membership, in other words, would cease to be an association good in equilibrium.

The fact that Sanskritization exists at all raises the question as to what the costs of Sanskritization are. Though the 'elites' of a society form a nebulous collection and no one charges an entry fee for joining them, there must exist hidden charges; and, indeed, there are. In the context of caste societies, these take the form of ridicule if one attempts Sanskritization and fails. Thus the cost is an *expected* cost but sure enough it is there. This is brought out very clearly in Srinivas's (1955) essay on a southern Indian village (p. 24): 'Discrimination against the Smiths occurs everywhere in peninsular India, *possibly as a result of their attempts in the past to rise high in the caste hierarchy by means of a thorough Sanskritization of their customs*' (my italics). He goes on to make similar observations about the *Kammálans* of Tamil Nadu.

Using the theories of association developed in this chapter, it ought to be possible to formalize the concept of Sanskritization. Such a formalization in conjunction with Akerlof's model of customs could give us some insights into the dynamics of customs and mores.

6.6. CONCLUSION

Association goods complicate policy questions. It is well-known that a lot of corruption (example, bribery) germinates from the existence of goods and services which are not distributed through the price mechanism. To this a standard response has been to suggest that we simply turn these goods over to the price mechanism. This prescription runs into difficulty if the good in question happens to be an association good. In that case, as discussed in Section 6.1, the value of the good itself may depend on the mechanism used to allocate it and may be diminished by a resort to a particular mechanism.

I shall, however, put aside policy issues here and briefly comment instead on two important subjects which I have not taken up in this chapter but which deserve analysis in future. These are general equilibrium and welfare. It would be valuable to construct a general equilibrium model where one commodity happens to be an association good. A simple way to model this would be to suppose that there are h individuals and n goods and the nth good is an association good. Let x_j^i be the number of units of good j consumed by person i. Let $x_n^{-i} = x_n^1, ..., x_n^{i-1}, x_n^{i+1}, ..., x_n^h$). Person i's utility function could be defined as follows:

$$u^i = u^i (x_1^i, ..., x_n^i, x_n^{-i}).$$

The utility function would have the usual restrictions plus the following one: if $x_n^i = 0$, then changes in x_n^{-i} cannot affect u^i.

The unusual variable in the utility function is x_n^{-i}. But its presence is easy to understand. Since n is an association good, the value of consuming this good to an individual depends on who else is consuming this good, that is, x_n^{-i}. One could, of course, impose more restrictions than the one imposed above. For instance, we could define *a priori* a set of people, among the h, who have social status, and then require that if $x_n^i > 0$, u^i will go up if x_n^{-i} changes such that the total amount of good consumed by those with social status increases.

If we assume now that each person has an initial endowment of each of the goods (as a special case, considering the possibility that one person owns the entire endowment of good n), we could conduct an analysis of some standard questions like whether an equilibrium exists and whether the equilibrium will be Pareto-optimal.

The existence and the welfare question gets much harder conceptually, if we allow for the possibility that for an association good there need not be an initial endowment in the same way that endowments are assumed to exist for goods in standard economic theory. This is because association goods can, in reality, often be *created*. For instance, giving people certificates or giving them honorary titles are acts which, in principle, any agent can undertake and with virtually no resource being used. It is difficult to think of a technological or resource-based upper bound on the number of certificates that can be given in an economy. It is necessary to think of the bounds on certificates, honours, and awards in very different terms from the bounds on guns, butter, or even haircuts.

These are some of the open problems which the present chapter brings to light. These problems are likely to be interesting but also conceptually difficult. Sufficiently so, to call this present chapter to a close.

NOTES

1. It is worth mentioning that in this chapter no distinction is made between an allocation rule and the final profile of its distribution. That is, if two different allocation rules result in the same distribution of the good in question then they are not two distinct allocation rules but the same one. This assumption is justified in a large and complex economy where people do not get to observe the actual process of decision as to how a good is allocated but infer it from the ultimate distribution which they can observe. This is what makes an 'association' good a special case of goods which are valued according to the allocation rule used.

2. Originally developed by Srinivas (1952), the concept has undergone several extensions and modifications. See, for example, Staal (1963).

3. Written by N.R. Kleinfield in the *New York Times*, Business section, 15 June 1986.

4. And here is Veblen on the reason for some people's demand for alcohol and stimulants (p. 70): 'Drunkenness and the other pathological consequences of free use of stimulants, therefore, tend in their turn to become honorific, as being a mark, at the second remove, of the superior status of those who are able to afford the indulgence'.

5. This influential concept was developed by Hirsch (1977), though he did not pursue its implications for market equilibria far enough. Similar ideas, albeit in more diluted form, can be traced further back in time to, in particular, Wicksteed (1910). A recent revival of this approach occurs in Frank (1985a); see also Frank (1985b).

6. The best-known work on this being that of Leibenstein (1950).

7. This is discussed in Section 6.2 of this chapter.

8. In Basu (1987a), I model the case where individuals value a good more if others seek but fail to acquire it. This could be for reasons of quality uncertainty or social status. Related ideas occur in Scitovsky (1944) and Leruth (1987).

9. There may be reasons, quite unconnected with status, why people want to belong to certain clubs or communities. This could be because a sense of belonging is often an end in itself (this is discussed by Hirschman 1985) or it is the basis of 'well-being' (Rainwater 1974). However, to the extent that people have preferences over belonging to different groups, the formal structure of my model would remain applicable. There is a large and interesting literature on clubs, beginning with Buchanan's (1965) investigation (see, for example, Ng 1973; Sandler and Tschirhart 1980). But clubs which people join for reasons of association, to wit, the kind of clubs I am discussing here, have an extremely brief literature (see McGuire 1972) but widespread existence in reality.

10. For someone like Groucho Marx who said he would never pay to join a club which would have him as a member, $v_i(M) \leq 0$, for all $M \in H(i)$.

11. What constitutes 'no discrimination' can have several formal interpretations (Basu 1987b) but here I take the simple meaning of 'same fees from all'.

12. Another useful direction of enquiry concerns the objective function of clubs and the determination of who the decision maker is. In Buchanan's (1965) model of clubs all individuals are identical and so a representative individual's attempt to maximize utility is what determines club size. With heterogeneous agents the problem is more serious. There can be models where there are fairly well-defined existing members who are the collective decision makers. This is the assumption in Walzer's (1983) construction, which deals with a broader notion of membership and goes into questions of not only clubs but immigration. There is an interesting theoretical question even here concerning dynamics. Suppose that at each stage the existing members decide on who will be the next batch of new entrants. Then, to the extent that the new entrants will have a say in future rounds about future entrants, the current incumbents will take into account the preferences of the outsiders in doing their calculus of deciding whom to admit.

13. I use this non-stochastic definition for simplicity. For a discussion of a criterion which allows for random errors and is a generalization of my definition, see Ashenfelter and Oaxaco (1987) and, in particular, their discussion of the interesting court case of *Castaneda v. Partida*.

14. This is implied by Sen's (1975b) observation '... people may in fact prefer to receive

income for work rather than be on the dole', because being on the dole could, in the abstract, be thought of as a certain 'job'.

15. For some indirectly corroborative evidence, see Jencks et al. (1988) and, especially, their reference to Siegel's findings.

16. This should make it clear that my p and o are not euphemisms for w and b. In models of racial discrimination each group prefers to cluster with its own types (Becker 1957; Schelling 1972). In addition, it is often assumed that employers prefer to employ labourers of their own race. While Akerlof's (1976, 1980) model is very different from this it is also very distinct from my model of status. In Akerlof, people have no *a priori* associative preference one way or the other. They have conjectures about interpersonal preferences. Though these conjectures have no exogenous basis, they are corroborated in equilibrium. Finally, it is worth clarifying that preferences are being taken as given and I am not concerned with the effects of discrimination on preferences.

17. There is an interesting analogy here with 'honorary degrees'. For these there are two types of recipients—those who are 'deserving' and those who have given a lot of money to the school. If the 'purchasers' are to consider this an honour, it is necessary that enough deserving types get the award. I am grateful to a referee for this example.

18. Demonstration effects, international or within a society (Duesenberry 1949; James 1987), are manifestations of a similar phenomenon in the domain of consumption.

REFERENCES

Akerlof, G. 1976. 'The Economics Caste and of the Rat Race and other Woeful Tales'. *Quarterly Journal of Economics* 84.

—— 1980. 'A Theory of Social Customs, of which Unemployment May Be One Consequence'. *Quarterly Journal of Economics* 94.

Arrow, K.J. 1973, 'Higher Education as a Filter'. *Journal of Public Economics* 2.

Ashenfelter, O. and R. Oaxaca. 1987. 'The Economics of Discrimination: Economists Enter the Courtroom'. *American Economic Review* (Papers and Proceedings) 77.

Basu, K. 1986. 'One Kind of Power'. *Oxford Economic Papers* 38.

—— 1987a. 'Monopoly, Quality Uncertainty and "Status"Goods'. *International Journal of Industrial Organization* 5.

—— 1987b. 'Disneyland, Monopoly, Interlinkage and Usurious Interest Rates'. *Journal of Public Economics* 34.

—— E.L. Jones, and E. Schlicht. 1987. 'The Growth and Decay of Custom: The Role of the New Institutional Economics in Economic History'. *Explorations in Economic History* 24.

Becker, G. 1957. *The Economics of Discrimination*. University of Chicago Press.

Buchanan, J. 1965. 'An Economic Theory of Clubs'. *Economica* 32.

Duesenberry, J. 1949. *Income, Saving and the Theory of Consumer Behaviour*. Harvard University Press.

Frank, R.H. 1985a. *Choosing the Right Pond: Human Behaviour and the Quest for Status*. Oxford University Press.

—— 1985b. 'The Demand for Unobservable and Other Nonpositional Goods'. *American Economic Review* 75.

Hirsch, F. 1977. *Social Limits to Growth*. Routledge and Kegan Paul.

Hirschman, A.O. 1985. 'Against Parsimony: Three Easy Ways of Complicating Some Categories of Economic Discourse'. *Economics and Philosophy* 1.

James, J. 1987. 'Positional Goods, Conspicuous Consumption and the International Demonstration Effect Reconsidered'. *World Development* 15.

Jencks, C., L. Perman, and L. Rainwater. 1988. 'What is a Good Job? A New Measure of Labor Market Success'. *American Journal of Sociology* 93.

Lazear, E.P. and S. Rosen. 1981. 'Rank-order Tournaments as Optimum Labor Contracts'. *Journal of Political Economy* 89.

Leibenstein, H. 1950. 'Bandwagon, Snob and Veblen Effects in the Theory of Consumers' Demand'. *Quarterly Journal of Economics* 64.

Leruth L. 1987. 'Product Differentiation through Price Differentiation: Equilibrium in a Duopoly Model'. CEME. Brussels. mimeo.

McGuire, M. 1972. 'Private Good Clubs and Public Good Clubs: Economic Models of Group Formation'. *Swedish Journal of Economics* 74.

Nalebuff, B.J. and J.E. Stiglitz. 1983. 'Information, Competition, and Markets'. *American Economic Review* 73.

Ng, Y.K. 1973. 'The Economic Theory of Clubs: Pareto Optimality Conditions'. *Economica* 40.

Rainwater, L. 1974. *What Money Buys: Inequality and Social Meanings of Income*. Basic Books.

Rosen, S. 1986. 'Prizes and Incentives in Elimination Tournaments'. *American Economic Review* 76.

Sandler, T. and J.T. Tschirhart. 1980. 'The Economic Theory of Clubs: An Evaluative Survey'. *Journal of Economic Literature* 18.

Schelling, T.C. 1972. 'A Process of Residential Segregation: Neighbourhood Tipping'. In H. Pascal, ed., *Racial Discrimination in Economic Life*. Lexington Books. 1972.

Scitovsky, T. 1944. 'Some Consequences of the Habit of Judging Quality by Price'. In T. Scitovsky, *Papers on Welfare and Growth*. Stanford University Press. 1964.

Sen, A.K. 1975a. *Employment, Technology and Development*. Clarendon Press.

—— 1975b. 'Employment, Institutions and Technology: Some Policy Issues'. *International Labour Review* (July).

Spence, A.M. 1973. *Market Signalling*. Harvard University Press.

Srinivas, M.N. 1952. *Religion and Society among the Coorgs of South India*. Oxford University Press.

—— 1955. 'The Social System of a Mysore Village'. In M. Marriott. ed. *Village India*. University of Chicago Press. 1955.

Staal, J.F. 1963. 'Sanskrit and Sanskritization'. *Journal of Asian Studies* 22.

Veblen, T. 1989. *The Theory of the Leisure Class*. Macmillan. (My page references are to the Allen and Unwin, 1925, edition.)

Walzer, M. 1983. *Spheres of Justice: A Defence of Pluralism and Equality*. Basic Books.

Wicksteed, P.H. 1910. *The Common Sense of Political Economy*, Vol. II. Macmillan.

7 Civil Institutions and Evolution
Concepts, Critique, and Models

7.1. INTRODUCTION

When studying the causes of the rise and fall of nations or the technological advance or stagnation of different regions, economists have usually looked for differences in resource availabilities, the appropriateness of government policies, and international relations. Thus, in planning to boost agricultural production in a region, we typically wonder whether we should intervene in the credit market to ensure the availability of cheap credit or provide agricultural extension services or stem the adverse movement of the terms of trade between agriculture and industry. What has not, however, been adequately discussed is the role of different norms. One community may be more prone to taking risks than another. Hence, one may be more likely to accept high-yielding varieties than the other.

Is such a difference in the attitude to risk between, say, the Punjab farmer and the farmer from Tamil Nadu an inherent difference? The answer may depend on how long a view we take of the matter. In the short run, of course, these are inherent differences. But if we take a sufficiently long view of history, it is entirely possible that these are merely different norms which have *evolved* from roots which were once similar.

In textbook economics, individuals choose from a set which is constrained by only what their money can buy. In reality, there are additional constraints imposed by the norms of the society or community to which one belongs. Norms can be

From *Journal of Development Economics* 46, 1995: 19–33.

This is a revised version of the paper presented at the conference on *State, Market and Civil Institutions: New Theories, New Practices and their Implications for Rural Development* held at Cornell University on 13–14 December 1991. For discussion and comments, I am grateful to V. Bhaskar, Bhaskar Dutta, Marcel Fafchamps, Ajit Mishra, Jeffrey Nugent, Eric Van Damme, Jorgen Weibull, and the participants at the conference in Abisko, Sweden, 4–7 May 1992, where a variant of this paper was presented.

economically progressive or regressive. From all accounts, the Protestant work ethic helps economic progress; Rastafarianism does not. Hence, the study of the survival and demise of norms may give us clues to the successes and failures of economies.

Let me explain this with an example. In Nugent and Sanchez's (1989) paper discussing the Castilian Mesta—the Spanish guild of shepherds with grazing rights so extensive that they often conflicted with the private property rights of landowners—one of the characters, Harry, argues as follows (p. 263): 'Although the preservation of inefficient institutions is not unheard of (Akerlof 1976; Basu et al. 1987), in view of the Mesta's very remarkable strength and longevity (having lasted from 1273 to 1836), I suspect that it was serving a socially useful purpose'.

But is there any *basis* to the suspicion of Nugent and Sanchez, alias Harry, that a social purpose was being served? Clearly 'longevity' *in itself* is no explanation. But there may indeed be an indirect link. The fact that a civil norm or institution has survived for a long time guarantees that the norm must have passed the test of natural selection and so must have some minimal usefulness. Hence 'Harry's' view can be given an evolutionary justification.

The formal analysis of evolution in economics is a relatively recent phenomenon. Its roots are to be found in biology, in particular in the seminal work of Maynard Smith and Price (1973) (see also Maynard Smith 1982). Their analysis of evolutionary games has caught the attention of economists and there has been an enormous outpouring of writings on it. This is indeed an important area for economists interested in development and the growth and decay of norms.

The study of the formation and persistence of social norms, though still in its nascency, has a substantial literature (to name just a few, Akerlof 1976; Basu 1986; Platteau and Abraham 1987; Nabli and Nugent 1989). But none of these papers use results and concepts from the literature on evolutionary games.

This chapter may be viewed as an attempt to provide a bridge between these two kinds of analyses.

Since evolutionary games have not yet found their way into the development literature (Bardhan 1993 being very much the exception), it may be useful to begin with a primer for development economists. This is attempted in Section 7.3. It is then argued that economists have got excessively involved in the technical solutions of evolutionary games, without paying adequate attention to how these may be adapted to the human context. I suggest ways in which this may be altered to be applicable to human conflict. Finally, I develop a new solution concept which identifies social norms that can survive the sieve of natural selection.

7.2. INSTITUTIONS AND NATURAL SELECTION: PRELIMINARY IDEAS

To give a more concrete idea of how evolution can help us understand certain civil institutions, let me begin with an example I have discussed elsewhere (Basu 1990). It is an example which tries to reject what is often referred to as 'functionalism' and replace it with what may be called 'minimal functionalism'. It has been noted by anthropologists that in most primitive societies people have 'possessory rights', that is, whoever first gets to possess a good has a right to it. Posner (1981: 182) has noted, however, that in primitive societies where investment is feasible, the investor is often protected by the grant of a non-possessory right. For instance, in a hunter–gatherer society, the trap-setter has the right to a trapped animal instead of the person who first finds the animal. Posner seems to be explaining with this example how societies choose institutions which are optimal for their lifestyles. There are others who have adopted more extreme 'functionalist' positions, arguing, for instance, that societies invariably choose laws and civil institutions which are functionally optimal or are ones for which benefits outweigh costs. Such naive transplanting of individual choice models on social domains has been rightly criticized by many (see, for instance, Bardhan 1989).

It is, however, possible to argue that though such extreme functionalism is best jettisoned, a 'minimal functionalism' can be defended by a very different route, namely evolution. If one finds that a society which has remained (and, therefore, survived) unchanged over a long stretch of history has certain norms, it is arguable that these norms cannot be too detrimental for the people. The fact that the people practicing this norm have survived such a long time ensures this. Turning to the above example, suppose that there is a hunter–gatherer economy where the trap-setter does not have the right to the trapped animal, but the first person to lay his hands on the animal gets to keep it. In such an economy people would either cease to set traps or, after setting a trap, wait there, forgoing all other activities (such as hunting and gathering). The productivity or 'fitness' of such an economy would be low and it is possible that the economy would not survive too many generations.[1] Hence, hunter–gatherer economies which survive to be analysed by anthropologists happen to be the ones which grant the trap-setter rights over the possessor. Thus, like the giraffe's long neck and the housefly's resistance to DDT, social groups have norms which serve minimal functions to ensure that they survive.

Unlike the colour of my shirt or the location of your house, the norms of a society cannot be explained in terms of human volition. Just as lions move in prides not because they choose to do so but because, if they did not, their hunting ability would fall drastically and they would not survive to be seen,[2] hunter–gatherer societies may have the norms they do because these norms have survived natural selection.

If we are to explain co-operative behaviour norms in a society, it seems useful to take the evolutionary approach. Unfortunately, it will be seen that Maynard Smith and Price's 'Evolutionarily Stable Strategy' or phenotype turns out to be necessarily a Nash equilibrium. I shall, however, demonstrate that my modified solution concept can admit non-Nash strategies and, therefore, may be better suited to explaining co-operation.

The above discussion is of an evolutionary process in which there is no explicit recognition of the strategic nature of interaction between agents. The advantage of the recent work on evolutionary games is that interpersonal interdependence is at the centre of the story. It has other shortcomings, though. But before taking these up, we must do a brief recapitulation of its main ideas.

7.3. EVOLUTIONARILY STABLE STRATEGIES

The social sciences had for a long time remained untouched by the rise of evolutionary models in the natural sciences. This is now changing as a consequence of Maynard Smith and Price's (1973) work. Their work on combining evolution with game theory had precursors—the most notable being Lewontin (1961). But in Lewontin's model a species plays games against nature. The distinguishing feature of the work on evolutionary games is that it allows for strategic interaction between players.

Let $G = (S_1, S_2, P_1, P_2)$ be a two-player normal-form game where S_i is player i's set of strategies and P_i the payoff function. G is an *evolutionary game* if the following is true:

(i) S_1 and S_2 have the same, finite number of elements. We shall write $S_i = \{1, ..., m\} = S$.

(ii) The payoff matrix is symmetric. That is, for all $i, j \in S$, $P_1(i, j) = P_2(j, i)$. Define $A(i, j) = P_1(i, j)$. Note that the entire payoff matrix can be deduced from the function A.

From now on we shall hold the S_i's as fixed. Hence an evolutionary game is fully defined by A. If we write a_{ij} for $A(i, j)$, then the information in A is also fully captured by the matrix $[a_{ij}]$. Distorting notation a little, I shall write $[a_{ij}] = A$. Hence A represents both a matrix and a function. It will be clear from the context as to which sense it is being used in.

Let $M(S)$ be the set of all mixed strategies open to player i. That is,

$$M(S) = \{x \in E^m \mid \Sigma x_i = 1; \ x_i \geq 0, \ i = 1, ..., m\},$$

where E^m is the m-dimensional Euclidean space. If $x \in M(S)$, it means that the player will play strategy $i \in S$ with probability x_i. More generally, if $T \subset S$, we define the set of all mixed strategies with support in T as $M(T)$.

If 1 and 2 play strategies x and y in $M(S)$, then player 1's (expected) payoff is $x^T A y$ which, again distorting notation a little, I shall also write as $A(x\,y)$.

Though an evolutionary game looks like any ordinary game with some symmetry conditions added on, its interpretation is very distinct. What are called 'strategies' here are not really the 'strategies' of von Neumann and Morgenstern but phenotypes. Each player is a certain phenotype. That is, we could think of each player as born to play a fixed strategy $p \in M(S)$. Moreover, a p-player's child is also a p-player.

Next, the payoff in an evolutionary game depicts not the level of happiness of agents, but their fitness. Indeed Maynard Smith (1982) refers to A as the fitness matrix. I shall, however, take it—as will be clear later—that utility coincides with fitness.

Though an evolutionary game is a two-player game, we should think of there being an infinite population. From this, players are randomly matched in pairs and made to play the game A. It is assumed that if in a certain population a strategy q (that is, a player who always plays q) gets a lower expected payoff than strategy

p, then q will gradually die out from the population because players of type q will have a lower reproduction rate than those of type p.

Now consider a monomorphic population of type $p \in M(S)$. That is, the entire population consists of agents who play p. Following the discussion in the above paragraph, we shall say that p *is immune* to $q \in M(S)$ if

(7.1) $A(p, p) \geq A(q, p)$ and

(7.2)   if $A(p, p) = A(q, p)$, then $A(p, q) > A(q, q)$.

Since immunity is such an important element in the definition of ESS, its motivation needs to be spelt out. The usual justification is in terms of 'small invasions' of mutants. I think this justification is best formalized in lexicographic terms. Since the bulk of the population consists of type p and a tiny invasion is of type q, if p does better against p than q does against p, it is reasonable to suppose that q will be less fit than p and will get destroyed. Performance against q is of secondary importance. If both p and q perform equally well against p, then q will be less fit than p if p does better against q than q does against q. (7.1) and (7.2) capture just this idea.

A strategy $p \in M(S)$ is an *evolutionarily stable strategy* (ESS) if p is immune to all $q \in M(S) - \{p\}$.

It is clear from (7.1) that an ESS has to be a Nash equilibrium and over and above that it must have the refinement that comes with (7.2). Indeed, subsequent analysis has shown that it is a very sharp refinement. As ESS is, in fact, not just a Nash equilibrium but also perfect and proper (Van Damme 1987: Theorems 9.3.1 and 9.3.4). And it is also true that there are games which do not possess any ESS.

Before proceeding with further discussion, note that in the above definition we allow for phenotypes to be mixed strategies. If we want to define an ESS under the presumption that players cannot play mixed strategies, it is easy to modify the above definition. In defining immunity and ESS we have to simply replace $M(S)$, wherever it occurs, with S. In what follows, it will be generally assumed that mixed strategies are allowed. Whenever an assumption to the contrary is used, I shall state it explicitly.

To illustrate this equilibrium concept at work, let us quickly review a special case of the well-known Hawk–Dove game (see Maynard Smith 1982: ch. 2) or Van Damme (1987: ch. 9).

A player can be aggressive (A) or timid (T). Player 1's payoffs are given by the matrix below.

Game G_1			Player 2	
			A	T
Player	A		−1	2
1	T		0	1

This game (2's payoffs are symmetric) has only one ESS: A strategy which plays A with probability 1/2 and T with probability 1/2. In other words, only a population of agents who are aggressive half the time is immune from the invasion of mutants.

Next, consider the game G_2 described below.

Game G_2		Player 2	
		x	y
Player	x	1	0
1	y	1	0

Consider a strategy $(p, 1 - p)$, which I shall refer to, in brief, as simply p. In this p is the probability of playing x. Is p an ESS? Note that $A(p, p) = p$, $A(q, p) = p$, for all q. Hence condition (7.1) for immunity is satisfied by p. Next, note that $A(p, q) = q$. So, since $A(p, q) = A(q, q)$, (7.2) cannot be satisfied. In other words, game G does not possess an ESS. This is somewhat unfortunate, because there is clearly something robust about strategy x. Fortunately, as we shall see later, with a very reasonable modification of ESS, x will be found to be evolutionarily robust. This will be so not just in the sense of 'neutral stability', which x satisfies, but in terms of a new solution concept—especially suited to analysing human conflict—defined below.

7.4. THE LOGIC OF HUMAN CONFLICT

In the above model a player exercises no choice. So players cannot be rational or irrational; their behaviour is inherited and unchanging. Standard game theory on the other hand gives players full freedom to choose from the set of strategies. In reality, human beings are somewhere in between. They choose and optimize over some strategies but also consider some strategies as out of bounds. These latter are determined by a person's inherited training on the norms of the society he lives in. Thus we may choose between several possible careers but may consider picking pockets as something we would not do, whatever the payoffs. There may be others who consider pickpocketing as a reasonable career—I have first-hand evidence of the existence of such persons. Similarly, in some communities, children are taught to always pay their taxes when they grow up; whereas in others children are taught that taxes ought to be paid if the expected penalty of not paying exceeds the amount of tax not paid. What we want to study is which of these norms will survive natural selection.

Let S be the set of all conceivable strategies open to a player. Taking a hint from the above discussion, I shall define a *civil norm* as any subset, T, of S. If an agent adheres to civil norm T it means that he *chooses* the optimal strategy from *within* T and considers strategies in $S - T$ as ones which one ought not to use. Norms, we shall assume, are inherited.

Under this reformulation, a civil norm is considered evolutionarily robust if it is immune to invasions of small numbers of agents with other civil norms. Note that an ESS would be a special case of this if the civil norms were restricted to unit sets (that is sets with only one member).

To appreciate the second problem of ESS, suppose that there is a planet (earth) and people live in different nations. A mutant in one nation is like a migrant. With the notion of a planet and nations interpreted in abstract terms, one can see the importance of the mutant everywhere. A small trickle of migrants from one area to another have at times flourished in the region of their adoption and at other times they have perished. The Marwaris in Bengal, the Gujaratis in Maharashtra, the English in India in the eighteenth and nineteenth centuries, the Indians in England today are the success stories. The stories where migrants have done poorly and have become negligible are many more.

It is arguable that in these examples, who succeeds and who fails is not so much a matter of inherent traits of a community as a question of chemistry. X may do well in a population of Y's. The reason why this is at least prima facie possible is because every society has its civil norms. I shall call these gaps in utility maximization a society's *normative loopholes*. These are things which a person would not do (or would do) purely because they are a norm in his society and irrespective of their utility or payoff consequences. Not breaking queues is a normative loophole of, for instance, Finnish society. I call it a 'loophole' because a mutant or a migrant from another society who does not have this norm can presumably exploit this and do well for himself. I believe that the English took such easy control of India in the eighteenth and nineteenth centuries because they exploited the normative loopholes of that India. The Spanish against the early American civilizations was a similar story. The natives were surprised by the range of actions which the invaders were willing to use.

Observe now that if a mutant in one society or nation is a migrant from another society, a mutant cannot have just any norm but must have a norm which is itself 'stable'. In other words, in defining a stable norm, to ensure that the norm is uninvadable by all *conceivable* norms is to err on the side of caution. We should instead simply check that it is uninvadable by other stable norms. But note that this introduces recursion in the definition of a stable norm. So we have to proceed with caution towards a set-valued solution concept.

Though in the end I shall suggest a solution concept which takes account of both these criticisms, it is pedagogically more transparent if it is done in two stages. Thus, in Section 7.5, I simply formalize the recursion idea. Then, in Section 7.6, I introduce the idea of a civil norm instead of a strategy as a phenotype, and go on to incorporate both these ideas simultaneously in the solution concept.

7.5. MUTANTS AS MIGRANTS

We shall say that $T \subset M(S)$ is a *conclave of evolutionarily stable* strategies (*CESS*) if

(I) for all $p, q \in T$, such that $p \neq q$, p is immune to q and

(II) for all $p \in M(S) - T$, there exists $q \in T$ such that p is not immune to q.

The idea of such recursive definitions which result in set-valued solution concepts is not a new one. It has, as already pointed out, been used in game theory in general, CESS being a definition in the spirit of von Neumann and Morgenstern's (1944) 'stable set'. And even in evolutionary contexts Swinkels (1992) has explored concepts which are related to CESS. Swinkels develops the concept of 'equilibrium evolutionary stability' (EES). This requires that the population be immune to invasions by mutants which are in *Nash* equilibrium. I prefer instead to look at mutants which are in equilibrium by the *same* criterion as the existing population. Swinkel's exercise is motivated in part by the urge to restore existence. I, however, do not treat the existence of equilibrium as an *objective*. The aim here is to look for reasonable solution concepts for the *human* context and then be prepared to accept the non-existence of solution for some games.

The technical properties of CESS need to be investigated; but that is not my intent here. Instead, let us check how CESS *performs* in practice. Consider game G_2, described above. Though that game, as shown earlier, has no ESS, it has a CESS. Indeed, the reasonable looking outcome $\{x\}$ happens to be CESS. Note that $\{x\}$ satisfies property (1)) of CESS trivially. Next, take any mixed strategy $q \in [0,1]$. It is easy to see that q is not immune against the pure strategy x (or equivalently against the mixed strategy $p = 1$).

What is interesting and worth noting here is that CESS allows us to explain how non-Nash equilibria could survive in reality. Hence, it gives us a new route for explaining co-operative behaviour in non-cooperative games. I illustrate this with an example.

Game G_3	A	B	C	D
A	2	1	1	3
B	1	2	3	1
C	1	3	1	0
D	3	1	1	0

Let us rule out the use of mixed strategies in game G. Note that G_3 has no symmetric Nash equilibria. That is, none of (A, A), (B, B), (C, C), and (D, D) is a Nash equilibrium. It will now be demonstrated that $\{A, B\}$ is a *CESS*. Check that A is immune to B and B is immune to A. Consider next a country of only C. This is not immune to B. Similarly, D is not immune to A.

It is not difficult to check that in this game $\{A, B\}$ is the unique CESS. Thus we may have some nations having only type A's and some only B's. Each will withstand the occasional invasion of the other. C and D will not exist. They are the *social* unicorns and mermaids. We can conceive of them but the earth is too hostile for their survival.

Finally, it is easy to check that CESS need not always exist. This will be demonstrated with an example in Section 7.7.

7.6. CIVIL NORMS

As discussed in Section 7.4, ideally we should model human beings neither as devoid of rationality, that is the ability to *choose* from among strategies (as in the original evolutionary model of Section 7.3 and also in Section 7.4), nor as devoid of civil norms which typically constrain the set of strategies from which a person chooses. Thus if $\{x, y, z\}$ are all conceivable strategies open to a person and z entails dipping into other people's pockets, especially in overcrowded buses, in search of M_1 then a civil norm could be $\{x, y\}$. This norm says that picking pockets is wrong. A person choosing from $\{x, y, z\}$ and endowed with this norm will maximize his utility by selecting a strategy from within $\{x, y\}$.

Consider game A. As before, the set of pure strategies is given by $S = \{1, ..., m\}$. I shall define a *restricted game* of A as (X, Y), where $X, Y \subset S$. The payoffs in this restricted game are simply the restriction of the payoff functions P_1 and P_2. Thus if the two players choose $(x, y) \in X \times Y$, then 1's payoff is $P_1(x, y) = A(x, y)$ and 2's payoff is $P_2(x, y) = A(y, x)$. Payoffs from mixed strategies are defined as before.

Suppose a person with civil norm $X \subset S$ meets another person with civil norm $Y \subset S$, what is the expected outcome? I shall here stay out of the problem of informational asymmetries by assuming that the civil norms of the two players are common knowledge among the two players. If the two players are rational, it may be reasonable to suppose that a Nash equilibrium of the restricted game (X, Y) will occur. But if (X, Y) has more than one Nash equilibrium, which one should we expect? I shall get around this by assuming that this is given in the description of the human evolutionary game defined below.

The *Nash equilibrium* of a restricted game (X, Y) is $p \in M(X)$ and $q \in M(Y)$ such that $A(p, q) \geq A(p', q)$, for all $p' \in M(X)$ and $A(q, p) \geq A(q', p)$, for all $q' \in M(Y)$.

Let us define 2^x as the collection of all non-empty subsets of X and recall that E is the set of real numbers.

A *human evolutionary game*, (A, N), is an ordered pair such that A is an evolutionary game and N is a mapping, $N: 2^s \times 2^s \rightarrow E$, such that, for all $(A, B) \in 2^s \times 2^s$, there exists one nash equilibrium in the restricted game (A, B) which gives players 1 and 2 payoffs of $N(A, B)$ and $N(B, A)$, and with the additional requirement that the Nash equilibrium be symmetric if $A = B$.

That every restricted game will have at least one Nash equilibrium is well-known. That a restricted game (A, B), with $A = B$, will have a Nash equilibrium with equal payoffs to both players follows from Lemma 9.2.1 in Van Damme (1987: 212). Hence, for every evolutionary game, A, we can define at least one human evolutionary game, (A, N).

Given a game (A, N), we define a *civil norm* as any subset T of S. We are interested in identifying civil norms which can withstand the arrival of mutants or migrants with other civil norms.[3] This can be easily defined following Maynard Smith and Price's method.

Let (A, N) be a human evolutionary game. The civil norm T is *immune* to civil norm X if

(7.3) $N(T, T) \geq N(X, T)$ and
(7.4) $[N(T, T) = N(X, T)] \rightarrow [N(T, X) \geq N(X, X)]$.

I shall describe a civil norm T as an *invasion-resistant set* (IRS) if T is immune to all $X \in 2^s - T$.

Note that an IRS is also a set-valued solution concept though it is so in a different sense from CESS. It is worth observing that by virtue of the use of the weak inequality in (7.4), the IRS is the set-valued counterpart of Maynard Smith's (1982) *neutrally stable strategy* (see also, Van Damme 1987: 212). I do this in order to prevent a trivial non-existence problem that can arise.[4]

As before, we can impose a recursion property on IRS in the same way as was done for ESS in Section 7.5, to get a meta-set-valued solution, which will be called CIRS.

We shall say that a collection of civil norms, $K = \{T_1, ..., T_n\}$, is a *conclave of invasion resistant sets* (CIRS) if,

(III)   for all $T, X \in K$, and $T \neq X$, T is immune to X, and

(IV)   for all civil norm $T \notin K$, there exists $X \in K$, such that T is not immune to X.

To illustrate how these solution concepts work and, in particular, how they work differently from standard solution concepts, consider the well-known Rock-Scissors-Paper game (see Maynard Smith 1982 and Van Damme 1987 for discussion) which is illustrated below as game G_4.

Game G_4	x	y	z	
x	ε	-1	1	
y	1	ε	-1	$0 \leq \varepsilon \leq 1$
z	-1	1	ε	

As is well-known, this game has no ESS and no neutrally stable strategy either. However, this game has an IRS. In particular, the civil norm $S = \{x, y, z\}$ is an IRS.

The restricted game $S \times S$ has only one symmetric Nash equilibrium in which each player earns $\varepsilon/3$. Consider now any single-strategy mutant, without loss of generality, say x. The restricted game $(\{x\}, S)$ has a unique Nash equilibrium in which S earns 1 and $\{x\}$ earns -1. Since $-1 < \varepsilon/3$, S is immune to $\{x\}$. Next consider two-strategy mutants. Without loss of generality consider the mutant civil norm $\{x, y\}$. The restricted game $(\{x, y\}, S)$, it can be checked, has a unique Nash equilibrium in which $\{x, y\}$ earns $(\varepsilon - 1)/(3 + \varepsilon)$. Since $(\varepsilon - 1)/(3 + \varepsilon) < \varepsilon/3$, S is immune to $\{x, y\}$. Hence S is immune to all invasions of civil norms $T \in 2^S - S$. Hence S is an IRS.

Next check that for all $T \in 2^S - S$, T is not immune to S. Thus $\{S\}$ is CIRS.

7.7. AN EXAMPLE: BETRAYAL AND CO-OPERATION IN BUSINESS

Consider a game where each individual has to decide whether to do business or to abstain (action *a*) and, if he opts for business, whether to co-operate (action *c*) with his business partner or to betray (action *b*) him. In other words, each individual can choose between *a*, *b*, and *c*.

Suppose two individuals meet who have both chosen to go into business; it will be assumed that they get locked into a Prisoner's Dilemma. If both play *c*, they get 1 unit each. If you co-operate while the other betrays, you get -2, while the other gets 2. If you both betray, you get -1 each. Hence the payoff is as follows.

Game G_5		b	c
	b	−1	2
	c	−2	1

If, on the other hand, you choose to abstain from business, you get a payoff of zero no matter what the other person does. Also, if the other person chooses to abstain, you get a zero payoff no matter what you choose, because it is being assumed that, to get a business started, you need two persons. The upshot is that the full game, G_5, is as shown below. Note that the Prisoner's Dilemma described above is embedded inside this game. In other words, what we have is a Prisoner's Dilemma with an option to stay out of it (by choosing a)

Game G_6		a	b	c
	a	0	0	0
	b	0	-1	2
	c	0	-2	1

If we think of the payoffs as profit from business, then the payoffs are reasonable. If even one player refuses to go into business, the business does not start and both earn zero profit. If both go into business and one player co-operates, while his partner betrays, the former makes a loss of 2. And so on.

The Nash equilibrium pay-off of this game is (0,0). Hence standard game theory would predict that at least one player would choose to abstain and so the business would not take off. It can be checked that recourse to the first ideas in evolutionary games do not help very much because this game does not have an ESS, CESS, or a neutrally stable strategy.

Once we turn to the concepts of IRS and CIRS more interesting results begin to emerge. It is easy to check that this game does have an invasion-resistant set. This is given by $\{a, c\}$; and in such a society each person gets a utility of 1, which is the co-operative outcome.

In other words, we can conceive of a society where citizens are taught the norm not to betray others. So they may choose to go into business and co-operate or to abstain from business. What is interesting is that this norm is evolutionarily stable. It is immune to invasion from people with other norms. The intuition is easy to see. When these people meet a mutant who does not mind betraying, they choose to abstain from going into business with the mutant. So mutants do badly. This suggests why adherence to honesty may be a useful norm, and nations which practise this may benefit in the long run.

The conclave of invasion-resistant sets is more time-consuming to compute. It turns out that $\{\{a, c\}, \{c\}\}$ is a CIRS. So in the long run there will be some societies where the norm is $\{a, c\}$ and some where the norm is $\{c\}$. Societies with other norms would not survive the evolutionary process in the long run. The payoffs in the equilibrium are once again non-Nash and co-operation seems to survive.

7.8. CONCLUSIONS

In the literature on development much has been written on the role of economic factors in ushering in technical progress. We have learnt of the role of credit availability, extension services, the terms of trade between sectors. What has, however, been seldom studied—though we do pay frequent lip service to it — is the role of social norms and civil institutions. In some societies, hard work is a cause of embarrassment, in others it is a source of pride. In some societies, honesty in speech is an ingrained habit, in others honesty is practised only when this is to one's advantage.

The purpose of this study was to develop a model for studying the strengths and weaknesses of civil norms. The model provides a bridge between the optimality claims of some schools of thought and its total negligence in others.

There are several directions that can be fruitfully pursued from here. My general discussion of evolutionary processes in Sections 7.1 and 7.2 often hints at the importance of 'group selection'. If a group of identifiable people (for instance, (those belonging to the same caste group) are committed to the same norm (for example, 'never tell lies') it may help the survival of the group vis-à-vis other groups with other norms. In the formal analysis of the chapter the idea of group selection was not pursued. This may, however, be a line of research which will yield rich dividends in the future.

It may appear at first sight that in this chapter I take too stationary a view of norms. After all, norms do change and undergo mutations. While it is true that I did not go into the dynamics of civil norms and institutions, an evolutionary model in no way denies this; and, in fact, may be particularly well-suited to examining such mutations.

An exogenous change that changes the underlying game could well trigger off the demise of existing norms and usher in new ones, just like in England, as industrialization increased, darker moths became better protected from their prey because they blended into the soot laden background and soon these darker moths became the dominant variety. Hence, though the present model is static, my 'human evolutionary games' can be adapted to study the dynamics of civil institutions.

NOTES

1. When I talk of a society 'not surviving' too many generations, I am not necessarily referring to the case of the society gradually facing Malthusian death. A society can fail to survive because its territories get taken over by pastoralists or colonial invaders. Indeed, the idea of survival in the face of invasions is central to the analysis of evolutionary stability as we shall see below.
2. This theory has been attributed to G.B. Schaller by Wilson (1975: 504).
3. Banerji and Weibull (1991) have modelled evolutionary games where phenotypes mingle with rational agents (that is, agents whose civil norms are the entire set of strategies, S). Their model can help us understand the survival chances of rational

agents. Phenotypes have the advantage of being able to make commitments, whereas rational agents have the advantage of being able to respond optimally.

4. This kind of weakening of the notion of stability has recently been justified by Binmore and Samuelson (1992). If a population consisting of a certain kind of agent is able to co-exist with a bridgehead of mutant invaders, where neither is able to hurt the other, then the original population is stable according to this weaker definition. Once we combine this idea with the possibility that there may be repeated invasions, interesting issues concerning dynamics and the stability of polymorphic populations arise.

REFERENCES

Akerlof, G. 1976. 'The Economics of Caste and of the Race and Other Woeful Tales'. *Quarterly Journal of Economics* 87: 355–79.

Banerji, A.V. and J. Weibull. 1991. 'Evolutionary Selection and Rational Behavior'. In A. Kirman and M. Salmon, eds, *Rationality and Learning in Economics*. Oxford: Basil Blackwell.

Bardhan, P. 1989. *Alternative Approaches to the Theory of Institutions in Economic Development*. In P. Bardhan, ed., *The Economic Theory of Agrarian Institutions*. Oxford: Clarendon.

—— 1993. 'Analytics of the Institutions of Informal Cooperation in Rural Development'. *World Development* 21: 633–40.

Basu, K. 1986. 'One Kind of Power'. *Oxford Economic Papers* 38.

—— 1990. *Agrarian Structure and Economic Underdevelopment*. Chur.: Harwood.

Basu, K., E. Jones, and E. Schlicht. 1987. 'The Growth and Decay of Custom: The Role of the New Institutional Economics in Economic History'. *Explorations in Economic History* 24.

Binmore, K.G. and L. Samuelson. 1992. 'Evolutionary Stability in Repeated Games with Finite Automata'. *Journal of Economic Theory* 57: 278–305.

Lewontin, R.C. 1961. 'Evolution and Theory of Games'. *Journal of Theoretical Biology* 1: 382–403.

Maynard Smith, J. 1982. *Evolution and the Theory of Games*. Cambridge: Cambridge University Press.

Maynard Smith, J. and G.R. Price. 1973. 'The Logic of Animal Conflict', *Nature* 246: 15–18.

Nabli, M.K. and J.B. Nugent. 1989. 'The Institutional Economics and Its Applicability to Development'. *World Development* 17: 1333–48.

Nugent, J.B. and N. Sanchez. 1989. 'The Efficiency of the Mesta: A Parable'. *Explorations in Economic History* 26: 261–84.

Platteau J.P. and A. Abraham. 1987. An Inquiry into Quasi-credit Contracts'. *Journal of Development Studies* 23: 461–90.

Posner, R.A. 1981. *The Economics of Justice*. Cambridge, MA: Harvard University Press.

Swinkels J. 1992. 'Evolutionary Stability with Equilibrium Entrants'. *Journal of Economic Theory* 57: 306–32.

Van Damme, E. 1987. *Stability and Perfection of Nash Equilibrium*. Berlin: Springer-Verlag.

von Neumann, J. and O. Morgenstern. 1944. *Theory of Games and Economic Behavior*. Princeton, NJ: Princeton University Press.

Wilson, E.O. 1975. *Sociobiology*. Cambridge, MA: Belknap Press.

PART III
Agrarian Organization

8 Technological Stagnation, Tenurial Laws, and Adverse Selection

This chapter explores the relation between the structure of property rights and output-augmenting activity, like investment and the adoption of new technology.[1] The principal weakness of most existing arguments is that they are one-sided. Consider Gale Johnson's (1950) suggestion that technological innovations do not occur in the agrarian sector of many less developed economies because of the landlord's inability to evict tenants. Because of this he cannot expect to reap the benefits of new investment since the old tenant will continue to pay the same rent. The trouble with this line of reasoning is that in making a case for why a landlord would not innovate, it inadvertently provides an explanation of why a rational tenant would innovate. After all, if a tenant is confident of not being evicted, he should be willing to spend on the innovation because he can appropriate the benefits.

Tenant-based explanations of technological stagnation (for example, Kalecki 1976: 19) suffer from the converse problem of inadvertently explaining why rational landlords would innovate.

A more complete theory of stagnation has to explain *simultaneously* why it will not be worthwhile for any agent (that is, the landlord or the tenant) to innovate. This turns out to be a more difficult task and is the subject matter of this chapter.

A common element of property-rights laws or customs in several countries is that the rights of *both* the landlords and tenants are circumscribed in important ways. In particular, it is frequently the case that landlords do not have the right to evict tenants. A tenant can occupy the land or house for as long as he wishes.

From *American Economic Review* 79, 1989: 251–5.

I have benefited from conversations with Albert Hirschman, Eric Jones, Siddiqur Osmani, and from seminars at the Indian Statistical Institute, Kolkata, and the Institute for Advanced Study, Princeton, NJ. I am grateful to WIDER, Helsinki, where a part of this work was done and to the Indian Council of Social Science Research for financial support.

However, he does not have the right to sublet the property or sell the tenancy rights to someone else.

It is being assumed that these legal tenets hold no matter what individuals may agree to among themselves This is certainly true in India. If a tenant promises to quit his landlord's house or land after a certain period and then at the end of the period refuses to go, the landlord has little hope of appealing to the law because the tenant's prior right to continue to occupy a house or land for as long as he wishes virtually nullifies their subsequent contract.

The innovation that I shall be considering is a 'sunk' investment in land. That is, once it has been adopted, it cannot be separated from the land and sold off without loss of value. Soil improvement, a new irrigation facility, and a deep tube-well are examples of such innovation. This model could be applied to urban housing. House maintenance is an example of a *sunk* investment. Though it is not stated in these terms, the model provides an explanation of the poor upkeep of apartments.[2]

8.1. ADVERSE SELECTION AND SUBOPTIMAL INVESTMENT

An innovation is an ordered pair (X, C), with the restriction $X - C > 0$, where C is the cost of adopting this innovation which has to be incurred 'now' and X is the benefit that will accrue subsequently, that is, after a time-lapse.

In between the adoption of a new technology and its bearing fruit the tenant may quit. If he does so, the landlord gets X. If he stays, the tenant gets X. This is our 'basic axiom' and it is assumed to be true in the ensuing analysis.

This axiom follows from the legal frame work assumed above.[3] If a tenant stays, given the fixed-rental system, he gets the additional output, X, that emerges from the land. If he quits, given that he cannot sell his tenancy rights, the landlord gets back full possession of his land. He can now rent it out again and charge his new tenant an additional rent of X.

Let q be the exogenously given probability of the tenant's quitting. It is now easy see that neither the landlord nor the tenant may wish to accept an innovation. If the landlord undertakes the innovation his expected profit is $qX - C$. If the tenant undertakes the innovation his expected profit is $(1 - q)X - C$. Clearly, each of these could be negative even though $X - C$ is positive.

As an explanation of suboptimal adoption of new technology the above argument is more powerful than the popular arguments described in Section I, but it is still far from adequate. This is because a simple cost-sharing arrangement can get the landlord and his tenant out of the problem. If the landlord offers to pay qC of the cost of innovation and asks the tenant to pay $(1 - q)C$, then both will profit from this innovation.

Fortunately a more compelling explanation becomes possible if we allow for the possibility that the landlord owns many plots of land and on each plot he has a tenant. Tenants may have different probabilities of quitting. An innovation (X, C) is suddenly available which can be adopted on each plot. It is assumed that the landlord announces the fraction of the cost he is willing to incur. It is then up to each tenant to accept the innovation or reject it. Of course each acceptor has to bear the remaining cost. Suppose a very high cost share is unprofitable for the landlord. If, then, he offers to pay a smaller fraction, the tenants who are likely to quit soon will reject the innovation. Hence the acceptors will be the less desirable tenants from the landlord's point of view, and the landlord may continue to find the innovation unprofitable. This adverse selection of tenants as the landlord's cost-share is lowered may result in a low level of innovative activity. This section formalizes this intuitive idea and explores its implications.

There is one landlord and he has T types of tenants. Let $H = \{1, ..., T\}$ be the set of the types of tenants. For each i belonging to H, let n_i be the number of tenants of type i and q_i be the probability that a tenant of type i will quit.[4] We follow the convention of labelling tenant types such that

$$(8.1) \qquad q_1 > q_2 > ... > q_T.$$

Note that if $q_i = q_{i+1}$, then i and $i + 1$ need not be distinguished. Hence not using *weak* inequalities in (1) imposes no restrictions.

Information is asymmetric. Each tenant knows his q. The landlord does not know this, though he knows how many types of tenants he has and how many of each type. The assumption of asymmetric information has been contested in the literature (Bardhan 1984; Eswaran and Kotwal 1985) on the grounds that relations in such economies are personalized. I would, however, give asymmetric information a chance to explain certain features of rural economies.[5] It is true that relations here are personalized. But as long as we assume less than perfect information (which seems an eminently reasonable assumption) it seems reasonable to suppose that i's information about j is worse than j's information about j.

Let d be the fraction of the cost of innovation (that is, C) which the landlord agrees to pay if a tenant adopts the innovation (X, C). Since to the landlord all tenants are identical, he does not discriminate between them and it is being assumed that he offers them all the same cost-sharing arrangements, that is d. A tenant will adopt the new technology only if he expects to make a profit as a consequence. Hence, the expected profit of a tenant of type i, R_i, is given by

$$(8.2) \quad R_i(d) = \max\{(1 - q_i)X - (1 - d)C, 0\}.$$

Let $A(d)$ be the set of tenant types who adopt the new technology

$$(8.3) \quad A(d) = \{i \in H \,(1 - q_i)X - (1 - d)C \geq 0\}.$$

Implicit in (8.3) is the assumption that a tenant who is indifferent between accepting the innovation and not, accepts it. This is a harmless tie-breaking assumption.

The landlord's profit, R_L, is given by

$$(8.4) \quad R_L(d) = \sum_{i \in A(d)} n_i[q_iX - dC].$$

The landlord's aim is to maximize $R_L(d)$ with respect to d. Hence the cost-sharing arrangement that will emerge in the equilibrium is given by d^*, defined as follows:

$$R_L(d^*) \geq R_L(d), \qquad \text{for all } d \text{ in } [0,1].$$

What is interesting is that in this model, at equilibrium, there may be severe underinvestment or widespread non-adoption of this new technology. The argument is essentially one of adverse selection. Consider first $d = 1$. As the landlord lowers d, the share of his cost falls, which seems to be good from his point of view [see (4)]. But as d is lowered, $A(d)$ becomes smaller, that is, fewer tenants accept the innovation. And note that the tenants who remain in $A(d)$ are the ones with low quit probability, that is, the ones with whom the landlord would least like to go into a cost-sharing venture. However, given that he cannot recognize tenant types in advance and that the legal system is such that he is not allowed to write contracts contingent on a tenant's quitting decision, he has no method of averting the adverse-selection problem. Hence as d becomes smaller, his profit may fall.

As a result of this, several interesting possibilities arise as the following theorems illustrate.

THEOREM 8.1: There are situations such that for all i belonging to H, there exists $d(i) > 0$ such that both the landlord and the tenant of type i can earn positive profit if they have a cost-sharing arrangement where the landlord pays fraction d(i) of the total cost; but nevertheless the landlord refuses to invest anything, that is, $d^* = 0$.

REMARK 8.1: In this case the only tenants who will invest will be those whose tenure is so certain, that is, q so small, that they find it profitable to 'go it alone'. It is easy to show that the adoption rate of the innovation may be suboptimal and, in fact, 'very low'.

PROOF: Let d_i be the smallest value of d which will induce group i to invest. Thus d_i is defined implicitly by

$$(8.5) \qquad (1 - q_i)X - (1 - d_i)C = 0.$$

It is easy to check that d^* must be either 0 or one of $d_1, ..., d_T$. I prove this by contradiction. If d belongs to the open interval (d_i, d_{i+1}), then it is possible to lower d a little without altering the set $A(d)$. Hence it follows from (8.4) that $R_L(d)$ will rise. Hence d could not have maximized $R_L(\cdot)$.

Given the observation in the above paragraph, it is easy to see how to construct an example which validates Theorem 1:

Let q_T be any number in the open interval $[0, 1 - (C/X)]$. Note that (8.5) implies that as q_i becomes larger, d_i becomes larger as well. Suppose now that q_{T-1} is sufficiently large so that d_{T-1} is such that

$$(8.6) \qquad q_T X - d_{T-1} C < 0.$$

Observe now that if the landlord sets $d = d_j$, then all tenants of type i, where $i < j$ will reject the new technology. Hence

$$(8.7) \quad R_L(d_j) = n_j(q_j X - d_j C) + n_{j+1}(q_{j+1}X - d_j C) + ... + n_T(q_T X - d_j C)$$

Given (8.1), (8.5), and (8.6), it follows that for all d_j belonging to $\{d_1, ..., d_{T-1}\}$,

$(q_T X - d_j C)$ is negative. Hence there exists a sufficiently large n_T, say $n_T(d_j)$, such that $R_L(d_j) < 0$ if $n_T = n_T(d_j)$. Suppose now that

$$n_T > \max\{n_T(d_1), \ldots, n_T(d_{T-1})\}.$$

Then $R_L(d_j) < 0$, for all d_j in $\{d_1, \ldots, d_{T-1}\}$. Since $d_T < 0$ and $R_L(0) = 0$, it follows that $d^* = 0$. Hence the landlord will not invest anything toward the adoption of the new technology (X, C). Clearly only those groups, j, for whom $q_j < 1 - (C/X)$, will implement this new technology, thereby ensuring under-adoption.

THEOREM 8.2: There are situations such that for all $i \leq T - 1$, there exists $d(i) > 0$ such that both the landlord and the tenant of type i earn a positive profit if they have a cost-sharing arrangement where the landlord pays $d(i)$ of the cost, but nevertheless for all $d > 0$, the landlord earns a negative profit.

REMARK 8.2: Theorem 8.1 established a case in which the landlord's preferred share of investment was zero. In Theorem 8.2, not only is each $d > 0$ rejected by the landlord, but for each such d the landlord actually earns a negative profit.

PROOF: Consider this example. There are only two types of tenants and these are characterized as:

$$q_1 = 1; \qquad n_1 = 10$$
$$q_2 = 0; \qquad n_2 = 1$$

In other words there are ten sure quitters and one sure 'stayer'. The innovation available is given by

$$(X, C) = (12, 11).$$

From the first paragraph of the proof of Theorem 8.1 we know that d^* in this case can be either 0 or 1. Now $R_L(1) = -1$ and $R_L(0) = 0$. Hence $d^* = 0$. It may be checked that for all $d > 0$, $R_L(d) < 0$. Since $X - C > 0$ (as is the assumption throughout this chapter), every plot will benefit from the implementation of this new investment. But in this case, at equilibrium only one tenant out of the eleven makes the investment, thereby illustrating the under-adoption problem.

Before stating the next proposition, I need to introduce some terminology. Consider two situations: one where $q = [q_1, \ldots, q_T]$ denotes the quit probabilities (of the T types of tenants) and another where $q' = [q'_1, \ldots, q'_T]$ denotes the quit probabilities. If for all i, $q'_i \geq q_i$ and there exists j such that $q'_j > q_j$, then we shall say that in the q-situation there is less mobility of tenants than in the q'-situation.

THEOREM 8.3: The relation between mobility of tenants and output is not monotonic. That is, with a decrease in the mobility of tenants, output may rise or fall.

REMARK 8.3: Hence in the absence of an arbitrary prior assumption that either landlords or tenants cannot innovate (an assumption which underlies a lot of conventional writing), one cannot monotonically relate adoption of technology to the likelihood of tenants' quitting. The proof is easily constructed using the example in the proof of Theorem 8.1 and is available in Basu (1987 b).

Finally, and this is related to Theorem 8.3, it is worth observing that the *level* of quit probabilities is not important for the under-adoption of technology. What matters are the differentials. The proof is easy and omitted.

THEOREM 8.4: Suppose in society 1 the quit probabilities are given by $(q_1 \dots q_T)$. Society 2 is identical to society 1 in every way excepting that its quit probabilities, $(q'_1, \dots, q'_T)$, are such that for all i, $q'_i = q_i - e$, where e is any number (satisfying the condition that $q'_i \in [0, 1]$ for all i). In this case the level of under-adoption of technology (or the number of people who adopt the technology) is identical in societies 1 and 2.

8.2. CONCLUSION

In a more elaborate model it will be essential to bring in time more explicitly and model behaviour as a sequence of moves. Contracts may then have the problem of subgame perfection because there may be advantages in not fulfilling one's part in the contract after the other agent has done his share. The law curtails this perfection problem by ensuring that there is no reneging on contracts which the law recognizes as valid. If the law recognizes only a limited range of contracts as valid, the problem of suboptimality crops up.

NOTES

1. Several writers have addressed this issue: D. Gale Johnson (1950); Amit Bhaduri (1973); David Newbery (1975); Michal Kalecki (1976); Pranab Bardhan (1984); and Avishay Braverman and Joseph Stiglitz (1986).
2. The various sections of the Delhi Rent Control Act (see DRCA 1958) read very much like the axioms of a theory of non-maintenance of houses.
3. What has been attributed to the law thus far could also be a consequence of social customs. As argued in Basu et al. (1987), customs, which emerge through long historical processes, could be sustained by and, at the same time, constrain individual behaviour in the same way as formally enacted laws.
4. Though quit probabilities are being treated as exogenous here, they can be modelled endogenously in terms of opportunities available to tenants elsewhere. This leaves the results unchanged as I have shown in Basu (1987b).
5. In Basu (1987a) I try to show that it plays an important role in understanding credit markets and interlinkage in rural economies.

REFERENCES

Bardhan, P. K. 1984. *Land, Labor and Rural Poverty: Essays in Development Economics*. New York: Columbia University Press.

Basu, K. 1987a. 'Disneyland Monopoly, Interlinkage and Usurious Interest Rates'. *Journal of Public Economics* 34, 1–17.

Basu, K. 1987b. 'Technological Stagnation, Tenurial Laws, and Adverse Selection'. Working Paper No. 14. WIDER, Helsinki.

Basu, K., E.L. Jones, and E. Schlicht. 1987. 'The Growth and Decay of Custom: The Role of the New Institutional Economics in Economic History'. *Explorations in Economic History* 24 (January): 1–21.

Bhaduri, A. 1973. 'A Study in Agricultural Backwardness under Semi-Feudalism'. *Economic Journal* 83,(March): 120–37.

Braverman, A. and J. Stiglitz. 1986. 'Landlords, Tenants and Technological Innovations'. *Journal of Development Economics* 23 (October): 313–32.

DRCA, *Delhi Rent Control Act, 1958.* Government of India, New Delhi.

Eswaran, M. and A. Kotwal. 1985. 'A Theory of Contractual Structure in Agriculture'. *American Economic Review* 75 (June): 352–67.

Johnson, D.G. 1950. 'Resource Allocation Under Share Contracts'. *Journal of Political Economy* 58 (April): 111–23.

Kalecki, M. 1976. *Essays on Developing Economies.* Hassocks: Harvester Press.

Newbery, D.M.G. 1975. 'Tenurial Obstacles to Innovation'. *Journal of Development Studies* 11 (July): 263–77.

9 The Market for Land
An Analysis of Interim Transactions

9.1. INTRODUCTION

In many less developed countries (LDCs) the market for buying and selling land distinguishes itself by its inactivity.[1] It is true that historically the structure of land rights in less developed countries has been extremely complex with different people having different kinds of rights on the same plot of land.[2] But as Bardhan (1984: 95) points out: 'Even with full property rights in land, the market for buying and selling of cultivable land is often rather inactive. Unless forced by extremely difficult circumstances, a resident villager does not usually sell his land'. Some micro-level studies—example, Rao (1972) and Bliss and Stern (1982)— have also corroborated this.

Several reasons for this alleged low turnover in the market for land have been discussed in the literature (see Chaudhuri 1975; Bhaduri 1976). One popular *explanation* is based on the *belief* that the possession of land leads to power and prestige. While the belief is probably valid, it does not support the explanation. The fact that possession of land leads to power explains why the demand for land is higher and supply lower than one would expect otherwise. Hence, as is evident from the simple demand–supply diagram, this explains why land price is high but not why turnover is low.

A more satisfactory argument I encountered in a conversation with—not surprisingly—a farmer from Midnapore, in West Bengal. On being asked whether he would sell his land if he got double the 'normal' price, he answered in the

From *Journal of Development Economics* 20, 1986: 163–77.

This paper was written while I was a visitor at the Development Economics Research Centre, University of Warwick In writing it I have benefited from a seminar at the London School of Economics and from the comments of Mrinal Datta Chaudhuri, Omkar Goswami, Jean Mercenier, and Nick Stern.

negative, arguing that he would not sell because he would not know what to do with so much cash and, unlike land, cash was a risky asset.[3] I persisted: if he got double the normal price, he could buy another larger plot. That, he regretted, is precisely what is not possible. In that region, he explained, land sales were very few—almost non-existent. So there was no guarantee of his being able to buy back land in the immediate future.

If all individuals reason in this way, a very interesting possibility arises: individuals hesitate to sell land because land turnover is low; and it is their hesitation which, in turn, reinforces the low turnover. It is this phenomenon which the present chapter tries to model, abstracting for the sake of clarity from other features of the market for land.

A sale of the above kind, that is, one where the seller intends to buy back the same commodity (not necessarily the same piece) in the near future, will be referred to as an interim sale or interim transaction. The concern of this chapter is with interim transactions in the market for land. Two qualifications ought to be kept in mind. First, it is possible to construct valid explanations of the inactivity of land markets which lie beyond the ambit of an interim-sales model.[4] Thus there is no attempt to deny that the ensuing theory deals with *one* of the many complex facets of land economics. Some of the broader issues are taken up briefly in a later section. Second, our interim-transactions model is, in itself, an abstract theoretical construct and hence there is no reason why its application ought to be confined to the market for land. A later section discusses how our model could be applied to different areas, including that of interlinkage and labour-tying in backward agriculture.

The model of interim transactions with reference to land is developed in Section 9.2. Some of the larger issues concerning land are examined in Section 9.3. The welfare consequences of our model are discussed in Section 9.4. This is followed by a sketch of alternative markets where the interim-transactions model may be applicable. Among other things we discuss labour-tying in the rural sector. The model of Section 9.2 is developed under fairly severe restrictions in order to keep its focus sharp. Appendix 9.1 discusses possible modifications of the basic model.

9.2. INTERIM TRANSACTIONS: THE BASIC MODEL

It will be assumed that land is available in indivisible units, with p denoting the price of each unit. At each price the total supply of land, S, is the aggregate of interim supply and 'regular' supply. Interim supply, as just explained, is undertaken with the hope of buying back land in the near future. Regular supply is the conventional once-and-for-all supply—for instance from those who are planning to migrate or have just learnt about the greater advantages of shares and debentures. In order to focus attention on interim transactions, we shall assume that regular supply, $\hat{S}$, is given simply as

$$(9.1) \qquad \hat{S} = \hat{S}(p), \hat{S}'(p) \geq 0.$$

Aggregate demand, D, also has two components. Since interim sales are undertaken with the hope of buying back land, at any point of time there will be some demand for land which arises from interim sales of the near past. This will be referred to as interim demand. Regular demand, on the other hand, is the conventional demand of a fresh buyer. Once again, to keep attention away from the latter, it will be assumed that the regular demand, $\hat{D}$, is given in the following conventional manner:

(9.2) $\qquad \hat{D} = \hat{D}(p), \hat{D}'(p) \leqq 0.$

and there exists $\bar{p}$ such that for all $p \geqq \bar{p}$, $\hat{D}(p) = 0$. The indivisibility of land, coupled with the fact that individual purchasing power has limits, guarantees the existence of such a price, $\bar{p}$, beyond which demand is zero.

We may now turn to a more detailed analysis of interim supply and demand. Assume there is a set, N, consisting of n individuals each of whom owns one unit of land and who are considering interim sales. Suppose person $i \in N$ has need for liquid money over the following year and let $a(i)$ ($\geqq 0$) be the benefit he derives from each rupee of *cash*. It may be convenient to imagine that each person, i, has a black box such that if he puts 1 rupee into it now it emerges at the end of the year as 1 rupee plus $a(i)$ units of benefit. Hence, by selling land now, he gets a net benefit of $a(i)p$. If i has no need for liquidity, $a(i) = 0$; if it is a drought year, and he needs cash for food, $a(i)$ will be very large. At the end of the year he recovers his solvency and, for simplicity, it is assumed that no further need for liquidity arises (that is, the black box vanishes). From then on, he would like to hold his wealth for use only at retirement. In keeping with our assumption that land is the safest asset, it will be supposed that everybody would ideally like to hold his wealth in the form of land. This may be formalized by assuming that one rupee held as land has a value of 1, while one rupee held as cash has a value of $c(i)(<1)$, for all $i \in N$.[5]

In order to do away with the complication of time, I will collapse the 'year' in the above description to a 'moment' by assuming that these same benefits [that is, $a(i)$, for all $i \in N$] accrue by selling land now and putting it in the black box, for just a moment. The trouble is that, once a person encashes (that is, sells) his land, he cannot be certain about being able to immediately buy back land. To keep the algebra simple, I will assume that he is either able to buy back land immediately or not at all. Suppose that an individual considers the probability of being able to buy back land to be ϕ.

Hence, i faces two options: he may sell land, pass money through the black box, and then try to buy back land. The net benefit he earns from this option is $a(i)p + \phi p + (1 - \phi)c(i)p$. Alternatively, he could play it safe and not sell his land at all. This will ensure that his wealth will be held as land throughout (that is, up to retirement). The net benefit from this option is p. Therefore, i will sell land if and only if[6]

(9.3) $\qquad a(i)p + \phi p + (1 - \phi)c(i)p - p \geqq 0$, or

$$d(i) \equiv \frac{a(i)}{1 - c(i)} \geqq 1 - \phi.$$

This implies that if the probability of being able to buy back land, ϕ, is high or if the preference for holding wealth as land is low [that is, $1 - c(i)$ is low] or if the need for liquidity is high [that is, $a(i)$ is large], then a person would be more likely to sell his land.

Given ϕ, the interim supply of land (which is equal to the total number of people willing to make interim sales) is

$$(9.4) \qquad \#\{i \in N \mid d(i) \geq 1 - \phi\} \equiv T$$

Since those who make an interim sale immediately try to buy back land, the interim demand for land equals interim supply and is given by (9.4). Clearly, therefore, the volume of interim transactions depends on ϕ. Since it is not clear, *a priori*, how the probability of being able to buy back land, ϕ, is determined, it is possible to consider alternative hypotheses and I do so in Appendix 9.1. In this section we shall develop a simple fixed-price model[7] with excess demand, that is, price is fixed at p where $\hat{D}(p) > \hat{S}(p)$. Since interim supply always equals interim demand, $\hat{D}(p) > \hat{S}(p)$ implies aggregate demand exceeds aggregate supply. Since price is fixed, in this section I shall denote $\hat{D}(p)$ and $\hat{S}(p)$ as, simply, $\hat{D}$ and $\hat{S}$.

We shall now assume that people take the probability of being able to buy land as given by the ratio of supply and demand or, more precisely, their expectation of this ratio, which may be denoted as $(S/D)^e$. Hence

$$(9.5) \qquad \phi = \left(\frac{S}{D}\right)^e.$$

Since aggregate supply, S, is the summation of regular supply, $\hat{S}$, and interim supply, T, and similarly for demand, we have

$$(9.6) \qquad \frac{S}{D} = \frac{\hat{S} + T}{\hat{D} + T}.$$

The essence of our argument is now transparent. Let sellers conjecture an aggregate supply–demand ratio. That, by (9.4) and (9.5), immediately determines the interim turnover, that is, T, and hence, by (9.6), the aggregate supply–demand ratio. If this corroborates the initial conjecture, then we have reached an *equilibrium*. In other words, at equilibrium,

$$\frac{S}{D} = \left(\frac{S}{D}\right)^e.$$

This, coupled with (9.4) and (9.5), gives us

$$(9.7) \qquad T = \#\left\{i \in N \mid d(i) \geq 1 - \frac{S}{D}\right\} \equiv T\left(\frac{S}{D}\right).$$

Therefore, *equilibrium interim sales* is a value of T which solves (9.6) and (9.7).

The interesting feature of this model is that there can be many equilibria. In particular, it is quite possible that both high and low turnovers are equilibrium activity levels. I shall merely present an intuitive argument here, since the example below establishes this formally: suppose S/D is lowered from an initial equilibrium level. Then people have less hope of being able to buy back land and so—as is evident from (9.7)—T is smaller. This, in turn, implies [from (9.6)] that S/D is lower and the new S/D may, therefore, well be an equilibrium.

The workings of the model are easier to illustrate if we assume that $d(\cdot)$ is defined on the interval $[0, n]$ (instead of merely on the integers in this interval), and suppose that the people are so arranged that $n_1 > n_0$ implies $d(n_1) < d(n_0)$.[8]

Given any S/D, define $\bar{i}$ such that

$$d(\bar{i}) = 1 - (S/D) \quad \text{or} \quad \bar{i} = d^{-1}(1 - (S/D)).$$

Since for all $i < \bar{i}, d(i) > d(\bar{i})$, it is clear that given S/D, exactly $\bar{i}$ people would want to sell land, that is, $T(S/D) = \bar{i}$. There is only one snag in writing it like this. It does not take into account the possibility of corner solutions. Taking these into account, the function $T(S/D)$ in (9.7) may be rewritten in full as

(9.8)
$$T = T\left(\frac{S}{D}\right) = \begin{cases} 0 & \text{if } d(0) \leqq 1 - \dfrac{S}{D}, \\ n & \text{if } d(0) \leqq 1 - \dfrac{S}{D}, \\ d^{-1}\left(1 - \dfrac{S}{D}\right) & \text{otherwise.} \end{cases}$$

Hence equilibrium interim sales is a value of T which solves (9.6) and (9.8).

In Figure 9.1, the smooth curve represents (9.6), where S/D is the dependent variable. In the same space we represent (9.8) by a broken line, remembering that

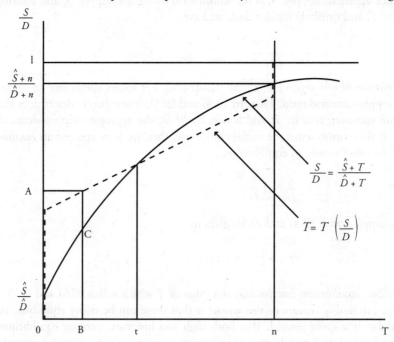

Figure 9.1

in this case T is the dependent variable. If $d(\cdot)$ is continuous, the existence of an equilibrium is ensured: note that the continuity of $d(\cdot)$ implies the continuity of $T(\cdot)$. If the broken line lies above curve (9.6) everywhere on $(0, n)$, then $T = 0$ is an equilibrium. If it lies everywhere below, $T = n$ is an equilibrium. If it lies somewhere above and somewhere below (which is the case illustrated in Figure 9.1), then continuity ensures the existence of $t \in (0, n)$ where the two curves intersect and thereby represent an equilibrium point.

To be able to talk about the *process* by which equilibrium is brought about, I shall suppose (ignoring the deeper problems of 'stability') that if at some T the dotted line lies above (below) the smooth one, T will tend to fall (rise). This is based on the standard 'phase diagram' argument; to start with, S/D ratio is given by point A. This would result in B interim sales. This would lead the S/D ratio to be lower than A—namely C. This leads to a lower interim sales, and so on. From this discussion it is clear that $T = t$ is an unstable equilibrium. What is interesting and easy to check is that in this model there must exist at least one stable equilibrium

In the case illustrated in Figure 9.2 there are three equilibria—at 0, t, and n. Of these, 0 and n are stable. Hence, ignoring the unstable case, we could assert that the market would be either very inactive, with zero interim sales, or be very active, with n interim sales. Which equilibrium actually occurs or whether there are any institutional factors which make one of these equilibria more likely are issues beyond the ambit of the present investigation, the main aim of which is to

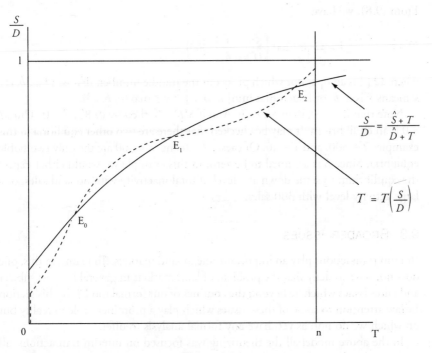

Figure 9.2

demonstrate how hyperactivity and inactivity of land transactions could both be thought of as equilibrium situations.

It ought to be emphasized, since Figure 9.1 and the example below may create an impression to the contrary, that the low-activity and high-activity equilibria need not coincide with, respectively, zero-activity and full-activity, Since the function $d(\cdot)$ can take different forms depending on the preferences of the individuals, the $T(S/D)$ function in Figure 9.1 can take different forms as well. It is immediately clear, and is illustrated in Figure 9.2, that none of the equilibria need coincide with $T = 0$ and $T = n$. In Figure 9.2 the three equilibria are E_0, E_1, and E_2, with E_0 and E_2 being stable. It is obvious that other kinds of equilibrium configurations—with more than three equilibria, with exactly one equilibrium, etc.—are possible depending on the nature of human preferences as embodied in $d(\cdot)$. The taxonomy is easy to work out (see Kaldor 1940 for an analogous taxonomy) and is, therefore, ignored here.

Example. This example illustrates how the situation depicted in Figure 9.1 may actually occur. Let $n = 300$, $\hat{S} = 0$, $\hat{D} = 100$. Let the function $d(\cdot)$ be as follows:

$$d = \frac{3}{4} - \frac{i}{1200}.$$

From (9.6), we have

(9.6′) $$\frac{S}{D} = \frac{T}{100 + T}.$$

From (9.8), we have

(9.8′) $$T = \Omega \left\{ 0, 1200 \left[\frac{S}{D} - \frac{1}{4} \right], 300 \right\},$$

where $\Omega \{.\}$ is an operator which picks out the middle number, that is, $\Omega \{a, b, c\} = x$ means x is a, b, or c such that $\min\{ a, b, c \} \leq x \leq \max\{a, b, c \}$.

Note that if $T = 0$, then $S/D = 0$. And if $S/D = 0$, then by (9.8′), $T = 0$. Thus $T = 0$ is an equilibrium. It may be checked that there are two other equilibria in this example: $T = 300$: and $T \approx 40$. Of these, $T = 0$ and $T = 300$ are the only two stable equilibria. Since $\hat{S}$ is assumed to be zero, in this example we would either expect the equilibrium to settle down at a level of total inactivity with no land sales, or a large activity level with 300 sales.

9.3. BROADER ISSUES

Interim transactions play an important role in land markets. To maintain this, one does not have to deny that the problem of land markets in general is a vast subject and raises issues which lie beyond the confines of our formal model. In this section I draw attention to some of these issues which play a prominent role in reality but on which we do not, as yet, have any formal analysis to offer.

In the above model all the theorizing was focused on interim transactions, all other kinds of buying and selling being tucked away under the residual category labelled 'regular' demand and supply. What this motley collection includes and how its different components behave would be worth investigating.

It was, for instance, mentioned that part of the regular supply of land in the rural sector emanated from villagers migrating to towns. An interesting corroborating evidence is provided by Rao's (1972) excellent study of land transfers in the *Ryotwari* areas of Maharashtra and Gujarat. He found that during 1956 to 1965, in all *talukas* and in almost all villages 'the land purchased by the resident community exceeded the land sold'. This appears paradoxical but, as Rao argues, this may be construed as evidence that some erstwhile villagers who migrated to towns sold off their land. It is, therefore true that while some landowners rent out their land when migrating to cities (in fact, this has been an important factor in the sub-infeudation of land in India), some prefer to sell off their land. How they decide between these two options is an open question which deserves attention in the future, given that it could help us understand the incidence of absentee landlordism.

A more momentous kind of land sale is what is popularly known as a 'distress sale'. Contrary to the impression created by popular usage, distress sales comprise an amorphous category. A poor labourer who sells his land to repay his burgeoning debt clearly makes a distress sale.[9] But what about the person who sells his land to marry off his daughter? The answer depends on his income level, on whether he is giving a dowry out of compulsion or choice, etc. Similarly, when a person sells his land for 'consumption or medical expenses' we tend to feel it must be a distress sale. Yet, as Cain (1981: 450–2) found out in his study of some regions of India and Bangladesh, most of these sales were made by the large landowners and that too for 'conspicuous or status consumption'. Despite these definitional reservations, it is clear that distress sales do occur in large amounts during periods of famines and other disasters. Mukherji (1971) notes that land sales in the district of his study (Birbhum in West Bengal) rose sharply in the early 1940s which is very likely a consequence of the Great Bengal famine. Similarly, Bose's (1970) study on Bihar revealed that a very poor rainfall was generally a precursor of high land sales.

Though distress sales are generally (not always) non-interim in nature, they provide an indirect corroboration of the theory developed in Section 9.2. Note first the interesting fact that the term 'distress sale' is almost always attached to *land* sales. The immediate reason is clear enough. It is widely believed that land is the last asset that a person parts with in distress. So a land sale by a poor person is taken to be the last act of desperation (see Cain 1981: 436). This apparently simple fact, however, hides a deep and puzzling question. If, for reasons of liquidity, a person has to run down a certain amount of his assets (which may include the capitalized value of his future labour), why this fuss if the asset happens to be land? Why would he prefer to sell a thousand rupees worth of jewellery rather than a thousand rupees worth of land? No definitive answer exists, but it seems plausible to argue that while jewellery is easy to buy back, it is not so with land because land sales are so few. And land sales are few precisely because land is the last asset people part with. This brings us back to the theory of interim transactions.

9.4. WELFARE IMPLICATIONS

To begin with, let us confine our attention to the basic model. The question which concerns us here is: Between a high-activity equilibrium and a low-activity equilibrium, which one is socially more desirable? Given the partial equilibrium nature of our model, no more than some tentative remarks are possible. By using the example in Section 9.2, I try to sketch the kind of considerations that go into evaluating alternative equilibria.

Consider the high-turnover equilibrium ($T = 300$)—using E_H to denote it and compare it with the low-turnover equilibrium ($T = 0$)—which I shall denote E_L. At E_H, 300 people sell their land. Since at equilibrium $\phi = \frac{3}{4}$, of these 300 people, 225 manage to buy back land and 75 do not. These 75 are, clearly worse off than they would have been at E_L. But, for these 75 people who have lost land and are forced to hold cash, there must exist 75 people who have got land. So the net benefit of this could be more or less depending on the interpersonal valuation of land. If the variations in such valuation are small, it may not be too wrong to suppose that the net benefit here cancels out with 75 people losing and 75 people gaining. Consider now the 225 people who sell land and manage to buy back. For one such person i, the net benefit of being in E_H compared to E_L is $a(i)$. Let $\bar{a}$ be the average of the $a(i)$'s of those 225 people. Then their net gain in E_H is $225\bar{a}$. Since the loss of the other 75 people could be supposed as approximately offset by the gains of those who acquire their land, we may suppose that the net gain to society of being at E_H is $225\bar{a}$.

Moving away from the specific example, if we consider a case where there are two equilibria—one more active than the other—we may suppose the active equilibrium is more advantageous with its additional benefit equalling the sum of $a(i)$'s of all i who sell and buy back land in the active equilibrium minus the sum of those who sell and buy back land in the inactive equilibrium.

What is interesting to observe is the nature of the benefit that confers with larger interim sales. Recall that $a(i)$ is the advantage that i gets from liquidity, that is from being able to cash his land asset temporarily. Thus a higher land turnover confers the same benefit which comes with greater liquidity. Thus, in some sense, the benefit of a high turnover is similar to the benefit of having more credit in an economy. In the absence of a high turnover, unless a person's need for cash is very high—that is, $a(i)$ very large—he does not sell his land. He tries, instead, to manage without this liquidity.

Let us consider a brief digression from the basic model: a preference for the high-turnover equilibrium over the low-turnover appears paradoxical when the sales in question are distress sales. Indeed sales where the sellers are unable to buy back land raise different welfare-theoretic questions from the ones above. These sales, unlike interim transactions; imply a redistribution of land from the poor to the rich; and it appears (and this is the conventional view) that in this case, a low-turnover state is welfare superior. But on reflection the verdict is not so clear. Suppose high land sales occur every time there is a famine because that is the way the poor stave off starvation. Now whether the low-turnover state is welfare-superior or not depends on whether (i) the low turnover reflects that there is no famine on, or (ii) there is a famine but people are unable to sell land—perhaps because there is a law prohibiting it (an entirely well-meaning legislation aimed at preventing a redistribution of land away from the poor). A low turnover of type (ii) is clearly socially undesirable.

9.5. APPLICATIONS

The basic model, viewed as an abstract theory, is applicable in many situations. We have so far discussed this in the context of land markets. In this section some other applications are considered.

Interim transactions have a significant role in shaping outcomes in markets with asymmetric information. Suppose used cars on sale can be of varying quality but command a single price, as in Akerlof (1970). Suppose a person buys a used car and discovers that its quality is below the average quality of used cars. Then he would be better off if he sold it and bought another used car. This has the interesting implication that as long as the used cars being sold are of a varying quality, the market for such cars cannot be in equilibrium. In other words, *at equilibrium*, the used-car price will reflect not just average quality but the exact one.

An obvious application is to the decision making of firms over business cycles. During a cycle, firms often have to take decisions (regarding, for instance, the buying and selling of inputs) which they know they will soon have to reverse, when the cycle turns. The decisions are, therefore, interim ones and they bring with them some of the considerations discussed in this chapter. A related matter and one of considerable interest to development economists is the seasonality of employment in backward agriculture.

The existence of seasonality could induce, as Bardhan (1984) has argued, the emergence of labour-tying contracts and interlinkage.[10] During the lean season landlords would ideally like to lay off workers. But of course they would be aware that once again, within a couple of months, they would have to rehire labourers. And, as with all interim transactions, their decision to lay off will crucially depend on what they reckon the chances are of being able to rehire workers.[11] If these are poor, they may not lay off workers even though there is not enough work for them.[12] A new twist to the standard labour-tying argument gets added and the model of Section 9.2 becomes relevant as soon as we make the realistic assumption that the probability of finding workers at the beginning of the peak season is positively related to the amount of unemployment in the lean season preceding it. Note that the amount of unemployment in the lean season depends on the number of workers laid off at the end of the preceding peak season. Hence, if the *aggregate* lay-off at the end of the peak season is high, it is worthwhile for each individual landlord to lay off workers. Conversely, if the aggregate lay-off is low, it means rehiring will be that much more difficult and so it may be best for each landlord not to lay off his workers. It is easy to formalize the above sketch of argument along the lines of Section 9.2 and check that there is a possibility of multiple equilibria with varying levels of lean-season unemployment. Thus different levels of labour tying could be thought of as equilibria in an interim transactions model. A detailed analysis of this could give us further insights into the institution of interlinkge and labour-tying and suggest policies for engineering the agrarian sector into one equilibrium rather than another.

It was argued in this chapter that interim transactions play a prominent role in several markets and they tend to generate multiple equilibria. Such markets could get caught at levels of low or even zero activity. A model of interim transactions was developed and its applications to different markets were examined. The structure of land markets which has received so much attention from economic historians and so little from theorists was discussed at length—both in the context of interim transactions and otherwise. Considerable scope for generalizing the basic model remains and one particular line is briefly pursued in Appendix 9.1.

APPENDIX 9.1

The basic model is one of no friction and perfect foresight. If $S = D$, then everybody is certain [see (9.5)] about being able to buy back land. Without being able to fully explain why, we know that in reality the *volume* of transactions is usually a good indicator of one's chances of being able to make a transaction. Thus when one asserts—as is often done in India—that it is easy to rent a flat in Delhi but not in Mumbai, one is not really saying that there is an excess demand for flats in Mumbai but not in Delhi. What one is probably saying is that the turnover in Delhi is larger. One way of capturing this is to assume [in contrast to (9.5) above] that,

(A9.1) $\phi = \phi(S^e)$, $\phi \geq 0$,

where S^e is the expected volume of aggregate supply.

If price is fixed at p, and expected total supply is S^e, then actual total supply will be

(A9.2) $S \equiv \hat{S}(p) + \# \{i \in M | \ d(i) \geq 1 - \phi(S^e)\}$

Equilibrium is obtained when

(A9.3) $S = S^e$.

With this alternative specification of the subjective probability function [that is, (A9.1) as opposed to (9.5)], it is easy to extend the analysis to one with flexible prices. With flexible prices, at equilibrium, aggregate supply [that is, (A9.2)] must be equal to aggregate demand. Since interim supply always equals interim demand, this means that regular supply must be equal to regular demand,

(A9.4) $\hat{S}(p) = \hat{D}(p)$.

Thus a *flexible price equilibrium* is obtained when (A9.2), (A9.3), and (A9.4) are true.

It is interesting to note that (A9.2)–(A9.4) is a recursive system. The equilibrium price, p^*, is determined entirely by the regular market. Once this is determined, the volume of transactions is determined by the interim sales behaviour [that is, (A9.2) and (A9.3)]. It is possible to represent the equilibrium diagrammatically, but we shall not go into that here.

While the subjective probability function used in this model, that is, (A9.1) is in some ways more realistic than (9.5), it has an important analytical lacuna. Given (A9.1), it is possible to have (i) $S = D$, and (ii) $\phi(S) < 1$. (i) and (ii) are, however, difficult to reconcile. (i) is usually taken to assert that all those who want to buy land can do so. In that case, it is difficult to see why individuals feel that the probability of being able to buy land, $\phi(S)$, is less than 1. One way of reconciling (i) and (ii) [and thereby making (A9.1) acceptable] is to interpret (i) differently. We could assume that it merely says that intended supply equals intended demand, though because of friction not every buyer (seller) necessarily finds a seller (buyer). A direct use of this approach would run into difficulties as not much is known about markets with this kind of friction, other than their widespread existence. Also, we would have to cope with the problem of uncertainty about being able to sell land, in addition to the uncertainty about being able to buy land.

These are sufficiently serious difficulties not to treat the model of this section as complete in any way. The model is meant to illustrate the kinds of difficulty which one has to face in analysing the flex-price case. If price is flexible and the subjective probability function is the one used in the basic model [as specified by (9.5)], then—it is easy to verify—the only equilibrium that would obtain is the high-activity one, which is a fairly uninteresting case. If the probability function is as in (A9.I), all the difficulties just discussed crop up. Yet (A9.1) has a certain appeal from our everyday experience. The line which needs to be pursued to construct a satisfactory flex-price model is either to formalize the notion of frictional unemployment which underlies the above exercise or to abandon both (9.5) and (A9.1) and search for alternative specifications of the subjective probability function.

NOTES

1. It ought to be clarified at the outset that the market for *renting* land is far from inactive in LDCs. All references to the market for land in this paper are to the market for full land rights.
2. Writing about land rights in East Bengal under the Permanent Settlement of 1793, Raychaudhuri (1969: 163) notes, '... rights of the various categories of interest in land were enmeshed in an incredible maze of crisscross relationships so that it is impossible to determine with any precision who was who or what was whose. Descriptions in the settlement reports indicate that those who owned land very often did not know what land it was they owned, and those who cultivated land often did not know the title or estate of their landlords'.
3. This view has had more scholarly adherents than my Midnapore farmer. Thus Raj (1970: 1) observes, '[Land] is the main form in which wealth is desired to be held in these economies ... In societies exposed to various kinds, of risk, ... land is an attractive asset to hold even if the pecuniary rate of return on the investment happens to be low'. In a historical context, Chaudhuri (1975) argued that land was the most convenient form of wealth because 'of the very limited existence of "other objects of speculation or investment" and also in view of land possessing "the quality of immovability"—"a very desirable quality when the system of police was defective, and the possession of valuable moveables was sure to tempt the cupidity of the numerous gangs of dacoits, which infested the country" ' (the sub-quotes are from Field 1884). It would, however, be an error to suppose that this was always the case. In India, before the establishment of British rule, land was in fact a very risky asset because of the absence of clear titles and rights. As Cohn (1969: 82) observed: 'One needed military force to support a claim to land and had to be willing to fight for it'.
4. One plausible explanation could be in terms of asymmetric information (Akerlof 1970). This, however, has the difficulty that in the personalized atmosphere of backward agriculture people are acquainted with not only one another's scandals but

also the quality of their lands. Hence information may not be *adequately* asymmetric to support an explanation on its own.

5. Suppose *i* expects to retire and cash his assets after *t* years, he has no time discount and he expects prices to remain unchanged. While land has no decay, cash has an expected decay rate of $100b$ ($b > 0$) per cent per annum (perhaps because of expected thefts). In this case the value of holding land is p and the value of holding cash, instead, is $p/(1-b)^t$. Using this interpretation, $c(i) = (1-b)^t$. In my model, however, I treat $c(i)$ as a 'primitive'.

6. This formulation implies risk-neutrality. It is easy to introduce risk-aversion by assuming that *i* maximizes expected utility and his utility function is concave. In such a case a person's decision to sell land would depend not only on $a(i)$, $c(i)$, and ϕ, but also on his degree of risk- aversion.

7. The fixed-price assumption is used here to keep the basic model uncomplicated. The issues which arise from relaxing this and also from using alternative specifications of (9.5), below, are explored in Appendix 9.1. It is worth noting that the strength and weakness of fixed-price modelling have been discussed extensively in the literature on the micro-foundations of macroeconomics. Also, the assumption is not as strong as it appears at first sight. It does not entail that prices do not change but simply that they do not change in response to short-run fluctuations in demand and supply. In Malinvaud's (1977: 9) words: [Q]uantitative adjustments are the first signals of changes in the demand–supply relations'. It should, therefore, be clear that our fixed-price assumption does not rule out the possibility of an inflation in all sectors. Of course, the model would have to be adjusted to take account of real balance effects.

8. The possibility of two persons having the same *d*'s is being ruled out. This is convenient and harmless.

9. The confiscation of land and other assets when the borrower fails to repay a loan is a problem which has been theoretically investigated: Bhaduri (1977), Basu (1984a).

10. The subject of interlinkage has received an enormous amount of attention. Interlinkage could arise for several reasons (see Basu 1984b for discussion and further references) and seasonal fluctuations in labour requirement is just one of them.

11. Problems of adjustment cost or the costs of employing new hands in place of old ones—issues which have been discussed in the ample literature on lay-offs and recessions in the context of industrialized economies (see, for example, Baily 1977)—are being ignored here.

12. As Kornai (1983: 67) argues: 'If there are shortages, supplies are uncertain. If supplies are uncertain, it is only rational behaviour to hoard inputs ... . You don't fire workers because maybe you can't find replacements tomorrow ... . It is all a vicious circle'.

REFERENCES

Akerlof, G. 1970. 'The Market for "Lemons": Quality Uncertainty and the Market Mechanism'. *Quarterly Journal of Economics* 84.

Baily, M.N. 1977. 'On the Theory of Layoffs and Unemployment', *Econometrica* 45.

Bardhan, P. 1984. *Land, Labour and Rural Poverty*. New York: Coluumbia University Press.

Basu, K. 1984a. 'Implicit Interest Rates, Usury and Isolation in Backward Agriculture'. *Cambridge Journal of Economics* 8.

Basu, K. 1984b. *The Less Developed Economy. A Critique of Contemporary Theory.* Oxford: Basil Blackwell.

Bhaduri, A. 1976. 'The Evolution of Land Relations in Eastern India Under British Rule'. *Indian Economic and Social History Review* 13.

—— 1977. 'On the Formation of Usurious Interest Rates in Backward Agriculture'. *Cambridge Journal of Economics* 5.

Bliss, C.J. and N.H. Stern. 1982. *Palanpur.* Oxford: Oxford University Press.

Bose, S.R. 1970. 'Land Sales and Land Values in Bihar'. *Indian Journal of Agricultural Economics* 25.

Cain, M. 1981. 'Risk and Fertility in India and Bangladesh'. *Population and Development Review* 7.

Chaudhuri, B.B. 1975. 'Land Markets in Eastern India 1793–1940. Part I: The Movement of Land Prices'. *Indian Economic and Social History Review* 12.

Cohn, B.S. 1969. 'Structural Change in Indian Rural Society'. In Frykenberg (1969).

Field, C.D. 1884. *Introduction to the Regulations of the Bengal Code.* Calcutta.

Frykenberg, R.E., ed. 1969. *Land Control and Social Structure in Indian History.* Madison, WI: University of Wisconsin Press.

Kaldor, N. 1940. 'A Model of the Trade Cycle'. *Economic Journal* 50.

Kornai, J. 1983. Interview to Forbes magazine, *Forbes*, (1 August).

Malinvaud, E. 1977. *The Theory of Unemployment Reconsidered.* Oxford: Basil Blackwell.

Mukherji, K. 1971. 'Land Transfers in Birbhum 1928-1955: Some Implications of the Bengal Tenancy Act, 1885', *Indian Economic and Social History Review* 7.

Raj, K.N. 1970. 'Ownership and Distribution of Land'. *Indian Economic Review* 5.

Rao, V.M. 1972. 'Land Transfers: Findings in a Ryotwari Region'. *Economic and Political Weekly* (Review of Agriculture) 7 (30 September).

Raychaudhuri, T. 1969. 'Permanent Settlement in Operation: Bakarganj District, East Bengal'. In Frykenberg (1969).

10 Disneyland Monopoly, Interlinkage, and Usurious Interest Rates

10.I. INTRODUCTION

There is a commonness in the schemes of (a) the Disneyland monopolist who charges a large entry fee before allowing people access to the joy rides in the park and (b) the rural landlord who gives credit only to those who are employed on his land or are his tenants: (a) relates to the well-developed literature on non-linear pricing[1] and (b) to the relatively recent and ongoing research on interlinkage in factor markets in backward agriculture.[2] The aim of this chapter is to analyse this commonness[3] and to shed new light on the causes and consequence of interlinkages in rural markets by drawing on results in the literature on non-linear pricing and optimal taxation.

Several explanations have been suggested for the existence of interlinkage. The fact that lending money to strangers can be risky may mean that a moneylender would give credit only to those with whom he has other dealings. This would lead to an explanation of interlinkage as a kind of insurance (Basu 1983; Platteau 1983). Another explanation could be that, since the effort or *effective* labour put in by a tenant is beyond the landlord's control, interlinkage is used by the landlord as an instrument of *indirect* control of labour effort. This is the basis of works such as Braverman and Stiglitz (1982) and Mitra (1983).

A different line is pursued in this chapter. Suppose rural credit markets are monopolistic. By this I do not mean that there exists only one moneylender in the rural region or locality, but simply that each borrower has access to only one moneylender. So there may be several moneylenders but each lender with his

From *Journal of Public Economics 34*, 1987: 1–17.

I have benefited from the comments of Angus Deaton, Jean Drèze, Raja Junankar, Nirvikar Singh and Nick Stern, and from seminars at Warwick and Berkeley. Financial support from the Development Economics Research Centre, University of Warwick, is gratefully acknowledged. A part of this work was done at the Institute for Advanced Study, Princeton.

borrowers forms a little 'credit island' with meagre—and for the formal analysis, no—flow of money between these islands. Given that historical ties[4] (example, the fact that i and j belong to the same caste and have lived in the same village since birth) generally reduce the risk of credit default, it is natural for a lender to prefer giving loans to those with whom he has historical ties. And this makes the description of a fragmented credit market a plausible one.

Focus now on one island with its monopolist moneylender, who, we shall assume, happens to be also a landowner, and several potential borrowers. It can be shown that one way in which the moneylender-landlord can increase the surplus extracted from the borrowers is by offering them an interlinked deal whereby they could work as labourers at a wage below the normal rate and also take credit at a certain interest rate. So interlinkage here is a result of monopoly in one market, namely the credit market. It exists for the same reason that 'leverage' and 'tie-in sales' exist in industry—or rather would exist in industry if not for the Sherman Act and other legal provisions (Bowman 1957). This idea is presented in Section 10.3.

Two shortcomings of the large recent literature on interlinkage are as follows. First, while there are models of high interest rates, in most models of interlinkage the natural tendency for rural interest rates is to get equated with the organized-sector interest rate (see, for example, Braverman and Srinivasan 1981; Basu 1983). Second, in most models, borrowers are *ex ante* identical. While this assumption is normally made to look innocuous, the popularity of its adoption is really caused by the fact that the case of non-identical borrowers is analytically difficult to model.

Interestingly, these two problems are closely related and solving one solves the other. It will be argued that one important cause of why interest rates are usurious or high is borrower heterogeneity. The modelling of interlinked markets with heterogeneous borrowers becomes tractable once we exploit the structural analogousness between interlinkage and non-linear pricing. I do this in Section 10.5. It is shown that with heterogeneous borrowers, rural interest rates may be above the organized-sector rate and also, given certain restrictions on inter-borrower preferences, interest rates will be lower for larger loans.

Interest rates could also be high because of certain kinds of fiscal policy. The existence of interlinkage means that a wage policy could have an immediate impact on the credit market and interest rates. Policy questions in general have received little attention in the literature on interlinkage, and consequently I go into these in some detail in this chapter. It is known that in the presence of interlinkage if we try to achieve a certain objective via labour-market policy, it might get dissipated or reversed via credit-market response. This has led to the extreme view that tampering with one market may be useless. The effects of an agricultural income tax and minimum-wage legislation are examined in this chapter. The impact on interest rate is carefully worked out. I also address the 'one market' problem. Can worker welfare be increased by raising wages or would such a policy always get offset by adverse changes in the credit market? These and other questions are the subject matter of Section 10.4.

The formal analysis is initiated by briefly presenting the model of two-part tariff monopoly in the next section. A subsidiary aim of the chapter is to offer some simple new geometry for analysing interlinked markets and two-part pricing.

10.2. THE GEOMETRY OF TWO-PART TARIFF MONOPOLY

Consider a monopolist selling hats to a single price-taking consumer. He charges a two-part tariff, (T, p), where T is the 'entry' charge and p is the per unit price. This implies that if the consumer buys x units of hats he will have to pay $T + px$, if $x >$ 0. Consider a two-good world where the other good has a price of 1 and the consumer has an income of y in Figure 10.1. If he does not buy hats, he can buy y units of the other goods and get a utility of $\bar{u}$. The indifference curve representing $\bar{u}$ is shown in the figure.

In the case where x_0 is the number of hats the monopolist plans to sell, the maximum that he can earn is given by GJ. This he does by setting p equal to the marginal rate of substitution at J and T equal to yA'. Then the budget set faced by the consumer is the point y and all points within $OA'B'$ and clearly the consumer would be willing to buy x_0 units and pay $GJ = yD$. It follows that if we draw a horizontal line through y and turn the diagram upside down, we could think of $\bar{u}$ as the total revenue (TR) curve faced by the monopolist charging a two-part tariff. Such a monopolist is called a Disneyland monopolist.

A monopolist who charges only a fixed price per unit (and has no entry charge)

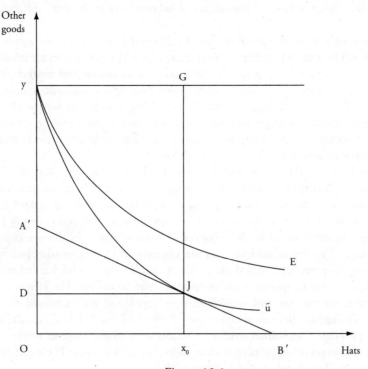

Figure 10.1

will be referred to as a traditional monopolist. In Figure 10.1, yE is the offer curve, that is, the locus of equilibrium points on all budget constraints that can be drawn through y. It is easy to see that yE is the TR curve (with the diagram turned upside down) for the traditional monopolist. Since the offer curve through y must lie above the indifference curve through y, a Disneyland monopolist necessarily earns more than a traditional monopolist.

To find out how much these two types of monopolists will produce, draw the total cost (TC) curve upside down with y as the origin. Each type of monopolist will produce that output which maximizes the vertical distance between the TC and the relevant TR curves. We may now move on to a central theme of this chapter, namely interlinkage and its geometry.

10.3. AN EXPLANATION OF INTERLINKAGE

Suppose there are n labourers. Each can produce an output of q units. They have access to a competitive labour market where the prevailing wage equals the marginal product of labour, that is, q. For credit, however, they can turn to only one landlord. The need for credit arises, in reality, for many reasons. Here, for the sake of simplicity, it will be assumed that there are two periods and wages are paid in period 2. In period 1, a labourer has to borrow to finance consumption. If a labourer receives a loan of L units in period 1 and has to pay it back in period 2 with interest, at a rate of i, and he gets a wage of w units, his consumption stream in the two periods is given by $(L, w - (1 + i)L)$. The utility that he gets from this is given by

(10.1) $u = u(L, w - (1+i)L), \quad u_1 > 0, \ u_2 > 0.$

The function is assumed to be strictly concave and differentiable. To start with, it is being assumed that all workers have the same preferences. This will be relaxed in Section 10.5. To find the labourer's demand function for loans we have to solve the following problem:

$$\max_{\{L\}} u(L, w - (1 + i) L).$$

By solving this we get the amount of loan demanded by a labourer to be a function of w and i:

(10.2) $L = L(w, i).$

Now consider the moneylender who has a monopoly in the credit market. It is assumed that he has access to the organized credit market where the interest rate is r. Hence the opportunity cost to the moneylender of giving credit in the rural sector is r. We shall begin by assuming that the moneylender cannot discriminate between loans in terms of interest rate. He has to fix an interest rate, i, which he cannot then vary across borrowers or loans. If he acts like a traditional monopolist he will, confronted by the demand curve for loans, lend up to the point where the marginal revenue equals the marginal cost of lending which, in this model, is r. He will then set i above r in the usual way.

He can, however, earn a larger profit if he uses his monopoly power in the credit market to offer joint deals in the credit and labour markets. By insisting that a person must be his employee in order to get his credit and by paying his employees less than the wage rate in the competitive labour market, he can emulate a two-part tariff monopolist and extract the entire surplus from the labourers. This is the essential cause of interlinkage in this model.[5]

Suppose the landlord offers a package (w, i). If a worker accepts this he has to work for the landlord for a wage of w and he can take as much credit as he wishes at an interest rate i. Assume the workers accept this package. Then the landlord's profit, Π, is given by

(10.3) $$\Pi(w, i) = n\{q - w + (i - r)L(w, i)\}.$$

Remember that each worker produces q units of output and confronted with (w, i), takes a loan of $L(w, i)$, as specified in (10.2). We shall refer to $n(q - w)$ as the production income and $n(i - r)L(w, i)$ as the usurious income of the money-lender-landlord. It is being assumed that the output, q, produced by each worker is realized in the second period, which is also when the wage is paid and the loan repaid. It is worth noting that $q - w$ here plays the role which the entry fee plays in the Disneyland model.

Note that if a labourer rejects the offer (w, i), he can always flee to the labour market where he gets a utility of $u(0, q) \equiv u$. This will be referred to as the reservation utility of the labourer. Clearly then the landlord, in designing his offer to the labourers, has to ensure that they get at least as much as their reservation utility. Hence, the landlord's problem is

$$\max_{\{w, i\}} \Pi(w, i)$$

s.t.

$$u(L(w, i), w - (1 + i)L(w, i)) \geq \bar{u}.[6]$$

Solving this we get (w, i) and, by using (10.2), we can then solve for L. Let the solution of this exercise be denoted by $(w^*, i^*, L^*) \equiv E^*$. E^* is, therefore, the equilibrium in this model. This completes the description of our basic model.

The characterization of E^* turns out to be a very easy exercise using the diagrammatic apparatus of Section 10.2. It is clear that the landlord can treat the reservation indifference curve, qe, as his TR curve with Figure 10.2 turned upside down and with q being the origin. If he lends L units to a labourer, the cost of this is $(1 + r)L$. Hence, if we draw a line through q with a slope of $1 + r$, we could think of it as the TC curve facing the landlord. His optimum is, therefore, given by point e where the slope of the reservation indifference curve equals $1 + r$. Hence the landlord should offer a wage of w, as shown in Figure 10.2, and set i equal to r. His profit from each labourer is given by qw in Figure 10.2 and hence his total profit is this multiplied by n.

Viewed in this manner several standard theorems on interlinkage are easily understood. In this model all labourers get the same utility and each labourer gets as much utility as he would have got if he did not transact with the monopolistic moneylender and went to the labour market instead. The only difference is that he

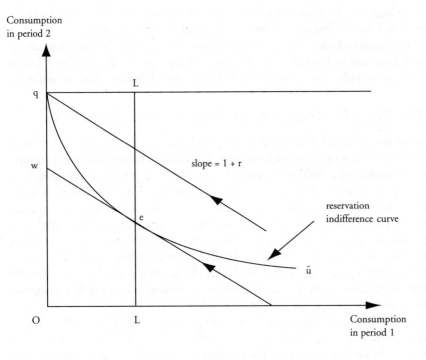

Figure 10.2

would be at point *e* in one case and *q* in the other. This is known in the literature as the utility-equivalence theorem.

In the above analysis the indifference curve representing *ū* touches the vertical axis (at *q*). It may appear more reasonable to assume that as the consumption in period 1 approaches 0, the indifference curve should asymptotically approach the vertical axis. After all, some consumption in each period is essential. Fortunately, there is no need to deny this in our model. We could simply assume that a certain minimum consumption in period 1 is guaranteed to the labourer (by, for example, his relatives) and what the horizontal axis in our diagrams show (and what the first argument in a labourer's utility function represents) is consumption in period 1 over and above this minimum guaranteed level.

Let us define the rural interest rate as *usurious* if *i* exceeds *r*. Note that in the above simple model the landlord would not charge usurious interest rates. However, this should not be equated with an absence of 'exploitation', for this landlord extracts more from the labourers than a traditional monopolist-moneylender.

In this model, interlinkage is an *outcome* of monopoly in one market. Interlinkage enables the landlord to extract the consumer's surplus from those who take credit from him or—to use legalistic jargon (Bowman 1957; Markovits 1967)—it enables him to exercise 'leverage'. In some early literature and occasionally even now (Wharton 1962; Bharadwaj 1974), it has been argued that interlinkage gives landlords greater power than monopoly. In a model such as the above one, this is an ambiguous observation because whatever earnings of the landlord can be attributed to interlinkage can, in turn, be attributed to monopoly.

The subject which we set out to explore now is the existence of usurious interest rates. There can be natural reasons for this but before going on to that, we focus on the effects of public policy on interlinked markets and, in particular, interest rates.

10.4. PRICE CONTROLS AND THE AGRICULTURAL INCOME TAX

Let us first consider a special kind of price control, namely a minimum-wage legislation. What I refer to as a legislation could instead be interpreted as a custom. The formal analysis will be the same. In the case of wages, many countries have minimum-wage laws but these are not always enforced in backward rural areas. There may also exist social sanctions against paying too low wages and these can often impose effective constraints. Irrespective of whether their origin is the law or custom, we shall consider here the effect of a restriction on paying wages below w_G. So now we have to think of the landlord as maximizing his profit subject to the constraint stated in Section 10.3 plus the constraint that $w \geq w_G$. For the problem to be interesting w_G must be above w^*. For simplicity I shall, throughout this section, assume $n = 1$

Let us denote the equilibrium wage and interest as $\hat{w}$ and $\hat{i}$ in the presence of such a minimum-wage restriction. It is simple to show that $\hat{w} = w_G$ and $\hat{i} > r$. Let us begin by assuming that $\hat{i} \leq r$. Clearly then the landlord cannot be earning more profit than $(q - w_G)$. This follows from (10.3) and is also obvious from Figure 10.3.

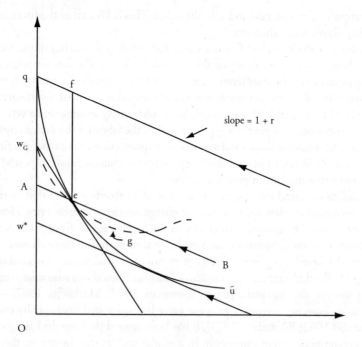

Figure 10.3

Now if the landlord sets w equal to w_G and i a little above r (taking care not to lose the customer), it follows from (10.3) that he will earn more than $(q - w_G)$. Hence the first situation could not have been a profit-maximizing one. This contradiction implies that $\hat{i} > r$.

Now suppose $\hat{w} > w_G$. We have already seen that $\hat{i} > r$. Now choose w and i such that (i) $w \in (w_G, \hat{w})$, (ii) $\hat{w} - w = (\hat{i} - i)L(\hat{w}, \hat{i})$, and (iii) $i > r$. It is easy to check that such (w, i) exists. Basically, (w, i) offers the labourer a Slutzky-compensated budget constraint. It follows from (ii) that $i < \hat{i}$. Since a Slutzky-compensated demand curve is downward sloping, it follows that $L(w, i) > L(\hat{w}, \hat{i})$. Using (10.3), we get

$$\Pi(w, i) - \Pi(\hat{w}, \hat{i}) = \hat{w} - w + (i - r)\, L(w, i) - (\hat{i} - r)L(\hat{w}, \hat{i})$$

$$= (i - r)(L(w, i) - L(\hat{w}, \hat{i})), \text{ by (ii)}$$

$$> 0, \text{ by (iii)}.$$

This is a contradiction. Hence $\hat{w} = w_G$. What we have proved is the following theorem.

THEOREM 10.1: If a minimum wage, w_G ($>w^*$), is imposed, the landlord will pay the minimum wage and charge usurious interest.[7]

It is interesting to examine the effect of a minimum wage on the worker's welfare. Let $\bar{u}$ be the reservation indifference curve of a labourer in Figure 10.3. Let e be the point of tangency of the budget constraint drawn through w_G with the indifference curve $\bar{u}$. If the landlord offers this budget constraint he will earn a profit of ef. Now draw the offer curve for the labourer when the budget constraint pivots around w_G. Clearly, this curve must pass through e. From Theorem 10.1 we know that the wage is equal to w_G. This offer curve represents the TR curve of the landlord (viewed upside down with q as origin). Through e draw a line, AB, which has a slope of $1 + r$. If the offer curve lies above this line to the right of e, then e is the best point from the landlord's point of view and equilibrium will occur there. In this case the worker's welfare remains unchanged because he remains on his reservation utility level. If the offer curve lies somewhere below AB, to the right of e, as does the broken curve in Figure 10.3, then there exist points on the offer curve which earn the landlord larger profits than e. In that case equilibrium will occur at a point like g where the labourer is on a higher utility level than $\bar{u}$. Hence, though a minimum wage restriction raises interest, it *may* leave the labourers better off on balance.

Based on this theorem one could hazard a tentative hypothesis about the movement, over time, of interest rates and wages. It has been argued that individual landlords find it difficult to give wages at variance with the prevailing norm (see, for example, Bliss and Stern 1982). Hence it may be argued that when wages fall, this is preceded by a period when a downward tension develops but wages nevertheless do not fall because of the working of social sanctions on each employer. It is only when the pressures of supply and demand become too much that wages fall. Hence, during the period before a wage decline it is as if there is a minimum wage legislation. Therefore, a wage decline should be preceded by a period when interest rates rise (by Theorem 10.1). And when wages actually begin to fall, it is like the lifting of a minimum-wage legislation, so interest rates would be expected to fall as well.

Finally, given the amount of controversy that has been generated in India regarding the agricultural income tax, it may be interesting to examine the impact of this in the context of our model. It is very likely that even if a government would ideally like to impose a tax on total agricultural profit, that is, $\Pi(w, i)$, sheer manageability considerations will make it unwise to try and tax usurious income. Also, such a case is analytically easy and uninteresting. So we shall focus here on a proportional income tax on production income only.

Let t be the fraction of production income which the landlord has to pay as tax. Hence the landlord's maxim and becomes:

$$\Pi(w, i) = (1 - t)(q - w) + (i - r)L(w, i).$$

The impact of such a tax is summarized in the next theorem.

THEOREM 10.2: If a proportional income tax is imposed on the landlord's production income, then the rural interest rate will exceed r and the wage will exceed w^*.

Let $(\hat{w}, \hat{i})$ be the equilibrium wage and interest after the tax t is imposed. We have to prove $\hat{i} > r$. Assume $\hat{i} \leqq r$. Define a function $w(i)$ implicitly by

$$\max_L u(L, w(i) - (1 + i)L) = \max_L u(L, \hat{w} - (1 + \hat{i})L).$$

Basically, as i is changed, $w(i)$ is the change in wage which keeps the labourer on the same indifference curve. Now define $\Omega(i) = \Pi(w(i), i)$. Hence, by (10.4), $\Omega(i) = (1 - t)(q - w(i)) + (i - r)l(i)$, where $l(i) = L(w(i), i)$. Hence,

$$\Omega'(i) = -w'(i) + tw'(i) + (i - r)l'(i) + l(i)$$

$$= tw'(i) + (i - r)l'(i), \text{ by Shephard's Lemma.}$$

If $i = \hat{i}$, then

$$\Omega'(\hat{i}) = tw'(\hat{i}) + (\hat{i} - r)l'(\hat{i}).$$

By the definition of function $w(i)$, it follows that $w'(i) > 0$. And since $\hat{i} \leqq r$, hence $W'(\hat{i}) > 0$. Hence $\hat{i}$ cannot be the optimum. This contradiction established $\hat{i} > r$.

Since the labourer must remain on or above the reservation indifference curve, if the interest rate is higher, so is the wage. This completes the proof of Theorem 10.2.

An income tax imposed on the landlord may or may not raise the level of labourers' welfare. The argument is similar to the case of minimum-wage legislation discussed above and is left to the reader to work out using a similar diagrammatic technique.

10.5. USURIOUS INTEREST RATES

A 'natural' explanation of usurious interest rates—as opposed to the policy-engineered ones discussed in the previous section—becomes possible once we drop the assumption, so widely used in the literature on interlinkage (Braverman and Srinivasan 1981; Mitra 1983; Basu 1983), that all labourers have identical preferences. The case of non-identical labour would have been very difficult to handle if we had to begin from scratch. But this becomes a simple exercise if we can suitably draw on the work on non-linear pricing with heterogeneous consumers. There can be various ways of dropping the assumption of homogeneous tenants. Braverman and Guasch (1984) have explored the case of heterogeneity in the productivity of labourers. In what follows, heterogeneity exists only in preferences. Also, in my model, credit is not rationed. Labourers are free to take as much credit as they wish.

Along with labour heterogeneity, we shall assume that there exist social sanctions against discrimination between labourers. For, if the landlord is free to discriminate, then it is best for him to set $i = r$ for all labourers and vary w so as to extract all consumer's surplus from each labourer, as in Section 10.2.

Non-discrimination can be modelled in various ways and two of these will be considered here. First, the case where the landlord has to offer a unique package (w, i) to all labourers is taken up. In the second case, we allow the landlord to offer many packages but he has to offer these packages to the labourers anonymously, that is, anyone can take up any package.

The case where the landlord has to offer a unique package can be intuitively analysed. Suppose there are different kinds of labourers, some who need credit more 'intensely' than others (in a sense to be made precise later). If now the landlord sets $i = r$, he earns nothing from his loans [see (10.3)]. His entire earning has to come from production income, that is, $q - w$. This means that he would not manage to extract more from those who need more credit. One way of extracting more from such people is to set i above r. It is in this that the idea of usurious interest lies.

Before going on to formalize this, it is worth noting that this idea has antecedents which go back to some writings on anti-trust law in the 1950s. I quote from a remarkably lucid paper by Bowman (1957: 23–4) where he is discussing a case between Heaton-Peninsular Button-Fasters Co. and Eureka Speciality Co.:

A machine was invented for stapling button to high-button shoes [and the] machine was worth more to the more intensive users. If the patentee attempted to sell it at different prices to different users, however, he would have encountered two problems. To determine in advance how intensively each buyer would use the machine would have been difficult; to prevent those who paid a low price from reselling to those who paid a high price might have proved impossible. A tie-in would resolve these difficulties. The machine might be sold at cost, on condition that the unpatented staples used in the machine be bought from the patentee. Through staple sales the patentee could obtain a device for measuring the intensity with which his customers used the machines. Hence by charging a higher than competitive price for the staples the patentee could receive the equivalent of a royalty from his patented machines.

Before going on to consider usurious interest let us first establish the more general proposition that if there is heterogeneity in the preferences of labourers and the landlord is not allowed to discriminate between labourers, the interest rate

charged by the landlord will (except in coincidental cases) differ from the organized sector interest rate. In other words, heterogeneity destroys perfect arbitrage
in the credit market. This is very easy to demonstrate diagrammatically.

Let $\bar{u}_1$ and $\bar{u}_2$ be the reservation indifference curves of persons 1 and 2, as in
Figure 10.4. Each curve consists of two straight-line segments. In each case the
steeper segment is steeper than $1 + r$ and the flatter segment flatter than $1 + r$.

Now consider the landlord's problem. If the landlord faced only labourer 1,
what (w, i) would he offer? It is easy to see that he would offer any package which
would make point E person 1's equilibrium point. Similarly, if he faced only
person 2, he would devise a (w, i) package so as to pin down labourer 2 at point
F. Now, if he faces both 1 and 2 together and has to offer a unique (w, i) package
to both, what should he do?

Clearly he should set w equal to OB and $1 + i$ equal to the slope of line BA
(which is formed by joining E and F and extending). In other words he offers
labourers the budget set OBA. Given this budget set, 1 will choose point E and 2
point F. Clearly, there is no reason why i should be equal to r. As in Figure 10.4,
i may be usurious, or i may be less than r. Hence, if we now look at the profile of
interest rates charged by different landlords we will get a diverse variety of interest
rates and they need not equal the organized sector rates.[8] Though I have established this with kinked indifference curves, these results will be valid in more
general cases. However, if indifference curves are smooth, the landlord will not be
able to extract the entire surplus from both labourers as in the above illustration.

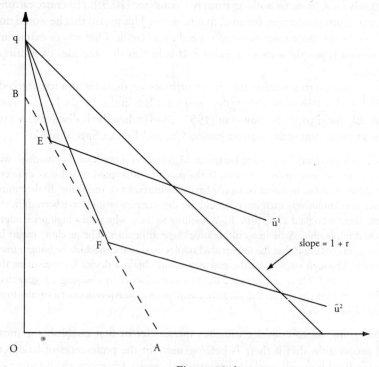

Figure 10.4

What we have is established is this:

THEOREM 10.3: If preferences among labourers vary and the landlord is constrained to offer a unique wage and interest, then there exist preference structures for which the interest rate is usurious.

Without violating labourer anonymity, the moneylender-landlord could be given another degree of freedom. We may consider the case where instead of offering a unique package the landlord offers a vector of packages. Anonymity or non-discrimination in this case requires that he does not differentiate between labourers, in the sense that the vector of packages is thrown open to all labourers and each is left free to choose any. What will the interest rates look like in such a situation? I give here an answer to this question using a well-known theorem in non-linear pricing (see, for example, Spence 1980) along with a generalization of it (see Basu 1985).

For the sake of easier exposition we need to introduce some notation. Instead of thinking of the landlord offering a wage and an interest, we shall think of an offer as a specification of consumption in periods 1 and 2. An offer $\langle L, C \rangle$ means that if a labourer accepts this he will have to work for the landlord and will get L units of consumption in period 1 and C units in period 2. Now while we do allow labour heterogeneity, we will impose some restriction on interpersonal preference differences. Let $s^i(L, C)$ be the (negative of the) slope of person i's indifference curve at (L, C). Now suppose that the n labourers can be grouped into t types of labourers. There are θ_j labourers of type j. Hence $\Sigma_{j=1}^t \theta_j = n$. We assume that for all ($\leq n-1$) a labourer of type $j+1$ needs credit with a greater intensity than a type-j labourer. This we assume to be true in the following sense. Let $u^i = u^i(L, C)$ be the utility function of a person of type i. It is strictly concave and differentiable. We assume that for all (L, C) and for all i:

$$\frac{u_1^i(L, C)}{u_2^i(L, C)} < \frac{u_1^{i+1}(L, C)}{u_2^{i+1}(L, C)},$$

which may be rewritten in brief as

$$s^i(L, C) < s^{i+1}(L, C).$$

The landlord offers T packages, $\{\langle L_1, C_1 \rangle, ..., \langle L_t, C_t \rangle\} \equiv \{\langle L_i, C_i \rangle\}$ and labourers are left free to choose any. It is a question of nomenclature and I assume that a labourer of type i chooses $\langle L_i, C_i \rangle$. That is,

(10.6) $u^i(L_i, C_i) \geq u^i(L_j, C_j)$, for all j,

and

(10.7) $u^i(L_i, C_i) \geq u^i(0, q)$

Expression (10.7) captures the fact that individuals are free not to accept any package and to go to the competitive labour market where a wage of q is assured.

The landlord's profit is given by

(10.8) $\Pi(\{\langle L_i, C_i \rangle\}) = nq - (1 + r) \sum_{i=1}^t \theta_i L_i - \sum_{i=1}^t \theta_i C_i.$

The landlord's aim is to choose a t-tuple of offers $\{\langle L_i, C_i \rangle\}$ so as to maximize (10.8) subject to (10.6) and (10.7). Let the solution to this problem be denoted by $\{\langle L_i^*, C_i^* \rangle\}$.

Our aim is to characterize this solution in terms of interest rates and wages. If a person j chooses a consumption stream $\langle L, C \rangle$ we may define the (implicit) interest rate, $i(L, C, j)$, and wage, $w(L, C, j)$ as follows:

$$i(L, C, j) = s^j(L, C) - 1,$$

$$w(L, C, j) = s^j(L, C) \cdot L + C.$$

These are called the interest rate and wage associated with point $\langle L, C \rangle$ for person j because it is easy to see (using Figure 10.2) that if a person j faces a wage-interest package given by $i(L, C, j)$ and $w(L, C, j)$, then he will optimally choose the point (L, C).

By a generalization of a well-known theorem in non-linear pricing, it can be shown that the maximization of (10.8) will yield a solution with the following properties:[9] the marginal rate of substitution of a person of type t at $\langle L_t^*, C_t^* \rangle$ equals $1 + r$, and for all $i < n$, the marginal rate of substitution of a person of type i at $\langle L_i^*, C_i^* \rangle$ is greater than $1 + r$. Translating these results, so as to state them in terms of interest rates, yields the following proposition.

THEOREM 10.4: If individuals have differing credit needs such that they can be arranged so as to satisfy (10.5) and if landlords are free to offer several packages but are not allowed to discriminate, then all persons with the greatest credit need will be charged an interest rate equal to the organized-market interest, that is, r; all other labourers will be charged usurious interest rates.

This theorem has an obvious, but in this context interesting, corollary. In Figure 10.5, let $\langle L_t^*, C_t^* \rangle$ be denoted by e_t. It, of course, lies on the indifference curve of a person of type t. Consider a person of type i ($i < t$) and let e_i denote $\langle L_i^*, C_i^* \rangle$. Obviously, e_i lies on the indifference curve of a labourer of type i. Let us label these two indifference curves u^i and u^t. At the point of intersection of u^i and u^t, i.e. at point z, u^t must be steeper than u^i because of (10.5). It follows that e_i lies to the left of z and e_t to the right. For, if e_t was to the left of z (and on the u^t curve), then labourers of type i would choose point e^t rather than e^i thereby contradicting constraint (10.6) of the maximization problem. A similar argument implies that e^i must be to the left of z. Hence, for all $i < t$, labourers of type i take a smaller loan than t. Since, by Theorem 10.4, labourers of type i pay a higher interest than those of type t, we have this proposition.

COROLLARY 10.1: Individuals who take the largest amount of loan pay the lowest interest rate. All those who take smaller loans, pay usurious interest rates.

10.6. CONCLUSION

Interlinkage is a phenomenon that can arise for various reasons. This chapter explored a line of argument in which monopoly in one market generates forces

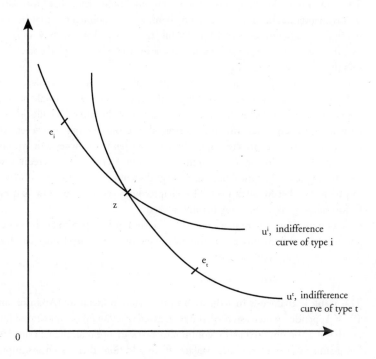

Figure 10.5

which lead to the interlocking of this market with another one. It is an institution which enables the landlord to extract consumer's surplus from his labourers. This kind of interlinkage is analogous to the tie-ins and two-part tariffs which have been a subject of much research in industrial pricing theory. This chapter made use of this structural commonness to explore the impact of various fiscal policies on a rural economy with interlink age between labour and credit markets, and also to examine the effect of *ex ante* heterogeneity among labourers on rural interest rates. It was shown that such heterogeneity in a labour market in which there are social sanctions against discrimination between workers could provide an explanation for the existence of usurious interest rates.

NOTES

1. The modern literature, especially the Disneyland version of it, originated in Oi (1971) and was followed by, among others, Adams and Yellen (1976), Spence (1977, 1980), Guesnerie and Seade (1982), and Braverman *et al.* (1983). Variants of this, namely the tying-in problem or block tariffs, were discussed by Burstein (1960) and Gabor (1955).
2. Bhaduri (1973), Bardhan (1980, 1984), Braverman and Srinivasan (1981), Braverman and Stiglitz (1982), Platteau (1983), Mitra (1983), Basu (1983, 1984), Gangopadhyay and Sengupta (1986), and others.

156 :: DEVELOPMENT, MARKETS, AND INSTITUTIONS

3.   The commonness between non-linear pricing and interlinkage that I formally analyse
     in this chapter has been noted earlier by Bardhan who pointed out that Burstein's 'tie-
     in sales' is analogous to interlinkage. While this is true, I try to show in this chapter
     that the analogousness is much more stark if, instead of Burstein's theory, we consider
     Oi's theory of two-part tariffs.

4.   It is important to distinguish between historical and economic ties (see Basu 1984:
     148). The fact that two persons belong to the same caste is an example of the former;
     the fact that one works for the other is an example of the latter. Default risk is reduced
     by lending to someone with either historical or economic ties. However, since eco-
     nomic ties can be contracted upon, if a person lends to those with whom he has
     economic ties, inerlinkage occurs immediately. But if a person gives credit to someone
     with whom he has historical ties interlinkage does not occur automatically (since there
     can be no market for such ties). This chapter however, tries to show that even here
     factor markets may eventually get interlocked.

5.   Given interlinkage, the moneylender and the landlord happen to be the same person,
     referred to in this chapter as moneylender, landlord, or moneylender-landlord.

6.   This may, alternatively, be expressed as:

$$\max_{\{L\}} u(L, w - (1 + i)L) \geqq \bar{u}.$$

7.   This result is analogous to a theorem in the taxation literature (Atkinson and Stern
     1974: Appendix) which asserts that if there is a restriction on the maximum lump-sum
     tax that may be imposed and if commodity taxes are optimal, then an increase in the
     lump-sum tax would enhance welfare. If, in addition, there is an assumption that
     taxpayers have a reservation utility below which they must not or cannot be pushed,
     then it follows that the commodity tax ought to be wielded only when there is a
     restriction on the lump-sum tax.

8.   This is consistent with the empirical findings reported in Bardhan and Rudra (1978).

9.   For a statement of the standard theorem, see Spence (1980) and Phlips (1983). This
     version makes crucial use of a strong restriction on individual utility functions. By
     using an alternative mode of proof this restriction can be shown to be redundant (Basu
     1985). Seade (1983) has established this result without the restrictive assumption on
     individual utility functions but assuming that there is an infinity (and, in particular, a
     continuum) of consumer types.

REFERENCES

Adams, W.J. and J.L. Yellen. 1976. 'Commodity Bundling and the Burden of Monopoly'.
     Quarterly Journal of Economics 90.
Atkinson, A.B. and N.H. Stern. 1974. 'Pigou, Taxation and Public Goods'. *Review of
     Economic Studies* 41.
Bardhan, P. 1980. 'Interlocking Factor Markets and Agrarian Development: A Review of
     Issues'. *Oxford Economic Papers* 32.
—— 1984. *Land, Labour and Rural Poverty*. Columbia University Press.
Bardhan, P. and A. Rudra. 1978. 'Interlinkage of Land, Labour and Credit Relations:
     Analysis of Village Survey Data in East India'. *An Economic and Political Weekly* 69
     (February).

Basu, K. 1983. 'The Emergence of Isolation and Interlinkage in Rural Markets'. *Oxford Economic Papers* 35.

—— 1984. *The Less Developed Economy: A Critique of Contemporary Theory*. Basil Blackwell and Oxford University Press.

—— 1985. 'Notes on Nonlinear Pricing and Monopoly'. Development Economics Research Centre Discussion Paper. University of Warwick.

Bhaduri, A. 1973. 'A Study in Agricultural Backwardness under Semi-fedalism'. *Economic Journal* 83.

Bharadwaj, K. 1974. *Production Conditions in Indian Agriculture*. Cambridge University Press.

Bliss, C. and N. Stern. 1982. *Palanpur*. Oxford University Press.

Bowman, W.S. 1957. 'Tying Arrangements and the Leverage Problem'. *Yale Law Journal* 67.

Braverman, A. and L. Guasch. 1984. 'Capital Requirements, Screening and Interlinked Share-cropping and Credit Contracts'. *Journal of Development Economics* 14.

Braverman, A. and T.N. Srinivasan. 1981. 'Credit and Sharecropping in Agrarian Societies'. *Journal of Development Economics* 9.

Braverman, A. and J.E. Stilitz. 1982. 'Sharecropping and Interlinking of Factor Markets'. *American Economic Review* 72.

Braverman, A., and J.L. Guasch, and S. Salop. 1983. 'Defects in Disneyland: Quality Control as a Two part Tariff'. *Review of Economic Studies* 50.

Burstein, M.L. 1960. 'The Economics of Tie-in Sales'. *Review of Economics and Statistics* 42.

Gabor, A. 1985. 'A Note on Block Tariffs'. *Review of Economic Studies* 23.

Gangopadhyay, S. and K. Sengupta. 1986. 'Interlinkages in Rural Markets'. *Oxford Economic Papers* 38.

Guesnerie, R. and J. Seade. 1982. 'Nonlinear Pricing in a Finite Economy'. *Journal of Public Economics* 17.

Markovits, R. 1967. 'Tie-ins, Reciprocity and Leverage Theory'. *Yale Law Journal* 76.

Mitra, P.K. 1983. 'A Theory of Interlinked Rural Transactions'. *Journal of Public Economics* 20.

Oi, W. 1971. 'A Disneyland Dilemma: Two-part Tariff for a Mickey Mouse Monopoly'. *Quarterly Journal of Economics* 85.

Phlips, L. 1983. *The Economics of Price Discrimination*. Cambridge University Press.

Platteau, J.P. 1983. 'Interlinkage of Contracts: The Interpenetration of Credit and Labour Relations in the Case of a Traditional Marine Fishing Village of South Kerala'. In I. Dobozi and P. Mandi, eds. *Emerging Development Patterns*. Budapest.

Seade, J. 1983. 'Nonlinear Pricing by Profit-maximisers'. Warwick University. Mimeo.

Spence, A.M. 1977. 'Nonlinear Prices and Welfare'. *Journal of Public Economics* 8.

—— 1980. 'Multi-product Quantity-dependent Prices and Profitability Constraints'. *Review of Economic Studies* 47.

Wharton, C.R. 1962. 'Marketing, Merchandising and Moneylending: A Note on Middlemen Monopsony in Malaya'. *Malayan Economic Review* 6.

11 Fragmented Duopoly
Theory and Applications to Backward Agriculture

with Clive Bell

11.1. INTRODUCTION

In certain trades trust is a precondition for exchange or transaction to occur. This would be true where information asymmetries are strong. In buying used cars most of us would prefer to make a purchase from friends and acquaintances (or at least from some of them!). It is well known that in informal credit markets, where formal legal institutions are weak, a person would lend money only to those whom he can trust or over whom he has some control. Thus a landlord may agree to lend money only to his labourers and a merchant may agree to lend only to his regular customers. This has led to a view that credit markets are 'fragmented'. [1] However, when it has come to actually modelling such a case the usual recourse has been to treat it as a case of several monopoly islands. Strictly speaking, however, the market just described is neither a monopoly nor a duopoly since the set of potential borrowers of the landlord would, typically, have some intersection with the set of potential borrowers of the merchant but the two sets would not be identical. What we have is a case in between a monopoly and oligopoly. It is this 'in between' case that is formally characterized and explored in this chapter.

Let us assume that there are n sellers of a certain commodity. Let S_i be the set of potential customers of seller i. To consumers outside S_i, i will never sell goods, irrespective of the price. Consider now two special cases. First, if it is true that

$$S_1 = S_2 = \ldots = S_n,$$

From *Journal of Development Economics* 36, 1991: 145–65.

This chapter has benefited from the comments of participants in a seminar at the Indian Statistical Institute, New Delhi, and Nirvikar Singh.

then we have a case of standard oligopoly with n firms. All firms are competing over the same set of customers.

If, on the other hand, $(S_1, S_2, ..., S_n)$ happens to be a partition over the set of all potential customers in the economy, then we have a case of n standard monopolies. Each seller has his own exclusive pool of customers. [2]

There is no reason why we have to restrict attention to these two polar cases. We may well have cases where for some i, j, the sets S_i and S_j have some common members but it is not the case that S_i is the same set for all i. We shall describe a market structure where this happens (along with the two polar cases just described) as a fragmented oligopoly.

Though we motivated the idea of fragmented oligopoly by talking about the role of trust and control in certain transactions, [3] we believe that this market structure could be usefully applied in many different areas. It clearly has relevance to models of industrial location. Indeed, certain features of location contribute to the fragmentation of rural credit markets when the pattern of settlement is nucleated, as in the case of South Asia's villages, rather than continuous, as in Hotelling's (1929) classic work. It is known, for example, that not all villages have resident moneylenders (RBI 1954) and that commission agents and traders often have 'territories' made up of several contiguous villages from which most of their clients in moneylending and trade are drawn. [4] Drawing upon these examples, suppose that there are three villages, A, B, and C, in a row. Moneylender 1 lives in village A; and moneylender 2 lives in C. If we suppose that the inhabitants of A would go only to their 'resident' money-lender and likewise for C, and that those of B would go to whoever charges less, then we have a case of fragmented duopoly. If N_X is a set of people in village X, then this is a special case of the above formal definition with $n = 2$ and $S_1 = N_A \cup N_B$ and $S_2 = N_C \cup N_B$. Thus, though the model that we construct does not belong to the class of location models based on Hotelling's (see, for example, D'Aspremont et al. 1979; and Bonanno 1987) and the properties that we investigate are distinct from the ones that a model of location would focus on, the abstract structure could be used as a basis for a model of locational duopoly.

Another view of our model is that of an oligopoly with switching costs (see, for example, von Weizsäcker 1984; Klemperer 1987a, b; and Bulow et al. 1985). Indeed our model may be viewed as an application of switching cost theory, with prohibitive switching costs once the 'domains' or 'territories' of firms have been established, to the study of backward markets and agrarian relations. Though our initial model, in abstraction, is a kind of switching-cost model, we develop it in some detail as our aim is to address issues in development and to persuade development economists of the relevance of such models of industrial organization to agrarian theory.

Models of fragmented oligopoly could also find application in activities where because of asymmetric information each seller has a predetermined clientele that trusts him. International trade with prior political fragmentation is another area of possible application of this theory. Though this chapter is an abstract analysis of fragmented duopoly and little depends on what actual motivation is used, our interest in the subject arose from an attempt to give a rigorous characterization of the idea of 'market fragmentation' which is so central to development economics and particularly the theory of agrarian structure. It is for this reason that much of the chapter dwells on problems of backward agriculture.

When firms possess captive segments of the market, it is natural to ask whether they can practise price discrimination between segments. This is indeed an open question. It is arguable that in fragmented agrarian markets, which are our central concern in this chapter, arbitrage is not easy and so price discrimination ought to be treated as feasible. One must, however, remember that in personalized rural markets of the kind described in Bardhan (1984), the possibility of price discrimination may be thwarted by social norms. In different societies, different kinds of discrimination are treated by the people as 'unjust'. The origins of these norms lie in distant history but are often powerful enough to make certain kinds of discriminatory pricing infeasible. That is, the cost in terms of political dissension is too high from the seller's point of view. It is for this reason that we have in this chapter devoted somewhat more attention to the non-discrimination model. We do, however, deal with the case of segment-specific price discrimination in separate sections.

The Cournot-Nash equilibria of a fragmented duopoly in which sellers cannot practise price discrimination are analysed in Section 11.2. Section 11.3 briefly describes the case where a seller can price-discriminate between market segments. In Section 11.4 a two-period model is constructed in which in the first period the players fight to establish their domains, that is, the S_1s and the S_2s. In the second period they treat S^1 and S^2 as given and play a quantity-setting game. The subgame perfect equilibria of such a two-period game, with and without price discrimination, are examined. The case with price discrimination is taken up in Section 11.5, and the possibility of rent-dissipation in this setting in Section 11.6.

11.2. THE NASH EQUILIBRIUM OF A FRAGMENTED DUOPOLY WITHOUT PRICE DISCRIMINATION

There are n identical consumers and each consumer's demand function for the commodity in question is given by

(11.1) $q = q(p)$,

where p is price and q is quantity demanded. We assume q is a continuous function and $q'(p) < 0$. The inverse demand function is written as follows:

(11.2) $p = p(q)$.

There are two sellers (or firms), 1 and 2. The n consumers are partitioned into three sets, N_1, N_2, and N_3, consisting of, respectively, n_1, n_2, and n_3 persons. Thus $n_1 + n_2 + n_3 = n$. The members of N_1 would buy goods from only firm 1. Members of N_2 would buy from only 2. The third group would buy from whoever offers better terms. These three groups will be referred to as the three *segments* of the market. N_i is firm i's *captive segment*, for $i = 1, 2$; and N_3 will be referred to as the *contested segment*.[5]

Both firms have the same cost function: A cost of c units has to be incurred to produce each unit of the good. An immediate consequence of this assumption is that were the firm able to charge the monopoly price, p^m, in its captive segment of the market, p^m would depend only on the shape of the individual's demand function and c. That is, p^m is then independent of the pattern of market segmentation. This is taken up further in Sections 11.3 and 11.5.

Consider now firm i's problem. It has to decide how much to supply to its captive segment, x_i, and how much to apply to the contested segment, q_i. To begin with, it will be assumed that a firm cannot discriminate between consumers in terms of the price charged. The consequence of relaxing this assumption is discussed in Section 11.3.

Suppose each firm has chosen a strategy. That is, we are given (x_1, q_1, x_2, q_2). Clearly the price of the good in the contested segment will be

$$p = p(q_1 + q_2)/n_3.$$

If $q_i > 0$, then the fact that a firm must charge the same price to all customers means that i must charge a price of $p((q_1 + q_2)/n_3)$ even in its captive segment. As price depends on the other firm's choice of q_j, the firm's choice of x_i may not be consistent with demand in the captive segment of its market. Thus i's total profit will be

(11.3)
$$\left[p\left(\frac{q_1 + q_2}{n_3} \right) - c \right] \left\{ q_i + \min\left[x_i, n_i q\left(p\left(\frac{q_1 + q_2}{n_3} \right) \right) \right] \right\}$$

Note that $n_i q(p((q_1 + q_2)/n_3))$ is the demand for the good in the captive segment when price is $p((q_1 + q_2)/n_3)$; and the shorter side of the market determines the volume of sales when supply is not equal to demand.

It is easy to see, however, that, given q_1 and q_2 (> 0), firm i's choice of x_i can be deduced therefrom. Hence we may define the profit of each firm in terms of only q_1 and q_2. Using π_i to denote firm i's profit, we have:[6]

(11.4)
$$\pi_i(q_1, q_2) = \begin{cases} \max_{x_i}\left[p\left(\frac{x_i}{n_i} \right) - c \right] x_i & \text{if} \quad q_i = 0. \\ \left[p\left(\frac{q_1 + q_2}{n_3} \right) - c \right]\left[q_i + \frac{n_i}{n_3}(q_1 + q_2) \right] & \text{if} \quad q_i > 0 \end{cases}$$

The interpretation of this profit function is as follows. Given (q_1, q_2), firm i supplies to its captive segment a profit-maximizing amount of goods. That is, given q_1 and q_2, price is determined by $p((q_1 + q_2)/n_3)$; so that if $q_i > 0$, then in its captive segment, firm i supplies exactly the amount that is demanded, which is equal to $(n_i/n_3)(q_1 + q_2)$. If $q_i = 0$, then the fact that a firm has to charge the same price to all its buyers places no restriction on the price it can charge in the captive segment. In such a case it can charge the monopoly price, p^m, and make monopoly profits. These features are captured in (11.4).

Let us define the Nash equilibrium of the game as a (q_1^*, q_2^*) such that $\pi_1(q_1^*, q_2^*) \geq \pi_1(q_1, q_2^*)$, for all q_1 and $\pi_2(q_1^*, q_2^*) \geq \pi_2(q_1^*, q_2)$, for all q_2.

It is useful to have a visual representation of the reaction functions. This would enable us to compare a fragmented duopoly with a traditional duopoly. In Figure 11.1, firm 1's reaction functions lie in the NE- and NW-quadrants. If q_2 is zero, firm 1 acts as a monopolist on both its captive segment and the contested segment. In that case, let OC be the amount it supplies on its captive segment and OA be the amount it supplies on the contested segment. As q_2 rises, firm 1's sales on the contested and captive segments are represented by the lines AB and CD. It will be shown later that AB will be steeper than the 45° line and CD will be a rising curve, as shown. As q_2 rises, supply in firm 1's captive segments deviates more and more from the monopoly output OC. This happens because a firm has to charge the same price to all customers. As q_2 keeps rising, a point will be reached where firm 1 would prefer to drop out of the contested market and sell the monopoly output to its captive segment. This happens when $q_2 = OG$. For all $q_2 > OG$, firm 1 sells $GE = OC$ units on its captive segment and zero in the contested market.

We have here drawn a case which gives a 'stable' Nash equilibrium (in the sense of Friedman 1977). It is later shown that this must always be the case. In

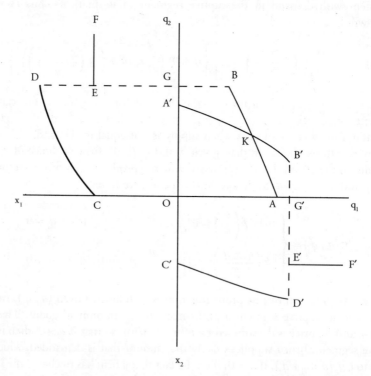

Figure 11.1: Reaction Functions and Equilibrium in a Fragmented Duopoly

Figure 11.1 we also depict firm 2's reaction functions: These are denoted by the same letters with primes on them. The above discussion makes it clear that for analysing the Nash equilibria of a fragmented duopoly we could concentrate exclusively on the NE-quadrant because the reactions in the captive segments (that is, the NW- and SE-quadrants) could be derived mechanically from the happenings in the NE-quadrant.

In the case depicted in Figure 11.1 there is only one Nash equilibrium. But since the reaction functions have breaks it appears as if we can have corner equilibria as in models with fixed costs (example, Spence 1979; Dixit 1979, 1980; Basu and Singh 1990) as illustrated in Figure 11.2. If E_1 had occurred, then firm 1 would be selling OE_1 on the contested segment, whereas firm 2 would be selling only to its captive segment. It can, however, be shown that such equilibria can never arise in this model and in order to have such corner equilibria it may be necessary to introduce some fixed costs (Mishra 1991). It seems to us that in practice, markets do often get partitioned into zones within which each firm acts like a monopolist.[7] However, as things stand, equilibrium is always unique and occurs with both firms supplying to the contested segment.

Let us now take note of a property of the reaction functions which has important implications for our model. Let the function $R_i(q_j)$ denote firm i's optimal [in terms of (11.4)] choice of q_i given that the other firm has chosen q_j. In case there is more than one q_i which satisfies this condition, we shall assume that R_i specifies the smallest of these qs. Thus in Figure 11.1, if $q_2 = OG$, then $R_1(q_2) = 0$.

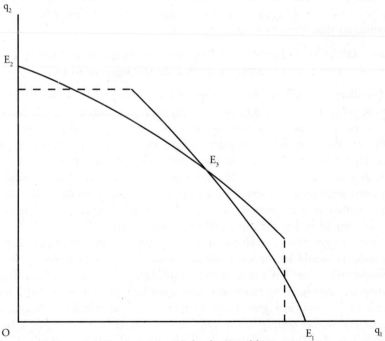

Figure 11.2: Multiple Equilibria

Suppose q_2 is such that $R_1(q_2) > 0$. Hence in maximizing π_1 we could [in equation (11.4)] concentrate on the case where $q_1 > 0$. That is,

$$\pi_1(q_1, q_2) = \left[p \left(\frac{q_1 + q_2}{n_3} \right) - c \right] \left[q_1 + \frac{n_1}{n_3} (q_1 + q_2) \right]$$

Maximizing π_1 with respect to q_1 gives us the following first-order condition:

$$(11.5) \qquad \frac{\partial \pi_1}{\partial q_1} = (p - c)\left(1 + \frac{n_1}{n_3}\right) + \frac{p'}{n_3} \cdot \left[\left(1 + \frac{n_1}{n_3}\right) q_1 + \frac{n_1}{n_3} q_2 \right] = 0.$$

This yields the following theorem.

THEOREM 11.1:   If $R_1(q_2) > 0$,   then $\partial R_1 / \partial q_2 > -1$,

If $R_2(q_1) > 0$,   then $\partial R_2 / \partial q_1 > -1$.

PROOF: See Appendix 11.1

Theorem 11.1 asserts that as long as both firms are operating on the contested segment, a decrease in q_2 by one unit causes an increase in $R_1(q_2)$ by less than one unit; symmetrically, the same applies to firm 2's reaction function.

Using Theorem 11.1 we can quickly establish some corollaries. Observe that our Nash equilibrium must be stable in the sense that the reaction functions intersect in the 'correct' direction. This is because Theorem 1 implies that in the NE-quadrant of Figure 11.1, firm 1's reaction function must be steeper (in magnitude) than firm 2's reaction function.

COROLLARY 11.1: As long as firm 1 operates on the contested market, a fall in q_2 would cause firm 1's supply on its own captive segment to fall.

Corollary 11.1 tells us that the slope of the CD curve will be in the direction shown. To see this, check that, by Theorem 11.1, as q_2 falls $q_2 + R_1(q_2)$ must fall. Hence price in the contested segment rises. Since the firm charges all its customers the same price, the price charged by firm 1 in the captive segment rises. Hence the amount sold on the captive segment must fall.

It is easily shown that if the entire industry (that is, all the captive and contested segments) was served by a monopolist, output would be less than or equal to that in a fragmented duopoly. It follows that price in a fragmented duopoly would be less than or equal to monopoly price.

First, observe that since all consumers are identical, the volume of output in the industry would be the same whether it was served by one monopolist or t monopolists. If firm 1 is a monopolist supplying $n_1 + n_3$ customers and firm 2 a monopolist supplying n_2 customers, firm would supply CA units and 2 would supply OC' units (in Figure 11.1). Hence a single monopolist selling to all n consumers would supply CA + OC' units. Let $(x_1^*, q_1^*, x_2^*, q_2^*)$ be the equilibrium of a fragmented duopoly. If $q_1^* = 0$ or $q_2^* = 0$, then clearly $x_1^* + q_1^*$

$+ x^*_2 + q^*_2 = CA + OC'$. If $(q^*_1, q^*_2) > 0$, that is, the industry is at a point like K, then Theorem 11.1 implies $q^*_1 + q^*_2 > OA$. Since OA is the monopoly output with n_3 buyers, price in the fragmented duopoly equilibrium is less than monopoly price; and output is greater than monopoly output. The above claim, along with Corollary 11.2 below, tells us that, in some sense, a fragmented duopoly lies where we expect it to lie—somewhere *between* a standard duopoly and a monopoly.

Let us now turn to the properties of the Nash equilibrium and do some comparative statics. If with n_2 and n remaining constant n_1 increases, what happens to firm 1's share in the contested market? In other words, how does the size of one's captive segment affect one's share in the contested segment? The next theorem asserts that this relationship is a negative one. There is here an interesting analogy with Fudenberg and Tirole's (1986: 23–4) analysis in which an incumbent firm, planning to deter entry, prefers not to have a large captive segment.

THEOREM 11.2: If n_1 increases with n and n_2 constant, then a Nash equilibrium, (q_1, q_2) where $(q_1, q_2) > 0$, changes such that 1's relative market share in the contested segment falls (that is, q_1/q_2 falls).

Since we are looking at a case where in the Nash equilibrium $(q_1, q_2) > 0$, (q_1, q_2) must satisfy (11.5) and, by symmetry, the following:

(11.6) $$(p - c)\left(1 + \frac{n_2}{n_3}\right) + \frac{p'}{n_3}\cdot\left[\left(1 + \frac{n_2}{n_3}\right)q_2 + \frac{n_2}{n_3}q_1\right] = 0.$$

Equations (11.5) and (11.6) imply

$$\frac{n_1 + n_3}{n_2 + n_3} = \frac{(n_1 + n_3)\,q_1 + n_1 q_2}{(n_2 + n_3)\,q_2 + n_2 q_1}.$$

Cross-multiplying and substituting $n - n_1 - n_2$ for n_3 we get

(11.7) $$\frac{q_1}{q_2} = \frac{n - n_1}{n - n_2}$$

The theorem is immediate.

Just before stating the theorem we claimed that we were going to look into the effect of n_1 on the market share. Clearly, this can be interpreted in several ways. What Theorem 11.2 examined was the effect of n_1 on q_1/q_2 with n_2 and n held constant. What, it may be asked, will be the effect of raising n_1 on q_1/q_2 if n_2 and n_3 are held constant? To answer this, note that (11.7) implies $q_1/q_2 = (n_2 + n_3)/(n_1 + n_3)$. Hence firm 1's market share falls if n_1 increases and n is also increased by the same amount.

Equation (11.7) tells us more than Theorem 11.2. Market shares in the contested segment in a Nash equilibrium are independent of c and approach equality as n increases with n_1 and n_2 constant.

THEOREM 11.3: The equilibrium price does not vary with changes in n_1 and n_2

as long as $n_1 + n_2$ and n remain unchanged, excepting in the special case where the change in n_1 and n_2 causes a firm to enter or withdraw from the contested market.

This is a somewhat surprising result. It asserts that in the determination of the industry's price and output, what matters is how much of the market is contested and how much is captive. Excepting the special case mentioned in the theorem, the exact break-up of the total captive segment into firm 1's and 2's segments is inconsequential.

To prove this, consider first an 'interior solution', that is, $(q_1, q_2) > 0$. Rewriting (11.5) and (11.6), and using (11.7), we get

$$(11.8) \qquad \frac{p'q_1}{p-c} = -(n-(n_1+n_2))\frac{(n-n_1)}{n},$$

$$(11.9) \qquad \frac{p'q_2}{p-c} = -(n-(n_1+n_2))\frac{(n-n_2)}{n}.$$

Writing z for $(q_1 + q_2)/(n - (n_1 + n_2))$, from (11.8) and (11.9) we get

$$(11.10) \qquad z = \frac{p(z)-c}{-p'(z)} \cdot \frac{2n-(n_1+n_2)}{n}.$$

Equation (11.10) implies that z will be unchanged as long as n, $n_1 + n_2$, and c remain unchanged. Since price depends on z, price remains unchanged as long as n, $n_1 + n_2$, and c remain unchanged.

If we have a corner solution, the monopoly price will prevail no matter how the segmentation occurs.

It is interesting to observe that (11.10) implies that we cannot predict the direction of changes in price induced by changes in n or $n_1 + n_2$, unless we impose restrictions on p''. It is easily checked using (11.10) that a rise in $(n_1 + n_2)$ will cause z to fall, and hence price to rise, if $p'' \leq 0$. In other words, as the contested segment becomes smaller, $p'' \leq 0$ is a strongly sufficient condition for the equilibrium price to rise towards the monopoly price. As a standard duopoly is characterized by $n_1 = n_2 = 0$, we also have

COROLLARY 11.2: If $p'' \leq 0$, industry output (price) in a fragmented duopoly will be less (greater) than that in a standard duopoly.

It is possible to use this model to do more comparative statics exercises and deduce other properties, but that is not the aim here. Instead we apply the theory of fragmented duopoly to a problem in backward agriculture and, in that context, explore how the captive segments of the market are established in a two-period setting. But before doing so, we make a brief digression to show how our model may be adapted to allow segment-specific price discrimination.

11.3. FRAGMENTED DUOPOLY WITH PRICE DISCRIMINATION

Let us assume, as before, that seller i chooses q_i and x_i but that he is free to set the price in his captive market, wherever he wishes.

Given profit-maximizing behaviour and given q_1, q_2, x_i, firm i will set a price of $p(x_i/n_i)$ in its captive market, and in the contested market, price will be given by $p((q_1 + q_2)/n_3)$. If we continue to assume a constant marginal cost, then all the segments get completely dismembered and equilibrium can be worked out separately for each. The monopoly price, p^m, will be charged in each of the captive segments, while the standard duopoly price will hold in the contested segment.

The problem is much more interesting if we suppose that firm i's total cost function, $c_i(\cdot)$, is increasing and convex. Firm i's profit, $\hat{\pi}_i$, is given as follows:

$$\hat{\pi}_i(q_1, q_2, x_i) = p\left(\frac{x_i}{n_i}\right) \cdot x_i + p\left(\frac{q_1 + q_2}{n_3}\right) q_i - c_i(q_i + x_i), \quad i = 1, 2.$$

Firm i maximizes this by choosing q_i and x_i. Its first-order conditions are:

(11.11)
$$\frac{x_i}{n_i} p'\left(\frac{x_i}{n_i}\right) + \left(\frac{x_i}{n_i}\right) = c_i'(q_i + n_i)$$

and

(11.12)
$$\frac{q_i}{n_3} p'\left(\frac{q_1 + q_2}{n_3}\right) + \left(\frac{q_1 + q_2}{n_3}\right) = c_i'(q_i + n_i).$$

The *Nash equilibrium* of a *price-discriminating fragmented duopoly* is given by the (x_1, q_1, x_2, q_2) derived from solving the four equations described by (11.11) and (11.12) and by setting i equal to 1 and 2.

Comparative-statics results may be derived in much the same way as in the previous section. For example, assuming that the marginal revenue curve is downward sloping [that is, the left-hand term in (11.11) falls as x_i rises and the left-hand term in (11.12) falls as q_i rises], Corollary 1 can be derived even for the price-discrimination model. Moreover, following Bulow et al. (1985), this model can be used to illustrate some surprising results, like how a subsidy in the captive segment of a seller can actually result in the seller being worse-off in equilibrium. With these remarks we turn to the analysis of agrarian relations and the determination of the size of the captive and contested segments. We return to the subject of price discrimination Section 11.5.

11.4. SUBGAME PERFECTION IN A TWO-PERIOD MODEL OF AGRARIAN RELATIONS

Since n_1 and n_2 influence the outcome of the one-period fragmented duopoly described in Sections 11.2 and 11.3, it is but natural that firms will try to influence n_1 and n_2 to the extent that they can. For the sake of illustration, consider a rural economy with n labourers and two landlords. In period 1, each landlord i decides on the number, n_i, of labourers he will employ on his land. [8] In period 2 the landlords supply credit to them and to the contested segment of the market for loans. This periodization reflects more the priorities of decision than the actual sequence of time. Moreover, in reality period 2 will be further split up involving a first subperiod when the loan is received by the labourers and a second subperiod when the wage is received and the principal and interest is repaid. We, however, ignore this further temporal partitioning of period 2.

We shall assume—and this is not unrealistic—that each landlord has the power to forbid his employees from taking credit from the other landlord. Further, this is in a setting where everybody knows everybody and the landlords consider it safe to give credit to any labourer from this set of villages. Thus the n_1 and n_2 chosen in period 1 become parameters in the second period in the fragmented credit market. Moreover n_1 and n_2 have the same significance as the n_1 and n_2 in Sections 2 and 3 above since landlord i can lend to $n_i + n_3$ labourers where $n_3 = n - n_1 - n_2$.

It is immediately clear that in this model landlord i may hire employees not just to work as labourers but keeping in mind that a larger n_i alters the kind of leverage he has in the credit market. Hence this theory provides a rationale for interlinkage, albeit of a very different kind from the ones found in the literature (for example, Braverman and Srinivasan 1981; Braverman and Stiglitz 1982; Basu 1983; Mitra 1983; Bell 1988).

The natural solution criterion to use in such a two-period model is that of subgame perfection. We shall first give an abstract characterization of this and then scrutinize a special case.

Let landlord i's production function be

$$X_i = X_i(n_i), \ X_i' \geq 0, \quad X_i'' \leq 0$$

To keep the model simple, we assume that labourers have access to other employment opportunities at an exogenous wage, w. In period 2 each landlord earns profits from production and interest from the credit market depending on what Nash equilibrium emerges from a fragmented duopoly characterized by n_1 and n_2.

In order to state this more formally, note that if in a fragmented duopoly n and c are fixed, the fragmented duopoly is defined entirely by (n_1, n_2).

Let us now define a Nash equilibrium correspondence, N, as follows. For every pair of non-negative integers n_1 and n_2 such that $n_1 + n_2 \leq n$,

$N(n_1, n_2) \equiv \{(q_1, q_2)|(q_1, q_2)$ is a Nash equilibrium in a fragmented duopoly defined by $(n_1, n_2)\}$.

A specification of which Nash equilibrium will occur in period 2 for each game (n_1, n_2) is a *selection*, f, from the Nash equilibrium correspondence N. That is, $f(n_1, n_2)$ is an element of $N(n_1, n_2)$, for all (n_1, n_2).

Given that c represents the opportunity cost of giving credit and p is the price of credit, we could use π_i as defined in Section 11.2 to be i's profit function in period 2.

For every selection, f, from the correspondence N, we can define each player's profit in the two-period game (assuming zero discounting) as

$$(11.13) \qquad \Omega_i(n_1, n_2, f) = X_i(n_i) - wn_i + \pi_i(f(n_1, n_2)), \quad i = 1, 2,$$

where the absence of price discrimination in the credit market implies that all labourers will pay the same price and hence that both landlords will pay their labourers the exogenous wage w.

The triple (n_1^*, n_2^*, f^*) is a (subgame-) perfect equilibrium if and only if

$$\Omega_1(n_1^*, n_2^*, f^*) \geqq \Omega_1(n_1, n_2^*, f^*) \qquad \text{for all } n_1, \text{ and}$$

$$\Omega_2(n_1^*, n_2^*, f^*) \geqq \Omega_2(n_1^*, n_2, f^*) \qquad \text{for all } n_2.$$

Distorting terminology slightly, we may refer to (n_1^*, n_2^*) as a 'perfect equilibrium' if there exists an f^* such that (n_1^*, n_2^*, f^*) is a perfect equilibrium.

In this setting, labourers are fully rational and make their choices after evaluating the consequences of joining one or other of the captive segments of the market, as opposed to dealing in the contested segment. However, we assume that n is large and labourers do not collude, so that each takes the pattern of segmentation (n_1, n_2) as exogenously given. As noted above, the assumption of a constant marginal cost of funds, c, for both landlords implies that the monopoly price p^m, is independent of the size of each captive market. Hence, if the labourer conjectures that the market will contain no contested segmented (i.e., $n_1 + n_2 = n$), he will face a price p^m from both landlords; and since the wage is exogenously given, he will, therefore, be indifferent between them. If, on the other hand, there is a contested segment, then in the absence of price discrimination, the same price will rule everywhere; and again he will be indifferent as to which segment he joins. That is to say, an interlinked wage and credit contract with either landlord will yield a labourer the same utility as an unbundled deal. Thus, although labourers are not strategic in the sense that the actual choice of n_i is effectively in the hands of the landlords alone, they are fully rational. In brief we model labourers in the same way as consumers are modelled in oligopoly theory.

We analyse the perfect equilibria of the two-period game in the special case where the demand schedule of an individual consumer is linear over the relevant range of outcomes:

$$(11.14) \qquad p = a - bq.$$

We assume that n is so large and the marginal product of labour, that is, $X_i'(n_i)$, falls so fast that landlords 1 and 2 will never choose n_1 and n_2 for which there is a Nash equilibrium where one firm abandons the contested segment totally. Hence, we could focus on the unique 'interior' Nash equilibrium that occurs for each relevant (n_1, n_2). Let $f(n_1, n_2)$ refer to such a Nash equilibrium.

Using (11.5), (11.6), and (11.14), we get

$$(11.15) \qquad \pi_i(f(n_1, n_2)) = \frac{(a-c)^2}{b} \cdot \frac{(n-n_j)n^2}{(3n-n_1-n_2)^2}, \qquad i = 1, 2.$$

Hence, using $\bar{\Omega}_i(n_1, n_2)$ to denote $\Omega_i(n_1, n_2, f)$ we have

$$(11.16) \quad \bar{\Omega}_i(n_1, n_2) = [X_i(n_i) - wn_i] + \left[\frac{(a-c)^2}{b} \cdot \frac{(n-n_i)n^2}{(3n-n_1-n_2)^2} \right], \quad i = 1, 2.$$

Clearly, if n_1^* and n_2^* are such that n_1^* maximizes $\bar{\Omega}_1(n_1, n_2^*)$ and n_2^* maximizes $\bar{\Omega}_2(n_1^*, n_2)$, then (n_1^*, n_2^*) is a perfect equilibrium.

The first interesting feature of the perfect equilibrium to note is that in equilibrium each landlord will be employing labour up to a point where the wage rate exceeds the marginal product of labour. Let $\hat{n}_i$ be such that

$$X_i'(\hat{n}_i) = w.$$

It is easy to see that for all n_2, and all $n_1 < \hat{n}_1$, $\bar{\Omega}_1(\hat{n}_1, n_2) > \bar{\Omega}(n_1, n_2)$. At $n_1 = \hat{n}_1$ a further increase in n_1 causes $\bar{\Omega}_1$ to rise since, at this point, the first expression within brackets in (16) is stationary and the second expression is rising. Hence, landlords always employ in excess of what pure marginal productivity and wage considerations would lead them to do. This result is quite in keeping with Klemperer's (1987b) finding of heightened competition in the 'first' period. It could also be thought of as providing a rationale for the idea that landlords have a penchant for maintaining an excessive number of dependent labourers (see, for example, Bhaduri 1983). In addition, this model gives some new insight into the phenomenon of disguised unemployment and surplus labour, since it is possible for marginal product to be not only less than w, but even zero (if X_i' vanishes for finite n_i).

From the first-order conditions of maximizing $\bar{\Omega}_1(n_1, n_2)$ with respect to n_1 and $\bar{\Omega}_2(n_1, n_2)$ with respect to n_2 and denoting the equilibrium values with a star, we have

$$X_1'(n_1^*) + \frac{2(a-c)^2 n^2(n-n_2^*)}{b(3n - n_1^* - n_2^*)^3} = w$$

and

$$X_2'(n_2^*) + \frac{2(a-c)^2 n^2(n-n_1^*)}{b(3n - n_1^* - n_2^*)^3} = w.$$

These, in turn, imply

$$(11.17) \quad \frac{X_1'(n_1^*) - w}{X_2'(n_2^*) - w} = \frac{n - n_2^*}{n - n_1^*}$$

Hence, if $n_2^* > n_1^*$, then $X_1'(n_1^*) > X_2'(n_2^*)$, since from the reasoning above we know that $X_i'(n_1^*) - w < 0$, $i = 1,2$. It is important to appreciate that this is true though the production functions of the two landlords need not be the same. If we use the extent of divergence of $X_i'(n_i^*)$ from w as an index of production inefficiency, then what we have established is that larger farms (in terms of numbers of workers employed) are the ones exhibiting greater production inefficiency. Also, larger farms have larger shares of the contested segment of the credit market,[9] and hence are larger overall.

11.5. EQUILIBRIUM IN AGRARIAN MARKETS WITH PRICE DISCRIMINATION

If landlords can practice price discrimination, the labourer who accepts an interlinked contract by going into a captive segment of the credit market knows that he will be charged the monopoly price, p^m, which exceeds that in the contested segment, p^o, should one exist.[10] Thus, in order to make an interlinked contract attractive to labourers, landlords will have to offer a wage premium, δ say, in compensation for the higher rate of interest. Landlords are, therefore, constrained by the utility equivalence condition

(11.18) $v(p^m, w + \delta) = v(p^o, w)$,

where $v(.)$ is the indirect utility of a labourer.

In this case, (11.13) becomes

(11.13′) $\Omega i(n_1, n_2, f) = [Xi(n_i) - (w + \delta)n_i] + \pi_i(f(n_1, n_2))$

with the reminder that f now pertains to the Nash equilibrium as in Section 11.3 (that is, with price discrimination allowed).

(11.19) $\pi_i(f(n_1, n_2)) = n_i p^m \cdot q(p^m) + p\left(\dfrac{q_1 + q_2}{n_3}\right) \cdot q_i - c(n_i q(p^m) + q_i)$,

where $(q_1, q_2) = f(n_1, n_2)$.

With a linear demand function,

$$p^m = (a + c)/2 \text{ and } q^m = (a - c)/2b.$$

In a standard duopoly, with $n_3 = n - n_1 - n_2$ given exogenously,

$$p^o = (a + 2c)/3 \text{ and } q^o = (q_1^o + q_2^o)/n_3 = 2(a - c)/3b,$$

and by symmetry,

$$q_1^o = q_2^o = n_3 q^o/2.$$

Substituting for $(p^m, q^m, p^o, q_1^o, q_2^o)$ in (11.19), some manipulation yields

(11.20) $\pi_i(f(n_1, n_2)) = \dfrac{(a - c)^2}{b} \cdot \left(\dfrac{5n_i - 4n_j}{36} + \dfrac{n}{9}\right)$ $i = 1, 2$ $i \neq j$,

which, unlike (11.15), is linear in (n_1, n_2).

The next step is to obtain the wage premium δ from (11.18). While the value of δ depends on $v(.)$, it follows at once from the fact that (p^m, p^o, w) are all independent of (n_1, n_2) that δ must be likewise. Hence, substituting for $\pi_i(\cdot)$ from (11.20) in (11.13′), we have

(11.21) $\bar{\Omega}_i(n_1, n_2) = [X_i(n_i) - (w + \delta)n_i] + \dfrac{(a - c)^2}{b} \cdot \left(\dfrac{5n_i - 4n_j}{36} + \dfrac{n}{9}\right)$, $i = 1, 2$.

As in Section 11.4, in equilibrium each landlord will be employing labour to a point where the wage rate (including the premium δ in this case) exceeds the marginal product of labour. For when $[X_i(n_i) - (w + \delta)n_i]$ is stationary, π_i is increasing in n_i. Denoting the values of (n_1, n_2) in equilibrium with a star, we have, from (11.21),

$$(11.22) \qquad X_i'(n_i^*) = (w + \delta) - \frac{5}{36}\frac{(a-c)^2}{b}, \qquad i = 1, 2.$$

Hence, unlike the case without price discrimination, the marginal product of labour is identical on the farms of both landlords.

This result is not very surprising in the light of the fact that the assumption of constant marginal costs makes all the parameters of an individual's wage and credit contracts independent of the pattern of market segmentation, if landlords can practice price discrimination. As we saw in Section 11.3, the cost functions (in this case for lending) must be increasing and convex for interesting situations to arise from the one-period game with (n_1, n_2) fixed. It is certainly plausible that the cost of lending, for example, is increasing and convex with the size of the captive market, since the landlord must prevent each of his captive clients from borrowing from the other landlord in period 2 and recover monopoly interest charges from them subsequently.

11.6. RENT DISSIPATION

There remains the question of whether competition for captive segments of the market in period 1 will more than dissipate the rents from lock-in in period 2 (Klemperer 1987a). Suppose, therefore, that interlinking was banned. In a standard duopoly with $n_1 = n_2 = 0$ and $n_3 = n$, the profit of each landlord from moneylending is, under the above assumptions about costs and demand,

$$(11.23) \qquad \pi_i^\circ = n(a - c)^2/9b.$$

In this case, the total profit of landlord i in equilibrium is

$$(11.24) \qquad \Omega_i^\circ = [X_i(\hat{n}_i) - w\hat{n}_i] + n(a - c)^2/9b,$$

where $X_i'(\hat{n}_i) = w$. Subtracting (11.24) from (11.21), we obtain

$$(11.25) \qquad \bar{\Omega}_i(n_1^*, n_2^*) - \Omega_i^\circ = [X_i(n_i^*) - wn_i^*] - [X_i(\hat{n}_i) - w\hat{n}_i] - \delta n_i^*$$
$$+ \frac{(a-c)^2}{b}\left(\frac{5n_i^* - 4n_j^*}{36}\right), \qquad i = 1, 2.$$

Since $\hat{n}_i$ maximizes $[X_i(n_i) - wn_i]$,

$$\xi_i \equiv [X_i(n_i^*) - wn_i^*] - [X_i(\hat{n}_i) - w\hat{n}_i] < 0$$

and the (algebraic) sum of the first three terms on the right-hand side of (11.25) is negative.

Now suppose that one landlord (1, say) has more land than the other, so that, by virtue of (11.22) and an assumption that land and labour are complementary, $n_1^* > n_2^*$. Now, if the difference in holdings is such that $n_2^* \leq 4n_1^*/5$, it follows at once that the landlord who has the smaller holding would be better-off if interlinking were banned.

In order to examine whether the combined rents from lock-in of both landlords are more than fully dissipated by heightened competition for captive segments in period 1, we sum over i in (11.25) and obtain

(11.26) $\sum_i [\bar{\Omega}_i (n_1^*, n_2^*) - \Omega_i^{\circ}(n_1, n_2)] = (\xi_1 + \xi_2) - (n_1^* + n_2^*) [\delta (a - c)^2/36b].$

Since $\xi_i < 0$, a strongly sufficient condition for the said rents to be more than dissipated is

(11.27) $\delta > (a - c)^2/36b.$

Now the loss in an individual's net consumer surplus that results from being charged the monopoly price as opposed to the duopoly price is

$$(p^m - p^\circ) (q^m + q^\circ)/2 = 7(a - c)^2/72b > (a - c)^2/36b.$$

Hence, as δ is the compensating variation with respect to the increase in price from p° to p^m, (11.27) will indeed hold if consumption in each period is a non-inferior good for a labourer. We have, therefore, shown that rents from second period lock-in can be more than dissipated in our model, a possibility which appears in other models in the related literature.

By way of comparison, we now examine whether this result will hold if landlords cannot practice price discrimination. Summing (11.18) over i and subtracting $(\Omega_1^{\circ} + \Omega_2^{\circ})$, we obtain, in this case,

(11.28) $\sum_i [\bar{\Omega}_i (n_1^*, n_2^*) - \Omega_i^{\circ}(n_1, n_2)] = (\xi_1 + \xi_2) + \dfrac{(a - c)^2 n}{b} \left[\dfrac{n(n + n_3^*)}{(2n + n_3^*)^2} - \dfrac{1}{9} \right].$

Since $9n(n + n_3^*) > (2n + n_3^*)^2$, strong claims about whether rents are more than fully dissipated cannot be made without knowledge of the shape of $X_i(n)$ over the domain $(\hat{n}_i, n_i^*)$, all of which determine the magnitude of ξ_i. We leave this as an open question.

11.7. CONCLUSION

This chapter started by analysing a market structure in which each firm has a *predetermined* set of potential customers. These sets may overlap but they need not coincide totally with one another. Such a structure could emerge in a location-model of oligopoly, but it emerges more naturally in trades where the problem of asymmetric information and moral hazard is high. Such markets were referred to as fragmented oligopolies, and the basic properties of a fragmented duopoly were analysed formally. The next step was to make each firm's set of potential customers endogenous by embedding a fragmented duopoly in a two-period model and then examine its perfect equilibrium. This was done in the context of labour and credit markets in backward agrarian economies. There emerged a rationale for interlinking, albeit of a sort quite different from that advanced in the extant literature on that subject.

Fragmented oligopolies, it was argued, are relevant in a wide variety of situations. The particular model constructed in this chapter was meant to be illustrative. By considering alternative strategy sets for firms and different solution concepts, a range of different models of fragmented oligopoly can be constructed. There is, in brief, room for much further exploration.

APPENDIX 11.1. PROOF OF THEOREM 11.1

Given the symmetric nature of the two parts of Theorem 11.1, it is clearly sufficient to prove either.

From the second-order condition we have

(A11.1) $\quad \dfrac{\partial^2 \pi_1}{\partial q_1^2} = 2\dfrac{p'}{n_3} \cdot \left(1 + \dfrac{n_1}{n_3}\right) + \dfrac{p''}{n_3^2} \cdot \left[\left(1 + \dfrac{n_1}{n_3}\right) q_1 + \dfrac{n_1}{n_3} q_2\right] < 0.$

Taking total differentials in (11.5), we get

$$p' \cdot \left(\dfrac{dq_1}{n_3} + \dfrac{dq_2}{n_3}\right)\left(1 + \dfrac{n_1}{n_3}\right) \dfrac{p''}{n_3} \cdot \left(\dfrac{dq_1}{n_3} + \dfrac{dq_2}{n_3}\right)\left[\left(1 + \dfrac{n_1}{n_3}\right) q_1 + \dfrac{n_1}{n_3} q_2\right]$$

$$+ \dfrac{p'}{n_3} \cdot \left[\left(1 + \dfrac{n_1}{n_3}\right) dq_1 + \dfrac{n_1}{n_3} dq_2\right] = 0.$$

Rearranging terms this may be rewritten as

(A11.2) $\quad \dfrac{dq_1}{dq_2} = -\dfrac{2\dfrac{p'}{n_3} \cdot \left(1 + \dfrac{n_1}{n_3}\right) + \dfrac{p''}{n_3^2} \cdot \left[\left(1 + \dfrac{n_1}{n_3}\right) q_1 + \dfrac{n_1}{n_3} q_2\right] - \dfrac{p'}{n_3}}{2\dfrac{p'}{n_3} \cdot \left(1 + \dfrac{n_1}{n_3}\right) + \dfrac{p''}{n_3^2} \cdot \left[\left(1 + \dfrac{n_1}{n_3}\right) q_1 + \dfrac{n_1}{n_3} q_2\right]}.$

Given (A.1) and $p' < 0$, it follows that $(dq_1/dq_2) > -1$. Since (11.5) implicitly defines the reaction function $R_1(\cdot)$, we have proved Theorem 11.1.

NOTES

1. See Bhaduri (1983), Basu (1983), Bardhan (1984), Platteau and Abraham (1987).
2. Such a model is developed in Basu (1987) where the rural credit market is modelled as a collection of independent credit islands.
3. Trust plays an important role not only in backward markets but in a whole range of interactions in any economy: see Dasgupta (1986).
4. This was revealed in conversations between commission agents and Bell in the course of fieldwork in Andhra Pradesh and Punjab, India.
5. This ought not to be confused with the concept of 'contestable' markets in the literature.
6. We assume throughout that $\max_{x_i} [p(x_i/n_i) - c]x_i > 0$, for $i = 1$ or 2. This ensures that production is profitable.
7. Recall that in this model both monopolists will charge the same price, since customers

are identical. If, however, we allow for heterogeneity among customers, then the prices may be different.

8. We shall assume that the parameters of the model are such that firm 1's chosen n_1 and firm 2's chosen n_2 never sum to greater than n.

9. From (11.5) and (11.6), we get $(q_1/q_2) = (n-n_1^*)/(n-n2^*)$. Substituting into (11.15) yields the required result.

10. This argument uses subgame perfection which rules out the possibility of landlords committing themselves to some price different from p^m.

REFERENCES

Bardhan, P.K. 1984. *Land, Labor and Rural Poverty*. New York: Columbia University Press.

Basu, K. 1983. 'The Emergence of Isolation and Interlinkage in Rural Markets'. *Oxford Economic Papers* 35: 262–80.

———. 1987. 'Disneyland Monopoly, Interlinkage and Usurious Interest Rates'. *Journal of Public Economics* 34: 1–18.

Basu, K. and N.Singh, 1990. 'Entry-deterrence in Stackelberg Perfect Equilibria'. *International Economic Review* 31: 61–71.

Bell, C. 1988. 'Credit Markets and Interlinked Transactions'. In H.B. Chenery and T.N. Srinivasan, eds, *Handbook of Development Economics*. Amsterdam: North-Holland.

Bhaduri, A. 1983. *The Economic Structure of Backward Agriculture*. London: Academic Press.

Bonanno, G. 1987. 'Location Choice, Product Proliferation and Entry Deterrence'. *Review of Economic Studies* 54: 37–45.

Braverman, A. and T.N. Srinivasan. 1981. 'Credit and Sharecropping in Agrarian Societies'. *Journal of Development Economics* 9: 289–312.

Braverman, A. and J.E. Stilitz. 1982. 'Sharecropping and the Interlinking of Agrarian Markets'. *American Economic Review* 72: 695–715.

Bulow, J.I., J.D. Geanakoplos, and P.D. Klemperer. 1985. 'Multimarket Oliogopoly: Strategic Substitutes and Complements'. *Journal of Political Economy* 93: 488–511.

Dasgupta, P. 1986. 'Trust as a Commodity'. Economic Theory Discussion Paper No. 101. Cambridge University, Cambridge.

D'Aspremont, C., J.J. Gabszewicz, and J.F. Thisse. 1979. 'On Hotelling's Stability in Competition'. *Econometrica* 47: 1145–50.

Dixit, A. 1979. 'A Model of Duopoly Suggesting a Theory of Entry Barriers'. *Bell Journal of Economics* 10: 20–32.

——— 1980. 'The Role of Investment in Entry-deterrence'. *Economic Journal* 90: 95-106.

Friedman, J. 1977. *Oligopoly and the Theory of Games*. Amsterdam: North-Holland.

Fudenberg, D. and J. Tirole. 1986. 'Dynamic Models of Oligopoly'. London: Harwood Academic Publishers.

Geertz, C. 1978. 'The Bazaar Economy: Information and Search in Peasant Marketing'. *American Economic Review* 68: 28–32.

Hotelling, H. 1929. Stability in competition, *Economic Journal* 39, 41–57.

Klemperer, P.D. 1987a. 'The Competitiveness of Markets with Switching Costs'. *Rand Journal of Economics* 18: 138–50.

——— 1987b. 'Markets with Consumer Switching Costs'. *Quarterly Journal of Economics* 102: 375–94.

Mishra, A. 1991. 'Clientelization and Fragmentation in Backward Agriculture: A Model Based on Forward Induction'. Delhi School of Economics. New Delhi. Mimeo

Mitra, P. 1983. 'A Theory of Interlinked Rural Transactions'. *Journal of Public Economics* 20: 169–91.

Platteau, J.P. and A. Abraham. 1987. 'An Inquiry into Quasi-credit Systems in Traditional Fisherman Communities: The Role of Reciprocal Credit and Mixed Contracts'. *Journal of Development Studies* 23: 461–90.

RBI (Reserve Bank of India). 1954. All India Rural Credit Survey, Vol. 1, Part 2 (Credit Agencies). RBI Bombay.

Spence, A.M. 1977. 'Entry, Capacity, Investment and Oligopolistic Pricing'. *Bell Journal of Economics* 8: 534–44.

von Weizsäcker, C.C. 1984. 'The Costs of Substitution'. *Econometrica* 52: 1085–116.

12 The Broth and the Cooks
A Theory of Surplus Labour

12.1. THE PROBLEM

Broadly speaking, an economy is said to have surplus labour or disguised unemployment if it is possible to remove a part of its employed labour force without causing a decline in the aggregate output. Although the subject had distant roots (Robinson 1937; Navarrete and Navarrete 1951), it was given a lucid theoretical structure by Sen in the mid-1960s (Sen 1966). The subject of surplus labour was once the centre of debates on subsistence economies and agrarian structure and had generated an enormous literature.[1] These models, however, were increasingly called into question and interest in the subject faded out.

The present chapter revisits this old subject in the belief that we can rigorously define and explain surplus labour by drawing on recent advances in the theory of efficiency wage. I am referring here to the class of efficiency-wage models which originate in Leibenstein's (1957,1958) work and will refer to these writings as the efficiency-wage literature.[2] The basic axiom used in this literature is that in low-income economies there exists a positive relation between the wages received by laboures and their productivity.

The suggestion that this basic axiom can explain surplus labour is not new. It was, in fact, an important motivation for Leibenstein's original exploration (see also Mazumdar 1959; Wonnacott 1962).[3] As the efficiency-wage literature advanced, however, it become clear that the basic axiom cannot explain surplus labour or disguised unemployment within the context of these models. It may

From *World Development* 20 (1), 1992: 109–117.

I am grateful to A.L Nagar, Siddiq Osmani, and Martin Ravallion for comments and discussion. The chapter benefited from a seminar at the Australian National University, Canberra.

be true that the withdrawal of a part of the labour force causes wages to rise and in turn causes the remaining laboures to be more productive. But it is very easy to show that in the existing models (example, Mirrlees 1975) this increased productivity can never be enough to fully compensate for the withdrawn labourers (see Basu 1984). What the efficiency-wage literature can explain well is open unemployment and recent focus has been in that direction.

The basic axiom, it will be argued here provides a basis for surplus labour. The efficiency-wage literature fails to explain surplus labour because whenever it uses the basic axiom it uses it in conjunction with another assumption, to wit, that the positive relation between wage and labour productivity is perceived fully at the level of each employer. I shall refer to this as the perception axiom.

To place the present model in perspective, it may be mentioned that there are related papers (example, Agarwala 1979; Stiglitz 1976; Guha 1989) which manage to explain surplus labour. Guha (1989), for instance, has in a lucid paper used a similar framework to explain surplus labour, although his argument is different from the one developed here. In Stiglitz (1976) also, there is a case where surplus labour can occur, but only when production is organized in family farms in which income is divided equally among the members.

It will be argued in this chapter that the basic axiom and the perception axiom are independent and there are situations where, even though the basic axiom is valid, the perception axiom is untenable. This is true somewhat in the same way that the aggregate demand curve faced by a perfectly competitive industry happens to be downward sloping even though it is not perceived to be so by each individual firm in the industry. Note that there is a time-lag, often quite long, between wages and productivity[4] (see Bliss and Stern 1978; Dasgupta and Ray 1991; Osmani 1991). Hence, in markets where landlords face a high labour turnover, there may be little relation between the wage paid by a particular landlord and the productivity of his or her workers even though the basic axiom may be valid at the aggregate level, that is between the equilibrium market wage and average productivity of labourers.[5] The extreme example is provided by the casual labour market where labourers are hired afresh each day. I shall assume that the casual labour market is one where there is no relation between wage and productivity at the level of each landlord and model this in Section 12.3. Not only does the casual labour market provide an analytically convenient polar case, but the widespread existence of casual labour markets in reality (see Binswanger and Rosenzweig 1984; Dreze and Mukherjee 1987) makes this model of some practical interest.[6]

The polar case provides a plausible and theoretically consistent explanation of surplus labour, raises some interesting policy issues (Section 12.4), and demonstrates the importance of modelling a case that has been ignored in the literature, where the basic axiom is valid but the perception axiom is not.

What happens between the two polar cases of the efficiency-wage literature and the model of Section 12.3, that is, where the wage–productivity link is not totally absent at the micro level but neither is it fully captured as required by the perception axiom? This issue is explored in Section 12.5. It is argued that in this case both open and disguised unemployment can be explained. Clearly, the exaggerated view of the non-existence of disguised unemployment originated from the fact that the entire efficiency-wage literature considers the polar case, which is also the only case, where disguised unemployment cannot occur.

In the theory that is constructed in this chapter, although the basic axiom is true, each employer may have little or no incentive to resist wage cuts. Such a possibility is consistent with experience (Rudra 1982; Dreze and Mukherjee 1987) and suggests that for explaining rigidities we may have to turn to labourers' preference and behaviour, rather than those of employers.

12.2. BASIC CONCEPTS

In this chapter we distinguish between efficiency units of labour, hours of labour, and labourers.[7] Efficiency units capture the idea of labour productivity. Production depends on the number of efficiency units of labour used. The number of efficiency units that emerges from each hour of labour depends on the wage rate (per hour), w, that the labourer earns:[8]

(12.1) $h = h(w),\ h'(w) \geq 0$

This assertion is usually justified on the grounds that w determines consumption and since we are referring to poor and malnourished labourers, it is natural to suppose that as a labourer's consumption rises so does his or her fitness and productivity (Leibenstein 1957, 1958).[9] It will be assumed throughout that there exist real numbers c and d such that, for all $w \leq c,\ h(w) = 0;$ for all

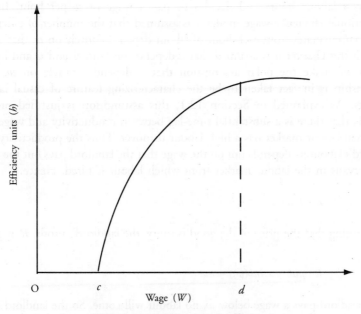

Figure 12.1: Wage and efficiency

w such that $c \leq w < d$, $h'(w) > 0$ and $h''(w) < 0$ and for all $w \geq d$, $h'(w) = 0$. In other words, there is a sufficiently low wage below which a labourer is totally unproductive; and h does not rise endlessly with w. For sufficiently high wages the relation ceases to be positive. A typical $h(\cdot)$ function is represented in Figure 12.1.

The output produced on a landlord's farm depends on the number of efficiency units of labour that are employed. If n hours of labour are employed and each hour of labour produces h efficiency units, then output, x, is given by:

$$(12.2) \qquad x = x\,(nh), x' \geq 0, x'' \leq 0.$$

It will be assumed that, for all real numbers r for which $x'(r) > 0$, it must be the case that $x''\,(r) < 0$.

12.3. A SIMPLE MODEL: THE CASUAL LABOUR MARKET

Consider a poor agrarian economy with k identical landlords and t identical labourers. The model is built in two stages. At first it is assumed that the market wage is somehow fixed at $\tilde{w}$. Each landlord believes he or she can hire as many labourers as desired at $\tilde{w}$. Using this assumption, the landlord's behaviour is modelled. This is referred to as the 'partial equilibrium' model. The second stage consists of endogenously explaining the market wage $\tilde{w}$ and is referred to as the 'general equilibrium'.

12.3.1. Partial Equilibrium

Let $\tilde{w}$ be the exogenously given market wage. Suppose a landlord decides to employ n labour hours and decides to pay a wage of w per hour. In the conventional efficiency-wage model it is assumed that the number of efficiency units that emanates from each hour of labour depends entirely on w, that is $h = h(w)$. In this chapter it is assumed that h depends on both w and $\tilde{w}$ and in this section we make the polar assumption that h depends entirely on $\tilde{w}$. This relationship is in fact taken to be the characterizing feature of casual labour markets. As explained in Section 12.1, this assumption is justified on the grounds that there is a substantial time-lag between productivity and wage and the casual labour market has a high labour turnover. Thus the productivity of a landlord's labourers depends not on the wage that the landlord pays but the wage that prevails in the labour market from which labour is hired. Hence,

$$(12.3) \qquad h = h(\tilde{w})$$

Assuming that the price of the good is unity, the landlord's profit, R, is given by:

$$(12.4) \qquad R\,(n,w) = x\,(nh(\tilde{w})) - nw$$

If the landlord pays a wage below $\tilde{w}$, no labour will come. So the landlord's aim is to maximize $R\,(n,w)$ subject to $w \geq \tilde{w}$.

It is easy to see that the landlord would like to pay as low a wage as possible. Hence he or she sets wage equal to $\tilde{w}$. Having done so, the landlord chooses n to maximize $R(n, \tilde{w})$. Clearly the value of n depends on $\tilde{w}$. So we write

(12.5) $n = n(\tilde{w})$

Since $n(\tilde{w})$ maximizes $R(n, \tilde{w})$, hence, using the first-order condition, we know:

(12.6) $x'(n(\tilde{w})h(\tilde{w})) = \dfrac{\tilde{w}}{h(\tilde{w})}$

Given equation (12.5) we can compute the aggregate employment in the economy by simply multiplying $n(\tilde{w})$ by k. This completes our description of the partial equilibrium. If the wage prevailing in the labour market is $\tilde{w}$, then each landlord pays a wage of $\tilde{w}$ and hires $n(\tilde{w})$ hours of labour, where $n(\tilde{w})$ is defined implicitly by equation (12.6). Our next task is to enquire into the determination of $\tilde{w}$.

12.3.2. General Equilibrium

In Section 12.3.1 we learned to compute the total demand for labour, given an exogenous $\tilde{w}$. If we do this experiment for different values of $\tilde{w}$, we derive the aggregate demand function for labour:

(12.7) $D = kn(\tilde{w})$,

where D is the total demand for labour.

To derive the equilibrium market wage, $\tilde{w}$, we have only to specify the

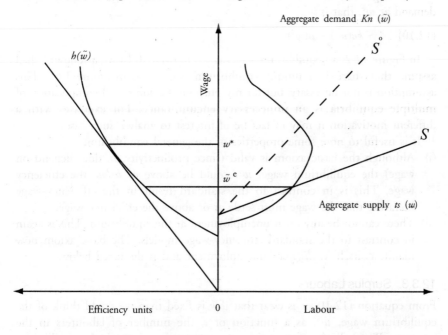

Figure 12.2: Aggregate Demand for and Supply of Labour

aggregate supply curve of labour and then find the wage at which demand equals supply. Before going on to such an exercise, let us analyse the shape of the demand curve. The basic axiom renders the shape unusual and our subsequent theorems require us to examine this anomaly.

It is useful to begin by locating what is known in the traditional literature as the efficiency wage, which is the wage at which $w/h(w)$ is minimized. We shall denote such a wage by w^*. In the left half of Figure 12.2, we reproduce the h-function of Figure 12.1 and illustrate the efficiency wage, w^*, clearly the point where the 'average' and the 'marginal' of the h-function coincide.

It will now be shown that for all $\tilde{w} \geq w^*$, the aggregate demand curve is downward sloping in the usual way, that is $\delta D/\delta\tilde{w} < 0$. Note that if $\tilde{w} \geq w^*$, then an increase in $\tilde{w}$ causes $\tilde{w}/h(\tilde{w})$ to rise. Since $x'' < 0$, it follows from equation (6) that as $\tilde{w}$ rises, $n(\tilde{w})h(\tilde{w})$ must fall. Since $h'(\tilde{w})>0$, it follows that $n(\tilde{w})$ falls. Thus $kn(\tilde{w})$ falls. This proof is easily verified geometrically in Figure 12.2. For $\tilde{w} < w^*$, an increase in $\tilde{w}$ could cause an increase or decline in demand.[10]

Now, let us turn to the supply curve. Consider one of the t identical labourers. I shall assume that the number of hours of labour, s, supplied by the labourer is positively related to the wage, $\tilde{w}$ that he or she receives. Thus

(12.8) $s = s(\tilde{w}), s'(\tilde{w}) \geq 0$

The aggregate labour supply, s, is therefore given by:

(12.9) $s = ts(\tilde{w})$

The wage, w^e, will be described as an equilibrium wage if supply equals demand at w^e, that is,

(12.10) $kn(w^e) = ts(w^e)$.

In Figure 12.2, an equilibrium wage, w^e, is illustrated. In what follows I shall assume that there is a unique equilibrium wage,[11] as in Figure 12.2. This assumption is not necessary, but for my purpose the additional complication of multiple equilibria is an unnecessary encumbrance. For exercises with a different motivation it may in fact be of interest to analyse such cases.

It is useful to note some properties of the general equilibrium:

(i) Although the basic axiom is valid (since productivity, h, does depend on wage) the equilibrium wage, w^e, could be above *or below* the efficiency wage. This is in contrast to the standard result in the efficiency-wage literature that the wage must settle at or above the efficiency wage.

(ii) There cannot be any open unemployment at the equilibrium. This is again in contrast to the standard efficiency-wage models. The basic axiom now manifests itself in *disguised* unemployment and is discussed below.

12.3.3. Surplus Labour

From equation (12.10) it is clear that if k is fixed than we could think of the equilibrium wage, w^e, as a function of t, the number of labourers in the economy. We shall, therefore, write $w^e = w^e(t)$, where $w^e(t)$ is the equilibrium wage given that the number of labourers is t. Clearly $w^c(t)$ is defined implicitly by:

$$k(w^c(t)) = ts(w^c(t)).$$

We shall say that there is surplus labour or disguised unemployment in the economy if a decline in the number of labourers results in output rising or remaining constant. A more formal definition could be given using the functions $n(w)$ and $w^c(t)$, as follows: An economy which has t labourers has surplus labour or disguised unemployment if there exists $t^\circ < t$ such that

$$X(t^\circ) = x(n(w^c(t^\circ))h(w^c(t^\circ))) \geq x(n(w^c(t)h(w^c(t))) = X(t),$$

where $X(t)$ is the total output in an economy with t labourers.

To prove that there can exist surplus labour in equilibrium, note that as the number of labourers declines, equilibrium wage must rise.[12] This is obvious from Figure 12.2. Clearly a decline in t causes the aggregate supply curve to pivot upward around its intercept on the wage axis. Thus, for instance, if $t^\circ < t$, the aggregate labour supply curve, given t°, will look like the broken line marked S°. Hence a decline in t causes the equilibrium wage to rise.

As a second step, note that as long as the equilibrium wage happens to be below the efficiency wage, w^*, every increase in the equilibrium wage results in an increase in aggregate output. As already shown, it follows from the nature of the h-function that if $w^* \geq w' > w^\circ$, then:

$$\frac{w'}{h(w')} < \frac{w^\circ}{h(w^\circ)}$$

This and equation (12.6) imply that:

(12.11) $x'(n(w')h(w')) < x'(n(w^\circ)h(w^\circ))$

Since $x'' < 0$, equation (11) implies:

$$n(w')h(w') > n(w^\circ)h(w^\circ).$$

We have established, therefore:[13]

(12.12) $w^* \geq w' > w^\circ \rightarrow kx(n(w')h(w')) > kx(n(w^\circ)h(w^\circ))$

Suppose now that t is such that $w^c(t)$ is below w^*. If a part of the labour force is removed, then, as shown above, the equilibrium wage will rise and equation (12.12) shows that output must rise as well. Thus there is surplus labour or disguised unemployment in the economy whenever the equilibrium wage happens to be below the efficiency wage (and there is no reason why this cannot happen).

Finally, in regard to the amount of surplus labour, in the empirical literature the amount of surplus labour is usually defined as the maximum number of labourers that can be removed without causing output to be smaller than the original output. We refer to this concept as *definition one*.

The model in this chapter suggests that there can be another definition.

Define t^* as the number of labourers that results in the aggregate output in the economy to be maximized. It is easy to check—using equation (12.12) and note 10—that t^* is defined implicitly by $w^c(t^*) = w^*$. According to *definition two*, the amount of surplus labour in an economy which has t labourers is max $\{t - t^*, 0\}$.

I draw attention to these two definitions in order to argue that, although definition one is the popular one, definition two is conceptually more attractive. The most important reason for this is that definition two satisfies a kind of path independence property. Clearly one property that we would expect a measure of surplus labour to possess is found in the following supposition: In a particular situation z labourers are found to be in surplus and $m(<z)$ of these labourers are removed. In this new situation we should have $z - m$ surplus labourers. It is easy to check that definition two satisfies this property and definition one does not.

12.4. Some Policy Issues

The original interest in surplus labour arose from policy matters, especially project evaluation and planning. If labour was to be drawn from the rural sector for industrial projects, how would it affect rural production? It was realized that if surplus labour existed then this withdrawal of labour was likely to be painless.

In this section, however, I analyse some other policy issues. It would seem from the above model that in the presence of disguised unemployment the correct policy is to somehow shore up the labourers' consumption level. This objective could be met indirectly by giving a wage subsidy or by the direct method of giving free food rations or stamps. In what follows both these policies are analysed. It is assumed throughout this section that the *status quo* equilibrium is one which has disguised unemployment.

The consequence of a wage subsidy is easy to analyse; let us consider it first. Suppose that the government announces that for each person employed the employer will be given a subsidy of D (> 0). The individual employer's profit function is now a little more elaborate than equation (12.4), and may be denoted as follows:

$$R\,(n, w, D) = x(nh(\tilde{w})) - n(w - D).$$

The landlord maximizes this profit by choosing n and w, subject to $w \geq \tilde{w}$. As before, the landlord sets $w = \tilde{w}$ and chooses n so as to satisfy:

$$x'(nh(\tilde{w})) = \frac{\tilde{w} - D}{h(\tilde{w})}$$

Let $n\,(\tilde{w}, D)$ be the solution. Since $x'' < 0$, it follows that as D rises, $n\,(\tilde{w}, D)$ rises. Hence the consequence of giving a wage subsidy (that is, raising D from zero to some positive number) is to shift the aggregate demand curve for labour rightward. Hence the equilibrium wage will rise, aggregate output will rise[14] and surplus labour will decline.

Somewhat surprisingly, the effect of the direct policy of giving food rations or stamps[15] is more ambiguous. It would raise aggregate output only under certain elasticity conditions. To state these simply, let us define the elasticity of the marginal product of labour with respect to efficiency units by m. That is,

$$(12.12) \qquad m = -x''(nh) \times \frac{nh}{x'(nh)}$$

Now suppose the government implements a free-food ration scheme (for example, the kind that was effective in Sri Lanka from the 1940s until the late 1970s). Each person is given f units of food. What will be the consequence of such a scheme on output and surplus labour? In the presence of such a policy an individual landlord's profit function (12.4) has to be modified to the following:

$$R(n, f) = x(nh(\tilde{w} + f)) - n\tilde{w}$$

Note that this function takes into account the fact that the landlord will always set w equal to $\tilde{w}$. The landlord maximizes this factor with respect to n. Hence, from the first-order condition, we have:

$$(12.13) \qquad x'(nh(\tilde{w} + f))h(\tilde{w} + f) = w.$$

First, we want to check the effect on demand for labour of an increase in f. Hence, by treating $\tilde{w}$ as constant and taking total differentials in equation (12.13), we get:

$$h(\tilde{w} + f)x''(nh(\tilde{w} + f))\{nh'(\tilde{w} + f)df + h(\tilde{w} + f)dn\} + x'(nh(\tilde{w} + f))h'(\tilde{w} + f)df = 0$$

Rearranging the terms and, for brevity, suppressing the arguments in the functions, we get:

$$\frac{dn}{df} = -\frac{nh'}{h} - \frac{x'h'}{x''h^2}$$

Since $x' > 0$, $h' \geq 0$, and $x'' \leq 0$, it cannot be signed unconditionally. Using equation (12.13), we see that $dn/df > 0$ if and only if

$$m < 1.$$

Hence only if the marginal product curve is sufficiency flat would a food-ration scheme cause an increase in the demand for labour, in the same way as a wage subsidy. Unlike in the case of a wage subsidy, however, we can talk about the effect on employment, wages, and surplus labour. A food-ration scheme is likely to affect the supply curve of labour as well.

Let us use the simple specification that a lumpsum subsidy decreases the supply of labour hours. That is, if an individual gets free food rations, his or her supply curve of labour shifts to the left. This trend is in keeping with the textbook theory of labour supply as long as leisure happens to be a normal good.

Now we can analyse the effect of implementing a free-food ration policy. If $m < 1$, the effect of a food-ration scheme is to shift the aggregate demand curve right and supply left. This effect is shown in Figure 12.3, which reproduces the

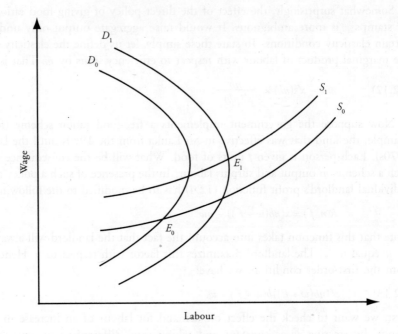

Figure 12.3: The Effect of Food Rationing

right side of Figure 12.1. The subscript 0 refers to the original position and 1 to the new one, and E_0 and E_1 are the old and new equilibria. The effect of the policy is to raise wages, decrease surplus labour, and increase output.[16]

If $m > 1$, the effect of a food-ration policy is not predictable. This outcome is easy to check using a diagrammatic exercise as in Figure 12.3. The popular intuition about what to do in the event of 'nutrition'-based disguised unemployment (see, for example, Robinson 1969: 375) is thus correct only conditionally. If landlords are price takers, then conditions on m are restrictions on technology. Thus the effect of this policy hinges on the nature of technology.

Finally, with reference to infrastructural investment, what would happen if the government invested in rural infrastructure? In much the same way as in the wage-subsidy case, it can be seen that this step would raise the aggregate demand for labour, assuming, of course, that improved infrastructure raises the marginal productivity of labour.[17]

This section briefly outlined the consequences of different kinds of policies, without attempting to rank them. The results in this section are necessary for conducting an exercise in ranking policies but not sufficient.

12.5. TOWARD A GENERALIZED MODEL

It was mentioned above that one reason an individual landlord may notice no relation between wage he or she pays and the productivity of labourers is because there is a time-lag between wages and productivity and the landlord's labour may be having a positive turnover. In this section we make this relation explicit and allow for the fact that the there may be *some* wage–productivity relation even at the micro level of an individual landlord.

Consider a very simple lag structure in which a worker's productivity in period t depends on his or her wage r periods ago:

$$h_t = h(w_{t-r})$$

Assume that q is the fraction of the labour force that quits a firm (or landlord) each period (and is replaced by new labourers) and $p(= 1 - q)$ is the fraction that stays on. There has been work on the determination of q in a general framework (example, Salop and Salop 1976) and also in a developmental context (see Stiglitz 1974; Basu 1984); but I shall here treat q as exogenous.

Now, if a landlord employs m labourers, the number of them that will remain after r years is $p^r m$. Suppose, as before, that there are k landlords and the reservation wage of labour is $\tilde{w}$. Let w be the wage paid by a landlord and n the number of labour hours employed by that landlord. Then, in a steady state, the landlord's output per period is:

(12.14) $x = x(p^r nh(w) + (1 - p^r)nh(\tilde{w}))$

The landlord's problem is to

(12.15) $\text{Max } R(n,w) = x(p^r nh(w) + (1 - p^r)nh(\tilde{w})) - nw$

subject to $w \geq \tilde{w}$.

To solve this, first ignore the constraint and derive the first-order conditions. Denote the solution of this by (n^o, w^o).
Note that (for all $w > c$):

$$\delta^2 R/\delta w^2 = x''(.)(p^r nh'(w))^2 + x'(.)p^r nh''(w) \leq 0$$

since $h'' \leq 0$ and $x'' \leq 0$. It follows that if w^o is not attainable because of the constraint, it is profit maximizing to get as close as possible to w^o. Hence, denoting the w which solves the landlord's problem by $\tilde{w}$, we know that:

$$\tilde{w} = \max \{w^o, \tilde{w}\}$$

Inserting $\tilde{w}$ in equation (12.15) we can solve for the optimum n. Call this $\tilde{n}$. Since $\tilde{w}$ and $\tilde{n}$ depend on $\tilde{w}$. I shall write these as $\tilde{w}(\tilde{w})$, $\tilde{n}(\tilde{w})$.

The model can be closed as before by aggregating the labour demand schedules of the k landlords and equating aggregate demand and aggregate supply. It is not difficult to see that under certain parametric situations there will be an excess supply of labour and in other situations there will be no excess supply and market clearing wages would be below w^*. In the former situation there is open unemployment and in the latter there is surplus labour.[18]

Given that surplus labour can occur if p^r is anywhere in the half-open interval [0,1], it is clear that our rejection of the possibility of surplus labour may have been exaggerated by virtue of the fact that the traditional literature is entirely based on the assumption of p^r being equal to one. This chapter's theoretical finding is not incompatible with the empirical evidence. While it is true that the evidence is mixed, a large number of economists have reported evidence of surplus labour—not just from densely populated Asian economies but also from Latin America (see de Janvry 1981; and, for a survey, Kao et al. 1964).

NOTES

1. See, for example, Georgescu-Roegen (1960); Schultz (1964); Islam (1965); Paglin (1965); Sen (1967, 1975); Desai and Mazumdar (1970); Agarwala (1979); Basu (1990). For surveys of this labyrinthine literature, see Kao et al. (1964); Mathur (1965); Robinson (1969).

2. The reference here is to the kinds of models that occur in Mirrlees (1975), Rodgers (1975), Stiglitz (1976), Bliss and Stern (1978) and Dasgupta and Ray (1986). This is, the reader ought to be warned, a mild abuse of tradition since the term 'efficiency wage' is generally used to describe *any* model where the downward stickiness of wage is explained in terms of the employer's preference.

3. Despite the understatement, the point is also quite clearly made by Streeten (1970) when he writes: 'it is not warranted to assume that … consumption at low levels of hiring has no effect on productivity'. Streeten goes on to suggest that a measure which cuts down the hours worked may raise worker productivity.

4. This point is well recognized in the efficiency-wage literature but is ignored for simplicity. It is, of course, the point of this chapter that the lag is not an inconsequential complication.

5. It is also possible that even though there is a link between wage and productivity at the level of each landlord, landlords do not necessarily perceive this.

6. It is true that the duration of labour–employer relation is usually longer than stipulated in a contract (see Bardhan 1984: 83–4), but in the absence of a long-term contract it may not be in the landlord's interest to increase wages with a view to enhancing labour productivity in the long run.

7. The importance of distinguishing between labour hours and labourers for studying disguised unemployment was recognized by Sen (1966) (see also Mellor 1967). The further differentiation with efficiency units arose with the incorporation of the basic axiom in labour-market theories.

8. The assumption that the relation is between h and per hour wage (instead of total wage earned by the labourer) keeps the algebra simpler. It is also not too strong an assumption in this model since it will be assumed that labourers choose voluntarily the number of hours they will work, given the per hour wage rate.

9. Myrdal (1968) also discusses this in his chapter on 'underemployment'.

10. If, for instance, $x'(0)$ is a positive real number, it can be shown that the aggregate demand for labour goes to zero for a sufficiency low $\bar{w}$, which is the case illustrated in Figure 12.2.

11. Note also that if the equilibrium is unique, it must also be 'stable' in the standard textbook sense.

12. This is always true if there is a unique equilibrium. If there are multiple equilibria then this is true for all stable equilibria.

13. Following the same method it is possible to show that:

$$w' > w^e \geq w^* \rightarrow kx(n(w')h(w')) < kx(n(w^e)h(w^e)).$$

Although this point is not important here, we need to refer to this in Section 12.5.

14. This is assuming, of course, that D is not so large, that the equilibrium wage rises well past the efficiency wage. In that case, it would have a depressing effect on output.

15. These policies are relevant to less-developed economies, especially the South Asian ones, as there is a long history of experimentation with alternative schemes in this class of policies (see Dreze and Sen 1991).

16. Subject to, of course, a similar qualification as in note 14.

17. This is indeed an assumption. It is often taken for granted that if there are two factors of production, an increase in one increases the marginal productivity of the other. That this need not be so is easy to see: if a factory employs red-haired and green-haired labour, there is diminishing marginal productivity for each labour-type and from the point of production the colour of a labourer's hair does not matter, then clearly an increase in greens must cause a drop in the productivity of reds.

18. A formal derivation of these is available from the author on request.

REFERENCES

Agarwala, N. 1979. 'On Leibenstein's Theory of Disguised Unemployment'. *Indian Economic Review* 14.

Bardhan, P. 1984. *Land, Labor and Rural Poverty*. New York: Columbia University Press.

Basu, K. 1984. *The Less Development Economy: A Critique of Contemporary Theory*. Oxford: Basil Blackwell.

—— 1990. 'Agrarian Structure and Economic Underdevelopment'. In J. Lesourne and H. Sonnenschein, eds, *Fundamentals of Pure and Applied Economics*. Chur. Harwood Academic Publishers.

Binswanger, H. and M. Rosenzweig. 1984. 'Contractual Arrangements, Employment, and Wages in Rural Labour Markets: A Critical Review'. In H. Binswanger and M. Rosenzweig, eds, *Contractual Arrangements, Employment and Wages in Rural Labour Markets in Asia*. New Haven: Yale University Press.

Bliss, C. and N. Stern. 1978. 'Productivity Wages and Nutrition: Part I, The Theory, Part II, Some Observations'. *Journal of Development Economics* 5.

Dasgupta, P. and D. Ray. 1986. 'Inequality as a Determinant of Malnutrition and Unemployment: Theory'. *Economic Journal* 96.

—— 1991. 'Adapting to Under-nourishment: The Clinical Evidence and Its Implications'. In Jean Dreze and Amartya Sen, eds, *The Political Economy of Hunger*. Oxford: Oxford University Press.

de Janvry, A. 1981. *The Agrarian Question and Reformism in Latin America*. Baltimore: Johns Hopkins University Press.

Desai, M. and D. Mazumdar. 1970. 'A Test of the Hypothesis of Disguised Unemployment', *Economica* 37.

Dreze, J. and A. Mukherjee. 1987. 'Labour Contracts in Rural India: Theories and Evidence'. Working Paper 7. DRP, London School of Economics. London.

Dreze, J. and A. K. Sen, eds. 1991. *The Political Economy of Hunger*. Oxford: Oxford University Press.

Georgescu-Roegen, N. 1960. 'Economic Theory and Agrarian Economics'. *Oxford Economic Papers* 12.

Guha, A. 1989. 'Consumption, Efficiency and Surplus Labour'. *Journal of Development Economics* 31.

Islam, N. 1965. 'Concept and Measurement of Unemployment and Underemployment in Developing Economies'. *International Labour Review* (March).

Kao, C.H.C., K.R. Anschel, and C. Eicher. 1964. 'Disguised Umemployment in Agriculture'. In C. Eicher and L. Witt, eds, *Agriculture in Economic Development*. New York: McGraw-Hill.

Leibenstein, H. 1957. 'The Theory of Underemployment in Backward Economies'. *Journal of Political Economy* 65.

—— 1958. 'Underemployment in Backward Economies: Some Additional Notes'. *Journal of Political Economy* 66.

Mathur, A. 1965. 'The Anatomy of Disguised Unemployment'. *Oxford Economic Papers* 17.

Mazumdar, D. 1959. 'The Marginal Productivity Theory of Wages and Disguised Unemployment'. *Review of Economic Studies* 26.

Mellor, J. 1967. 'Towards a Theory of Agricultural Development'. In H.M. Southworth and B.F. Johnson, eds. *Agricultural Development and Economic Growth*. Ithaca: Cornell University Press.

Mirrlees, J. 1975. 'Pure Theory of Underdeveloped Economies'. In L.G. Reynolds, ed. *Agriculture in Development Theory*. New Haven: Yale University Press.

Myrdal, G. 1968. *Asian Drama*. New York: Pantheon.

Navarrete, A. and I.M. Navarrete. 1951. 'La subocupacion en las economies poco desarrolladas'. *El Trimestre Economico*. English translation in *International Economic Papers* 3.

Osmani, S. 1991. 'Nutrition and the Economics of Food: Implications of Some Recent Controversy'. In Dreze and Sen (1991).

Paglin, M. 1965. 'Surplus Agricultural Labour and Development'. *American Economic Review*, 55.

Robinson, J. 1937. *Essays in the Theory of Employment*. Basingstoke: Macmillan.

Robinson, W. 1969. 'Types of Disguised Rural Unemployment and Some Policy Implications'. *Oxford Economic Papers* 21.

Rodgers, G. 1975. 'Nutritionally Based Wage Determination in the Low-income Labour Market'. *Oxford Economic Papers* 27.

Rudra, A. 1982. *Indian Agricultural Economics: Myths and Realities*. New Delhi: Allied Publishers.

Salop, J. and S. Salop. 1976. 'Self-selection and Turnovers in the Labour Market'. *Quarterly Journal of Economics* 40.

Schultz, T. 1964. *Transforming Traditional Agriculture*. New Haven: Yale University Press.

Sen, A.K. 1966. 'Peasants and Dualism with or without Surplus Labour'. *Journal of Political Economy* 74.

—— 1967. 'Surplus Labour in India: A Critique of Schultz's Statistical Test'. *Economic Journal* 77.

—— 1975. *Employment, Technology and Development*. Oxford: Clarendon Press.

Stiglitz, J. 1974. 'Alternative Theories of Wage Determination and Unemployment in LDCs: The Labour Turnover Model'. *Quarterly Journal of Economics* 11.

Stiglitz, J. 1976. 'The Efficiency Wage Hypothesis, Surplus Labour and the Distribution of Labour in LDCs'. *Oxford Economic Papers* 28.

Streeten, P. 1970. 'An Institutional Critique of Development Concepts'. *Archives Europeennes de Sociologie* 11.

Wonnacott, P. 1962. 'Disguised and Overt Unemployment in Underdeveloped Economies'. *Quarterly Journal of Economics* 26.

13 Limited Liability and the Existence of Share Tenancy

13.1. INTRODUCTION

The early laws of aerodynamics had seemed to suggest that the bumble-bee cannot fly. Consequently, the flight of the bumble-bee has been a source of provocation and advance in the study of aerodynamics. Something similar is true of share tenancy. The axioms of textbook economics suggest that share tenancy cannot exist. Its existence—which is fairly widespread in backward economies[1]—has, therefore, been a source of puzzlement and provoked a large literature.[2] This has enhanced our understanding of not just tenancy but agrarian structure and sharing arrangements in general.

After the early realization[3] that a landowner could do better if, instead of leasing out his land on a share rental basis, he leased it out on fixed rental, it was believed that we could explain the existence of sharecropping if we allowed for uncertainty in our models. But it was proved later that just having one kind of exogenous uncertainty (for example, that due to the weather) could not explain sharecropping. A more complicated argument, which brought in labour-market uncertainty as well, was needed (Newbery 1977).

Similarly, attempts to explain share tenancy by introducing variations in entrepreneurial skills and asymmetric information have proved to be futile. It has been shown that there must be at least two factors of production for which quality is uncertain and the information among buyers and sellers is asymmetric (Hallagan 1978; Allen 1982; Basu 1984).[4]

From *Journal of Development Economics* 38, 1992: 203–20.

For comments and discussions I am grateful to Anna Cook, Gaurav Dutt, Robert Evenson, James Heckman, Siddiq Osmani, V.K. Ramachandran, Elizabeth Sadoulet, and T.N. Srinivasan. The chapter has benefited from seminars at Berkeley, Yale, Princeton, the Indian Statistical Institute, Delhi, and the World Bank.

The aim of the present chapter is to contribute to this debate by providing a new and simple theory of the dominance of share over fixed rents by using the concept of 'limited liability', in particular the version of it which was used by Stiglitz and Weiss (1981). In a recent paper, Shetty (1988) lucidly explains the role of limited liability in the context of agrarian relations. The *limited liability axiom* asserts that if i has some financial commitment towards j (for example, a loan to be repaid or rent to be paid) but happens to be bankrupt, then j has to forgo his claim.[5] We could defend this axiom by referring to the law (in many countries bankruptcy is a legitimate reason for reneging on certain kinds of contracts) or social sanctions, which can be compelling on individuals, as described in Basu (1986). But if we treat the word 'bankrupt' literally as a state of total insolvency, then the axiom becomes almost self-evident. In a multi-period model claims need not necessarily be forgone but can be carried over to the future, but, as will be shown later, this leaves my argument intact.

A landowner is considered who cannot be present on his land to directly supervise hired labour. So his problem is to devise a suitable tenancy contract (share, fixed, or a mixture) and lease out the land. It is assumed that underlying any tenancy contract is an implicit limited-liability clause. That is, if the weather fails and the harvest is sufficiently poor, then the landlord would not be able to claim his full rent. We already know from the Stiglitz–Weiss theory that the presence of a limited-liability clause introduces a certain tension between the two agents. As will be shown below, in the presence of limited liability, the tenant would prefer risky projects (that is, his behaviour will mimic that of a risk-loving person) whereas the landlord would act like a risk-averse person even if they are innately risk-neutral agents. It will be shown that share tenancy has the advantage of minimizing this tension. In other words, by offering a *share*-rental contract, the landlord is able to 'direct' the tenant's choice of project towards the kind that the landlord prefers, to wit, the less risky ones.

In traditional models, a tenant chooses the volume of inputs, like labour, to be used and the principal moral hazard problem stems from the landlord's inability to monitor input use. I shall here refer to this as *labour moral hazard*. The term 'labour' will often be dropped though, since traditionally a reference to moral hazard is a reference to labour moral hazard.

In the present model the tenant does not have to decide on the intensity of labour use, but chooses from among techniques or projects which are differentiated only in terms of riskiness. The landlord's inability to monitor the tenant's choice of technique may be referred to as *technique moral hazard*. It is the presence of technique moral hazard that distinguishes this model from related ones like Kotwal (1985) and Shetty (1988).

The central aim of this chapter is to highlight the rather surprising theoretical result that the presence of technique moral hazard (which has not been given much prominence in agrarian studies) coupled with the limited liability axiom (which has been used earlier, for example, in Shetty 1988) helps us explain the existence of share tenancy.

It should be emphasized at the outset that I shall establish the dominance of share tenancy by focusing exclusively on the above problem and by ruling out features which tilt the argument in favour of fixed-rental tenancy (example, the well-known problem of moral hazard in labour use). Hence, in the context of a real agrarian economy, this chapter may be viewed as providing *one* reason why share tenancy may be preferred. What will actually come into existence in reality will then depend on the nature of the economy, that is, on whether the features I focus on in this chapter dominate or features like the moral hazard problem in the use of inputs are more prominent.

This can be the basis of a theory of what kinds of tenurial contracts we could expect in different economic situations. The last section of this chapter provides a tentative discussion of this problem.

13.2. LIMITED LIABILITY AND ATTITUDE TO RISK

In order to discuss a whole range of possibilities I shall begin with a 'mixed'-rental contract, of which share tenancy and fixed-rental tenancy appear as two polar extremes. The aim is to isolate conditions under which the polar end of *share* tenancy will come to prevail in equilibrium.

A mixed contract is defined by (r, R), where r is the fraction of the gross output and R the lumpsum which the tenant has to pay the landlord after the harvest. In other words, if the harvest yields X units of output, the landlord will get a total rent of $rX + R$ and the tenant will get $(1 - r)X - R$, given that they have agreed to the mixed contract (r, R). It is obvious that if $R = 0$ and $r > 0$ then we have a case of pure share tenancy and if $r = 0$ and $R > 0$, it is a fixed-rental contract. The case of $R < 0$ is ruled out by assumption since we are considering absentee landlordism.

In this chapter we study the effects of the limited liability axiom. I shall, therefore, assume that underlying all contracts is the limited-liability clause which says that the tenant has a prior right to output level S; and he fulfils his contract only after guaranteeing himself S. This S can be as low as one wishes, and may or may not be treated as subsistence consumption. Nothing hinges on its interpretation.

Given this limited liability clause and a mixed contract (r, R), if the harvest yields X units of output, the tenant's income, Y_T, is given by

(13.1) $Y_T(r, R, X) = \max\{(1 - r)X - R, S\}$

and the landlord's income, Y_L', is given by

(13.2) $Y_L(r, R, X) = \min\{rX + R, X - S\}$.

It is easy to check that $Y_L = X - Y_T$.

Now, even if we assume—and I do make such an assumption—that individuals are innately risk-neutral, given the limited liability clause, the tenant and the landlord will behave *as if* they have non-neutral attitudes to risk. The tenant will act risk-loving and the landlord will act risk-averse. In fact, they

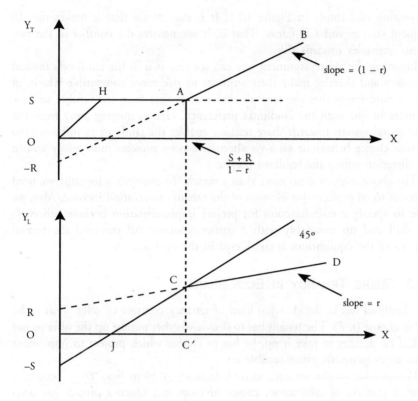

Figure 13.1: Limited Liability and the Existence of Share Tenancy

would behave thus even if the former was mildly risk-averse and the latter mildly risk-living. This is transparent as soon as we represent equations (13.I) and (13.2) on a diagram as in Figure 13.1.

In Figure 13.1, SAB represents Y_T as a function of X and $-SCD$ represents Y_L as a function of X. What limited liability has done is to concavify the landlord's earnings curve. Hence the conflicting attitudes towards risk.

Suppose there are two projects the tenant can choose from: (i) cultivate by traditional method and (ii) use high-yielding varieties. For simplicity, let us assume that the expected output in both cases happens to be the same, but uncertainty is greater in (ii). That is, if the weather is good, (ii) implies an output of x_2 and (i) implies an output of x_1 and $x_2 > x_1$ and if the weather fails (ii) implies an output of x'_2 and (i) implies an output of x'_1 and $x'_2 < x'_1$. Assume also that $x'_1 < (S + R)/(1 - r) < x_1$. It is very easy to check that the tenant will select the riskier project, that is (ii) whereas the landlord would have preferred if the safer project, that is, (i), was selected.

To give the reader an early insight as to why a landlord may prefer share tenancy, suppose we have a mixed-rent tenancy (r, R) to start with. Now if r becomes smaller and goes towards zero, this could be thought of as a gradual move away from share tenancy towards the pure fixed-rental system. What does a lowering of r imply in Figure 13.1? It is easy to see that it makes the AB segment steeper and CD flatter. That is, it accentuates the conflict in the two agents' attitudes towards risk.

Inverting the above argument one can see that it is in the landlord's interest to raise r and thereby make their attitudes to risk more compatible which, in turn, would imply that the tenant's choice of project from his feasible set may be more in line with the landlord's preference. Hence, moving away from the fixed-rental system towards share tenancy enables the landlord to influence the tenant's choice behaviour vis-à-vis alternative risky projects more easily and in the direction which the landlord prefers.

The above analysis is no more than a sketch. To establish it formally we need to resort to an explicit specification of the tenant's reservation income. Also, we have to specify a cost function for project implementation because otherwise we shall end up invariably with a corner solution. All this and the formal analysis of the equilibrium is conducted in the next section.

13.3. SHARE TENANCY IN EQUILIBRIUM

The landlord has to decide what kind of tenancy contract to offer. That is, he has to choose (r, R). The tenant has to decide whether to take up the offer or not and, if he decides to take it up, he has to choose which project to implement from an exogenously given feasible set.

Let us take on the tenant's second decision problem first. By a 'project' I mean a method of cultivation, choice of crop, etc. Once a project has been chosen, the output will depend on the weather; and for simplicity I shall assume that each project can be either successful or a failure.[6] I shall denote a project by D. If project D is chosen, then it means that if the project is successful, output will be D units. If it fails output is F (F is the same for all projects).[7] In order to give the limited-liability clause some bite, it is assumed that a failed project would necessitate the invoking of the limited-liability clause. That is, we are restricting ourselves to the case where

(13.3) $\qquad S > (1 - r)F - R.$

A sufficient condition using only exogenous variables, which ensures (13.3) is discussed later (see note 10).

To keep the focus exclusively on the uncertainty aspect of projects, it will be assumed that all projects have the same expected income, E. Hence, the probability, $p(D)$, of project D's success is given by

(13.4) $\qquad p(D) = (E - F)/(D - F).$

It is being assumed that D can take any value above E.

We use $c(D)$ to denote the cost of implementing project D. Since the tenant chooses the project it is natural—and that is what I am assuming—that the tenant incurs the cost of its implementation. In any case since the project choice cannot be monitored by the landlord, if he paid for it, the tenant would take the money and choose the project which is most advantageous from the tenant's point of view.

Given (r, R) if the tenant takes up the tenancy offer and implements project D, his *expected net income*, denoted by Z_T, is

$$(13.5) \qquad Z_T(r, R, D) = (1 - p(D))S + p(D)((1 - r)D - R) - c(D).$$

It is being assumed that in the event of success, the tenant's income exceeds S.[8] That is, $(1 - r)D - R > S$. This coupled with assumption (13.3) and equation (13.1) gives us equation (13.5), since $Y_T(r, R, F) = S$ and $(1 - r)D - R = Y_T(r, R, D)$.[9]

The tenant's choice of project, given (r, R), will be denoted by $D(r, R)$ and this is defined as

$$(13.6) \qquad D(r, R) = \underset{D}{\arg\max} \, Z_T(r, R, D).$$

In order to ensure that an optimal D exists and can be derived by the use of standard first- and second-order conditions, it is sufficient to assume—and from here on I am making this assumption—that $c(D)$ is twice differentiable and everywhere strictly convex, more specifically, $c'(D) > 0$ and $c''(D) > 0$.

It is worth noting that the convexity of $c(D)$ is a very reasonable requirement. This is because (i) it is sensible to assume that there exists an upper limit to the output that can emerge from a plot of land no matter how congenial the weather and as we try to implement projects which strive towards this upper limit, costs become arbitrarily high; and (ii) as D approaches E (from the right) the probability of success approaches unity and it may be argued that such projects, for which success is near certain, are arbitrarily costly.[10]

The solution to (13.6) is now easy to see. Substituting (13.4) into (13.5) and differentiating, we get

$$\frac{\partial Z_T}{\partial D} = [(E - F)(S - F(1 - r) + R)]/(D - F)^2 - c'(D)$$

and

$$\frac{\partial^2 Z_T}{\partial D} = [-2(E - F)(S - F(1 - r) + R)]/(D - F)^3 - c''(D)$$

Given (13.3) and $c''(D) > 0$, it follows that $\partial^2 Z_T / \partial D^2 < 0$. Hence Z_T is strictly concave in D. It follows that in order to maximize Z_T, it is enough to work out the first-order condition.

Given a mixed contract (r, R) and the tenant's choice of project D, the landlord's *expected net income*, denoted by Z_L, is

$$(13.7) \qquad Z_L(r, R, D) = (1 - p(D))(F - S) + p(D)(rD + R).$$

Recall that one of the things that the tenant has to decide is whether to at all take up the tenancy offer or not. It will be assumed that the tenant has a reservation (net) income of Z^* and he would take up the landlord's offer as long as he expects at least Z^* out of it.

Hence the landlord's problem is to choose $r \in [0, 1]$ and $R \geqq 0$, so as to

$$\max Z_L(r, R, D),$$

subject to (i) $D = D(r, R)$,

(ii) $Z_T(r, R, D(r, R)) \geqq Z^*$.

The first constraint takes account of the fact that it is the tenant who chooses the project and (ii) takes account of the tenant's freedom not to accept the landlord's contract, (r, R).

Let (r^*, R^*) be the solution to the above maximization problem. Then (r^*, R^*) is the tenancy contract that will prevail in equilibrium. We are now in a position to state the main theorem of this section.

THEOREM 13.1: In the above model share tenancy is the dominant tenurial arrangement. That is, in equilibrium, R is always set equal to zero.

PROOF: Suppose (r^*, R^*) is the tenancy contract that prevails in equilibrium and $R^* > 0$. The proof is completed by constructing another (r, R) which satisfies (i) and (ii) and for which the landlord earns a larger net income Z_L.

Define (r', R') such that $R' = 0$ and

(13.8) $\quad r' = r^* + R^*/D(r^*, R^*)$.

It will first be shown that

(13.9) $\quad Z_T(r', R', D(r', R')) \geqq Z^*$.

From (13.8) and $R' = 0$, it follows that

$$Z_T(r', R', D(r^*, R^*))$$

$$= (1 - p(D(r^*, R^*)))S$$

$$+ p(D(r^*, R^*))(1 - r^* - R^*/D(r^*, R^*))D(r^*, R^*) - c(D(r^*, R^*))$$

$$= Z_T(r^*, R^*, D(r^*, R^*))$$

$$\geqq Z^*, \text{ since } (r^*, R^*) \text{ is an equilibrium.}$$

From the definition of the mapping $D(\cdot)$ [see (13.6)], we know

$$Z_T(r', R', D(r', R')) \geqq Z_T(r', R', D(r^*, R^*)).$$

Hence, (13.9) must be true.

What remains to be proved is that

(13.10) $\quad Z_L(r', R', D(r', R')) > Z_L(r^*, R^*, D(r^*, R^*))$.

The first step towards this entails noting that

(13.11) $\quad D(r', R',) < D(r^*, R^*)$.

From the definition of $D(\cdot)$ and applying the first-order condition to (13.5), we know

(13.12) $\qquad \dfrac{\partial Z_T}{\partial D} (r^*, R^*, D(r^*, R^*))=0.$

It is easy to check using (13.5), (13.8), and $R' = 0$, that

$$\frac{\partial Z_T}{\partial D} (r', R', D(r^*, R^*)) = \frac{\partial Z_T}{\partial D} (r^*, R^*, D(r^*, R^*)) - p(D(r^*, R^*))R^*/D^*$$

$$< 0, \qquad \text{by (13.12)}.$$

Hence it follows from the second-order condition that if D' is such that

$$\frac{\partial Z_T}{\partial D} (r', R', D') = 0,$$

then $D' < D(r^*, R^*)$. Since $D' = D(r', R')$, we get (13.11).

Now, it may be checked that (13.10) is true if and only if

(13.13) $\qquad (1 - (E-F)/(D'-F))(F-S)+((E-F)/(D'-F))(r'D' + R').$

$$> (1 - (E-F)/(D^*-F))(F-S) +((E-F)/(D^*-F))(r^*D^* + R^*),$$

where $D' = D(r', R')$ and $D^* = D(r^*, R^*)$. Substituting (13.8) and $R' = 0$ in (13.13) and using (13.11), it can be checked that (13.13) is true if and only if $S/F > 1 - r^* - R^*/D^*$. But the latter must be true, given assumption (13.3). Hence (13.10) must be true. Q.E.D.

It must be pointed out that while my model uses the Stiglitzt–Weiss formulation of limited liability, a more elaborate formulation would assert that under limited liability a tenant would be assured of S units of output *only as long as this does not entail the landlord actually having to pay the tenant.* Let us call this 'weak limited liability'. Note that our limited-liability clause could require that not only does the landlord forgo his rental claim but in some really bad years he may actually have to pay the tenant. This would happen if X is less than J in Figure 13.1. The *weak* limited-liability clause does not go that far. If we had used the weak limited-liability clause, (13.2) would have to be written as follows:

$$Y_L(r, R, X) = \max \{0, \min \{rX + R, X - S\}\};$$

and (13.1) also would have to be changed since $Y_L = X - Y_T$.

In terms of Figure 13.1, the landlord's income function would be $OJCD$ and the tenant's income would be shown by $OHAB$.[11]

As will be immediately transparent, we now have a more complicated picture of when share tenancy will dominate 'and when the fixed-rental system will dominate. If the bad and good output levels occur between, respectively, OJ and JC', fixed rentals will dominate. But it is clear that share tenancy could still dominate over the fixed-rental system in many cases. This would happen for sure if a failed project yields an output between J and C'.

Hence, using the weak limited-liability clause, we could have a more sophisticated model of the domination of alternative tenurial arrangements, but in this chapter I shall continue to focus on our more simple model.

A question which naturally arises is that if instead of a one-period model, as above, we had a multi-period model, would my analysis still be valid? Would not the ability of agents to carry over imbalances in account in one period to the next one affect the argument? More specifically, would we not expect that in such a model a system like the one discussed by Kotwal (1985) which entails a fixed rental with positive and negative side payments to compensate for fluctuations in output caused by the weather to dominate over other tenurial arrangements?

The answer is no for two reasons. First, in Kotwal's model, the random term in the production function is additive which allows for easy identification of output shifts caused by the weather. Secondly, and more importantly; Kotwal's tenant does not confront a choice of technique problem and so his model does not have any scope for technique moral hazard which is central to my model.

Suppose we do have several periods. It is true that a non-payment of rental over a few periods may be carried over. But this cannot be done endlessly. A debt carried over for too many periods may be construed as a case of bonded labour in terms of the legal definition (see Government of India 1976) and a landlord must entertain the possibility of not being able to recover the full rent for reasons of society or law. Moreover, a tenant's life being finite, there is no way of guaranteeing that a tenant will owe the landlord no unpaid rents at the time of his death. And since the practice of making a child work off a father's debt is no longer a common practice, a multi-period model cannot rule out the possibility of a tenant being unable to pay the full rent because of extreme poverty. If we do allow some transfers from one period to another, all we would have to do is to work with *present values* of income, instead of income. Thus in equations (13.5) and (13.7) we would have to use the present values of, respectively, the tenant's and the landlord's incomes over time, instead of Z_T and Z_L. With this and with the tenant choosing between projects or techniques (instead of an input, as in Kotwal 1985) we would, as before, get the result that in some situations, share tenancy would be dominant.

It is also noteworthy that tenancy relationships are often of brief durations. Walker and Ryan (1990: 173) in their detailed study of India's semi-arid tropics observe: 'The brief duration of most leases represents one feature of tenancy that is widely shared by the study villages. The majority, or about 60 per cent of the sharecropping and fixed-rent contracts, were for only one cropping season.' They go on to suggest that the fear of tenants acquiring permanent rights on land is probably what prompts landlords to go in for short-duration contracts. But for us the upshot is that in the light of this, the scope for multi-period levelling out of income fluctuations may not be very large in practice. Hence my focus on a single-period relation need not be too untenable an abstraction.

Finally, I wish to draw attention to the fact that, as in Shetty's (1988) model, I have restricted attention to 'linear landlease contracts'. Hence R is restricted to non-negative values and non-linear contracts are ruled out by assumption. A wage-labour system, which amounts to $r = 1$ and $R < 0$, was thus ruled out by assumption. This seems reasonable in a model of absentee landlordism (see also Shetty 1988: footnote 7) but, given that Theorem 13.1 suggests that in equilibrium R takes corner value, to wit, zero, for purely theoretical reasons, it is interesting to check what would happen if no non-negativity constraint is placed on R.

To understand this, it is useful to first find out the Pareto-optimal contracts. Clearly if project D is implemented, the total income of the landlord and the tenant is $E - c(D)$. That is,

$$Z_L(r, R, D) + Z_T(r, R, D) = E - c(D).$$

Hence, for Pareto optimality, it is necessary that project $\tilde{D}$ gets chosen, where

$$\tilde{D} = \text{argmin } c(D).$$

Let us write $\tilde{c}$ for $c(\tilde{D})$. Next, note that if (r, R) is such that

(13.14) $(1 - r)F - R \geqq S,$

then the limited-liability clause has no bite and the tenant will choose the most efficient project, namely $\tilde{D}$, since the tenant's gross income will be $(1 - r)E - R$ no matter which project is chosen. Hence, if the landlord chooses (r, R), satisfying (13.14), Pareto efficiency is ensured.

Hence, if the landlord wants to maximize his own income, he should ensure that (r, R) satisfies (13.14) and in addition that the tenant gets only his reservation income, that is

(13.15) $(1 - r)E - R - \tilde{c} = Z^*.$

Thus any $r \in [0, 1]$ and any real number R which satisfy (13.14) and (13.15) will be selected by the landlord in equilibrium, if we do not place a non-negativity requirement on R.

It is easy to check that, if $\tilde{c} + Z^* \geqq S$, then $R = -\tilde{c} - Z^*$ and $r = 1$ is a solution to this problem. That is, a wage labour system with wage equal to $-\tilde{c} - Z^*$ is a solution. There are other solutions but [given (N.1) in note 10] it follows that all these entail a negative R. It may be argued that with an absentee landlord and $r = 1$, there would be very serious labour moral hazard problems. This was not modelled explicitly because, as was explained earlier, inputs like labour and effort were kept out of the model in order to focus attention on the technique moral hazard problem. But, just to get a glimpse into the problem, suppose a tenant has to put in effort into the land for success. That is, without effort, no matter which project is chosen, output will be F. In such a situation it is obvious that if a contract has $R = -\tilde{c} - Z^*$ and $r = 1$ (that is, a tenant's income has no relationship with yield), then the tenant will put in zero effort. In order to induce effort out of him r has to be less than 1. How much less will depend on the cost of effort. As r becomes less than 1, R will go from $-\tilde{c} - Z^*$ towards 0. While it is conceivable that we will get an equilibrium with $R = 0$ and $0 < r < 1$, what is most reasonable to expect is an equilibrium with $R < 0$ and $0 < r < 1$.

This in itself is interesting. It amounts to a system of sharecropping with a fixed side payment of R. It will not resemble a wage-contract system since typically R will be less than S, and so, in the event of a failure, the fixed payment of R will go unnoticed since it will anyway be more than made up by the remission under the limited-liability clause. In the event of success the tenant will get $(1 - r) D - R$.

In brief, if we restrict attention to only linear landlease contracts, share tenancy would come out as dominant. If, however, we allow the fixed payment to be negative and take account of labour moral hazard, the dominant system would typically be share tenancy with a fixed side payment from the landlord to the tenant. There remains, however, much work to be done on combining the present model with labour moral hazard in a more explicit and rigorous fashion.

13.4. CONDITIONS FOR THE DISAPPEARANCE OF SHARE TENANCY

The above model may be described as the pure risk model because the principal decision there is of how to respond to the uncertainty inherent in nature. In such a model, it has been proved, share tenancy would be the dominant tenurial arrangement. If we combine this risk model with what I shall label as the 'productivity' aspect of decision (which allows us to bring in the well-known Marshallian arguments against share tenancy), then we get a framework in which the fixed-rental system, share tenancy or the mixed-rental system could dominate depending on whether the risk or the productivity considerations are larger, and larger by how much. Such a construction would allow us to discuss the conditions under which we could expect share tenancy to disappear. This section takes an informal look at this problem.

The way we can introduce the productivity problem in the above model is to assume that a tenant can choose to put in different amounts of labour, L (or any other input or vector of inputs, for that matter). What this does is to shift the expected yield from land, $E(L)$. Having chosen the amount of labour, he can choose between projects of different riskiness [but with the same expected yield of $E(L)$]. This latter decision problem is identical to what we have encountered in the previous section.[12] It is of course expected that labour is costly. If w is the market wage then w can be treated as the opportunity cost of each unit of labour.

The decisions of labour use and riskiness of project may be described as, respectively, the productivity and the risk decisions. If in a particular economy the former problem was not there, then, as we already know from Theorem 13.1, share tenancy would prevail in equilibrium. If, on the other hand, the only decision problem of the tenant was the productivity one, then, as we know from Marshall, fixed-rental tenancy would dominate. This is simply because in share tenancy the tenant gets a fraction of the yield from land but he bears the entire cost of inputs.[13] This introduces a wedge in the marginal calculus and results in an inefficient use of inputs.

It is now easy to see the conditions under which we would expect share tenancy to give way to the fixed-rental arrangement. Our analysis suggests that share tenancy will be less predominant in areas (i) where production is relatively weather-independent (for example, irrigated areas) or (ii) where the cultivator has little latitude in terms of the choice of projects of varying riskiness. Also, if (iii) there is considerable substitutability between land and other inputs, the fixed-rental system will be more prominent. To see this one has to simply consider the other extreme where inputs have to be used in fixed proportions. In that case, once the amount of land is specified the amount of other inputs that can be used is well defined. The productivity decision is, therefore, trivial and the risk aspect is dominant, thereby laying out the basis of Theorem 13.1.

Finally, (iv) in relatively well-off areas, where incomes are unlikely to drop too low even in bad weather, share tenancy is unlikely because the limited-liability clause in such an area may not have to be invoked. So that clause cannot influence the tenurial structure.

It should be clear that as a condition for the disappearance of sharecropping, (iv) has a different status from (i)–(iii), because (iv) also happens to be the precondition for explanations of the incidence of share tenancy of the kind captured in (i), (ii), and (iii).[14] This is because, in this chapter the focus is on the consequences of the limited liability axiom. Where the axiom is void, there may be other reasons for share tenancy[15] but the explanation in this chapter is certainly not the relevant one.

There remains considerable scope for expanding the institutional context of the debate between share tenancy and the fixed-rental system, by recognizing the role of law and social sanctions. Basu (1989) demonstrates that under legal institutions which are quite widespread in developing economies and which do not allow for the adjustment of rents over time, the fixed-rental system can have an adverse effect on innovative activity. One possible line of research which may yield insights into the dynamics of tenurial systems is the relation between innovative activity and alternative tenurial systems. This relation would however depend critically on the nature of legal and social institutions.

13.5. CONCLUDING REMARKS

Returning to the subject with which this chapter began, I would like to reiterate that in LDCs the limited liability axiom need not be a matter of law or social custom but is nevertheless a reasonable assumption. Before going into this, it is worth noting that a class-based explanation of the limited-liability clause has been discussed in the literature (see Adnan 1985). The argument is based on the fact that the landlords *as a class* and in the long run may not benefit from exploiting tenants to the point that is feasible in an *immediate* context. This is because such extreme exploitation may in the long run destroy the very class structure which makes the exploitation possible. However, from this to conclude that exploitation will not be pressed to its immediately feasible limit it is necessary to explain why what is in a landlord's *class*-interest would also be in his

204 DEVELOPMENT, MARKETS, AND INSTITUTIONS

self-interest or to explicitly defend the position that individuals act in their class interest whether or not that goes against their self-interest.

Custom-based explanations have also been made in the literature. Even in exploitative relationships, patronage has often been a prominent element (see, for example, Epstein 1967; Breman 1974), which entails that the landlord or the employer has some responsibility to provide subsistence consumption to a tenant or a labourer in bad years.[16] This could take the form of direct assistance or the remission of a part of the rent. Writing about pre-war Japan, Ishikawa (1975: 463) remarks that even fixed-rental contracts turned out to have an element of the 'ordinary cropsharing arrangement' because in years of crop failure there would occur some reduction in rent.

While these are indeed cases of the limited-liability clause at work, even in the absence of class-based or custom-based explanations, the limited-liability clause must automatically be *potentially* there in a sufficiently poor economy because in the event of a crop failure (or two or more successive crop failures) a tenant may just not *have* the wealth to fulfil his contract. In such a case, rent remission becomes inescapable.

I use the word 'potentially' because in such a poor economy, landlords would take precautions to minimize the likelihood of losing out on rent because of crop failure. This is one reason why landlords prefer tenants to be relatively better-off—a consideration which does not seem to appear in hiring wage labour. Shetty (1988) builds a model where wealthier tenants are offered better terms by the landlord. Though his argument is different, it is interesting that limited liability is an essential feature of his model.

NOTES

1. See, for example, Rao (1971), Reid (1975), Bell (1977), Pearce (1983), and Boyce (1987).
2. To cite a few references: Cheung (1968, 1969), Bardhan and Srinivasan (1971), Stiglitz (1974), Mazumdar (1975), Roumasset (1976), Bell and Zusman (1976), Hallagan (1978), Allen (1982), Basu and Roy (1982), Binswanger and Rosenzweig (1984), Quibria and Rashid (1984), Bardhan (1984), Braverman and Guasch (1984), Singh (1987).
3. For a clear statement, see Marshall (1920).
4. See also Newbery and Stiglitz (1979). The more recent model of Allen (1985) pursues a very different line of argument and what it establishes is the existence of share tenancy *with side payments* and not of share tenancy, pure.
5. As a concept, limited liability originated outside economic theory: see Jensen and Meckling (1976) for discussion of it in the context of corporate finance. See also the discussion on bankruptcy in Brealey and Myers (1988: Sec. 18.3).
6. It is possible for some projects to be more resilient, that is, these projects would succeed under a wider range of weather conditions.
7. This assumption is inconsequential and made only for algebraic simplicity. Thus the example in Section 13.2 involving projects (i) and (ii) does not fit into this framework. But it can be checked that even if it were true that increasing risk meant that

bad-weather output is worse (as, for instance, is the case with some high-yielding varieties) our general result would continue to be true though the class of available projects would be different from the one just assumed.

8. The case where this is not so is uninteresting and will, therefore, be ignored here. This will be obvious as we go along.

9. Note that I am applying the limited-liability clause on the gross yield from harvest. Another possibility would have been to first deduct $c(D)$ from the harvest and then check whether this net yield is above S or not and then apply the limited-liability clause. For the theorem 13.1 below it does not matter which convention is followed, so I choose what appears to be mathematically simpler.

10. This does not prove the convexity of $c(D)$ but urges us towards it. It proves that if we have to choose between $c(D)$ being convex everywhere and concave everywhere, it can only be the former. If D is represented on the horizontal axis of a diagram, $c(D)$ would typically be a U-shaped curve on the interval between E and X marked on the horizontal axis, where X is the highest possible output under the best of weather conditions. It is now possible to state a condition on exogenous variables which ensures (13.3) holds in equilibrium. Let $\tilde{c} \equiv \min c(D)$. Consider:

(N.1) $\qquad S > (Z^* + \tilde{c})F/E$

where Z^* is as defined immediately after equation (13.7). It is easy to show that if (N.1) is true and R is restricted to non-negative values then (13.3) must be true in equilibrium. The essential step involves noting that if (N.1) is true, then whenever (r, R) is such that $(1 - r)E - R = Z^* + \tilde{c}$ is true, it cannot be that $(1 - r)F - R \geq S$.

11. I owe this observation to Siddiq Osmani.

12. While, for ease of exposition, I speak as if the two decisions [(i) how much labour to use and (ii) which project to implement] are taken in a sequence, actually these will be simultaneous and indeed one decision may well depend on the other.

13. I am, of course, ignoring here the case of input-sharing share tenancy, which could, in some circumstances, remove the distortion.

14. This could mitigate what would otherwise appear to be conflicting between my theoretical findings and Rao's (1971) empirical observations.

15. Recently, de Janvry et al. (1989) have considered an environment similar to that in my model, namely one with 'highly risky income, extreme levels of poverty, and lack of insurance'. Their model of share tenancy is, however, very different from mine and assumes 'safety-first behaviour'. Another approach to explaining sharing risks is to explicitly consider the repeated nature of most agrarian relations. This is done by de Janvry et al. (1989) and also by Coate and Ravallion (1989), though the two papers end up reaching very different conclusions concerning efficiency. There ought to be considerable scope for empirical investigation into the relation between tenurial forms and yield uncertainty. Though there has occurred some fairly meticulous work in this area the evidence that exists and has been analysed (for example, in Anderson and Hazell 1989) does not seem to be suited for testing the kind of hypothesis suggested in this chapter. But this is an objective worth keeping in mind.

16. Even in non-hierarchical relationships one can find the institution of reciprocity functioning as a mechanism of insurance against economic disaster (see Platteau and Abraham 1987).

REFERENCES

Adnan, S. 1985. 'Classical and Contemporary Approaches to Agrarian Capitalism'. *Economic and Political Weekly* 20. 27 July.

Allen, F. 1982. 'On Share Contracts and Screening'. *Bell Journal of Economics* 13.

—— 1985. 'On the Fixed Nature of Sharecropping Contracts'. *Economic Journal* 95.

Anderson, J. and P.B. Hazell, eds. 1989. *Variability in Grain Yields: Implications for Agricultural Research and Policy in Developing Countries*. Baltimore, MD: Johns Hopkins University Press.

Bardhan, P. 1984. *Land, Labor and Rural Poverty*. New York: Columbia University Press.

Bardhan, P. and T.N. Srinivasan. 1971. 'Crop Sharing Tenancy in Agriculture: A Theoretical and Empirical Analysis'. *American Economic Review* 61.

Basu, K. 1984. *The Less Developed Economy: A Critique of Contemporary Theory*. Oxford: Basil Blackwell.

—— 1986. 'One Kind of Power'. *Oxford Economic Papers* 38.

—— 1989. 'Technological Stagnation, Tenurial Laws and Adverse Selection'. *American Economic Review* 79.

Basu, K. and P. Roy. 1982. 'Share, Size and Subsistence: Revisiting Some Old Controversies on Tenancy'. *Economic and Political Weekly* 17. 24 July.

Bell, C. 1977. 'Alternative Theories of Sharecropping: Some Tests Using Evidence from Northeast India'. *Journal of Development Studies* 13.

Bell, C. and P. Zusman. 1976. 'A Bargaining Theoretic Model of Cropsharing Contracts'. *American Economic Review* 66.

Binswanger, H.P. and M.R. Rosenzweig. 1984. 'Contractual Arrangements, Employments, and Wages in Rural Labour Markets: A Critical Review'. In H.P. Binswanger and M.R. Rosenzweig, eds. *Contractual Arrangements, Employment and Wages in Rural Labour Markets in Asia*. New Haven, CT: Yale University Press.

Boyce, J. 1987. *Agrarian Impasse in Bengal: Institutional Constraints to Technological Change*. Oxford: Oxford University Press.

Braverman, A. and L. Guasch. 1984. 'Capital Requirements, Screening and Interlinked Sharecropping and Credit Contracts'. *Journal of Development Economics* 14.

Brealey, R.A. and S.C. Myers. 1988. *Principles of Corporate Finance*, 3rd edition, New York: McGraw-Hill.

Breman, J. 1974. *Patronage and Exploitation*. Berkeley, CA: University of California Press.

Cheung, S.N.S. 1968. 'Private Property Rights and Sharecropping'. *Journal of Political Economy* 76.

—— 1969. *The Theory of Share Tenancy*. Chicago, IL: Chicago University Press.

Coate, S. and M. Ravallion. 1989. 'Characterization and Performance of Informal Risk-sharing Arrangements'. Harvard University, Cambridge, MA. Mimeo.

de Janvry, A., S. Fukui, and E. Sadoulet. 1989. 'Efficient Share Tenancy Contracts under Risk: The Case of Three Rice-growing Villages in Thailand'. University of California, Berkeley, CA. Mimeo.

Epstein, T.S. 1967. 'Productive Efficiency and Customary System of Rewards in Rural South India'. In R. Firth, ed. *Themes in Economic Anthropology*. London: Tavistock Publications.

Government of India. 1976. 'Bonded Labour System (Abolition) Act of 1976'.

Hallagan, W. 1978. 'Self-selection by Contractual Choice and the Theory of Sharecropping'. *Bell Journal of Economics* 9.

Ishikawa, S. 1975. 'Peasant Families and the Agrarian Community in the Process of Economic Development'. In L.G. Reynolds, ed., *Agriculture in Development Theory*. New Haven, CT: Yale University Press.

Jenson, M.C. and W. Meckling. 1976. 'Theory of the Firm: Managerial Behavior, Agency Costs and Capital Structure'. *Journal of Financial Economics* 3.

Kotwal, A. 1985. 'Consumption Credit and Agricultural Tenancy'. *Journal of Development Economics* 18.

Marshall, A. 1920. *Principles of Economics*, 8th edition. London: Macmillan.

Mazumdar, D. 1975. 'The Theory of Sharecropping and Labour Market Dualism. *Economica* 32.

Newbery, D.M.G. 1977. 'Risk-sharing, Sharecropping and Uncertain Labour Markets'. *Review of Economic Studies* 44.

Newbery, D.M.G. and J.E. Stilitz. 1979. 'Sharecropping, Risk sharing, and the Importance of Imperfect Information'. In J.A. Roumasset, J.M. Boussard and I. Singh, eds, *Risk, Uncertainty and Agricultural Development*. New York: Agricultural Development Council.

Pearce, R. 1983. 'Sharecropping: Towards a Marxist View'. *Journal of Peasant Studies* 10.

Platteau, J.P. and A. Abraham. 1987. 'An Inquiry into Quasi-credit Contracts: The Role of Reciprocal Credit and Interlinked Deals in Small-scale Fishing Communities'. *Journal of Development Studies* 23.

Quibria, M.G. and S. Rashid. 1984. 'The Puzzle of Sharecropping : A Survey of Theories'. *World Development* 12.

Rao, C.H.H. 1971. 'Uncertainty, Entrepreneurship, and Sharecropping in India'. *Journal of Political Economy* 79.

Reid, J.D. 1975. 'Sharecropping in History and Theory'. *Agricultural History* 49.

Roumasset, J.A. 1976. *Rice and Risk: Decision Making among Low-income Farmers*. Amsterdam: North-Holland.

Shetty, S. 1988. 'Limited Liability, Wealth Differences and Tenancy Contracts in Agrarian Economies'. *Journal of Development Economics* 29.

Singh, N. 1987. 'Theories of Sharecropping'. In P. Bardhan, ed., *The Economic Theory of Agrarian Institutions*. Oxford: Oxford University Press.

Stiglitz, J.E. 1974. 'Incentives and Risk Sharing in Sharecropping'. *Review of Economic Studies* 61.

Stiglitz, J.E. and A. Weiss. 1981. 'Credit Rationing with Imperfect Information'. *American Economic Review* 71.

Walker, T.S. and J.G. Ryan. 1990. *Village and Household Economies in India's Semi-arid Tropics*. Baltimore, MD: Johns Hopkins University Press.

PART IV
International Labour Standards and Child Labour

14 Compacts, Conventions, and Codes
Initiatives for Higher International Labour Standards

14.1. INTRODUCTION

The International Labour Standards (ILS) movement is meant to be an initiative to promote better working conditions and higher living standards for workers in the Third World. It therefore seems baffling that the most vociferous opposition to ILS comes from the Third World, and not just from elite groups and governments, but also from workers and grass-roots activists. However, this opinion from the South, encountered all over developing countries, gets little representation in international fora and global meetings. Is the dissent from the South based on the South's misperception of its own interests? Or is it founded on a realistic perception of global politics and power? The purpose of this chapter is to argue the latter—that the Southern apprehension is understandable and to ignore this while drafting policy for the well-being of the workers will not only be an injustice, but it will give rise to global tensions and instability.

The contemporary world has seen a bewildering number of initiatives for ILS, the latest being the UN's Global Compact, which attempts to make big firms and corporations join hands in a voluntary contract to adhere to certain minimal labour standards. This stands in contrast to the effort of the International Labour Organization (ILO) to make *nations* ratify 'conventions' which then require them to enforce minimal labour standards within their national boundaries; and, in even sharper contrast to the proposed plan, to introduce a 'social clause' in the World Trade Organization (WTO) agreements, which

From *Cornell International Law Journal* 34, 2001: 487–500.

would allow the international community to place trade sanctions on countries that violated minimal labour standards.

This chapter will argue that, on the whole, the existing ILS initiatives are ill-conceived and likely to have undesirable fall-outs. This is true even though global opinion has become more sophisticated and nuanced in recent years and some of the more recent proposals, such as the UN Global Compact, are better than some earlier plans. For any ILS effort to succeed and to actually help those it is meant to help, it is imperative to take account of the opinions of developing nations. Accordingly, the chapter ends with a discussion of global democracy.

In summary, it is argued that at this stage ILS is best left to individual nations and only a minimal global co-ordination, and, further, that this global co-ordination is best done through the ILO and the UN. The WTO, *the way it currently functions*, is not the appropriate body for enforcing labour standards. In the long run, there must be an effort to democratize global organizations and institutions such as the WTO. Only when that is done, or at least when the process is reasonably under way, can global organizations be seriously entrusted with the task of promoting higher international labour standards.

14.2. THE ISSUES AND THE HISTORICAL BACKGROUND

Most people, when they think of labour standards, think of the law as its natural handmaiden. If workers are to be better off, avoid excessively hazardous work, keep their children out of the workplace, and so on, our natural tendency is to think of the law as the natural instrument for achieving these. Thus we may think of direct laws (such as minimum wage legislation and the legal prohibition of child labour) and indirect laws, which enhance worker power (such as the right to bargain collectively), as essential instruments for raising worker welfare.

A large part of mainstream economics is a warning that this kind of reasoning is faulty. It reminds us that the absence of government action does not necessarily mean that labour standards will remain low. As productivity and the demand for labour rise, workers can achieve higher living standards through the forces of the market. The mere threat that a worker may quit his or her job could ensure that he or she will be paid well and not be exposed to excessive risks, made to work excessive hours, and so on. Of course, some economists go overboard and argue that the well-being of the worker can be left entirely to market forces.

In reality, there are two broad reasons why interventions may be called for. First, markets often fail because of externalities, asymmetric information, or the difficulties of monitoring, and we may need laws to correct for these failures. And even when markets do not fail, the market outcome may be more inequitable than we are willing to tolerate. Second, even when each nation prefers a higher labour standard this may be impossible to achieve unless several nations co-ordinate their behaviour. When this happens, not only do governments immediately come into play, but the need arises for an internationally co-ordinated effort. The subject of ILS pertains to this second kind of intervention.[1]

The historical roots of the labour standards movement go far back into history, beginning with Sir Robert Peel's introduction of the English Factory Act of 1802, which is now treated as a landmark. The problem of inter-country co-ordination in the context of labour standards dates back to 1818, and in particular to the writings of Robert Owen, which were soon followed by the advocacy of numerous French intellectuals and activists (see Engerman 2001; also Charnovitz 1987: 565). Awareness of the inter-regional nature of the labour standards problem, increased through the nineteenth century and early twentieth century as the Federal Government of the United States battled to curb inter-state competition and adopt common labour standards. (see Kelly 1905: 3–104). The US historical experience nicely mirrors the current global problems.

In the US, the first child-labour legislation was enacted by the state of Massachusetts in 1837. Thereafter, different states brought in different legislation, often backing down for fear that firms and capital would leave and go to states where labour laws were more lax. Some of this history is nicely recounted by Florence Kelley (1905) (see also Moehling 1999: 72, 74–8). The openness of this inter-government competition is transparent from the following account in her book:

For lack of uniformity, progress has been hindered in many states, notably in the glass industry which, during 1904, successfully represented to the legislature of New Jersey that, if deprived of the privilege of employing boys under the age of sixteen years at night, it would migrate to Delaware and West Virginia, where no such restrictions yet await it (Kelly 1905: 91).

The inter-state competition came to an end as recently as 1938 with the passing of the first nationwide law in the US to monitor labour standards—the Fair Labor Standards Act (see Bhagwati 1995: 745).

After the Second World War, and especially in the last one or two decades, as the process of globalization gathered momentum and labour and capital began to move more freely across nations, the labour standards concern spilled beyond national and regional boundaries and became properly an international matter. Ever since the formation of the ILO in 1919 there has been a forum for these international concerns. But for a long time the ILO was an ineffective body, with some doubts about its survival. Initially it had only forty-four member nations. Membership grew slowly until 1946 when the ILO became an agency of the United Nations, and its membership grew rapidly thereafter. By 1969 it had 174 members (Engerman 2001).

The globalization of these concerns led to the codification of labour standards. The standards were classified under four kinds of 'rights' (1) Basic Rights, which included the right against involuntary servitude and injunctions against exploitative child labour and discrimination; (2) Civic Rights, which gave workers the freedom of association and collective bargaining rights; (3) Survival Rights, which ensured a minimum wage, accident compensation, and the right not to be exposed to excessive hazards; and (4) Security Rights, which placed restrictions on employers from firing workers and gave workers the right to retirement benefits (Portes 1990: 219; Maskus 1997: 4–7; Singh 2001).

Resisting the tendency for proliferating labour standards and recognizing that if the same standards are to be imposed on all regions, from sub-Saharan Africa to Western Europe, the requirements have to be fairly minimal, there has now emerged what is often referred to as the list of 'core labour standards'.[2] These consist of (1) prohibition of forced labour, (2) prohibition of discrimination in employment, (3) right to freedom of association, (4) right to bargain collectively, and (5) prohibition of exploitative child labour (Swinnerton 1997).

While the core labour standards are much more reasonable and realistic, the crux of the matter is not the agreement, in the abstract, of the importance of these minimal standards—most reasonable people will accept these—but the practical interpretation of these precepts and the methods used to implement them.

14.3. EXISTING INITIATIVES AND THEIR SHORTCOMINGS

There are two broad classes of global actions that have been used thus far to promote higher ILS. Following my earlier usage (Basu 1999b: 1083), I shall call these *extra-national* and *supra-national* actions.

Extra-national action is action taken by a nation within its own territory that creates incentives in other countries to improve ILS. An example of an extra-national action is Harkin's Bill, more formally known as the Child Labor Deterrence Act, which has, fortunately, remained a bill (S. 613, 103rd Cong. 1993). The aim of this bill was to enable the United States to put a ban on any import that has a child labour input. The law works within the United States but creates incentives in other nations to keep children out of the labour force because nations who do not do so will be prohibited from exporting to the United States. One can go further and argue that children should be empowered as actors in the process of decision making concerning their own rights.[3]

The weakness of the bill is its failure to recognize that (1) parents do not typically send their children to work out of sloth but out of desperation, and (2) it is possible for children to suffer a worse fate than labour, such as starvation. In the poorest nations, an abrupt halt to child labour is likely to cause children to suffer acute poverty and hunger.[4] Clearly, we must not be so single-minded in eradicating child labour that we are prepared to do so by making children starve. Additionally, this kind of extra-national action is likely to drive children away from the export sector to other sectors, which may be worse for their welfare. There is now mounting evidence from Nepal's carpet industry and Bangladesh's garment industry that the anticipation of legislative and other punitive actions by industrialized nations has driven children away from labour to prostitution (see UNICEF 1995; Brown et al. 1999).

The trouble with such bills is that even if they are inspired by a genuine concern for workers in the South, as they often are, they enable protectionism in the North. Interestingly, while the current versions of the Harkin's bill appeal only to the welfare of the child in motivating the legislation, the early versions of the bill had open reference to the fact that child labour in the Third World may cause unemployment in the North.[5] An implication of the analysis in this chapter is that more effective solutions would attack child labour at a nation-wide level, rather than in the exports sector alone (see Basu and Van 1998: 412).

A supra-national action is an action undertaken by a collectivity of nations to sanction against the violation of minimal labour standards. Two prominent examples of supra-national actions are the UN Global Compact and the various ILO conventions. In the case of the Global Compact, companies voluntarily agree to abjure certain practices. In the case of the ILO conventions, countries commit to adhere to certain standards. The important difference between these two voluntary schemes is that they place the primary responsibility of ILS on different agencies. The Global Compact places the responsibility on multinationals and big corporations while the ILO conventions place the responsibility on the nations, and primarily the Third World nations since these are the potential violators of the standards.

Perhaps the most potent form of supra-national action contemplated is to have a social clause in the WTO provisions, which would allow the WTO to impose trade sanctions on an erring country (Staiger n.d.). The risk of empowering the WTO thus is that this will become a powerful instrument of protectionism in the North.[6] Powerful lobbies may have already misused similar well-meaning legislation (Moffett 1998: A1). An interesting case in point is the use of the Sander's Amendment against the Brazilian company Sucocitrico Cutrale (Moffett 1998). The charge was that the company was using children to pluck oranges. However, as the *Wall Street Journal* pointed out, this was probably an act of reprisal headed by the Teamsters Union against Cutrale for downsizing some Minute Maid plants it had bought from Coca-Cola Co. in Florida (Moffett 1998).

The problem is not just that the power of the WTO will be misused, but that, as things stand, it is likely to be used disproportionately by industrialized nations against developing countries simply because the latter do not have the resources—money or expertise—to fight out cases in Geneva. Hence, the across-the-board negative reaction of developing countries to the idea of empowering the WTO seems to have some basis.

Faced with these criticisms, there is a groundswell of opinion in the industrialized nations, at least among the intelligentsia, to use more informal, and therefore flexible, arrangements to raise labour standards.[7] What has caught a lot of the liberal attention is the idea of 'product labelling', that is, to have stickers on 'suspect' goods that declare these goods are 'child-labour free' or, more generally, produced under circumstances that meet a minimal ILS.[8] Hence, the ultimate decision whether or not to boycott such a product is left as a decision of individual consumers. In fact the UN Global Compact is likely to have a very similar effect. By publicizing the list of companies that are signatories to this compact it can create a sense among consumers about which companies meet minimal labour standards and consumers can then boycott the others or buy from them only when there is a substantial price advantage.

Such informal schemes can be deeply unfair. There is, first of all, the large question of whether moral judgements ought to be dispensed through the markets. At first sight, this may appear to be an instance of consumer's sovereignty. But a preference against a carpet that uses child labour is not quite the same thing as one's preference for red apples or against green apples. The former is intimately tied to the urge to sanction a certain kind of behaviour. It is a moral preference of a particular kind, which may be called a 'sanctioning preference'.

While social sanctions do play important roles in civic life, it is not obvious that they are always the right method for dispensing justice. And there is good reason for this. When we express an interest in one good over another as a form of our sanctioning preference, our aim is not just to gratify a personal hedonism, but to punish or reward some people (for instance, those involved in the production of a certain good who, in the process, violate or adhere to certain standards). But what we really want is that those who violate certain standards should be punished to a certain degree, for instance by losing a certain percentage of their business—say 40 per cent. But there is no way for a *single* consumer to express this preference in the market. If he boycotts the good in an effort to hurt the producer and all those involved in the manufacture of a certain product, how does he know that all other consumers will not do the same and so end up drying up 100 per cent of the business, instead of exactly 40 per cent? Likewise, when a consumer decides to buy a particular brand name to reward the manufacturer a certain amount, there is no way to ensure that the right amount of consumers will do the same and so the reward will be commensurate with the good act. In brief, there is a huge co-ordination problem in the dispensing of justice that cannot be solved by the atomistic decisions of thousands of individual consumers.

Hence punishments dispensed through informal social sanctions often turn out to be witch-hunts causing disproportionate pain to some and too little pain to others. Not surprisingly, when it comes to justice, most societies prefer to use a centralized, non-democratic system, namely that of the courts and the judiciary. The free market is not the right instrument for passing moral judgements.

More specifically, the method of product labelling has the disadvantage of being too blunt an instrument. It treats all countries on a par. Take, for instance, child labour. Some sub-Saharan African countries, such as Ethiopia, have a huge dependence on child labour, with close to 45 per cent of all children in the age group 10 to 14 years working. On the other hand, in most Asian countries, including China and India, the participation rates are much lower (respectively, 11 per cent and 14 per cent).[9] If consumers in industrialized nations begin to totally boycott goods with a child-labour input, it is arguable that some of these countries where the participation rates are low will suffer, but be able to withstand the boycott. On the other hand, for several African countries and even some Asian and Latin American countries—the poorer ones—there may be a major adverse impact on the economy, causing a disproportionate suffering for all, including the children, who were meant to be protected by this action.

Additionally, this action is likely to be biased in favour of large manufacturers. Consider a small producer of soccer balls in Pakistan. For him the production unit is likely to double up as factory shed and bedroom. For such a producer to persuade a labelling agency that it does not use child labour and so should get a label will be very hard, since the children are never far away from the areas of production. On the other hand, a large producer can centralize its production and prevent children from even entering the factory. This is in fact exactly what Reebok International has done in Sialkot, Pakistan.

Finally, these informal methods of product boycott share the problem of extra-national action discussed above, which drive bad practices, such as the use of child labour, from the export sector of developing countries to the indigenous sectors where conditions are often worse.[10]

What then are we to do to improve labour standards?

14.4. RECOMMENDATIONS

One general recommendation for upholding labour standards that economists make is the importance of keeping trade channels from the Third World open. It is the greater demand for goods from the Third World that translates into a higher demand for labour, which raises the bargaining power of workers. This argument has been made so many times (for example, Dixit 2000; Jafarey and Lahiri 2001) that there is no reason to dwell on it beyond endorsement.

A related and more specific recommendation, in the context of child labour, is for policies that improve conditions in the adult labour market. While some early work held parents responsible for child labour, it was argued in Basu and Van (1998) that a child's non-work is likely to be a luxury good in a household's decision making.[11] In other words, parents do not like to send their children to work if they can help it; it is only when they are driven by acute economic hardship that they send their children to work.[12] This argument does not deny that there are exceptions in the form of abusive parents who buy their own leisure by making their children work and that other factors, such as the availability of decent schooling, have a large influence on the incidence of child labour. But, in general, when child labour is a mass phenomenon, as in contemporary developing countries, it is wrong to equate child labour with child abuse. It follows that a policy for eradicating child labour should treat the parent as an ally in this task rather than as an adversary. Hence, if we can intervene to reduce adult unemployment and raise adult incomes, parents on their own will withdraw children from the labour market. There will be no need to use the stick to achieve this. So, somewhat paradoxically, the one policy always worth using to combat *child* labour is to improve the conditions of *adult* labour.

All these policy interventions through the market are desirable but will clearly take a lot of time to implement. Even if we use them in the long run, we have to think of more direct interventions in the short run. What should these be? We have seen above how it is likely to be better to rely on conventions such as the ones adopted by the ILO or compacts such as that of the UN, rather than to use the social clause of the WTO. Yet even these are not good enough. Nor is it a good idea to leave sanctions to the consumers.

As things stand, the main agency for labour standards policy has to be with the national governments, which can tailor the policy to each nation's specific needs and context. Yet this alone is not enough, since labour standards have an important inter-country dimension. The tension is not between the North and the South but between the South and the South, as argued in Basu (1999) and Kanbur and Chau (2000). With globalization it is now easier for capital to move from one country to another. It is only natural that when one developing country contemplates raising a particular standard it has to worry that it may drive capital to another developing country.

This was borne out quite strikingly when, because of political reasons, the US stopped importing carpets from Iran. With one developing country's exports cut off, another developing country took over the business. In this case, India became the largest exporter to the US. It is this very fear that exports will shift to another developing nation that ties the hands of individual governments of developing countries from taking more action. On the other hand, the chances of an export activity shifting from a developing nation to an industrialized nation because of the raising of labour standards are negligible because the two types of nations have such widely differing comparative advantages. There is, therefore, need for multi-country co-ordinated action, but the co-ordination has to be among the developing countries in their own collective interest.

Hence we need a global organization to do the co-ordination. The difficulty stems from the fact that there is no organization that adequately represents the opinion and interests of developing nations. A prerequisite for handing over labour standards policy to an international organization is the democratization of the organization. Indeed, the WTO, in principle, could be an enforcer of ILS, if developing countries felt it represented their interest adequately. So, though for now we do not have too many options, other than relying or market-oriented policies, such as bolstering the demand for adult labour in developing nations and keeping open trade channels, and for some effort by national governments, there has to be a major effort to democratize international organizations such as the WTO, so that they can then be entrusted with the important task of crafting and implementing policies for better labour standards.

The democratization of international organizations is a large topic. The concluding section of this chapter is a brief incursion into this complicated subject.

14.5. RESTRUCTURING INTERNATIONAL ORGANIZATIONS

One concomitant of globalization and technological progress that has either gone unnoticed or has been hushed up by those who did notice it is that it has a natural corrosive effect on global democracy. As a consequence of this phenomenon, even if individual countries become democratic, the aggregate of global democracy may well be on the wane. Democracy entails many things—the existence of a variety of political and legislative institutions, avenues for citizens to participate in the formation of economic policies that affect their lives and, in the ultimate analysis, a certain mindset. Yet, at the core of it and in its simplest form, democracy requires: (1) that people should have the right to choose those who rule them and (2) the principle that the vote of each person should count as much as another person's vote.

Note that globalization, almost by definition, means that nations and people can exert a greater influence on other nations and the lives of citizens in other nations. Moreover, this power of one nation to influence another is by no means symmetric. The US for instance, can cut off virtually all the trade lines of Cuba. It can do so not only by curtailing its own trade with Cuba but by threatening punitive action against those who trade with or invest in Cuba. This is not just a hypothetical possibility; the Helms-Burton Act in the US is testimony to how this can actually happen.[13] Cuba, on the other hand, can do little to hurt the American economy or polity. Likewise, China can do things to Taiwan, which Taiwan can in no way reciprocate.

As the world shrinks and powerful governments develop a variety of instruments and ways to influence the lives of citizens in other nations, it is no longer enough for people to be able to choose the leaders of their own nations. Since transnational voting does not happen (and even its hypothetical suggestion sounds absurd to us), globalization is bound to cause a diminution of global democracy.

Thanks to globalization there are a variety of instruments that nations can use to influence outcomes elsewhere. For the purposes of the current chapter the most important is the cessation of international trade, such as would happen if the WTO were empowered to enforce ILS. International trade (after a slowdown in the years between the two World Wars) has risen steadily. These global linkages have fuelled unprecedented growth rates of national incomes (during the 1990s China grew at around 8 per cent per annum and India 6.5 per cent), but they have also created new vulnerabilities. Governments and international organizations can now use the threat of disrupting these flows (or the lure of releasing greater flows of money or goods) to enforce conformity to certain kinds of behaviour. And such threats have been used. International organizations have given money while insisting that the developing countries fulfil certain conditions, many of which have had nothing to do with ensuring repayment. These conditionalities have, at times, even been contradictory, such as requiring the debtor nation to practice democracy and to privatize certain key sectors, unmindful of the fact that this may be against the collective wishes of the people.

Some of these conditions have been blatantly in the interest of the donor nation. In 1998, during the Asian crisis, the rescue package put together with money from several industrialized nations, most prominently Japan and the US, had clauses that required Korea to lift bans on imports of certain Japanese products (which Japan had long been trying to sell to Korea) and to open up its banking sector to foreign banks (an item that had long been on America's bilateral agenda with Korea). Some of these demands may well be good for the borrower, but that is not the issue here. From the point of view of assessing global democracy, what is relevant is that people of the weaker nation have very little say in the imposition of these policies.

Given that the benefits of democracy are ample, as academic research has shown and non-academics always knew, this erosion of global democracy must have negative fallouts. Indeed, it is arguable that the rise in global unrest and instabilities are a manifestation of this retreat of democracy. And the inchoate demands of the protestors in the streets of Seattle and Washington may be founded in an intuitive but ill-articulated perception of this erosion of democracy.

What can be done about the erosion of global democracy? Utopian schemes, such as a global government or a global bank that is answerable to all nations in the world, are a distant dream. The process of globalization will course on, and inter-country democracy will continue to get bruised. It will be some time before this can bring us to discussing global governance and banking. In the meantime, what is open to us are small measures, namely those of strengthening the democratic structure of global institutions, such as the World Bank, the IMF, and the WTO. These are small measures, but extremely important.

Therefore, the appropriate measures are, ironically, quite different from the dismantling of these organizations, which is what the protestors in Seattle and Washington, and also some arch conservative groups in industrialized nations, want. On the contrary, we need to restructure these organizations and recognize that they have an especially important role to play today. Of course there will be need for vigilance. There is enough evidence that powerful politicians in powerful nations like to think of international institutions as valuable only to the extent that they can use them to their own advantage.

On 20 January 2000, Senator Jesse Helms, arguably the most important congressional voice in the US, told the council members of the UN:

If the United Nations respects the sovereign rights of the American people, *and serves them as an effective tool of diplomacy, it will earn and deserve their respect and support.* But a United Nations that seeks to impose its presumed authority on the American people, without their consent begs for confrontation and, I want to be candid, eventual US withdrawal.[14]

Helms went on to express distaste for 'supranational institutions', including the international criminal court which was created in 2000. What is most damaging about this kind of remark is that any organization that meets with Jesse Helms' approval immediately becomes suspect from the point of view of the world as a whole. The last thing that a credible international organization will now want is Jesse Helms' blessing. A WTO or a UN that has Helms' blessing and is entrusted with enforcing international labour and environmental standards will immediately be unacceptable to other nations, especially the developing countries whose interests are often orthogonal to those of industrialized nations.

We need to work to give nations, rich and poor, equal say, at least in international organizations that are supposed to play a mediating role in world economics or international relations. This horizontal equity is violated in most organizations through at least one of two routes. First, there is the open channel, which gives a larger share of votes to the nations contributing more to these organizations. This is certainly true of the IMF and the World Bank. The second route is through the lack of transparency of decision making. One can see the importance of this for democracy by looking at policy making within a country. If the process of decision making is visible to all, it becomes difficult for any group or lobby to hijack the agenda. The same holds true for international organizations. Big and powerful nations, by virtue of contributing senior personnel and money to these organizations, have much greater access to them. If decisions occur behind opaque walls, powerful nations are much more able to divert the agenda to suit their own interests. Take the case of the WTO. While it does follow the important principle of one-country one-vote, it is widely perceived as a preserve of powerful and rich nations. This is in part because of what some analysts call the 'green room' process, that is, what goes on behind the scenes (see Schott and Watal 2000: 283, 285–6). It is the green room where the agenda is set and what is to appear on the table for all member nations to discuss and vote on is determined. Many of the end results are determined at that stage. If the WTO is to become a more democratic institution, it must not allow its green room to be hijacked by a few.

This problem is nowhere more obvious than in the drafting of international labour standards. These are ostensibly designed in the interests of the workers of developing countries. But the form that these standards are tending to take— and the increasing talk of using trade sanctions to impose these standards—is close to what protectionist lobbies in industrial nations seek. This is not surprising given the greater access that the lobbies of rich countries have in the corridors of power in international organizations.

Most sound surprised by this criticism of global institutions. The fact that *the questioning* of the practice of richer nations (who contribute more funds) exercising more voting power in these organizations sounds outrageous simply shows how far away we still are from *global* democracy. It does not at all seem outrageous that Bill Gates does not have multiple votes in the US elections on the ground that he contributes more to government coffers. In fact, the suggestion that he could have more votes sounds outrageous. This is because democracy within a nation is a much more settled idea.

Fortunately, opinions change. Multinationals nowadays talk in terms of environmental responsibility and the importance of respecting labour standards, even when that implies taking a cut in profits. This seems to violate age-old beliefs and also the textbook description of multinational corporations.

When the one-person one-vote idea first came about, the rich feudal landlords must have been shocked and cried foul at this blatant injustice and the chaos in the process of decision making that this would cause. But no longer does this democratic principle *within a nation* seem strange.

Now, with the call for restructuring international organizations ringing out from the streets of Seattle and Washington and also congressional committees, such as the commission headed by Allan Meltzer (Report of the International Financial Institution Advisory Commission 2000) this is a good time for us to think through some of these issues. We must consider these issues not just from the point of view of economic efficiency and greater cost effectiveness, but also from the point of view of representation of the poor. It is only when we manage to make these changes in the structure of international organizations that we will be able to entrust them with important tasks such as monitoring labour and environmental standards across the globe.

NOTES

1. This view of ILS is explicit in Basu (1999a: 80, 89); Chau and Kanbur (2000).
2. For discussion, see Swinnerton (1997: 73, 76–84)
3. This is argued by Boyden and Levinson (2000).
4. There is a lot of evidence that it is poverty that drives households to send their children to work. For cross-country evidence, see Krueger (1997). And for evidence based on intertemporal micro data, see Edmonds (n.d.) and see also note 12.
5. A superior extra-national legal action is the Sander's Amendment of the Tariff Act of 1930, which seeks to ban imports of goods that use forced child labor. This move towards distinguishing between different forms of child labor is a move in the right direction.
6. Much has been written about the dangers of giving the WTO the power to uphold ILS. Example, Bhagwati (1995: 745); see also Srinivasan (1996).
7. For a very interesting suggestion of how to organize a flexible system, see Fung *et al.* (2001: 4). Their scheme shares the spirit of the UN Global Compact in one respect—they both place the primary responsibility for upholding standards on the corporations. However, the scheme does have important flaws. See Bardhan (2001); Broad (2001); Levinson (2001), Moberg (2001); Standing (2001); White (2001); and Basu (2001).
8. For analyses of product labelling, see Brown (2000); Basu *et al.* (2000); Bachman (2000: 30).
9. These and other statistics were compiled by the ILO. See ILO (1996).
10. For an interesting study in the context of Bangladesh of how global monitoring can backfire, see Kabeer (2000).
11. See also Swinnerton et al. (1999: 1382). Very different kinds of problems arise with street children, but unfortunately on this there are as yet few studies, an exception being Myers (1988).
12. There is ample evidence for the luxury axiom. For empirical studies that shed light on this axiom see, for instance, Ray (2000); Bhalotra (2000); Emerson and Portela (2000); Freije and Lopez-Calva (2000).

13. I have discussed the role and consequences of 'triadic' threats in Basu (2000).
14. *http://www.conservative.org/columnists/helms01202000.htm* (last visited 10 October 2001) (my italics—but also my hunch that those would be Helms' italics).

REFERENCES

Bachman, S.L. 2000. 'The Political Economy of child Labor and Its Impact on International Business'. *Business Economics* 35.

Bardhan, P.2001. 'Some Up, Some Down'. *Boston Review* (February/March).

Basu, A.K. et al. 2000. 'Guaranteed Manufactured without Child Labor'. Working Paper 2000–4. Cornell University.

Basu, K. 1999a. 'International Labour Standards and Child Labour'. *Challenge* 42.

—— 1999b. 'Child Labour: Cause, Consequence, and Cure, with Remarks on International Labour Standards'. *Journal of Economic Literature* 37.

—— 2000. *Prelude to Political Economy: A Study of the Social and Political Foundations of Economics.* Oxford and New York: Oxford University Press.

—— 2001. 'The View from the Tropics'. *Boston Review* (February/March).

Basu, K. and Van P. H. 1998. 'The Economics of Child Labor'. *American Economic Review* 88.

Bhagwati, J. 1995. 'Trade Liberalization and 'Fair Trade' Demands: Addressing the Environmental and Labour Standards Issues'. *World Economy* 18.

Bhalotra, S. 2000. 'Is Child Work Necessary?'. University of Cambridge. Mimeo.

Boyden, J. and D. Levison. 2000. 'Children as Economic and Social Actors in the Development Process'. EGDI Working Paper No.1. Available at *http://www.egdi.gov.re/pdf/workpaper.pdf.*

Broad, R. 2001. 'A Better Mousetrap'. *Boston Review* (February/March).

Brown, D. 2000. 'A Transactions Cost Politics Analysis of International Child Labor Standards'. In A.V. Deardorff and R.M. Stern, eds. *Social Dimensions of US Trade Policy.* Ann Arbor: University of Michigan Press.

Brown, D. et al. 1999. 'US Trade and Other Policy Options and Programs to Deter Foreign Exploitation of Child Labor'. Discussion Paper No. 433. University of Michigan. Available at *http://www.spp.umich.edu/RSIE/workingpapers/wp/html.*

Charnovitz, S. 1987. 'The Influence of International Labour Standards on the World Trading Regime: A Historical Overview'. *International Labour Review* 126: 565.

Chau, N.H. and R. Kanbur. 2000. 'The Race to the Bottom, from the Bottom'. CEPR Working Paper No. 2687. Cornell University. Available at *http://www.arts.cornell.edu/poverty/Kanbur/ck 15.pdf 2001.*

Dixit, A. 2000. 'Comment on a Transactions Cost Politics Analysis of International Child Labor Standards'. In A.V. Deardorff and R.M. Stern, eds, *Social Dimensions of US Trade Policy.* Ann Arbor: University of Michigan Press.

Edmonds, E. n.d. 'Will Child Labour Decline with Improvements in Living Standards'. Dartmouth College. Mimeo. Available at *http://www.dartmouth.edu/~eedmonds/vnivc.pdf.*

Emerson P. and A.S. Portela. 2000. 'Is There a Child Labor Trap? Intergenerational

Persistence of Child Labor in Brazil'. Cornell University. Mimeo. Available at *http:// econ.cudenuer.edu/emerson/childlabor/pdf.*

Engerman, S. 2001. 'The History and Political Economy of International Labour Standards'. Rochester University. Mimeo. Available at *http://www.egdi/gov.de/pdf/ study/.pdf.*

Freije, S. and L.F. Lopez-Calva. 2000. 'Child Labor School Attendance and Poverty in Mexico and Venezuela'. Cornell University. Mimeo.

Fung, A., D. O'Rourke, and C. Sabel 2001. 'Realizing Labor Standards: How Transparency, Competition, and Sanctions Could Improve Working Conditions Worldwide'. *Boston Review* (February/March).

International Labor Organization (ILO). 1996. *Economically Active Populations: Estimates and Projections 1950–2010.* CD-Rom. ILO.

Jafarey, S. and S. Lahiri. 2001. 'Will Trade Sanctions Reduce Child Labour? The Role of Credit Markets'. University of Essex. Mimeo.

Kabeer, N. 2000. *The Power to Choose: Bangladesh Women and Labor Market Decisions in London and Dhaka.* London: Verse Press.

Kelly, F. 1905. *Some Ethical Gains through Legislation.* The Citizen's Library of Economics Politics and Sociology, New York.

Krueger, A. 1997. 'International Labour Standards and Trade'. In M. Bruno and B. Pleskovic, eds, *Annual World Bank Conference on Development Economics 1996.* Washington: World Bank.

Levinson, M. 2001. 'Wishful Thinking'. *Boston Review* (February/March).

Maskus, K.E. 1997. 'Should Core Labor Standards Be Imposed through International Trade Policy?'. Policy Research Working Paper. The World Bank, Development Research Group.

Moberg, D. 2001. 'Union and the State'. *Boston Review* (February/March).

Moehling, C.M. 1999. 'State Child Labor Laws and the Decline of Child Labor'. *Explorations in Economics History* 36.

Moffet, M. 1998. 'Citrus Squeeze: US Child Labor Law Sparks a Trade Debate Over Brazilian Oranges'. *Wall Street Journal* (9 September).

Myers, W. 1988. 'Alternative Services for Street children: The Brazilian Approach'. In A. Bequele and J. Boyden, eds. *Combating Child Labor.* International Labor Office, Geneva.

Portes, Alejandro. 1990. 'When More Can be Less: Labor Standards, Development and the Informal Economy.' In US Department of Labor, Labor Standards and Development in the Global Economy 219.

Ray, R. 2000. 'Child Labor, Child Schooling, and their Interaction with Adult Labor: Empirical Evidence for Peru and Pakistan'. *World Bank Economics Review* 14.

Schott, J.J. and J. Watal. 2000. 'Decision Making in the WTO'. In J.J. *Schott,* ed. *The WTO After Seattle.* Institute for International Economics. 283, 285–6.

Singh, Nirvikar. 2001. 'The Impact of International Labor Standards: A Survey of Economic Theory'. University of California, Santa Cruz. Mimeo. Available at *http:// www.egdi.gov.re/pdf/study/study2.pdf.*

Srinivasan, T.N. 1996. 'International Trade and Labor Standards from an Economic Perspective'. In P. Van Dijck and Faber, eds. *Challenges to the New World Trade Organization.*

Staiger, R. n.d. 'The International Organization and Enforcement of Labor Standards'. University of Wisconsin. Mimeo. Available at *http://www.egdi.gov.se/pdf/study/study4. pdf.*

Standing, G. 2001. 'Human Development'. *Boston Review* (February/March).

Swinnerton, K.A. 1997. 'An Essay on Economic Efficiency and Core Labour Standards'. *World Economics* 20: 73, 76–84.

——— et al. 1999. 'The Economics of Child Labor: Comment'. *American Economic Review* 89.

UNICEF. 1995. *Girls in Especially Difficult Circumstances: An Action Report.* Kathmandu: UNICEF.

White, H. 2001. 'Educating Workers'. *Boston Review* (February/March).

15 The Economics of Child Labour

with Pham Hoang Van

According to the International Labour Organization (ILO), in 1990 there were almost 79 million children around the world who did regular work (see Ashagrie 1993: 16). This estimate of child labour would vary depending on how we define work, how we define a child, and how we collect the data, but no matter which estimate we take, the inescapable fact remains that this is a problem of gigantic proportions. Moreover, the magnitude of the tragedy is not captured by numbers alone, since the conditions of child labour can vary. There are children who work in hazardous industries, risking accident and injury; there are others working in conditions that take a slower but definite toll on their health.

As people become informed about child labour, the natural reaction is to seek ways to banish child labour. The easiest way to banish it—or so it seems—is to ban it. And across the world there has been an increasing chorus of opinion seeking a ban on child labour. Details of the proposals have varied. In the United States, the so-called Harkin's bill (Child Labor Deterrence Act of 1997) seeks to ban the import of those goods which have used child labour as input. International organizations and many citizens fora have talked about labelling products which are free from child labour inputs so that individuals, by confining their consumption to such goods, can bring about an effective ban. It will be argued later that many of these well-meaning interventions can be counterproductive.

From *American Economic Review* 1998: 412–27.

This chapter has benefited from seminar presentations at Boston University, Cornell University, the Delhi School of Economics, DELTA, Georgetown University, Pennsylvania State University, the University of California-Berkeley, the University of Namur, and Yale University. We would like to thank Dilip Abreu, Jim Albrecht, Pranab Bardhan, Valerie Bencivenga, François Bourguignon, Martin Browning, Veena Das, Rajat Deb, Ron Ehrenberg, James Foster, Patrick Francois, Albert Hirschman, Alain de Janvry, Heraklis Polemarchakis, Debraj Ray, T.N. Srinivasan, Erik Thorbecke, John Toye, Susan Vroman, and Henry Wan, Jr. for comments and criticisms at different stages of this work.

This is a field of study where prescription has outstripped analysis by a wide margin. It is the aim of this chapter to construct a model of child labour which can then be used to ask and answer some policy questions. There is one central idea which is at the heart of our model. The next two paragraphs give an intuitive sketch of this idea.

In the popular mind, child labour is very often equated with child abuse. The phenomenon is taken to be a product of avaricious entrepreneurs seeking cheap labour and selfish parents who would prefer enjoying leisure while their children work. It seems to us that while this popular description of entrepreneurs may well be accurate, the parents are mischaracterized. We argue instead that the traditional model of the household, where parents take their children's interests into account, while somewhat idealistic, is a better model. Thus, while not denying that child abuse does occur in all societies, we take the position that when we have children working as a mass phenomenon as in many less-developed countries, it is much more likely that this reflects not a difference in the attitude of the parents but the problem of stark poverty where the parents are compelled to send the children to work for reasons of survival. Even in England, which witnessed some of the worst excesses of child labour in the late eighteenth and early nineteenth centuries, a parliamentary report noted that 'parents were desperately unhappy about the situations their children were in but could do nothing about it. The social system allowed them no choice' (Horrell and Humphries 1995).

Once we accept this description of household decision making, the case for declaring child labour illegal gets considerably weakened, but in some situations there may nevertheless be a more complicated and equilibrium-based reason for declaring child labour illegal. If we agree that sending children out to work is an act of desperation on the part of the parents, it seems reasonable to expect that parents would not send their children to work if their own wages were higher or employment prospects better. Now do the following experiment. Suppose all children are pulled out from work, say, because of a total ban. What effect will this have? Clearly, the first effect of this will be a shortage of labour. And given that child and adult labour are usually substitutes, the wages of adults will rise in response to the excess demand for labour.[1] But as adult wages rise, it is possible, given our above assumption, that parents will not now want to send their children to work. Hence the ban may become redundant. In brief, once a ban is imposed, the ban may become unnecessary. Essentially what we are claiming is that the labour market may be characterized by multiple equilibria—one in which wages are low and children work and another in which wages are high and children do not work.

In the scenario described here, the purpose of government intervention is very different from that in conventional models. In our model, intervention does not create a new equilibrium but simply jolts the economy out of one equilibrium to another *pre-existing* equilibrium. In this model, partial bans can have unexpected adverse effects.

Economists seeking government intervention in the child-labour market have typically justified their recommendation by claiming that there are externalities to child labour or that private returns to education are smaller than social returns.[2] But such arguments need to be substantiated since 'externalities' are too often treated as a catch-all. What our model demonstrates is that in certain specific situations there may be a rigorous case for a ban simply based on the child-labour market's natural tendency to exhibit multiple equilibria.

There are many other aspects of child labour which are important—its dynamic implications, its relation to education and human capital, and its medical aspects. But those are not our concern here. Our focus is on the multiple equilibria which seem to be natural and inherent (potential) characteristics of child-labour markets but have eluded researchers and observers in this field.

The plan of the chapter is as follows. Section 15.1 presents some basic information on child labour and some accounts of historical experience which are relevant as backdrop to our model. Section 15.2 presents a basic model and introduces a diagrammatic technique for depicting equilibria. Section 15.3 suggests ways of generalizing the basic model. Policy questions and the subject of legislation form the subject matter of Section 15.4. Section 15.5 considers the implications of the model for the economics of fertility and suggests ways of extending this kind of modelling to other areas.

15.1. FACTS AND EXPERIENCE

To begin with the current scenario, the only thing that one can be certain about are the broad parameters of the problem. We known that a very large number of children—meaning persons below the age of 15 years—work. Most of these working children are in the Third World, with the exception of child prostitution, the incidence of which can be high even in industrialized nations. The bulk of child labourers belong to the 10-to-14 year age category; but there is also a substantial number of children below 10 years of age who work.

As we go behind such broad generalizations to actually construct numbers, we run into controversy. Employment surveys typically do not have respondents below 15 years of age. Some countries, such as India, have tried to officially count the number of children who work. But one can get very different answers depending on which source one turns to (for discussion, see Weiner 1991; Grootaert and Kanbur 1995). For instance, in 1983 the National Sample Survey (NSS) estimates showed that 17.4 million children worked, whereas a study by the Operations Research Group, conducted at the behest of the Ministry of Labour, estimated the number to be close to 44 million.

For an overall statistical picture, one can turn to the ILO estimates of 1993 collated and quoted in Ashagrie (1993: Table 4). Among children between 10 and 14 years of age, 70.9 million are labourers. If we look at 'participation rates', that is the *percentage* of children who work among all children of that age-group, the figures can be quite alarming. For the world as a whole for the 10-to-14 year age-group, the participation rate is 13.7 per cent, and in some parts of central Africa the figure can be as high as 32.9 per cent.[3]

Historically, child labour was not the preserve of Africa, Latin America, and Asia. Some of the worst excesses occurred in Europe in the late eighteenth and early nineteenth centuries and especially in Britain during the Industrial Revolution.[4] According to most sources, the participation rates in Britain during its industrial revolution were very high—higher than the contemporary rates in all regions of the world with the sole exception of middle Africa. According to the 1851 Census, in England and Wales 36.6 per cent of boys aged 10–14 and 19.9 per cent of girls in the same age-group were working. It is striking to note that these high participation rates in 1851 existed despite the main Factories Acts (of 1833 and 1844), which placed curbs on child labour, being already in place, and child labour arguably being on the wane.[5]

One important question is: what effect did the Factories Acts have on the incidence of child labour? The answer to this will help us speculate about the consequences of the many laws which are currently either in effect or under consideration. A study by Grootaert and Kanbur (1995) suggests that the incidence of child labour was declining even before the Factories Acts. Given that the non-poor people in poor countries do not send their children to work, could we assert that child labour in Britain would vanish anyway as British prosperity rose, with or without laws to curtail children's employment? The model we develop should help us ponder such questions, but in the remainder of this section let us try to elicit information from the historical literature in order to give shape to some of the *assumptions* that we use to build our model.

The popular instinct among most sections of our society is to support ideas such as those outlined in Senator Harkin's bill in the United States, which seeks to ban the import of child-labour tainted products. This popular instinct stems from the presupposition that the existence of child labour is the product of greed on the part of employers who employ the children and the parents who send the children to work. As stated in the introduction, we reject this view of the parents. And indeed there is overwhelming support for this rejection.

The first and foremost evidence is the contemporary fact that the children of the non poor seldom work even in very poor countries. This phenomenon is best explained by supposing that parents withdraw their children from the labour force as soon as they can afford to do so. In other words, children's leisure or, more precisely, non work[6] is a luxury good in the household's consumption in the sense that a poor household cannot afford to consume this good but it does so as soon as the household income rises sufficiently. In our second model, we use the Stone–Geary utility function to capture this idea.

Another source of evidence comes from the late-nineteenth century census data for Philadelphia. Claudia Goldin's (1979) analysis of this data leads her to conclude (p. 124): 'The higher the father's wage, the lower the probability of the child participating in the labor force'; and also: 'The father's unemployment sent both boys and girls into the labour force, with a stronger impact on the former'. A different kind of evidence comes from David Vincent's (1981) study of working-class autobiographies. The study showed that children who worked rarely blamed their parents, believing instead that it was poverty that drove the parents into making the children labour (see also Anderson 1971).[7]

By attributing to each household one utility function, our analysis does abstract from reality. There is evidence, for instance, that household consumption patterns differ depending on who takes the decisions and who earns the money.[8] Despite this abstraction, it is worth emphasizing that our model does not conflict with recent evidence and theories which ask for the rejection of the 'unitary model' of the household. This is because we assume that a child's labour-supply decision is taken by a parent. There is no attempt to deny that this decision could be different if the decision making were shifted to another member of the household.

More generally, all we want is to give primacy to the household or family wealth as a determinant of child labour. There has been some recent attempt to model parents and the children as being involved in bargaining conflicts (Moehling 1995; Gupta 1998). Such investigations are worthwhile but, if we were to have one representative model for analysing child labour we do not consider the bargaining model to be the right one. The model presented in the next section captures the essentials of our main theoretical idea.

Finally, it is important to emphasize that the phenomenon of child labour has important sociological and psychological issues at stake. The child-labour market does not always operate on the basis of voluntary exchange but involves coercion and psychological pressures (see Silvers 1996: 82). Nevertheless, we have stayed away from many of the larger issues and confine our attention to a rigorous economic analysis because it is not clear to us how we can take on board different aspects of this important phenomenon—economic, sociological, psychological—all at once. There is no choice but to dissect such a large phenomenon into several parts and to analyse these one at a time. Moreover, we hope that our chapter demonstrates how well-meaning spontaneous recommendations can often backfire. This is an area where what seems obviously the right thing to do may turn out, on deliberation, to be quite the opposite. As a consequence, this is also an area where individuals and groups, with their own self-interested agenda, can garner mass support for policies which actually benefit them while superficially appearing to help the cause of the labouring children. Formalism and scientific inquiry can be a bulwark against this.

15.2. CHILD LABOUR: A BASIC MODEL

What is nice about the results derived from this model and the one in the next section is that they are based on very weak assumptions. The two essential assumptions may be codified as the following two axioms.

THE LUXURY AXIOM: A family will send the children to the labour market only if the family's income from non-child-labour sources drops very low.

THE SUBSTITUTION AXIOM: From a firm's point of view, adult labour and child labour are substitutes. More specifically child labour can be substituted by adult labour.

In constructing the models we shall use many special assumptions and functional forms but those are all expositional devices. They keep the analysis tractable. All our main results are, we believe, essentially derived from the luxury and substitution axioms. It is worth stressing here that the luxury axiom that we need is weaker than the word 'luxury' suggests. (This is clarified in note 11.) These assumptions are not in themselves sufficient for generating multiple equilibria but they are sufficient for giving us a model with a *potential* multiplicity of equilibria. We discuss the conditions under which multiple equilibria actually occur, after describing the model formally. The above assumptions are built into the preference relations and production functions that we specify in this and the next section.

Assume that there are N identical families (or households) in the economy and that each family consists of one adult and one child. The latter of course may be simply a convention whereby *we call* the two parents 'one adult' and the two children 'one child'. The family's preference, $\succ$, is described by a binary relation defined on the set

(15.1) $\{(c, e) \mid c \geq 0, e \in \{0,1\}\},$

where c is consumption by each family member and e is the child's work effort which can only take on values of 0 or 1. We are assuming that the adults always work, no matter what the wages are. And for simplicity, child and adult consumptions are presently assumed to be equal.

We shall now impose an assumption which is in keeping with the luxury axiom and the arguments presented in this section. It is, however, very strong. This is only for reasons of simplicity and is relaxed later. The assumption is as follows. A family prefers to send the child to work if and only if, in the absence of income from the child, each individual's consumption falls below a certain exogenously fixed subsistence level, s. More formally, for all $\delta > 0$,

(15.2) $(c, 0) \succ (c + \delta, 1)$ if $c \geq s$,

and $(c + \delta, 1) \succ (c, 0)$ if $c < s$.

The household's aim is to choose c and e so as to maximize its preference subject to the following budget constraint:

(15.3) $2c \leq ew_c + w_A,$

where w_C and w_A are the market wages for, respectively, child and adult labour. Each household treats these wages as given.

The solution to the household's maximization problem, therefore, is as follows:

(15.4) $c(w_A) = \begin{cases} \dfrac{w_A}{2} & \text{if } w_A \geq 2s \\ \dfrac{w_A + w_C}{2} & \text{if } w_A < 2s ; \end{cases}$

$$(15.5) \qquad e(w_A) = \begin{cases} 0 & \text{if } w_A \geq 2s \\ 1 & \text{if } w_A < 2s . \end{cases}$$

It follows that labour supplies of adults and children, denoted by S^A and S^C, are given by:

$$(15.6) \qquad S^A = N;$$

$$(15.7) \qquad S^C(w_A) = \begin{cases} 0, & \text{if } w_A \geq 2s \\ N, & \text{if } w_A < 2s. \end{cases}$$

Our next step is to derive the market demand for adult and child labour. To do so we invoke the substitution axiom and make the simplifying assumption that adults and children are substitutes in production, subject to an adult-equivalent scaling, given by γ, where $0 < \gamma < 1$. So assume there are n identical firms, each producing a single consumption good. Each firm i's production function is given by:

$$(15.8) \qquad x_i = f(A_i + \gamma C_i), f' > 0, f'' < 0,$$

where x_i is firm i's output of the consumption good, and A_i and C_i are respectively the numbers of adult and child labourers employed by firm i. The firm is a wage taker. Hence, firm i's problem is as follows:

$$(15.9) \qquad \max_{\{A_i, C_i\}} f(A_i + \gamma C_i) - A_i w_A - C_i w_C.$$

The solution to (15.9) is straightforward. If $w_A < w_C / \gamma$, then the firm will employ only adults. If $w_A > w_C / \gamma$, then it will employ only children. If $w_A = w_C /\gamma$, then it will be indifferent between adults and children. We call w_C /γ the 'effective child wage' that is, the market child wage per adult-equivalent. In addition, each firm will always ensure that

$$(15.10) \qquad f'(A_i + \gamma C_i) = \min\left\{w_A, \frac{w_C}{\gamma}\right\}.$$

The aggregate demands for adult and child labour, D^C and D^A, are derived by multiplying each firm's demand by n. Hence, $D^A = D^A(w_A, w_C)$ and $D^C = D^C(w_A, w_C)$ are given implicitly by the following.

$$(15.11) \qquad \text{If } w_A > \frac{w_C}{\gamma} \text{ then } D^A = 0$$

$$\text{and } f'\left(\frac{\gamma D^C}{n}\right) = \frac{w_C}{\gamma}.$$

$$\text{If } w_A < \left(\frac{D^A}{n}\right) \text{ then } D^C = 0$$

$$\text{and } f'\left(\frac{w_C}{\gamma}\right) = w_A.$$

$$\text{If } w_A = \frac{w_C}{\gamma}$$

then $f' \left(\dfrac{D^A + \gamma D^C}{n} \right) = w_A = \dfrac{w_C}{\gamma}$

A labour-market equilibrium in this simple model is a pair of wages, $(w_A{}^*, w_C{}^*)$, such that

(15.12) $D^A (w_A{}^*, w_C{}^*) = N$,   and

$D^C (w_A{}^*, w_C{}^*) = S^C (w_A{}^*)$.

At first sight it may seem that what we have described is a *partial* equilibrium. However, it is easy to embed this model in a general equilibrium framework without having to modify the above description. One way is to think of this as an economy where the firms' profits are not shared with the households but instead are consumed entirely by the entrepreneurs of the firms. In that case the labour market equilibrium would fully characterize the closed-economy general equilibrium.[9] Alternatively, we could assume this to be a small open economy which would imply that the goods market will trivially clear and the same results would derive. One implication of viewing this as a general equilibrium will be that both equilibria will be Pareto efficient by the fundamental theorem of welfare economics, though, of course, the labour households may be better off in one equilibrium rather than another.

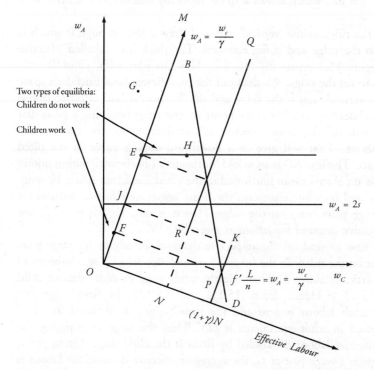

Figure 15.1: Equilibrium in the Child- and Adult-Labour Markets

We now develop a diagrammatic technique for depicting this equilibrium. The geometry, apart from aiding intuition, turns out to be a very useful instrument for doing policy analysis. It also helps us see very clearly how this model *may* exhibit multiple equilibria so that in the same economy, children working and children not working can be part of equilibrium behaviour.

In Figure 15.1, consider first the (w_A, w_C)-space. The axes of this space are marked Ow_C and Ow_A. For wage pairs above the horizontal line $w_A = 2s$, children will not work, $e = 0$; and below this line $e = 1$. In this space draw the graph of the function $w_A = w_C / \gamma$. This is the line OM. Since $\gamma < 1$, this line is steeper than 45°. This is a very significant and will be referred to here as the 'ridge'. If (w_A, w_C) is above the ridge, then the demand for adult labour is zero; if (w_A, w_C) is below the ridge, then the demand for child labour is zero. What happens if the market wages lie on the ridge? Let us define the *'effective labour'* used or demanded by a firm to be the total amount of labour measured in adult-equivalents being used or demanded by the firm. So if a firm i employs A_i adult labourers and C_i child labourers, its *effective* labour employment is $A_i + \gamma C_i$. If the market wages for adult and child labourers lie on the ridge then we know from (11) that each firm's effective demand for labour, L_i, is given by $f'(L_i) = w_A = w_C / \gamma$. In other words, firm i facing such a (w_A, w_C) will be willing to employ any combination of adult labour A_i, and child labour C_i, as long as $A_i + \gamma C_i = L_i$. Since all n firms are identical, the aggregate effective labour demand in the market is $L = nL_i$, which allows L to be implicitly defined by $f'(L/n) = w_A = w_C/\gamma$.

Consider the ridge as the 'vertical' axis and draw a line through 0 which is orthogonal to the ridge and going eastward. The thick line, labelled 'effective labour' in Figure 15.1 represents this line. Now, to start with, consider only wages which lie on the ridge. We shall call the two-dimensional Euclidean space in which the 'vertical' axis is the ridge and the 'horizontal' axis effective labour the 'tilted Euclidean space'. For every point on the ridge (showing a particular wage pair) mark off the firms' effective labour demand on the axis marked 'Effective Labour'. That will give us a downward-sloping curve in the tilted Euclidean space. The line BD is an n-fold 'horizontal' ('horizontal' within quotes will from now on always mean horizontal in the tilted Euclidean space) blow-up of such a line and therefore represents the firms' aggregate effective demand for labour for wage pairs lying on the ridge. Hence, if (w_A, w_C) is point E, the aggregate effective demand for labour is given by ON.

It is now easy to read off the respective demand for labour for wage pairs which are not on the ridge. In the (w_A, w_C) -space, suppose (w_A, w_C) happens to be a point vertically above E. Then, clearly, adult wage exceeds effective child wage, $w_A > w_C / \gamma$. Hence, from (15.11) and (15.12), the firms' aggregate demand for adult labour is zero and the firms' aggregate demand for child labour expressed in adult-equivalents is ON. Thus the wage determining the amount of effective labour demanded by firms is the child wage. Or, to put it differently, given a wage pair at G, the aggregate effective demand for labour is given by moving vertically down from G to E on the ridge and then 'horizontally' to the line *BD*. Hence, the effective demand is *ON*. For points above the ridge the effective demand is exclusively effective demand for *child* labour. The reader should satisfy himself or herself that for wage pairs below the ridge the same exercise is carried out by moving horizontally to the ridge and, of course, the demand for labour is now exclusively for adult labour. Hence, given a wage pair at *H*, the demand for child labour is zero and the demand for adult labour is *ON* .

In Figure 15.1, let us now draw the effective labour supply (that is, aggregate labour supply measured in adult-equivalents) corresponding to wage pairs that lie on the ridge. Note that for all wage pairs on the ridge and above J, the supply of child labour is zero [see (15.7)]. Hence, for all such wage pairs, the effective supply of labour is *ON*, where $ON = N$ (that is, the number of adults in the economy). If the wage pair is below *J*, the aggregate effective supply of labour is given by $N + \gamma N$ since all children are now out to work. Hence, the aggregate, effective supply of labour in the tilted Euclidean space is given by the two line segments *QR* and *KP*.

We shall first locate equilibria that may lie on the ridge. This is done simply by looking at the tilted Euclidean space and the points of intersection between the aggregate (effective) demand and supply curves. In the case illustrated in Figure 15.1 there are two equilibria given by the wage pairs *E* and *F*. At *F* both adults and children work, adult wage is very low and children's wage even less. At *E*, adult wage is high, no children offer labour on the labour market, and the entire demand for labour is met by the supply of adults.

To complete the search for equilibria, we must now check if there are any equilibria off the ridge. Using the 'ridge equilibria' as benchmark, this is easy to do. All wage pairs on the horizontal line through *E* and *H* and to the right of *E* constitute equilibrium wage pairs. Since, in this simple model, these are trivial extensions of the equilibrium at *E*, we shall in the remainder of this section focus attention only on the 'ridge equilibria'.

The occurrence of multiple equilibria is by no means necessary in this model. If a country's labour force becomes more productive (because of better technology, for instance), so that the aggregate demand curve, *BD*, shifts to the 'right' (that is, in the tilted Euclidean space), we shall soon have an economy with a unique equilibrium where only adults work. We believe that industrialized countries are in such a situation. If on the other hand, labour is very unproductive, so *BD* shifts to the 'left', we could have a unique equilibrium and child labour is a necessary phenomenon.[10]

There may not be a case for banning child labour in such a situation. As can be checked from Figure 15.1, a ban in such a model will raise adult wage but will nevertheless be less than 2*s*. As long as this new adult wage is less than the previous adult wage plus the child wage, all labouring households will be worse off. The popular support for a child labour ban in such situations usually stems from other hidden agenda such as protectionism or misguided concern for labour. Any argument for a ban has to be much more sophisticated. We discuss this matter in detail in Section 15.4.

Return now to the case of two equilibria as shown in Figure 15.1, and suppose that the economy is currently at the 'lower' equilibrium—that is, at F. While a model is never an exact mirror of reality, it is possible that Europe towards the end of the nineteenth century, in the last years of its industrial revolution, resembled this equilibrium better than any other. Wages were low; children worked for wages but labour productivity was moderately high.

The policy issue here is very interesting. A ban on child labour can very well be justified. If there is a total ban on child labour, effectively, the supply curve of labour in Figure 15.1 will be the 'vertical' line from Q through R, all the way down to N. Hence, the equilibrium at F ceases to be an equilibrium. The only possible equilibrium occurs at E. At this equilibrium there is no child labour. What is interesting, however, is that the legislation banning child labour which has so big an effect moving the economy from F to E, ceases to be a legislation of any consequence after this change. That is, even if the legislation were to be subsequently revoked, the economy would remain at E. This is a consequence of multiple equilibria. 'Interventionist policy' clearly acquires a new meaning in economies with multiple equilibria. Such a policy will be called *benign* intervention, since such a policy ceases to constrain anybody's behaviour simply by virtue of being there. Its entire effect is in terms of its *initial* impact. We return to further discussion of policy and welfare in a later section.

At the cost of more algebra, several aspects of this model can be generalized. A model which allows for a more realistic utility function and larger family size is developed in the next section. One can also raise the question of heterogeneity in family size, preferences, and productivity. To the extent that our central claim is an existential one, that is, one that asserts that there may exist multiple equilibria, it is not essential for our purpose to pursue such a generalization. Also the model in this section and the next makes it evident that our model is not critically dependent on the homogeneity of agents. However, to raise *further* questions of policy and impact on different kinds of households it will be natural to generalize along these lines in the future.

15.3. CHILD LABOUR: SKETCH OF A GENERAL MODEL

In the general model each household is assumed to have one adult and m (≥ 1) children; and each child consumes β (< 1) of what the adult in the household consumes. Let c be the adult's consumption, and $e \in [0, 1]$, each child's effort. Hence, $1 - e$ is each child's leisure. Effort is now chosen from a continuum of possibilities. We shall represent the household preference by the Stone–Geary utility function:[11]

$$(15.13) \quad u(c,e) = \begin{cases} (c-s)(1-e), & \text{if } c \geq s, \\ c-s, & \text{if } c < s, \end{cases}$$

where $c \geq 0$, $e \in [0,1]$ and $s > 0$ is a parameter. The household maximizes u with respect to c and e, subject to the budget constraint:

(15.14) $\qquad c + m\beta c = mew_C + w_A.$

From the first-order conditions we get the following effort function.

(15.15) $\qquad e(w_A, w_C, m) = \begin{cases} 0 \text{ if } s + sm\beta + mw_C \le w_A \\ 1 \text{ if } s + sm\beta - mw_C \ge w_A \\ \dfrac{mw_C - w_A + s + sm\beta}{2mw_C} \quad \text{otherwise.} \end{cases}$

The aggregate labour-supply functions for adult and child labour are, respectively:

(15.16) $\qquad S^A = N$

$\qquad S^C(w_A, w_C, m) = mNe(w_A, w_C, m).$

The demand for adult and child labour is exactly the same as in Section 15.2. Hence, with, m held constant, we define $(w_A{}^*, w_C{}^*)$ to be an equilibrium if

(15.17) $\qquad D^A(w_A{}^*, w_C{}^*) = N,$ and

$\qquad D^c(w_A{}^*, w_C{}^*) = S^C(w_A{}^*, w_C{}^*, m).$

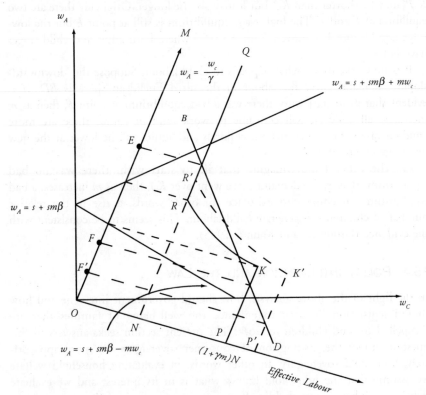

Figure 15.2: Equilibrium with Variable Effort and Family Size

It is worth noting here that equilibrium wages depend on m and, at times, we shall refer to the equilibrium wages as $w_A^*(m)$ and $w_C^*(m)$ to emphasize this dependence.

Using the geometric technique developed in Section 15.2 we can represent the aggregate effective labour supply and demand. Supply is given by the line *QRKP* in Figure 15.2. By inserting the demand curve for labour, *BD* (as before), it is clear that we shall have odd number k of equilibria, of which $(k + 1)/2$ will be stable. The stable equilibria are denoted by points E and F.

The generalized model can be used to analyse policy as well as the effect of changing age structure of the population on child labour. To do this note that the length of *NR* in Figure 15.2 in terms of the adult wage at point R is clearly given by $s(1 + m\beta)/(1 - m\gamma)$.

First assume $1 - m\gamma > 0$. Then as m increases, *NR* becomes longer, and beyond some point an equilibrium where children do not work at all will vanish. This can, somewhat approximately, be paraphrased to say that child labour is more likely to occur in a society with relatively more children. If $1 - m\gamma \le 0$ or $1/\gamma \le m$, it is evident from Figure 15.2 that the equilibrium where children do not work does not exist anyway.

More generally, check that as m increases, the supply curvy of labour, *QRKP*, moves (weakly) to the 'right' to, for instance, the broken line *QR′K′P′*, where *K′P′* may be shorter than *KP*, but it may also be longer. Originally there are two equilibria at E and F. The high-wage equilibrium is still at point E but the low-wage equilibrium has moved from F to F' where both adult and child wages have fallen.

It is now easy to see what happens to child labour. Suppose the 'downward-sloping' demand curve for labour in the tilted Euclidean space is *BD*. It is evident that if, to start with, there was a bad equilibrium at point F, then as m increases, all children will continue to work (and of course there are more children now) and wages of both children and adults will be lower at the new low-wage equilibrium F'.

On the other hand, imagine that if, to start with, there was no bad equilibrium (that is, the demand curve went over K), then as m increases, a bad equilibrium can come into existence. In other words, a rise in the relative number of children can generate child labour. This seems to be consistent with the evidence (Grootaert and Kanbur 1995).

15.4. POLICY INTERVENTION AND THE LAW

In the light of the above analysis, how should government intervene and how should legislation be used to enhance the well-being of families that are compelled to send children to work? The present section seeks answers to this question under the assumption of consumer sovereignty or, more appropriately, household sovereignty. In other words, in evaluating household welfare we assume that the household knows what is in its interest and we evaluate policies to enhance household welfare.

We are aware that our assumption does get violated in some situations. We wish to comment here on one kind of violation, brought to our attention by Albert Hirschman.[12] In gist, the argument is that certain impositions on consumer sovereignty are at times desirable because they may result in a genuine shift in consumer preference or morality. Much of what we consider moral or immoral depends on what we are used to. We may call this 'acquired morality'. Certain practices in faraway societies or times which look obviously immoral to us may not appear so to those societies. Likewise it is worth being aware that we may have certain common practices in our society which will appear shockingly immoral to our descendants when they look back at the late twentieth century. These acquired moralities then influence our behaviour and preference. Corporal punishment for children is a good example of such moral relativism. To some societies such punishments are natural or even desirable, and to others abominable. This may explain why child labour is not only tolerated in certain societies but considered natural and nothing to protest about. But if our aversion to child labour is an acquired morality, then one way to remove child labour is to try and make it customary for children not to work. If, for instance, child labour is banned for some time, then it is conceivable that our judgment in that matter will change—so that after some time, even if the law is revoked, we would not *want* to send our children to work regardless of household income.

This leads also to multiple equilibria working through social norms. This is an eminently plausible argument. However, in what follows, we work within the confines of traditional economics, where household preferences or judgments do not change. Our aim is to argue that, *despite* this, we reach non-traditional policy conclusions.

One of the central policy conclusions is the important role of benign policy interventions. Consider Figure 15.2 and suppose there is an aggregate demand curve, *BD*, that cuts through *QR* and *KP*. Then there are at least two potential equilibria. Suppose an economy is caught in the bad equilibrium, that is, at point *F*. Then a total ban on child labour could deflect the equilibrium all the way to the good equilibrium at point *E*. Hence, all working-class households would be better off. And the policy is self-liquidating in the sense that once in place it plays no role and constrains no one's behaviour. This is, of course, a consequence of there being more than one equilibrium. All this we have discussed in Section 15.2 and so we need not dwell on this anymore.

Suppose now that there is only one equilibrium, the bad one. This is because the aggregate demand curve (for labour) travels below point *R* and cuts the supply curve exactly once, on the segment *KP*. What will be the effect of a total ban on child labour?[13]

The ban will clearly cause adult wage to change from $f'((N + \gamma m N)/n)$ to $f'(N/n)$. Since $f'' < 0$, all we know is that the ban will cause adult wage to rise. The extent of the rise could vary depending on the nature of the production function, f. To see if the ban helps or hurts worker households, describe the utility levels of the household with and without a ban by, respectively, U^B and U^N. Since with no ban we have a bad equilibrium,

$$(15.18) \qquad U^N = \frac{[m\gamma + 1]\, f'\!\left(\dfrac{N + \gamma m N}{n}\right)}{m\beta + 1} - s.$$

In the case with the ban, consumption per person is

$$(15.19) \qquad c = \frac{f'\!\left(\dfrac{N}{n}\right)}{1 + m\beta}.$$

If this consumption level exceeds s, clearly the household benefits from a ban. If $c < s$,

$$(15.20) \qquad U^B = \frac{f'\!\left(\dfrac{N}{n}\right)}{1 + m\beta} - s.$$

Hence, a ban on child labour hurts workers if

$$(15.21) \qquad f'\!\left(\frac{N}{n}\right) < (m\gamma + 1)f'\left(\frac{N + \gamma m N}{n}\right)$$

Clearly we can find parameters under which this inequality may or may not hold. Hence, a ban could hurt worker households and also benefit them.[14]

Let us consider the case where a total ban cannot be implemented. This could be because of difficulties in monitoring. Children can be stopped from labouring in factories but there is little that government can do to stop children labouring on their own family farms. Similarly, Senator Harkin's bill in the United States can conceivably drive child labour out of the export industries in the Third World but can do precious little to prevent child labour in industries which produce for the domestic market. In anticipation of this bill becoming law, the Bangladesh Garment Manufacturers and Exporters Association took steps to fire children from their factories. 'The children went from jobs in garment factories to much worse jobs, such as breaking bricks in the hot sun or, even worse, prostitution' (Bachman 1995: 3). Another problem with some of these well-meaning suggestions for intervention is that they can provide a refuge for people and lobbies with other agendas that are not as well meaning, such as protectionism.

It is, therefore, important to investigate the effect of partial bans. To model such an intervention, let us introduce an innocuous difference between the n firms in the above model. Suppose n_1 firms are run by redheaded entrepreneurs and n_2 ($=n - n_1$) firms by greenheaded ones. Government, we assume, can only administer a ban on the 'red' firms. What will be the effect of such a ban?

So we start from a bad equilibrium ($w_A{}^*$, $w_C{}^*$) and then have a ban announced for the n_1 red firms. The consequence of this depends on the size of n_1.

Note that each firm's demand for effective labour in the equilibrium is $(1 + m\gamma)N/n$. Hence, total demand for labour from the red firms is $n_1(1 + m\gamma)N/n$. Suppose that the number of red firms, n_1, is so few that the following is true:

$$(15.22) \qquad \frac{n_1(1 + m\gamma)N}{2} \le N.$$

In other words, define $n' \equiv n(1 + m\gamma)$; and suppose $n_1 < n'$. Then the ban has no effect. All the red firms employ adults and the green firms employ the remaining adults and all the mN children.

Now suppose $n_1 > n'$. Evidently the pre-ban demand for labour by the banned red firms exceeds the supply for adult labour. Hence the pre-ban equilibrium cannot be sustained since we now have an excess demand for adult labour (and excess supply of child labour). Several possibilities arise in this case. One interesting situation would arise if there exists $(\tilde{w}_A, \tilde{w}_C)$ such that

$$(15.23) \qquad \tilde{w}_A < s + sm\beta - m\tilde{w}_C;$$

$$(15.24) \qquad f'\left(\frac{N}{n_1}\right) = \tilde{w}_A;$$

$$(15.25) \qquad f'\left(\frac{\gamma m N}{n_2}\right) = \frac{\tilde{w}_c}{\gamma}$$

Combining (15.23)–(15.25), we can equivalently write the following condition:

$$(15.26) \qquad f'\left(\frac{N}{n}\right) \le s + sm\beta - \gamma m f'\left(\frac{\gamma m N}{n - n_1}\right).$$

If n_1 satisfies (15.26) then we have, after the ban, an equilibrium where adult wage is $\tilde{w}_A$ and child wage $\tilde{w}_C$. The red firms employ only adults, the green firms only children. All children still work. And since $\tilde{w}_C$ is clearly less than w_C^*, child wage is less after the ban. From the point of view of banishing child labour, the ban would, in this case, have to be considered a failure. It does not diminish child labour, only child wage. This is the possible predicament that one has to worry about in recommending a legislation which can only effect a partial ban. It is worth noting, however, that even if (15.26) is satisfied and the ban is a failure from the point of view of controlling child labour, it may or may not lower the utility of the worker households. That depends on the following. If (15.26) is satisfied and $\tilde{w}_A$ and $\tilde{w}_C$ are such that

$$(15.27) \qquad \tilde{w}_A + \tilde{w}_C < w_A^* + m w_C^*,$$

then the ban not only worsens the child-labour condition but it lowers household utility as well. If the inequality in (15.27) is reversed, then household utility rises. If, on the other hand, n_1 is very large, and close to n, it is easy to see that the ban works *as if* it were a total ban and the labour market would settle at the good equilibrium.

The above discussion is at best a surrogate analysis of what would happen in a developing country if its exports which use child labour were banned. A fuller model can potentially be used to address a variety of policy questions in this regard. Suppose, for instance, the export industry is competitive and, therefore, runs on a slender profit margin and this is a small country and so it faces a fairly elastic demand. Then a ban on child labour can increase the cost of production and cause the export industry to shrink sharply, leaving the worker households worse off. But, for a formal analysis, we need to build on our simple model more complicated structures so that such questions can be formally taken up.

There are many other kinds of policy—taxes, subsidies, and other restrictions—the effects of which can be checked out using our model.

To sum up, bans are a powerful instrument but by no means unequivocally desirable. One has to be very careful about the empirical context before using this instrument. If there are multiple equilibria in the labour market, a ban is a benign policy intervention and worthwhile. But if the market has only one equilibrium which is likely in very poor countries, then a ban can worsen the condition of the labour households. Partial bans are especially likely to backfire and cause deterioration in labour conditions. The first-best policy is to attack the problem at its source. This entails improving the condition and scope for adult labour.

15.5. CONCLUDING REMARKS: FERTILITY AND GENDER

The model built in this chapter has implications for analysing fertility and population policy. It seems likely that the multiple equilibria in the labour market could bring about a multiplicity of equilibria pertaining to fertility choices of the household, once such choices are endogenized.[15] If our conjecture is right, then this will have implications for the kinds of population policy that we espouse.

Suppose an economy is at an equilibrium where fertility is high and children work. It is pointless in such a situation to send extension workers to households to explain to them the irrationality of large households. This is because the large family is a conscious, rational decision. This is, of course, a widely held view. What is interesting is that even though there is no individual irrationality at this equilibrium, the equilibrium may well be exhibiting *group* irrationality. Everybody would not only be better off if everybody had small families, but every individual family may prefer to be small if other families were small. Hence, the policies we would have to conceive of would attempt to deflect the economy from the high-fertility equilibrium to the low-fertility one.

More generally, the framework developed in this chapter, including the diagrammatic technique, should be applicable to several areas other than child labour. Whenever we have two or more variables being supplied by one decision maker, some of the same issues discussed here are likely to crop up. Several gender-related matters belong to this category. Traditional households, where the husband decides not only about his own work but also that of his wife's, may give rise to female labour-supply functions such that we would have multiple equilibria with women being excluded totally from the labour market in some of the equilibria. There is, however, a caveat to this noted in the next paragraph. If the policy maker does not share the husband's judgement, then she could use this kind of model to decide how best to intervenue in the market in order to enhance or curb women's employment. There may also be important issues of gender within the domain of child labour. There is evidence that the labour-supply response of girls and boys to changes in labour-market conditions can be very different (see, for example, Goldin 1979). Our model can, in principle, be extended to study the markets of boy-labour and girl-labour.

If we do use this kind of a model to analyse gender issues and, in particular, the supply of female labour, one important real-life difference needs to be kept in mind. There is some evidence that when women begin to work outside the household and contribute to the household's income they also have more influence on household choices and decisions (see, Strauss and Thomas 1995; Riley 1997). Hence, it is natural to expect that a man will take this into account when he decides to send his wife out to work. In addition, even if the initial decision about whether a women works or not belongs to her husband, once she begins working the decision whether she continues to work or not may cease to be the husband's decision. This anticipated shift in decision making is likely to introduce some important complications to modelling female labour, as distinct from child labour.

Finally, one important area of practical concern to which models such as these can be brought to bear is the debate on international labour standards. Because of the importance of this topic in international politics, there is now a growing literature commenting on it (see, for example, Fields 1994; Rodrik 1995). These are matters which, despite the growing interest, are still discussed without an accepted formal analytical framework. Combining the model of this chapter with trade could take us towards a formal framework.

NOTES

1. In case wages are rigid we would expect adult unemployment to decline.
2. A more sophisticated claim is that child labour is a manifestation of failures in other markets, such as the market for capital or insurance (Grootaert and Kanbur 1995).
3. For a survey of the contemporary world situation pertaining to child labour, which goes beyond numbers and looks at institutional details, see Bequele and Boyden (1988).
4. We confine most of our historical observations to Britain. The reader may refer to Weiner (1991) for a brief description of the experience of other European nations and also Japan and the United States.
5. A district-wise breakdown of this data is reported in Cunningham (1990). Though we say that child labour was on the decline by 1851, it is possible that the number of children who did some work peaked in 1874 (see Nardinelli 1990). However, the mitigating factor was that, by the late nineteenth century, most children were

working only half-time. This was in response to the requirement of the Factories Act of 1874 that children attend school on at least a half-time basis.

6. Since the alternative to work may not necessarily be leisure. It could, for instance, be education.

7. The only exception to these findings occurs in the case of alcoholism on the part of parents. It is difficult to get data on alcoholism. We have simply been able to determine that in 1800, an average person in England and Wales consumed 27 gallons of beer per annum (Nardinelli 1990). But it is difficult to judge from this alone (without information on the distribution of this consumption and the consumption of other types of alcohol) as to how heavy the drinking was. However, the sociological and historical writings cited above do not give the impression of alcoholism being particularly high and, therefore, the cause of mass child labour.

8. For discussion on this see, for example, Sen (1990); Browning et al. (1994); and Udry (1996).

9. We are grateful to Heraklis Polemarchakis for discussion on this.

10. It is arguable that Britain in the early nineteenth century had only the bad equilibrium; then in the mid-nineteenth century the bad and good equilibria; and by the start of the twentieth century only the good one. Policy intervention would be important mainly in the middle case. It would be redundant by the century's end, and very difficult to effectively implement and also of dubious welfare consequences at the start of the nineteenth century.

11. It is easy to check that this implies that the child's leisure is a luxury good because a doubling of household wealth (from non-child-labour sources) leads to a more than doubling of child leisure. However, as will be transparent as we go along, we do not really need the child's leisure to be a luxury good 'everywhere'. Essentially what we need is that there exists a positive household wealth where children begin to consume leisure and a higher wealth where they cease to work.

12. Personal communication to K. Basu, dated 15 February 1995.

13. It is interesting to note that some of the same effects of a ban on child labour can be achieved through the implementation of a minimum-wage law.

14. We have in our analysis ignored the fact that a small but non-negligible number of children belong to no family. They are 'abandoned', and make their own decision to work or not work. A blanket ban on child labour, without any provision for such children, will almost always work against the interest of these children. A model that explicitly deals with the problem of 'street children' (for an empirical account, see Myers 1988) would have to be based on very different assumptions from the ones we have used here.

15. The link between the market for child labour and fertility behaviour has been studied in the literature (see, for instance, Cain and Mozumder 1981) but the possibility of multiple equilibria in this context seems to have been overlooked.

REFRENCES

Anderson, M. 1971. *Family Structure in Nineteenth Century Lancashire*. Cambridge: Cambridge University Press.

Ashagrie, K. 1993. 'Statistics on Child Labour'. *Bulletin of Labour Statistics* 3. International Labour Organization: 11–24.

Bachman, S. L. 1995. 'Children at Work' (Commentary). *San Jose Mercury News* 16 July: 3.

Bequele, A. and J. Boyden, eds. 1988. *Combating Child Labour*. Geneva: International Labour Organization.

Browning, M., F. Bourguignon, P. Chiappori, and V. Lechene. 1994. 'Income and Outcomes: A Structural Model of Intrahousehold Allocation'. *Journal of Political Economy* 102 (6, December): 1067–96.

Cain, M. and A.B.M. Khorshed Alam Mozumder. 1981. 'Labour Market Structure and Reproductive Behaviour in Rural South Asia'. In Gerry Rodgers and Guy Standing, eds, *Child Work, Poverty, and Underdevelopment*. Geneva: International Labour Organization: 245–87.

Cunningham, H. 1990. 'The Employment and Unemployment of Children in England c. 1680–1851'. *Past and Present* 126 (February): 115–50.

Fields, G.S. 1994. 'Labor Standards and International Trade'. Cornell University. Mimeo.

Goldin, C. 1979. 'Household and Market Production of Families in a Late Nineteenth Century American Town'. *Explorations in Economic History.* 16 (2, April): 111–31.

Grootaert, C. and R. Kanbur. 1995. 'Child Labour: An Economic Perspective'. *International Labour Review*, 134 (2): 187–203.

Gupta, M.R. 1998. 'Wage Determination of a Child Worker: A Theoretical Analysis'. *Review of Development Economics.*

Horrell, S. and J. Humphries. 1995. 'The Exploitation of Little Children: Child Labour and the Family Economy in the Industrial Revolution'. *Explorations in Economic History* 32 (4, October): 485–516.

Moehling, C.M. 1995. 'The Intrahousehold Allocation of Resources and the Participation of Children in Household Decision Making: Evidence from Early Twentieth Century America'. Northwestern University. Mimeo.

Myers, W. 1988. 'Alternative Services for Street Children: The Brazilian Approach'. In Bequele and Boyden, L., eds. *Combatting Child Labour*. Geneva: International Labour Organization: 125–43.

Nardinelli, C. 1990. *Child Labour and the Industrial Revolution*. Bloomington, IN: Indiana University Press.

Riley, N.E. 'Gender, Power, and Population Change'. *Population Bulletin.* 52(1, May): 2–46.

Rodrik, D. 1995. 'Labor Standards and International Trade: Moving Beyond the Rhetoric'. Columbia University. Mimeo.

Sen, A.K. 1990. Gender and Cooperative Conflict'. In I.Tinker, ed. *Persistent Inequalities: Women and World Development*. New York: Oxford University Press: 123–49.

Silvers, J. 1996. 'Child Labor in Pakistan'. *Atlantic Monthly* (February): 79–92.

Strauss, J. and D. Thomas. 1995. 'Human Resources: Empirical Modelling of Household and Family Decisions'. In J. Behrman and T.N. Srinivasan, eds. *Handbook of Development Economics, Vol. IIIA*. Amsterdam: Elsevier: 1883–2023.

Udry, C. 1996. 'Gender, Agricultural Production and the Theory of the Household'. *Journal of Political Economy* 104 (5, October): 1010–46.

Vincent, D. 1981. *Bread, Knowledge and Freedom: A Study of Nineteenth-century Working Class Autobiography*. London: Europa Publications.

Weiner, M. 1991. *The Child and the State in India: Child Labour and Education Policy in Comparative Perspective*. Princeton, NJ: Princeton University Press.

16 A Note on Multiple General Equilibria with Child Labour

16.1. INTRODUCTION

Consider a poor country in which children are viewed as potential workers and there is no law—at least none that is properly enforced—that prohibits child labor. The fact that around 250 million children work the world over (see Basu 1999) suggests that the case we are considering is the norm rather than the exception. There is now quite a substantial empirical literature demonstrating that the typical parent sends a child out to work only when threatened by extreme poverty (see, for example, Grootaert and Patrinos 1999; Ray 2000). There is also a small analytical literature which argues that if a child's non-work is a luxury good (as the above empirical findings suggest) then the economy is likely to have multiple equilibria with one equilibrium in which children do not work and another in which they do (Basu and Van 1998; Swinnerton and Rogers 1999; Bardhan and Udry 1999; Lopez-Calva 1999). However, in the existing literature this result is established in a partial equilibrium framework.

If this theoretical claim is generally valid, then it has important policy implications. It will mean that a legal ban can (under some circumstances) be an effective way to deal with the problem; because the ban could prevent the economy from getting into the equilibrium in which children work and deflect it to the equilibrium where they do not. This has implications also for international policy initiatives, such as those concerning labour standards (Brown 2000; Dixit 2000; Jafarey and Lahiri 1999).

From *Economics Letters* 74; 2002: 301–8.

For helpful comments I am grateful to David Easley, Ron Jones, Tapan Mitra, Henry Wan, and the seminar participants at Rochester University.

The aim of this chapter is to construct a general-equilibrium model of an economy in which children are potential workers and then show that under some natural restrictions on preference, multiple equilibria are indeed likely in this model. The chapter also develops the simple geometric idea of a 'wage bill curve' and shows how this can be used to understand the possibility of multiple equilibria. While there has been some attempt to bring elements of general equilibrium argument into the picture (Swinnerton and Rogers 1999; Baland and Robinson 2000; Ranjan 2000), there has as yet been no full general-equilibrium treatment of the problem of child labour. Hence the objective of this chapter is essentially a methodological one—to show how arguments made in the context of partial equilibrium models can be extended to a general equilibrium framework. Viewed in the abstract, the model considers the possibility of multiple equilibria when a single decision-making unit (household) decides on the labour supply of more than one agent.

16.2. THE MODEL

We consider an economy with one worker household, one capitalist household, and one firm. These are all price-takers and so the restriction of there being one of each kind causes no loss of generality.

Each worker household has one adult and one child. The adult has an endowment of labour equal to 1 unit and the child has an endowment of labour equal to γ unit, where $\gamma \in (0, 1]$. Using c to denote aggregate household consumption and ℓ aggregate leisure, the household's utility function is given by

$$u = u(c, \ell)$$

where $c \geq 0$, $\ell \in [0, 1 + \gamma]$, where leisure ℓ is simply the amount of household labour endowment that is not sold. Hence, if it consumes ℓ units of leisure, it supplies $1 + \gamma - \ell$ units of labour. It will be assumed that when the household supplies e units of labour, it begins with the adult's labour, and supplies child labour only after it has supplied the 1 unit of adult labour. This means that it does not matter if the child's leisure is measured in some units different from adult leisure (see Basu 2000). This assumption also means that as soon as we know how much leisure, ℓ, the household consumes, we know not only how much labour the household supplies $(1 + \gamma - \ell)$ but how much child labour is supplied (max $\{\gamma - \ell, 0\}$).

Next consider the following assumptions concerning the household's utility function.

ASSUMPTION 16.1. The utility function u: $\Re_+ \times [0, 1+ \gamma] \to \Re$ is continuous, (weakly) monotonic, and quasi-concave.

We shall on some occasions use a stronger concavity assumption as follows:

ASSUMPTION 16.2. The utility function u is strictly quasi-concave.

Let p be the price of the consumable good and w the price of labour. Let α be the share of the firm owned by the worker household. Hence, if the total amount of profit earned by the firm is π, the worker household's problem is as follows:

$$\max_{c,\,\ell} u(c,\ell)$$

subject to $pc \leq w(1 + \gamma - \ell) + \alpha\pi$, $c \geq 0$, and $\ell \in [0, 1 + \gamma]$.

Assumptions 16.1 and 16.2 ensure that for every p (> 0), w and $\alpha\pi$, there is a unique solution to the above problem. Also, since we confine our attention entirely to Walras equilibria, it is harmless to normalize and set $p = 1$. We do so from now on; and hence write the solution to the above problem as follows.

$$c = c(w, \alpha\pi)$$

$$\ell = \ell(w, \alpha\pi)$$

Next let us turn to the capitalist household. This household never supplies labour. We may equivalently assume that this household has no endowment of labour. This assumption causes no loss of generality. As a matter of fact we could have assumed the capitalist household to be exactly like the worker household, excepting for the fact that it has rights to a larger share of the firm's profits. Then there could be price ranges where the capitalist household's profit share is so large that it *prefers* not to send the child to work. Continuing with our description of the capitalist household, let us assume that it owns a share $(1 - \alpha)$ of the firm. Since its utility depends only on its consumption, c', and its budget constraint is given by

$$c' \leq (1 - \alpha)\pi$$

we know that this household will choose c' so that

$$c' = (1 - \alpha)\pi$$

The firm's production function is given by

$$x = f(L)$$

where L is the amount of labour used and x the amount of output produced. The production function is required to satisfy the following.

ASSUMPTION 16.3: The production function $f: \Re_+ \to \Re_+$ is strictly monotonic, strictly concave, bounded from above, and has the properties that $f(0) = 0$ and there exists $b > 0$ such that $f(L) \leq bL$, for all $L \geq 0$.

The firm's problem is to:

$$\max_{L} \hat{\pi} = f(L) - wL$$

Given Assumption 16.3, for every $w \in \Re_+$ there is a unique L chosen by the firm. We denote this by

$$L = L(w)$$

Define

$$x(w) \equiv f(L(w))$$

and

$$\pi(w) \equiv x(w) - wL(w)$$

In this chapter, an economy, Ξ, is fully described by u, f and α. Hence

$$\Xi = \langle u, f, \alpha \rangle$$

Given an economy, $\Xi = \langle u, f, \alpha \rangle$, we define w^* to be a Walras equilibrium if

(16.1) $\qquad c(w^*, \alpha\pi(w^*)) + (1 - \alpha)\pi(w^*) = x(w^*)$

In stating the Walras equilibrium in this manner we are making use of the Walras law of markets, which ensures that if the goods market is in equilibrium (that is, (1) is true) then the labour market must be in equilibrium.

To ensure that we are not working in a vacuum it is worth noting:

THEOREM 16.1: Every economy, $\Xi = \langle u, f, a \rangle$, satisfying Assumptions 16.1–16.3, has at least one Walras equilibrium.

PROOF: Define $z(w) \equiv c(w, \alpha\pi(w)) + (1 - \alpha)\pi(w) - x(w)$. That is, $z(w)$ is the excess demand function for the good. Assumptions 16.1–16.3 guarantee that z is a function.

Choose $b > 0$ such that $f(L) \leq bL$, $\forall L \geq 0$. This exists by Assumption 16.2. It is obvious that if $w = b$, $x(w) = 0$, $\pi(w) = 0$. Hence, $z(b) = b(1 + \gamma - \ell(b, 0))$, from the definition of $z(.)$ and the worker-household's budget constraint. Hence $z(b) \geq 0$. If $z(b) = 0$, then $w = b$ is a Walras equilibrium.

So suppose $z(b) > 0$.

Clearly, $\exists \hat{w} < b$ such that

$$L(\hat{w}) > 1 + \gamma$$

$$\rightarrow L(\hat{w}) > 1 + \gamma - \ell(\hat{w}, \alpha\pi(\hat{w}))$$

$$\rightarrow x(\hat{w}) - \pi(\hat{w}) > w[1 + \gamma - \ell(\hat{w}, \alpha\pi(\hat{w}))]$$

$$\rightarrow z(\hat{w}) < 0$$

by the worker-household's budget constraint. It is easy to check that c, π and x are continuous functions. Hence, z is continuous and so $\exists w^* \in [\hat{w}, b]$ such that $z(w^*) = 0$.

16.3. MULTIPLE EQUILIBRIA

To see how multiple equilibria can arise in this model and how that is more plausible if households treat child leisure (or, more generally, non-work) as a luxury good, I will develop a diagrammatic representation of the above model.

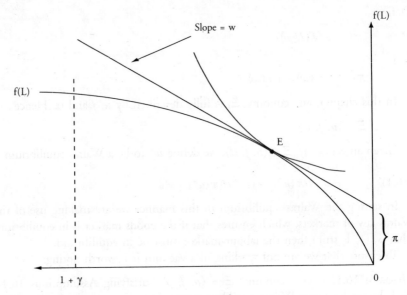

Figure 16.1

In doing so, we will consider the two polar cases $\alpha = 1$ and $\alpha = 0$. If $\alpha = 1$, it is as if there is only one household—the worker household. The geometric depiction of the Walras equilibrium in this case is fairly standard (Mas-colell et al. 1995: 15). In Figure 16.1, the horizontal axis measures the amount of labour used by the firm. The production function is as shown. If we treat the point marked $1 + \gamma$ as the origin and measure the household's leisure consumption in the eastward direction and goods consumption along the broken vertical line, we can depict the household's indifference curves in this space. The figure assumes $p = 1$.

Given Assumptions 16.1 and 16.2, there will exist a unique point where the production function is tangential to an indifference curve. E denotes this point in the figure. By a well-known argument, the slope of the tangent at E is the Walras equilibrium wage rate. The profit earned by the firm is shown by the vertical intercept of the tangent on the $f(L)$-axis. What Figure 16.1 clarifies is that, if the workers earn all the profits, the economy will have a unique equilibrium. Hence, we know that a necessary condition for the existence of multiple equilibria is that $\alpha < 1$. This is quite a realistic assumption, since one cannot think of any country in the world where workers earn all the profits.

While the possibility of multiple equilibria arises, as soon as we have $\alpha < 1$, for ease of exposition, I will consider the polar extreme of $\alpha = 0$. Hence there is a separation between the labouring households and the capitalist households. But once the logic of my argument and the diagrammatic technique is understood, it will be evident that the analysis carries over to all cases of $\alpha < 1$.

Now, every time we are given a w, the (worker) household's budget constraint is given by a line having a slope of w (a negative slope of w to be more precise), *through point 0*. There will be no positive intercept, such as π shown in

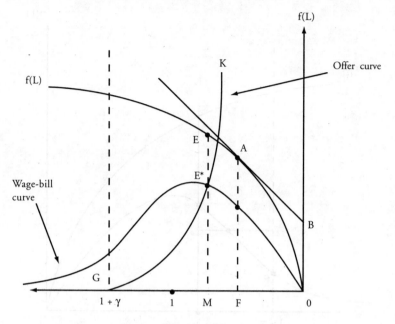

Figure 16.2

Figure 16.1, since the household earns no profit. So if the household's leisure consumption is $1 + \gamma$, its income is zero.

A crucial instrument in depicting a Walras equilibrium in this case is what will be called the 'wage-bill curve'. This is illustrated in Figure 16.2 and it is derived as follows. Consider any point on the graph of the production function, such as A. Consider the wage, w, for which A would be the profit-maximizing point of the firm. Let $\pi(w)$ be the profit of the firm at that w. Hence this is given by OB in Figure 16.2.

From the line segment AF, starting from point A, deduct the profit. The point one gets by so doing (D in Figure 16.2) is a point on the wage-bill curve. By varying A we get a locus of points like D. That locus is the wage-bill curve.

Since $f(0) = 0$, the wage-bill curve must start at 0 in Figure 16.2. Since by assumption 2, f is bounded from above, as L becomes large, the wage-bill curve converges to zero. This explains the shape of the wage-bill curve shown in Figure 16.2.

In brief, if the wage is such that the firm chooses point A, then the height of the wage-bill curve (DF) is the total wage bill generated at that point and the vertical gap between the production function and the wage-bill curve at that point (namely, AD) depicts the aggregate profit in the economy.

Next consider the worker household's problem. Treating the point $1 + \gamma$ as its origin, let us measure its leisure on the horizontal axis and goods consumption on the vertical axis (the broken line). Now consider all possible budget constraints through point 0 and on each budget constraint mark the household's optimal point. By joining such points we get the standard offer curve. Let us suppose that the offer curve is GK. There is no reason to suppose that G will

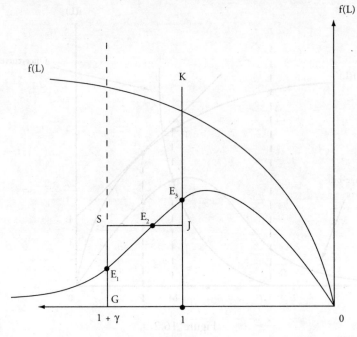

Figure 16.3

coincide with the point marked 1 + γ. The figure suggests this purely for reasons of aesthetics.

THEOREM 16.2: The Walras equilibria of an economy, $\Xi = \langle u, f, 0 \rangle$, are depicted by the points of intersection between the offer and wage bill curves.

To see this consider point E^* in Figure 16.2 where the wage-bill curve intersects the offer curve. Suppose the wage rate w^* is given by the slope of the line joining E^* and 0. Clearly, given w^*, the household will choose leisure and consumption depicted by E^*, since E^* lies on the offer curve. Since EE^* is the total profit in the economy, and a line of slope w^* at E has an intercept on the $y(L)$ axis equal to EE^*, given w^*, the firm chooses point E. Since the capitalist household uses the entire profit to consume goods, the total demand for goods $(EE^* + E^*M)$ equals total supply of goods EM.

It is now easy to see how multiple equilibria can arise. All one needs is for the offer curve to intersect the wage-bill curve more than once as, for instance, illustrated in Figure 16.3.

It has been often suggested that parents send their children to work only when that is necessary in order to attain some critical minimum consumption, S. This was called the 'luxury axiom' in Basu and Van (1998). One formal and somewhat extreme interpretation of this is as follows.

ASSUMPTION 16.4. There exists $S > 0$, such that, if $S \geq c \geq c' \geq 0$, then $u(c, \ell) \geq u(c', \ell')$, for all $\ell, \ell' \in [0, 1 +]$.

This axiom simply asserts that the offer curve rises vertically at G, at least up to S. The offer curve GSK in Figure 16.3 satisfies Assumption 16.4. A familiar example of a utility function satisfying Assumption 16.4 is the Stone–Geary utility function.

I had argued in Basu (1999) that there is a large literature and evidence that supported this axiom. It is worthwhile exploring the implications of this axiom in a general equilibrium model of an economy. The next theorem states a necessary and sufficient condition for the existence of a Walras equilibrium in which the children of worker households do full-time work.

THEOREM 16.3: Suppose $\Xi = \langle u, f, 0 \rangle$ is an economy satisfying Assumptions 16.1 and 16.3. For this economy to have a Walras equilibrium in which worker-household children do full-time work it is necessary that Assumption 16.4 be satisfied. This becomes a sufficient condition if (assuming $f(\cdot)$ is differentiable) $f'(1 + \gamma)(1 + \gamma) \leq S$.

The condition $f'(1 + \gamma)(1+ \gamma) \leq S$ simply says that, when all adults and children of worker households work, the marginal product of labour is so low that wage bill is less than the subsistence wage bill. The proof of Theorem 16.3 is obvious by using the diagrammatic technique developed above.

Note that Assumption 4 implies that child leisure is a luxury good. Hence, to have a Walras equilibrium in which worker-household children do full-time work it is necessary for child leisure to be a luxury good.

16.4. POLICY

If an economy is as depicted in Figure 16.3, and suppose it is, currently, in equilibrium at E_1, a ban on child labour would push the economy to the sole remaining equilibrium at E_3. It is obvious that at E_3 worker households are better off. Note also that once the equilibrium has moved to E_3, the legal ban is not, strictly speaking, needed any more. Legislative actions of this kind, which, once put into effect, can be removed without the economy reverting back to the original situation may be called 'ratchet legislation'. This model suggests that if child labour is driven by subsistence needs, it is possible that there will be multiple equilibria, and in that case there is scope for putting an end to child labour through the use of ratchet legislation.

This general-equilibrium analysis sheds light on an important policy question, which remained unclear in the partial-equilibrium model. It makes it plain that, in an economy in which child labour is prevalent, a ban on child labour could result in an equilibrium outcome which is Pareto optimal but, nevertheless, a ban on child labour cannot be justified on a purely Paretian ground. As is obvious from Figure 16.3, all equilibria in this economy are Pareto-optimal. We have to think of social welfare functions, which attach a special weight to workers' welfare or a negative weight to child work, in order to justify a ban. The welfare function can be Pareto-inclusive, but the inclusion of the Pareto criterion is not sufficient.

REFERENCES

Baland, J.M. and J. Robinson, 2000. 'A Model of Child Labor'. *Journal of Political Economy* 108: 663–79.

Bardhan, P. and C. Udry. 1999. *Development Microeconomics.* Oxford: Oxford University Press.

Basu, K. 1999. 'Child Labor: Cause, Consequence and Cure, with remarks on International Labor Standards'. *Journal of Economic Literature* 37: 1083–119.

—— 2000. 'The Intriguing Relation between Adult Minimum wage and Child Labor'. *Economic Journal* 110: C50–C61.

Basu, K. and P.H. Van. 1998. 'The Economics of Child Labor'. *American Economic Review* 88: 412–27.

Brown, D. 2000. 'A Transactions Cost Politics Analysis of International Child Labor Standards'. In A. Deardorff and R. Stern, eds. *Social Dimensions of US Trade Policies.* Ann Arbor: University of Michigan Press.

Dixit, A. 2000. 'Comments'. In A. Deardorff, and R. Stern, eds. *Social Dimensions of US Trade Policies.* Ann Arbor: University of Michigan Press,

Grootaert, C. and H. Patrinos. 1999. *The Policy Analysis of Child Labor.* New York: St. Martin's Press.

Jafarey, S. and S. Lahiri. 1999. 'Will Trade Sanctions Reduce Child Labor? The Role of Credit Markets'. Paper No. 500. Department of Economics, University of Essex.

Lopez-Calva, L.F. 1999. 'A Social Stigma Model of Child Labor'. CAE Working Paper No. 99–13. Cornell University.

Mas-colell, A., M. Whinston, and J. Green. 1995. *Microeconomic Theory.* Cambridge, MA: The MIT Press.

Ranjan, P. 2000. 'Credit Constraints and the Phenomenon of Child Labor'. *Journal of Development Economics.*

Ray, R. 2000. 'Child Labor, Child Schooling and Their Interaction with Adult Labor: Empirical Evidence for Peru and Pakistan'. *World Bank Economic Review* 14: 347–67.

Swinnerton, K. and C.A. Rogers, 1999. 'The Economics of Child Labor: Comment'. *American Economic Review* 89: 1382–5.

17 The Intriguing Relation between Adult Minimum Wage and Child Labour

17.1. MOTIVATION

There is now considerable evidence and some theoretical reason for believing that, in developing countries, improvement in the condition of adult workers results in the decline of child labour, since parents can then 'afford' to take their children out of the labour force (Goldin 1979; Horan and Hargis 1991; Bonnet 1993; Basu 1999a; Ray 1999). Hence *one* route to curbing child labour is to intervene in the adult labour market. However, much depends on *how* we intervene. If we adopt policies which raise the marginal productivity of adult workers, thereby raising wages and employment, all is well. On the other hand, the effect of a minimum-wage legislation to bolster adult wages can be complicated. In some circumstances this may cause a drop in the incidence of child labour. But the analysis gets complex if the increase in wage causes adult unemployment to increase. This is because in most developing countries unemployment benefits are non-existent; so it is likely that adults who are unemployed will send their children to work. So a minimum wage can result in a higher supply of child labour. This will typically cause an increase in child employment, which, in turn, will cause further losses in adult employment and further additions to the supply of child labour. The full impact of this

From *The Economic Journal*, 110, March 2000: C50–C61.

I have benefited from seminars at Yale University, University of California at Berkeley, and University of Chicago. For helpful comments and discussion I would like to thank Pranab Bardhan, Gary Becker, Alain de Janvry, Garance Genicot, Sajal Lahiri, Ayal Kimhi, Elizabeth King, Joseph Stiglitz and especially, Elizabeth Sadoulet.

multiplier-like process can be large. This chapter develops a model which helps us predict the net effect of such interventions.

While my focus here is on child labour, models of this kind are useful for analysing the impact of minimum-wage legislation or other kinds of wage rigidities on adult unemployment and job search (see Basu et al. 1999). There is a large empirical literature on this subject (see, for instance, Ashenfelter 1980; Layard et al. 1980; Card and Krueger 1995). This research is based on the presumption that children do not work, which is realistic for industrialized countries, but not for poor nations. According to International Labour Organisation (ILO) estimates, around 250 million children do full-or part-time work in the world, almost all of them in poor countries. When children are potential workers, standard results may undergo reversion, as this chapter tries to show theoretically. It is hoped that this will inspire empirical work in developing countries,[1] which investigates the effect on child labour of legislation meant for the adult labour market.

17.2. A COMMENT ON LABOUR STANDARDS

The argument in this chapter is of some significance in the context of the ongoing debate on international labour standards and the need for a 'social clause' in world trading arrangements. The case for trying to achieve minimal labour standards for workers the world over is unexceptionable. Workers should have the right to collective bargaining; children below a certain age, usually 15 years, should not have to work; no one should be forced to work; workers should not be exposed to undue hazards; workers should be able to earn a living wage. All these and many other suggestions have been put forward over the years and debated extensively (see, for instance, Bhagwati 1995; Rodrik 1996; Maskus 1997; Basu 1999b).

Troublesome questions arise as soon as we try to make these broad principles operational. Should trade sanctions be used to punish countries that violate some core labour standard? Would that lead to the standards issue being misused for protectionist purposes? Does the idea of labour standards run counter to the principle of comparative advantage?

The present chapter touches on the debate on labour standards differently. It raises the question of consistency among labour standards. It is true that many of the standards support one another. For instance, if workers have the right to collective bargaining, they may themselves refuse to work under excessively hazardous conditions. However, there may be some standards, which, when upheld, tend to undermine other standards. One class of labour standards that is discussed under the label 'survival rights' (see Portes 1990) often includes a minimum wage for adult workers. What the present chapter shows is that this right and the demand for the abolition of child labour—often made under the provision of 'basic rights', may have a complicated relationship, with the achievement of one being made more difficult by the success of the other.

This chapter is not on labour standards and no attempt is made here to stress one objective over another, but it draws attention to an issue that has received little attention—the inter-connections between different labour standards. In the light of the results in this chapter one may question the wisdom of using minimum wage as a part of international labour standards, But my main concern is that, *given* that minimum wage laws *are* routinely used and have been discussed in the context of international labour standards, we need to analyse the effect of such laws. The problem is also analytically interesting because its impact on child labour is less than obvious.

17.3. MODEL

Consider an economy with H identical households. Each household has 1 adult and m children. Adult supply of labour is assumed to be inelastic; more specifically, adults always want to work. Concerning child labour, we will assume that, if the household income from non-child labour sources rises sufficiently high, the households will of their own accord withdraw the children from the labour force. For a general statement of this assumption and its justification, see Basu and Van (1998). In the present chapter, this assumption will be simplified as follows: [1] There is a critical number, s, such that children are sent to work if and only if adult wage drops below s.

[1] is easy to derive from a utility function if it is assumed that: [2] The labour market is such that a child can either work or not work (that is, there is no scope for part-time work), [3] household norms are such that, all m children are either sent to work or none.

To see this, assume that the household maximizes the Stone–Geary utility function:

$$u = \begin{cases} (c - s)(1 - e), & \text{if } c \geq s \\ c - s, & \text{if } c < s, \end{cases}$$

where u denotes household utility, c total household consumption, and e each child's work decision, with $e = 0$ being the decision not to work and $e = 1$ being the decision to work.

Denoting the wage for child labour prevailing on the market by w_c and the wage for adult labour by w, the household's budget constraint is given by:

$$c \leq w + mew_c.$$

It is evident that if a household maximizes u, subject to the above constraint, by choosing $c \geq 0$ and $e \in \{0, 1\}$, [1] will turn out to be true.

[2] and [3] are, however, unrealistic assumptions. The informal sector, where children usually work has a lot of flexibility and so it is *possible* for children to work a few hours each day (see, for instance, Grootaert and Patrinos 1999). In other words, e can take fractional values. Moreover, parents are in reality free to send only some children to work. Can we *allow* for these possibilities and still derive [1]? The answer is yes, and this is shown at the end of this section.

Let us now assume that a child's labour and an adult's labour are two factors of the same kind. The difference is simply that a child produces a fraction γ (< 1) of an adult's labour. It may be convenient to think of this in the following way. There is a factor called labour (or effective labour, for emphasis) and each adult produces 1 unit of labour, while each child produces γ units of labour. This being so, it is obvious that, whenever both children and adults work, the prevailing adult and child wages must satisfy the following condition:

(17.1) $\qquad w_c = \gamma w.$

If this condition did not hold, firms could do better by substituting one kind of labour for another.

Given this simplifying assumption, it is clear that when adult wage is w, child wage must be γw, and what a firm will care about is the total amount of labour it has. What this total is composed of, that is, how much adult labour and how much child labour, is unimportant to the firm. Hence, we could write the aggregate demand function for labour in the economy as follows:

(17.2) $\qquad D = d(w),$

where D is the aggregate labour demanded by all firms in the economy. We will assume that $d'(w) < 0$. This demand curve is illustrated by the line marked D in Figure 17.1.

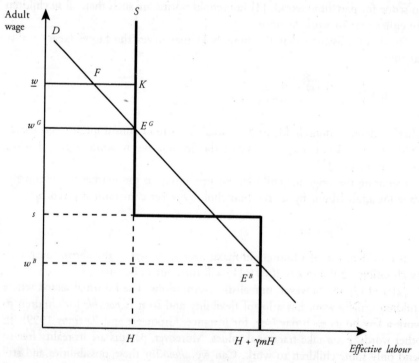

Figure 17.1

From the description of households, above, it follows that the aggregate labour-supply curve, as a function of the adult wage, is given by the step-shaped line marked S in Figure 17.1. Note that if w exceeds s, only adults supply their labour. There being H adults in the economy, the labour supply is given by H. If w drops below s, the mH children in the economy are out searching for work. Since they provide γ units of labour each, the total supply of labour is given by $H + \gamma mH$.

The remainder of this section constructs a household utility function, which does not use assumptions [2] and [3] but nevertheless results in a supply curve like Figure 17.1. What we need is a utility function that generates indifference curves of the kind shown by the unbroken lines in Figure 17.2. This is a somewhat unusual figure. The vertical axis represents household income, and the horizontal axis the total amount of 'leisure' enjoyed by the household. This leisure is, however, normalized; that is, leisure is measured as the complement of the total *effective* labour that the household can supply. Thus if the adult does not work, the leisure gained is 1, but if a child does not work the leisure gained is γ. This is not an assumption but simply a convenient way of representing leisure and work on the same axis. Hence, the maximum (normalized) leisure that a household can consume is given by $\gamma m + 1$. The horizontal axis in Figure 17.2 should be thought of as representing first the children's leisure (up to the point marked γm) and then the adult's leisure.

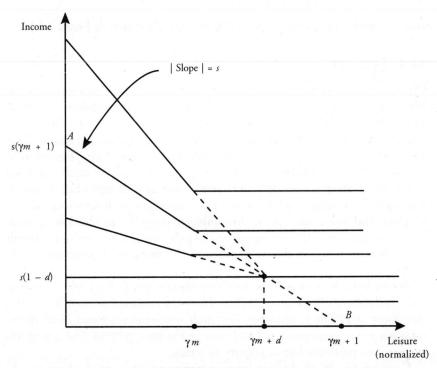

Figure 17.2

The lowest indifference curves are horizontal. Then, as we move to higher indifference curves, the segments to the right of γm remain horizontal, but to the left become steeper. If the adult wage is s (and so by definition each unit of effective labour costs s) the budget constraint is given by the line AB and it is clear that the household is indifferent between supplying any amount of labour between $\gamma m + 1$ and 1 (or, equivalently, buying any amount of leisure between 0 and γm). By inspecting the figure, it is evident that if wage rises above s, labour supply from each household will be 1 and if wage is below s labour supply from each household will be $\gamma m + 1$.

To describe Figure 17.2 mathematically, use L to denote the amount of normalized leisure consumed by the household (implying that the amount of labour supplied by the household is $\gamma m + 1 - L$). Choosing any number $d \in (0, 1)$ consider the following utility function:

$$u(c, L) = \begin{cases} c, & \text{if } L \geq \gamma m \text{ or } c \leq s(1 - d) \\ [dc + (\gamma m - L)s(1 - d)] / (\gamma m + d - L), & \text{otherwise.} \end{cases}$$

The second line of the utility function is simply a mathematical representation of the fact that the indifference curves in Figure 17.2, above the line $s(1 - d)$ and to the left of γm, are rays fanning out of the point $(\gamma m + d, s(1 - d))$.

Maximizing this utility function, subject to the budget constraint,

$$c \leq w(\gamma m + 1 - L),$$

yields a supply curve with property [1], which is illustrated in Figure 17.1.

17.4. RESULTS

Observe that in this model there can be more than one stable equilibrium in the labour market. An economy can get caught in the 'bad' equilibrium, E^B, where adult wage is w^B and child labour is high, even though a 'good' equilibrium, E^G, where adult wage is w^G and children do not work, is available (see Figure 17.1). My concern here is with the possibility of using minimum-wage legislation to get out of the bad equilibrium. This is an important question because a direct ban on child labour is very difficult to implement. And though adult minimum wages are also hard to implement, most countries have such legislation already in place and some mechanism for implementing it. In addition, if such legislation makes it in the *parents'* interest to pull their children out of the labour force, then one may be able to get around the problem of monitoring child labour.

At first sight, it looks as if any legal minimum wage, $\underline{w}$, for adults, as long as it is strictly above s (see Figure 17.1), will help the economy to move to E^G. But that is not true. The relation between adult minimum wage and child labour turns out to be complicated, as I had indicated in Basu (1999a). The aim of this chapter is to push this line of enquiry to a close.

Consider first of all the case where government sets $\underline{w}$ at or above w^G. To analyse the effect of minimum wage legislation we need to distinguish between the case where

(17.3) $\gamma m < d(\underline{w})/H$

holds and where it does not. Since γ is likely to be small for work that requires skill, this condition is more likely to hold for skilled work. In reality γ rises with the age of the child[2] (a detail that we have ignored in our model). Therefore, since smaller children are usually employed in family farms. (17.3) is likely to be satisfied by family farms.

Let us first consider the case where (17.3) holds. How many adults will find employment? By looking at Figure 17.1 and supposing that $\underline{w}$ is as shown, one may at first believe that $d(\underline{w})$ (shown in the figure by the line segment $\underline{w}F$) adults will find work. This is, however, not true. To see this let us use E to denote the number of adults who find employment. Then $H - E$ adults are unemployed, which means that in $H - E$ households the income earned by the adults will be zero. Therefore, the children from all these households will be looking for work. Hence, the aggregate supply of child labour is $\gamma m(H - E)$. Given that the wage is $\underline{w}$, the aggregate demand for labour is $d(\underline{w})$. Since E adults find work, the demand for child labour will be $d(\underline{w}) - E$. Hence there will be equilibrium in the child-labour market if:

$$\gamma m (H - E) = d(\underline{w}) - E.$$

Solving this for E, and writing the solutions as $E^*(\underline{w})$, have:

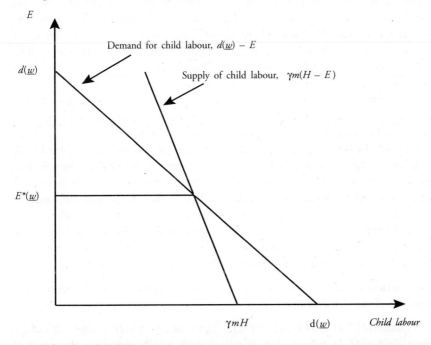

Figure 17.3

(17.4) $E^*(\underline{w}) = [d(\underline{w}) - \gamma mH\,]\,/\,(1 - \gamma m)$.

If E adults work, the evidence of child labour, as we just saw, is given by $m(H - E\,)$. Hence, if the legal minimum wage is __, the amount of child labour in the economy, $C(\underline{w})$, is given by $m[H - E^*(\underline{w})]$. Using (17.4), we have:

$$C(\underline{w}) = m[H - d(\underline{w})]\,/\,(1 - \gamma m).$$

Since $\underline{w} \geq w^G$, $d(\underline{w}) < H$. This coupled with (17.3), implies that $1 - \gamma m > 0$. Hence, $C(\underline{w}) \geq 0$ and as $\underline{w}$ increases, $C(\underline{w})$ increases.

PROPOSITION 17.1: If $\underline{w} \geq w^G$ and (17.3) is true, then a rise in $\underline{w}$ results in a rise in the incidence of child labour.

It is interesting to note that just as in standard textbook models, it is price that moves up and down to bring about equality in demand and supply, in our model it is the amount of adult employment, E, which adjusts till the point where demand for child labour is equal to the supply of child labour. Keeping this in mind we can draw the demand and supply of child labour as a function of E. These are shown in Figure 17.3. These curves are understood by following the reasoning preceding equation (17.4). The position of these curves depends on $\underline{w}$ (in addition, they are drawn under the assumption that $\underline{w} \geq w^G$) and so the curves will shift as $\underline{w}$ is changed.

In the case illustrated in Figure 17.3, which follows from the assumptions $\underline{w} \geq w^G$ and (17.3), the equilibrium adult employment, $E^*(\underline{w})$, and therefore the equilibrium child labour, $C(\underline{w})$, are, in a sense, stable. Observe first that the supply curve necessarily cuts the demand curve from above. Now, suppose, for the moment, that E adults, where $E < E^*(\underline{w})$, have found jobs. Then the demand for child labour will exceed the supply of child labour. Hence employers will end up employing more adults. Thus E will move up, towards $E^*(\underline{w})$. One can do a similar exercise starting with an E greater than $E^*(\underline{w})$.

As remarked earlier, though at the minimum wage, $\underline{w}$, the supply of adult labour exceeds the demand for labour, more adults get unemployed than the extent of the excess supply. In Figure 17.1, let the minimum wage be at $\underline{w}$. Then the supply of labour is given by the line segment $\underline{w}K$ and the demand for labour is given by the segment $\underline{w}F$. It may therefore appear that $\underline{w}F$ adults will find employment, with FK being unemployed. But that is not so. The fact of FK adults being unemployed will send the children of their household out in search of work. This will displace some more adults from their work, sending some more children out in search of work, and so on. The employment level of adults which finally occurs, $E^*(\underline{w})$, must therefore be less than the line segment $\underline{w}F$ in Figure 17.1. A statement and proof of this proposition follows.

PROPOSITION 17.2: If $\underline{w} > w^G$ and (17.3) is true, then adult employment is less than the demand for labour.

Equation (17.4) implies: $(1 - \gamma m)E^*(\underline{w}) = d(\underline{w}) - \gamma mH < d(\underline{w}) - \gamma md(\underline{w})$, since $d(\underline{w}) < H$. It follows that $E^*(\underline{w}) < d(\underline{w})$, which completes the proof of Proposition 17.2.

Next we turn to what would happen if (17.3) did not hold. So assume

(17.5) $\gamma m \geq d(\underline{w}) / H.$

If (17.5) were true, then the minimum wage would have quite a dramatic effect (we are continuing with the case where the minimum wage is set at or above w^G). To see this define w^* implicitly by

(17.6) $d(w^* / \gamma) = \gamma mH.$

This and (17.5) imply:

(17.7) $\underline{w} \geq w^* / \gamma.$

It is now easy to check there is an equilibrium in which child wage is w^*, no adults are employed, and all the children work. To see this, observe that adults cannot undercut the child wage because of (17.7). Hence, if child wage is w^*, no adult will find work. Hence all the mH children in the economy will be looking for work; and labour supply from children will equal γmH. Therefore, by (17.6), the supply of child labour will be equal to demand. So what we have established may be summed up as follows.

CLAIM 17.1: If $\underline{w} \geq w^G$ and (17.3) is false, then there is an equilibrium in which all adults are unemployed and all children work.

Let us now turn to the case where the legal minimum wage is set below w^G. Let us consider $\underline{w} \in (s, w^G)$. This is quite a real possibility. Since s is the level of adult wage below which households find it necessary to send their children to work may well consider setting a minimum-wage floor above s.

As before, suppose E adults are employed, adult wage is at w and child wage is at γm. Since adult wage is above s, all households where the adult finds work will not send their children to work; other households will. Hence, $m (H - E)$ children look for work and so the supply of labour by children is given by $\gamma m (H - E)$. The demand for labour from children is $d(\underline{w}) - E$. Hence, as before, the child-labour market is in equilibrium if $\gamma m (H - E) = d(\underline{w}) - E$. Thus the equilibrium employment of adults is given by (17.4).

Consider first the case where $\gamma m > d(\underline{w})/H$. Then $\gamma m > 1$, since $d(\underline{w}) > H$. It follows from (4), that $E^*(\underline{w}) \in [0, H]$. Hence, we have an equilibrium in which wage settles at $\underline{w}$ and both adults and children work.

PROPOSITION 17.3: If $\underline{w} \in (s, w^G)$ and (17.3) is violated, then there exists an equilibrium where wage settles at $\underline{w}$ and both adults and children work.

This is, at first sight, perplexing. Even though there is a market-clearing wage above the minimum wage (since $w^G > \underline{w}$), a new equilibrium gets created once a minimum wage is implemented. Though normally at that wage, demand for labour would have exceeded supply, now the fact of there being a minimum wage creates conditions for labour supply to increase (with children joining the labour market) up to the point where demand is equal to supply.

The utility function at the end of Section 17.3 is an example of where this can happen. One can also think of intuitive reasons for it. If a household is poor because the adult wage is low or the adult is unemployed, the children may have to be sent out to work a certain amount. But this could jeopardize the child's schooling prospect and, once this happens, the opportunity cost of child labour falls and so the supply of child labour increases further. Goldin (1979) has, in the context of late-nineteenth century Philadelphia, discussed the response of a child's labour and schooling to the father's unemployment; and her findings are consistent with the above.

Yet another route to explain this paradoxical result is to note that the children's supply response is somewhat like an 'added worker effect'. To model this entails a much more elaborate setting than the one described here. The idea is that, if there is a certain amount of unemployment expected to prevail in the labour market, some risk-averse households, fearing that the main breadwinner may lose his or her job, may send out more workers than they would have at that wage if they were assured of full employment in the economy. That is the line followed by Basu et al. (1999).

When the hypothesis of Proposition 17.3 is true, there is another possible equilibrium, in which adults are fully displaced by the children. Define w' to be such that $d(w' / \gamma) = \gamma mH$. Hence, $d(w' / \gamma) > d(\underline{w})$. It follows that $w' / \gamma < \underline{w}$. So, now suppose that children get a wage of w'; all firms will prefer children; adults are unable to undercut the wage because of the minimum-wage legislation; and $d(w' / \gamma) = \gamma mH$ implies that demand for child labour is equal to the supply. So we have an equilibrium, which may be summed up as follows.

CLAIM 17.2: If $\underline{w} \in (s, w^G)$ and (17.3) is false, then there is an equilibrium in which all adults are unemployed and only children work.

Claims 17.1 and 17.2 may now be combined to state the following proposition.

PROPOSITION 17.4: If $\underline{w} > s$ and (3) is false, then there is an equilibrium in which all adults are unemployed and only children work.

Finally, while still assuming that $w^G > \underline{w} > s$, let us consider what happens if $d(\underline{w}) / H > \gamma m$. It can be verified that either $E^*(\underline{w})$ is negative (if $\gamma m > 1$) or greater than H (since $d(\underline{w}) > H$). Since both those are infeasible, it follows that there is no equilibrium in which adult wage is at $\underline{w}$ and adults work. So this is the case where the good equilibrium is unequivocally reached, to wit, adult wage rises to w^G and only adults work. Hence, in this case the minimum wage law would certainly work.

What Proposition 17.4 and the above paragraph say is quite interesting. Suppose a minimum wage is imposed somewhere above s and below w^G in Figure 17.1. At first sight it appears that since there were two equilibria in the labour market, E^G and E^B, and the latter is no longer feasible, the only possible equilibrium is E^G. What we have just established is that, though E^G may well be achieved, the very imposition of a minimum-wage law can bring into existence a new equilibrium—one in which the wage settles at $\underline{w}$ and child labour expands to the maximum possible in the economy, while adults are unemployed.[3]

Hence, if one is using legislative action in an economy with multiple equilibria, it seems safer to use a ban on child labour, instead of the more indirect method of setting laws regarding the level of wages.[4]

17.5. INTERPRETATION

Observe that minimum-wage legislation tends to backfire most seriously (the case of Proposition (17.4) when (17.3) is false, that is, when γm is large. Indeed note that our results in general are very sensitive to the magnitude of γm. What does this variable represent? As it turns out this is quite an economically significant variable. It denotes the amount of effective labour that the children of a single household can supply.

In a modern economy, typically, fertility is low, and so m will be small. Also jobs being more skilled, children are a poorer substitute for adults; so γ happens to be small. It is conceivable that for even the least skilled of computing jobs, for instance, word-processing, γ will be very small. On the other hand, for certain kinds of labour-intensive work, such as making hand-knotted carpets, γ will be quite high (see Levinson et al. 1998). Hence, γm will tend to be small in a modern, industrialized economy, and large in a developing economy. In other words, (17.3) is more likely to be violated and so Proposition (17.4) is more likely to be relevant in a poor country. Therefore, the suggestion of using a minimum-wage legislation in developing countries as a form of international labour standard has the risk of exacerbating the problem of child labour.

NOTES

1. Bardhan (1984) does study the effect of unemployment on the household labour-supply decision in a developing country (India), but he pays no special attention to child labour.
2. Cain (1977) has calculated how in rural Bangladesh γ rises with age and reaches 1 by around the age of 13 years.
3. The simplicity of the model makes the result look more extreme than it will be in reality. In reality the labour market is usually segmented and our model could be thought of as pertaining to the unskilled end of the segments. Viewed in this way, what the result says is that children will tend to replace adults in the bottom end (skill-wise) of the labour market.
4. Of course, one can use a combination of minimum-wage laws for both adults *and* *children* to ensure that children do not work, but surely that is more cumbersome a route than simply declaring child labour illegal.

REFERENCES

Ashenfelter, O. 1980. 'Unemployment as Disequilibrium in a Model of Aggregate Labour Supply'. *Econometrica* 48: 547–64.

Bardhan, P.K. 1984. *Land, Labour and Rural Poverty*. New York: Columbia University Press.

Basu, K. 1999a. 'Child Labour, Cause, Consequence and Cure, with Remarks on International Labour Standards'. *Journal of Economic Literature* 37: 1083–119.

—— 1999b. 'International Labour Standards and Child Labour'. *Challenge* 42: 80–93.

Basu, K., G. Genicot, and J.E. Stilitz. 1999. 'Household Labour Supply, Unemployment, and Minimum Wage Legislation'. Policy Research Working Paper. No. 2049. The World Bank.

Basu, K. and P.H. Van. 1998. 'The Economics of Child Labour'. *American Economic Review* 88: 412–27.

Bhagwati, J.N. 1995. 'Trade Liberalization and 'Fair Trade' Demands: Addressing the Environment and Labour Standards Issue'. *World Economy* 18: 745–59.

Bonnet, M. 1993. 'Child Labour in Africa'. *International Labour Review* 132: 371–89.

Cain, M.T. 1977. 'The Economic Activities of Children in a Village in Bangladesh'. *Population and Development Review* 3: 201–27.

Card, D. and A. Krueger. 1995. *Myth and Measurement: The New Economics of Minimum Wage*. Princeton: Princeton University Press.

Goldin, C. 1979. 'Household and Market Production of Families in a Late Nineteenth-Century American Town'. *Explorations in Economic History* 16: 111–31.

Grootaert, C. and H. Patrinos. 1999. *The Policy Analysis of Child Labour: A Comparative Study*. New York: St. Martin's Press.

Horan, P.M. and P.G. Hargis. 1991. 'Children's Work and Schooling in the Late Nineteenth-Century Family'. *American Sociological Review* 56: 583–96.

Layard, P.R.G., M. Barton, and A. Zabalza. 1980. 'Married Women's Participation and Hours'. *Economica* 47: 51–72.

Levison, D. et al. 1998. 'Is Child Labour Really Necessary in India's Carpet Industry?'. In R. Anker et al., eds. *Economics of Child Labour in Selected Industries of India*. New Delhi: Hindustan Publishers.

Maskus, K. 1997. 'Should Core Labour Standards be Imposed through International Trade Policy?'. Policy Research Working Paper. No. 1817. The World Bank.

Portes, A. 1990. 'When More Can Be Less: Labour Standards, Development, and the Informal Economy'. In *Labour Standards and Development in the Global Economy*, US Department of Labor, Washington, DC.

Ray, R. 1999. 'Child Labour, Child Schooling and Their Interaction with Adult Labour: The Empirical Evidence and Some Analytical Implications'. *World Bank Economic Review*.

Rodrik, D. 1996. 'Labour Standards in International Trade: Do They Matter and What Do We Do about Them?'. Policy Essay. No. 20. Overseas Development Council, Washington, DC.

18 Child Labour
Cause, Consequence, and Cure, with Remarks on International Labour Standards

18.1. INTRODUCTION

According to the Bureau of Statistics of the International Labour Organization (ILO), in 1995 at least 120 million of the world's children between the ages of 5 and 14 years did full-time, paid work (ILO 1996; Ashagrie 1998). Many of them worked under hazardous and unhygienic conditions and for more than ten hours a day. This is not a new problem. In different parts of the world, at different stages of history, the labouring child has been a part of economic life. In particular, children have worked in large numbers in factories from the time of the industrial revolution in Europe and from the mid-nineteenth century in America. In contemporary times, the incidence of child labour is very high in Third World countries, and it has been that way for several decades now.

What has increased is the awareness of and concern for children who work as labourers. This is caused, in part, by the increasing globalization of the world, which has brought not only more information about the condition of labour in different nations to academics and activists the world over, but also

From *Journal of Economic Literature* 37(September), 1999: 1083–1119.

For useful comments and suggestions, I am grateful to Jens Andvig, Kebebew Ashagrie, Alaka Basu, Clive Bell, Francois Bourguignon, George Boyer, Dan Bromley, Jean Dreze, Patrick Emerson, Gary Fields, Garance Genicot, Noemi Giszpenc, Subbiah Kannapan, Ayal Kimhi, Elizabeth King, Luis-Felipe Lopez- Calva, Dani Rodrik, Pham Hoang Van, and Henry Wan. I have also benefited from seminar presentations at the Indian Statistical Institute in New Delhi, the Stockholm School of Economics, the Indira Gandhi Institute of Development Research, the University of Wisconsin, Notre Dame University, the World Bank, and the NEUDC Conference at Yale University.

goods produced by children in faraway lands into the hands of consumers in high-income countries. This has, in turn, brought two very different kinds of people onto the same platform—individuals who are genuinely concerned about the plight of children in poor countries, and those who comprise the forces of protectionism in developed countries. The two have rallied together to support a variety of interventions in Third World labour markets, ranging from banning imports into industrialized nations of products 'tainted' by child-labour inputs, through setting international labour standards to be monitored by international organizations such as the World Trade Organization (WTO) or ILO, to labelling products that involved child labour so as to give the consumer the option to boycott them.

Any such intervention is likely to have not just an impact on the well-being of children, but also spillover effects on others. It is imperative, therefore, that policy in this area be based on careful analysis and research, and not just emotion or impulse.

The literature on child labour is enormous, but it is scattered across the social sciences and piecemeal, lacking a common theoretical foundation. The aim of this chapter is to provide an analytical survey of this field, keeping in mind that this is an area where the primary reason for theorizing is ultimately to influence policy. The main policy debates and options are summarized in Section 18.3. Section 18.2 provides the factual background of the problem, drawing on large-scale data sets and on the substantial literature rooted in formal and informal micro studies. Thanks to the enormity of the problem in the last century, there is also a sizeable historical literature on the subject.[1] I draw on this, not comprehensively, but keeping in mind contemporary concerns and the analytical focus of this chapter, and report on this in Section 18.2.2.

Sections 18.4 through 18.7 are on models and theories related to child labour. The traditional argument for government intervention in child labour markets is based on the standard claim of externalities. Such arguments are recapitulated in Section 18.4, which also summarizes the early theoretical ideas of some classical economists. Conventional models treat the household as a single decision-making unit (Becker 1964); but once we recognize that there may be divergence of interests within the household, there is scope for arguing that children are victimized. There is now a whole range of bargaining models available for analysing intra-household decision making, some of which explicitly look into the question of child labour (for example, Moehling 1995; and Gupta forthcoming). These models are summarized in Section 18.5, along with some suggestions for extensions. If there are no externalities and no divergence of interest in the household, can there still be a case for intervention? Section 18.6 sketches a model (Basu and Van 1998) showing that, for a class of situations, the answer is yes, because of the labour market's propensity to have multiple equilibria. The model of Section 18.7 sketches an argument against harassment and shows how this kind of analysis can be used in thinking about child-labour legislation.

Child-labour regulation is an important part of the current debate on international labour standards. Section 18.8 discusses some questions concerning international labour standards in which the problem of child labour arises explicitly. Section 18.9 consists of brief concluding remarks.

18.2. THE EMPIRICAL CONTEXT

To place this analytical survey in context and also to keep our focus on real world policy concerns, it is useful to begin by briefly recounting the world's actual experience with child labour. This exercise is broken up into two subsections, one describing contemporary macro aggregates, and another describing the historical roots of the problem.

18.2.1. Contemporary

Any estimate of child labour depends on how we define 'child' and 'labour' and on the quality of statistics available. The ILO's Convention No. 138 specifies 15 years as the age above which, in normal circumstances, a person may participate in economic activity.[2] Following this, most studies treat a person of age less than 15 years as a 'child'. As a study by the US Department of Labor notes, while ILO Convention 138 'has been ratified by only about one quarter of the ILO membership, it has nevertheless been internationally recognized and used as a blueprint for national policy and practice with respect to child labor'. (US Department of Labor 1993: 5). This observation carries even greater weight because the US itself is not a signatory to the convention.

A child is classified as a 'labourer' if the child is 'economically active' (Ashagrie 1993).[3] Governments and international organizations usually treat a person as economically active or 'gainfully employed' if the person does work on a regular basis for which he or she is remunerated or that results in output destined for the market. The Indian census, for instance, explicitly uses such a convention. We know from micro studies that if we instead include those 'invisible' workers who do unpaid work that finds no market outlet, such as work within the household, the estimates of child labour can shoot up. Jayaraj

Table 18.1: Child Labour: Aggregate and Distribution

	Number of children (below 15 years) Working (in thousands)		
	1980	1985	1990
World	87,867	80,611	78,516
Africa	14,950	14,536	16,763
Americas	4122	4536	4723
Asia	68,324	61,210	56,784
East Asia	39,725	33,463	22,448
South East Asia	6518	6079	5587
South Asia	20,192	19,834	27,639

Source: Ashagrie (1993).

and Subramanian's (1997) recent calculations for the state of Tamil Nadu, India, show that for the 5–14 age group in 1983, if they use the restrictive definition of the kind that the ILO uses, 13 per cent of all children were labourers. Using the more liberal definition, the figure jumps to 33 per cent.[4]

Even after the definitions are sorted out (to the extent that they can be) official data on child labour tend to be deficient because of the likelihood of under-reporting. In most countries there are laws that place restrictions on child labour, ranging from an outright ban (as in most industrialized countries) to other kinds of limitations such as an outright ban on child labour for very small children, and for all children in hazardous industries (as, for instance, in Bangladesh, India, and Pakistan). Thus it is natural for guardians and employers to hide the information of 'illegal' work by children.

Keeping all these caveats in mind, and cobbling information from various sources, Ashagrie (1993; see also Grootaert and Kanbur 1995) was the first to put together an international data set on child labour. He found that in 1990 there were nearly 79 million children who were economically active. Most of them (57 million) were in Asia, However, over the previous ten years, he found that the absolute number of children working was declining in Asia but rising in the Americas and Africa, sharply in the latter. These data are summarized in Table 18.1.

It is worth pointing out that while Ashagrie's (1993) estimates, as summarized in Table 18.1, have the virtue of comprehensiveness, they generally give lower values for the incidence of child labour than other existing estimates. Indeed, more recent works by Ashagrie (1998) and the ILO (1996a), which were based on detailed experimental surveys in Ghana, India, Indonesia, and Senegal, have resulted in upward revisions of these figures. In addition, it must be kept in mind that all figures quoted in this section relate to full-time work. Recent ILO estimates suggest that if 'child labour' is taken to include those who do part-time work, the numbers, more than double. Thus the 1995 figure for child labour, quoted at the start of this chapter would rise to 250 million.

Table 18.2: Participation Rates For Children: 10–14 Years

	1950	1960	1970	1980	1990	1995	2000	2010
World	27.57	24.81	22.30	19.91	14.65	13.02	11.32	8.44
Africa	38.42	35.88	33.05	30.97	27.87	26.23	24.92	22.52
Latin America & Caribbean	19.36	16.53	14.60	12.64	11.23	9.77	8.21	5.47
Asia	36.06	32.26	28.35	23.42	15.19	12.77	10.18	5.60
Europe	6.49	3.52	1.62	0.42	0.10	0.06	0.04	0.02
Ethiopia	52.95	50.75	48.51	46.32	43.47	42.30	41.10	38.79
Brazil	23.53	22.19	20.33	19.02	17.78	16.09	14.39	10.94
China	47.85	43.17	39.03	30.48	15.24	11.55	7.86	0.00
India	35.43	30.07	25.46	21.44	16.68	14.37	12.07	7.46
Italy	29.11	10.91	4.12	1.55	0.43	0.38	0.33	0.27

Source: ILO (1996b).

The Asian figures are very large, but it has to be kept in mind that Asia's population is very large. So to get a better idea of the magnitude of the problem, we may wish to look at the 'participation rate', that is, the percentage of children of the relevant age group who work as labourers. In terms of participation rates, for the 10–14 years category, the problem in 1990 was most serious in Africa, with a figure of 27.87 per cent. The participation rate for Asia was 15.19 per cent. These statistics are available from the ILO (1996b), which has now compiled inter-country data on child labour from 1950 to 1995, along with projections up to 2010. A summary of this information is provided in Table 18.2 and Figure 18.1. The first five rows of Table 18.2 show the distribution of child labour across the main continental regions of the world. In addition, a sample of five nations, from among those that had a participation rate of over 20 per cent in 1950, is represented in the table to give the reader a glimpse of how varied the experience of different nations has been.

As the graph and table show, the problem is enormous, but the trend, fortunately, is in the right direction. For some countries, such as China, India, and especially Italy, the decline in the participation rate of children has been quite rapid. For most Latin American nations, such as Brazil, the decline is notable but less marked. The problem has been extremely persistent in large parts of sub-Saharan Africa, as illustrated by Ethiopia, but even here the trend is downwards. For China, interestingly, the decline is most rapid between 1980

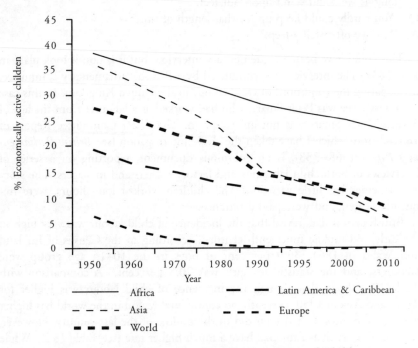

Figure 18.1: Trends in the Participation Rates of Children
10–14 Years of Age

and 1990, which happens to coincide with the period of very rapid growth in incomes.[5]

The overall growth of an economy is by no means the only factor, nor for that matter the most important factor, in the mitigation of child labour. Changes in technology, improvement in the conditions of the adult labour market, and the availability of decent schooling can all lead to children being voluntarily withdrawn from the labour force. Levy (1985), in a study of rural Egypt, found that mechanization did contribute to a diminution in child labour and also in fertility. The cultivation of cotton, especially weeding and picking, has conventionally been child-labour intensive in Egypt. So changes in cropping pattern, away from cotton, played a role in curbing child labour.

We shall return to the subject of how to curb child labour later. Let us, before that, take a look at the historical backdrop of the contemporary situation just described.

18.2.2. Historical

Here is an excerpt from an interview with a child labourer.

Q. 'What were your hours of labour, do you recollect, in that mill?'
A. 'In the summer season we were very scarce of water.'
Q. 'But when you had sufficient water, how long did you work?'
A. 'We began at 4 o'clock in the morning and worked till 10 or 11 at night; as long as we could stand upon our feet.'
Q. 'You hardly could keep up for that length of time?'
A. 'No, we often fell asleep.'

This could have been a contemporary interview, but it is not; it took place in June 1832. The interview was conducted by a British Parliamentary committee, investigating the conditions of child labour in the United Kingdom. In this case the interviewee was Peter Smart, who had worked as a labourer from the age of 5 years. Peter Smart was not an exception. The Select Committee Report of 1831–2 from which I have taken the above interrogation (see *British Parliamentary Papers* 1968: 338), is an enormous document, reporting on a series of interviews of both child labourers and factory owners and managers. The story that emerges has little variation. The children worked long hours, were frequently beaten, and were paid a pittance.

British census data reveal that the incidence of child labour was very high in the early and middle nineteenth century. According to the Census of England and Wales in 1861, 36.9 per cent of boys in the 10–14 age group were labourers, and the statistic for girls was 20.5 per cent.[6] A comparison with Table 18.2 shows that though the incidence of child labour was higher for Africa and Asia in 1950, currently no continental region in the world has higher participation rates than Britain did in the middle of the last century. However, some *nations*, such as Ethiopia, have a much higher rate (see Table 18.2). While the participation of children in the labour force may have been particularly high in Britain, the experience of other industrializing nations, such as Belgium, the

US, and Japan was not very different (De Herdt 1996; Parsons and Goldin 1989; and Saito 1996).[7]

While, historically, attention was drawn to the child labour problem during the industrial revolution, there are scholars who have argued that the problem was not especially acute during this time. According to them, child labour was comparably widespread even in the early eighteenth century, though the children did not work in factories at that time. But most of such observations are based on impressions rather than statistics. Moreover, the experience of working on farms, alongside one's parents, is arguably less grim than working in factories for fourteen hours at a stretch (Cunningham 1990), as suggested by the interview quoted above.

This view finds reinforcement in a contemporary study conducted by researchers at the Delhi School of Economics[8] and the Indian Social Institute which shows that child labour in *rural areas* is often 'light', so much so that these children ought to be able to get education without seriously cutting into their work commitments, *if* they had access to proper schools (Bhatty et al. 1997). This study, based on interviewing 1221 rural Indian parents, found that among the out-of-school children, about half worked less than three hours on the day preceding the survey and only 18 per cent worked more than eight hours. The story is very different for *factory* workers and organized child labour, as, for instance, in the match industry of Sivakasi (Kothari 1983; Kulkarni 1983).

The large incidence of child labour in the industrialized nations in the last century gave rise to a lot of debate and ideas from which we can benefit today.[9] What is quite striking and noteworthy is that child labour has not always been thought of as an evil. There have been times when it was treated as unpleasant to the child, but nevertheless desirable, somewhat akin to our contemporary view of education. Thus we find an eighteenth-century writer observing that 'parents, whose childhood was spent in idleness, have contracted every absurd prejudice against the employment of children, as unnatural, cruel and unprofitable'.[10] Hutchins and Harrison (1903) have recounted many instances of this attitude. They quote, for instance, a 1770 document which argues that:

being constantly employed at least twelve hours in a day ... we hope the rising generation will be so habituated to constant employment, that it would at length prove agreeable and entertaining to them ... [From] children thus trained up to constant labour we may venture to hope the lowering of its price [Hutchins and Harrison 1903: 5].[11]

Nevertheless, as the excesses of child labour increased through the early nineteenth century, opposition also mounted. And by the late nineteenth century, child labour was on the decline. It is true that this institution would soon be 'exported' out of the industrialized nations, as the practice of child labour got shifted to the colonies, but within the boundaries of industrialized nations, it was undeniably on the way out.

How did this happen? There is no consensus on this. On the one hand, there was a series of legislative acts limiting child labour and ultimately declaring it unconditionally illegal, and there were also rules about compulsory education which made it difficult for children to work full time. On the other hand, the increasing prosperity of Europe, the USA, and Japan made it easier for parents to pull children out of work without having to fear that this would commit the household to poverty.

All these factors must have played a role with important regional and sectoral differences. Scholliers' (1995: 208) study of child labour in Ghent, Belgium, revealed that by the mid-nineteenth century 'the number of children under twelve had diminished substantially, and this without any legislative intervention'. By contrast, the law played an important role in the decline of child labour in the cotton mills of Manchester (Bolin-Hort 1989). Brown et al. (1992), in their study of the fruit and vegetable canning industry in the US between 1880 and 1920, found that the decline in the incidence of child labour was due to both natural economic reasons and legal factors, though the economic forces were the stronger explanatory variable.

There is, however, some agreement on one matter. If one is using legislative fiat to fight child labour, it is more effective to legislate for compulsory education instead of simply banning child labour (Weiner 1991). One good reason for this is that a child's presence in school is easier to monitor (and thus ensure) than a child's absence from work.

There were others who, in the context of the historical debate, felt that legislation, whether it be for compulsory education or a direct ban on child labour, cannot be as effective as economic progress, and that the right policy is to wait for economic progress. Such a position is associated with Nardinelli (1990; and, for discussion, see Cunningham and Viazzo 1996a).

One of the more systematic investigations of the historical role of law in the decline of child labour occurs in the work of Moehling (1998). Her focus of study is the United States from 1880 to 1910. This is part of the period during which the incidence of child labour dropped off rapidly. It was also a period of activism against child labour. In 1900 twelve states had a minimum age limit of 14 years for manufacturing employment. By 1910 thirty-two states had such a restriction. The question Moehling investigates is whether it was the legislation that caused the decline in child labour or it was the diminishing dependence of industry on child labour that made the judicial activism possible.

The method that she uses is the 'difference of difference of difference' (DDD). A more standard method (for instance, one used by Angrist and Krueger 1991; and Margo and Finegan 1996) would have required her to compare the difference in the difference in the occupation rates of children aged 13 years and 14 years in states that have a law debarring those below 14 years old from working in manufactures- and states that have no such law, to see if the law had an impact. What Moehling does is to add another layer of differencing by looking at the difference-in-difference before and after some states adopted such legislation. This presumably nets out the effect that there may be differences between different states, stemming not from law but more inherent traits, such as industrial structure. Using national random samples of households from the censuses of 1880, 1900, and 1910 and the method of

DDD, Moehling concludes that minimum-age restrictions had little impact on employment in the US at the turn of the century.

The finding is important but not conclusive. Once one begins to go the route of adding on differences, strictly speaking, there is no stopping. Just as there may be innate differences between states, there may be innate differences (in particular, ones that are not the product of law) in changes over time across states.

Turning to the subject of state intervention, one must, in assessing the efficacy of a law, distinguish between the case where the law is not properly implemented, and one in which the law is implemented but its net effect on society is not desirable. What Moehling's study points to is the inadequate implementation of the US law. This does not mean that the law is not the right method of intervention for eradicating child labour. Another country at another point in history may be able to implement a law that had, allegedly, failed elsewhere in the late nineteenth century. An important policy question facing us is whether a legislative intervention is a desirable one. Does it promote welfare when properly implemented? To answer such questions, it is essential to have a theoretical model for analysing child labour. Later, when we have studied such models, we will see that there is scope for using both legislative and non-legislative interventions. Policy toward child labour has to be more nuanced and context specific than what governments and international organizations have attempted. But before we get to such a conclusion it is useful to recapitulate what the major policy options are and the role of different institutions.

18.3. THE POLICY QUESTIONS

In the battle against child labour, a variety of laws and interventions have been tried and even more discussed. In recounting this debate, it is useful to distinguish between three kinds of interventions and institutions: intra-national, supranational, and extra-national.

Intra-national effort consists of the laws that a country enacts and interventions that it plans in order to control child labour within the national boundary. This invariably comes with a certain amount of institutional paraphernalia, such as organizations set up to administer the law and otherwise dissuade child employment. Contrary to the popular view, the question is not just between banning and not banning child labour. Instead, a range of different instruments have been tried. This varies from one of the earliest pieces of legislation, such as the child labour law enacted by the state of Massachusetts, USA, in 1837, which prohibited firms from employing children under the age of 15 years who had not attended school for at least three months in the previous year, to contemporary laws, such as Nepal's Labour Act of 1992 and The Children's Act of 1992, that place restrictions on indigenous child labour.[12] Many countries also have important non-governmental, intra-national efforts to curb child labour. The Daughters' Education Programme (DEP) in northern Thailand is one such effort. The DEP tries to prevent young girls from going into prostitution by providing education and mobilizing local opinion literacy programmes and compulsory education, to the extent that these get in the way of labour, may also be viewed as an intra-national intervention. I return to the subject of education below.

Supranational interventions are those attempted through international organizations such as the ILO, the WTO, and United Nations International Children's Education Fund (UNICEF), which by establishing conventions, and encouraging and cajoling nations to ratify them, have tried to curb child labour. The most powerful, and also controversial, instrument that the supranational institutions can use to curb child labour is the imposition of 'international labour standards', that is, a set of minimal rules and conditions for labour which all countries are expected to satisfy. Since the adoption of such standards makes it possible to take punitive action (such as imposing trade sanctions) against defaulting nations, these can be potentially quite effective. Labour standards are discussed in Section 18.8.

Thanks to controversy and a divergence of opinion, the world has been slow to adopt international labour standards. This has led some developed countries to consider legislation and other action in their own countries that could curb child labour in developing nations. Such actions are what I label as *extra-national*. Consider, for instance, the Child Labor Deterrence Act, or the so-called 'Harkin's bill' which has been debated extensively in the US Congress. In a nutshell, this is a law that seeks to disallow the import into the US of goods that have been produced with the help of child labour. The law will work within the US but is nevertheless expected to have a strong deterrent effect in developing countries. There are variants of the Harkin's bill that have been considered and debated in the US. The 'Sanders' amendment' which seeks to amend the Tariff Act of 1930 so as to deter the import of goods produced by unfree or bonded child labour, is another (and, to me, a more reasonable) example of extra-national intervention, as are recent efforts to have imported goods that are 'child-labour free' to be labelled as such.

The trouble with such extra-national interventions is that these can come to be misused by lobbies and protectionists representing narrow sectarian interests. It is possible to take different views about the original motivation behind a bill. Krueger (1997), for instance, did an unusual test of the hypothesis that it is protectionism that prompted the Harkin's bill (see also Rodrik 1997). His study was based on checking what kinds of constituency the sponsors of the bill come from; and he concluded that the motivation for the bill was humanitarian concern. On the other hand, while the recent versions of the Harkin's bill have no mention of trade and protection, giving the impression of its only concern being the humanitarian one regarding the plight of children, an early version of the bill had openly appealed that adult workers in the United States and other developed countries should not have their jobs imperilled by imports produced by child labour in developing countries (US Department of Labor 1992: 5; see also Basu 1994; and Harkin 1994).[13] Fortunately, the original motivation is not the relevant question. What one has to be aware of is that such laws *can* be misused by the forces of protection.

An intra-national intervention which deserves to be discussed separately is education and compulsory schooling. Historically this has been considered a major instrument for eradicating child labour. The relation between education and child labour has been an area of active empirical investigation.[14] The important finding is that not only are these not mutually exclusive activities but there may be important complementarities between them. Psacharopoulos' (1997) study, using household survey data from Bolivia and Venezuela, shows that, though working children contribute substantially to household incomes, the educational attainment of children who work is significantly lower than that of non-working children. Patrinos and Psacharopoulos' (1997) research using Peruvian data, however, reveal that child labour is not detrimental to schooling and leaves the authors wondering if in some cases 'working actually makes it possible for the children to go to school' (p. 398). Presumably they are referring here to part-time work which leaves children the time to go to school. Hence, a restricted amount of child labour and schooling can actually be complementary. This is especially true in rural areas and the urban informal sector where work hours are not rigid. In this study of child labour in rural Bengal, Maharatna (1997) found that male (female) children, aged 10–15, worked on average 7.78 hours (4.59 hours) a day, and of that only 3.01 hours (0.01 hours) were spent on formal wage employment. The importance and possibility of work-and-school among the very poor is also brought out well in Grootaert's impressive empirical study of child labour in Cote d'Ivoire. This does not detract from the fact that compulsory education can play a role in limiting child labour (Weiner 1991). Morever, even if the education is not compulsory, the mere availability of good schools can do a lot in diverting children away from long hours in the work place (Dreze and Gazdar 1996; Addison et al. 1997).

In debating policy questions, in particular the use of compulsive measures, such as legal bans and compulsory education, it has to be kept in mind that for a child to work is not the worst thing that can happen. So when we stop child labour, there must be reason to believe that this will not make children worse off, for instance, by causing starvation or bodily harm.[15]

Even if *legal* intervention in the child-labour market is found to be undesirable, this does not mean government should sit back and wait for natural economic growth to gradually remove children from the labour force. Government can intervene in the market to create a variety of incentives, such as providing better and more schools, giving school meals, and improving conditions in the adult-labour market, which result in a reduction of child labour.

The justification for a lot of these interventions depends on whether we believe that the state is more concerned about the well-being of children than are the parents of the children. I believe that such a presumption would be wrong when child labour occurs as a *mass phenomenon* as distinct from cases of isolated abuse. This is not to deny that there are contexts where legal bans, total or sectoral, are desirable. But one needs careful, theoretical analysis to identify the contexts where these are likely to be beneficial.

18.4. EARLY THEORETICAL IDEAS

Given the widespread prevalence of child labour in the last century, it is not surprising that the origins of our contemporary mathematical models and theoretical constructs can be found, albeit in a much more primitive form, in the contributions of earlier writers such as Karl Marx, Alfred Marshall, and Arthur Pigou.

Marx, writing at a time when the incidence of child labour in factories was at a peak, had a lot to say on the subject. Focusing here on the theoretical ideas, it is interesting to note how Marx in *Capital* (1954 [1867] : vol. 1, ch 15, sec.3) virtually outlined a formal model of the cause of child labour. He first noted how, with the rise of new technology, in particular machinery, there arose scope for employing those 'whose bodily development is incomplete, but whose limbs are all the more supple. The labour of women and children was, therefore, the first thing sought by capitalists who used machinery' (Marx (1954) [1867]: 372).

The availability of machinery can, in an ideal world, create more time for leisure. But Marx noted that since the machinery was owned by one agent and labour by another, a diminished need for labour would tend to depress wages,[16] so much so that (1) it may be worthwhile for the capitalist to use labour liberally and (2) it may be necessary for workers to have their entire family work in order to make ends meet. Marx (1954 [1867]: 373) writes: '[Machinery] thus depreciates [the man's] labour power .... In order that the family may live four people must now, not only labour, but expend surplus-labour for the capitalist'. This argument is very close to ideas that we pursue later, and can give rise to the possibility of multiple equilibria, as shown in Section 6.1.

Marx also noted the long-term debilitating consequences of child labour.[17] But it was Marshall who pursued this idea, to the point of sketching a dynamic argument. Marshall (1920 [1890]: 620), with his characteristic fastidiousness, observed that children had laboured even before the industrial revolution but the moral and physical misery and disease caused by excessive work under bad conditions reached their highest point in the first quarter of the [nineteenth] century'. He noted (p. 469) that 'the most valuable of all capital is that invested in human beings'.

Most interestingly, he showed awareness of the dynamics of these observations:

The less fully [the children's] faculties are developed, the less fully they realize the importance of the faculties of their children, and the less will be their power of doing so. And conversely any change that awards to the workers of one generation better earnings, together with better opportunities of developing their best qualities, will increase the material and moral advantages which they have the power to offer to their children Marshall 1920: 468).

Some of the features of this quote will be captured in a formal model in Section 18.6.4.

On policy, most early writers ranged from favouring a ban on child labour to placing severe restrictions on the quantity and quality of child labour. Pigou (1962), who favoured a ban, was aware that a ban could cause poor families to dip below their subsistence level, and also argued that a ban should be coupled with social welfare being provided by the state to the neediest families. He did not tell us what his prescription would be if such social welfare was not forthcoming.

On what theoretical grounds did these early writers support government intervention in this matter? As we shall see later more formally, there is a host of possible arguments, but for a long time the most popular has been that of 'externalities'. Keeping a child away from education may mean missing out on benefits for society at large which do not accrue to the parent who takes the decision. For one, the main benefit goes to the child. As Marshall (1920 [1890]: 470) noted: 'Whoever may incur the expense of investing capital in developing the abilities of the workman, those abilities will be the property of the workman himself: and thus the virtue of those who have aided him must remain for the greater part its own reward'. John Stuart Mill also stressed the positive externality of education, arguing that for a parent not to educate the child is a breach of duty not only towards the child but 'towards the members of the community generally, who are all liable to suffer seriously from the consequences of ignorance and want of education in their fellow citizens' (Mill 1970 [1848]: 319). By extension, he concluded (p. 323): 'Children, and young persons not yet arrived at maturity, should be protected ... from being over-worked. Labouring for too many hours in the day, or on work beyond their strength, should not be permitted.'

Externalities are such a well-known argument for intervention that it is often used too cavalierly by economists and non-economists. It is frequently used as a facade when the real reasons are more self-serving. In the context of child labour, the externality argument needs to be made carefully for it to command attention. An excellent statement of this occurs in the recent work of Grootaert and Kanbur (1995).They consider the possibility that the social returns to education may exceed private returns. So government intervention to direct children away from work and to the classroom may be desirable. The ideal policy for achieving this, according to them, is to bolster the returns to education. They consider a ban on child labour to be a second-best intervention.

An extreme case of externality arises in the model of Gupta (1998) in which there is a total bifurcation between agency and welfare, since parents and employers take the child-employment decision entirely in their self-interest. The child is simply an instrument of their bargain. The model in Section 18.5.2 may, therefore, be viewed as a model of extreme externality.

18.5. BARGAINING MODELS

The formal analysis of child labour is closely related to the modelling of household behaviour. The early ventures in this direction (for instance,

Rosenzweig and Evenson 1977; Goldin 1979) were models of household decision-making, which tried to simultaneously explain decisions of consumption and child labour and, at times, also child schooling and fertility. The specifications were kept simple enough to allow for this greater generality and also to allow for empirical testing. Subsequent work moved away from this to allow for the possibility that a household's behaviour is not determined by one benevolent dictator, but instead is the outcome of internal bargains and power struggle. Models involving bargaining can and have been used to explain child labour and the level of well-being of children, though by and large such efforts treat child labour not as the focus of analysis but a fallout of general household modelling. In this section, I present the main outline of these models, focusing on and drawing out their implications for child labour.

Bargaining models of child labour may be classified into two distinct kinds, depending on who the agents involved in the bargain are. According to one view, the bargain occurs within the family, between the parent and the child. The other approach treats the employer and the parents of the child as the agents involved in bargaining.[18] These two models are the subject matter of the next two sub-sections, respectively.

18.5.1. Intra-Household Bargaining

The traditional model of the household, known as the unitary model, characterizes the household as a single unit of decision making (Becker 1964). This is a valid model if one person in the household happens to be a dictator or all persons have the same utility function.

There is, however, increasing evidence that a household's consumption pattern tends to change as the composition of who earns how much changes, even when the total earnings of the household are unchanged (see, for example, Thomas 1990; Strauss and Thomas 1995; and Moehling 1995). This is usually taken to indicate that the household is not a single conflict-free unit of decision making but, instead, an area of bargaining, where a person's bargaining power depends on the resources one brings to the household and one's fall-back options.[19]

A general representation of these approaches occurs in what is known as the collective model (Bourguignon and Chiappori 1994). Moehling (1995) has adapted this model further by taking explicit account of the child. For a simple version of this model, we could think of the household as being characterized by one parent (agent 1) and one child (agent 2). Since I am here not interested in the demand functions for different products, I shall assume that there is only one good in the economy and x_i is the amount consumed by agent i. Let the unit of the good be chosen such that its price happens to be 1. As in Moehling's model, suppose each agent in the household is concerned about the consumption of all members of the household.[20] Let u_i be person i's utility function.

The household's utility function is a weighted average of u_1 and u_2 where the weight attached to the parent's utility, α, depends on the incomes of the parent and the child, denoted respectively by y_1 and y_2. In other words, in a household's utility function, who gets how much weight depends on who brings how much money.[21] Hence, in the collective model, the household's decision-problem is as follows:

$$\max_{\{x_1, x_2\}} \alpha(y_1, y_2)u_1(x_1, x_2) + [1 - \alpha(y_1, y_2)]u_2(x_1, x_2),$$

subject to $x_1 + x_2 \leq y_1 + y_2.$

It is assumed that

$$\frac{\partial \alpha}{\partial y_1} \geq 0, \frac{\partial \alpha}{\partial y_2} \leq 0, \frac{\partial u_1}{\partial x_1} > 0, \frac{\partial u_1}{\partial x_2} \geq 0,$$

$$\frac{\partial u_2}{\partial x_1} \geq 0, \frac{\partial u_2}{\partial x_2} > 0 \text{ and } 0 \leq \alpha \leq 1.$$

Moehling estimates a closely related model using household data from early twentieth-century urban America, and finds that working children receive a larger share of household resources than non-working children.

This model can be taken further to explain a child's participation in the work-force. To see this, note that, strictly speaking, members of a household consume not just goods and services but also leisure. For simplicity, assume that the adult always works. Let e be the work done by the child, where $e \in [0, 1]$. The child's consumption of leisure is, therefore, $1 - e$.

Given that each person's utility depends on x_1, x_2, and e, a natural extension of the above model is to think of the household as facing the following decision problem, which I shall call the 'collective-maximization problem':

$$\max_{x_1, x_2, e} \alpha(y_1, y_2)u_1(x_1, x_2, e) + [1 - \alpha(y_1, y_2)]u_2(x_1, x_2, e),$$

subject to $x_1 + x_2 \leq y_1 + y_2.$

This is, however, a more complicated problem than appears at first sight, since the child's income, y_2, depends on the choice of e. Thus it is not clear that y_2 can be thought of as an exogenous variable.

There are two alternative routes that one can take from here. One way out of this is to treat α as a function of the price vector, as in Bourguignon and Chiappori (1994). Then, since the wage rate is a price, α will turn out to be a function of the wage rates of adults and children (w_1 and w_2) rather than y_1 and y_2. And of course the budget constraint will now be:

$$x_1 + x_2 \leq w_1 + ew_2,$$

keeping in mind that the adult always works full-time.

This gives us a straightforward optimization problem, which avoids the complication of simultaneity. The empirical plausibility of this approach, however, seems open to question. It implies that a person's bargaining power in the household depends not on the person's actual share of the household income but on the wage that one could earn, if one worked full-time. Sociological studies, on the other hand, suggest that a woman's bargaining power in the household is diminished if a woman does not do outside work (Riley 1997).

A second way out of this difficulty is one that rectifies this weakness and assumes that a person's power depends on how much income the person actually brings to the household budget. This is, however, technically more complicated. Note that in the collective maximization problem the decision maker is, effectively, an amalgam of the members of the household with the preference of each member receiving some weight. Once the child's effort (or, for that matter, anybody's effort) is thrown in as one of the variables over which a decision has to be reached, the weights that individuals receive (here captured by α and $1 - \alpha$) depend on what decision gets taken. In other words, who the decision maker is depends in part on what the decision is. Hence the collective-decision problem cannot be thought of as a normal-form game, since in such a game the players or the decision makers are primitives. One direction that one can pursue is to take y_2 as exogenous and have the household decide on x_1, x_2 and e; and then check whether we recover the same y_2. If we do, then we have a 'household equilibrium'.

In order to do this, let us take a child's wage rate to be w; that is, a full unit of work by a child yields a wage of w. If a child works for e units, his total income, y_2, is ew. It is assumed that, as far as the household is concerned, w is given exogenously. With y_1 and w given exogenously, we describe $(x_1{}^*, x_2{}^*, e^*)$ to be a *household equilibrium* if $(x_1{}^*, x_2{}^*, e^*)$ is the solution to the above collective-maximization problem, with $y_2 = e^*w$.

This equilibrium is not necessarily unique, nor is it obvious that it always exists. The existence problem is best understood by converting the household's problem to a search for a fixed point of a correspondence.

Let $\Phi = [0,1] \rightarrow [0,1]$ be a correspondence defined as follows. Given any e' $\varepsilon[0,1]$, we can take $y_2 = e'w$ (recall w is given exogenously). Now solve the collective-maximization problem taking y_2 to be $e'w$. (recall y_1 is given exogenously). All values of e that are a part of such a solution are the set $\Phi(e')$. This is what defines the correspondence Φ. It is now plain that a household equilibrium exists if and only if Φ has a fixed point.

Given that the maximand in the collective maximization problem need not be concave, Φ need not be convex-valued and we are not able to use Kakutani's fixed-point theorem. Indeed it is possible to construct reasonable examples where Φ has no fixed points. On the other hand, it is also possible to think of restrictions on the parameters which ensure that an equilibrium exists. One simple example of this is the textbook case of selfish individuals: Let us assume

$$u_1(x_1, x_2, e) = f_1(x_1)$$

$$u_2(x_1, x_2, e) = f_2(x_2) - c(e)$$

That is, the parent is interested in his own consumption, the child in the child's own consumption. It is worth emphasizing that this is still a collective model of the household, since the household's maximand continues to be a weighted average of the utilities of the members of the household. Hence, the allocation of resources continues to be Pareto efficient. Let us also, as is usual, assume, $f_1', f_2', c' > 0, f_1'', f_2'' < 0$, and $c'' > 0$.

These assumptions ensure that for every y_1 and y_2, there is a unique (x_1, x_2, e) which solves the collective maximization problem, and that the solution varies continuously with y_2. Thus, ignoring other variables, we can write $\Psi(y_1, y_2)$ to be the value of e which solves the maximization problem, given y_1 and y_2. Since for every $e \in [0, 1]$, $y_2 = ew$, we can define $\Phi(e) = \Psi(y_1, ew)$. Since Φ is a continuous function from $[0, 1]$ to $[0, 1]$, by Brouwer's fixed point theorem, there exists e^* such that

$$(18.1) \qquad e^* = \Phi(e^*) = \Psi(y_1, e^*w)$$

e^* is the amount of labour that the child will supply in equilibrium.

Note that e^* can be written as a function of y_1 and w, by using (1). Thus

$$e^* = e^*(y_1, w),$$

In other words, the child's labour supply depends on the adult wage (y_1) and child wage (w) that prevail on the market. It is possible to develop a more elaborate model with more exogenous variables. It will be interesting to draw out the empirical implications of such a model and put them to test. Another direction that can be pursued is to model the interaction between household members as a sequential game in which a player's power in period t depends on his income share in period $t - 1$. Instead of pursuing this here, I shall instead move on now to discuss models that were developed explicitly to explain child labour. One such model is that of Gupta ...

18.5.2. Extra-Household Bargaining

Citing a survey work currently afoot in some villages of West Bengal, India, Gupta (2000) argues that a child has negligible bargaining power in the household and is, effectively, an instrument for the parent's maximization effort. In addition, he assumes that parents are entirely selfish in the sense of being uninterested in the well-being of the children per se. While a parent owns his child's labour, he is unable to make the child work productively for want of complementary resources, such as land or cattle. He found that in West Bengal villages the bulk of child labour is directed to the maintenance of cattle. So for work the child has to go to an employer, who has the resources.

The bargaining that occurs in this model is between the parent and the employer over (i) the wage, w, that is to be paid for the child's work and (ii) the fraction, λ, of the wage that is to be paid in the form of food to the child. Gupta (1998) assumes that the parents spend the cash component of the wage entirely on themselves. I believe that this is empirically questionable, but let us go along with it as a simplifying assumption.

Using an efficiency-wage argument, assume that the output, x, produced by a child labourer is a function of his consumption. So

$$x = x(\lambda w),$$

where $x(\lambda w) = 0$, for λw less than some positive number, b, and concave thereafter. That is, for all $\lambda w > b$, $x'(\lambda w) > 0$ and $x''(\lambda w) < 0$.

Let us assume that if the bargain fails, the parent and the employer earn Y_p and Y_E respectively. Hence, the threat point of the bargaining problem is given by (Y_p, Y_E). If the parent and the employer agree on (w, λ), their incomes are, respectively, $(1 - \lambda)w$ and $x(\lambda w) - w$.

Therefore, the Nash bargaining problem consists of solving the following problem:

$$\underset{[w, \lambda]}{\text{Max}} \; [(1 - \lambda)w - Y_p][x(\lambda w) - w - Y_E]$$

This gives us the first-order conditions:

$$[(1 - \lambda)w - Y_p]x'(\lambda w) - w \, [x(\lambda w) - w - Y_E] = 0$$

$$[(1 - \lambda)w - Y_p][x'(\lambda w)\lambda - 1] + (1 - \lambda)[x(\lambda w) - w - Y_E] = 0$$

By rearranging these we get:

(18.2) $x'(\lambda w) = 1$

and

(18.3) $x(\lambda w) + \lambda w = 2w + (Y_E - Y_p)$

Since λw is, effectively, the child's wage, (18.2) says that the child's marginal product is set equal to 1. This is the standard result of efficiency wage. To see this, use V to denote a child's wage. Then the net income generated by a child is given by $x(v) - v$. If v is chosen to maximize this, we get $x'(v) = 1$, which is exactly what (18.2) is. In other words, in this model a child is paid a wage, λw, that maximizes net returns. The value of this is independent of the threat point. Once we know the value of λw, we can use (18.3) to solve for the value of w. This depends on Y_p and Y_E. As $(Y_E - Y_p)$ increases, w falls and λ increases, as is evident from (18.3).

It is now possible to derive comparative statics results by postulating how Y_E and Y_p get set and considering variations of this. Gupta (2000), for instance, considers the case where Y_E depends on the adult wage that prevails on the market. In particular, he assumes that Y_E falls as adult wage rises. This implies that as adult wage rises, the child's wage, w, will rise.

One can, however, hypothesize other explanations for Y_E and Y_p and derive other theories of how w will depend on the parameters of the model. What is interesting about this model is how sharply it contrasts with the model that we are about to encounter, one in which the parent is altruistically concerned about the child's welfare. In the model just described, the child's welfare is nobody's concern. The child is valued in the same way as the goose that lays the golden eggs.

18.6. MULTIPLE EQUILIBRIA AND GOVERNMENT INTERVENTION

What the early models seemed to overlook is that a labour market, where children are potential workers, will be prone to having more than one equilibrium, and if it did, then this would raise a variety of interesting policy questions. This is demonstrated in the model of Basu and Van (1998). It is worth asking why the model of Section 18.5.1 overlooked the possibility of multiple equilibria. Note that the collective-maximization problem reduces to the unitary model of the household if (i) $u_1(x_1, x_2, e) = u_2(x_1, x_2, e)$, or (ii) $\alpha(y_1, y_2) = 1$, for all y_1, y_2, or (iii) $\alpha(y_1, y_2) = 0$, for all y_1, y_2. But in allowing for this generality, what the model glosses over are some natural restrictions on the utility function, which is the starting point of the model of Basu and Van (1998). The latter is based on the unitary model. That is, it assumes that (i), (ii), or (iii) is valid, but this is not its distinguishing mark. I would conjecture that the model's central results would remain valid even if we allowed for bargaining within the household. A simplified model of Basu and Van is presented in subsection 18.6.1. Subsections 18.6.2–18.6.4 discuss the relation between child labour and, respectively, social norms, adult unemployment, and dynamics.

18.6.1. Model with Altruism

I shall here demonstrate, following Basu and Van (1998) but using some very special assumptions, the possibility of multiple equilibria. The special assumptions are for reasons of convenience. The only two essential assumptions are the following:

LUXURY AXIOM: A household would not send its children out to work if its income from non-child labour sources were sufficiently high.

SUBSTITUTION AXIOM: Adult labour is a substitute for child labour, or more generally, adults can do what children do.

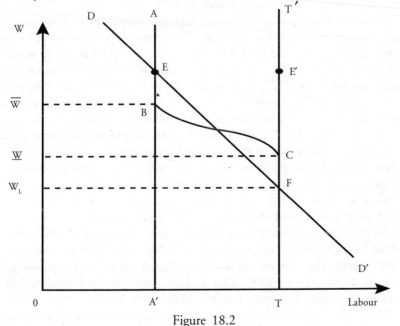

Figure 18.2

To give the simplest sketch of this model, let me strengthen these two assumptions to assert that (i) for every household i, there exists a critical wage, W_i, such that the household will send its children out to work if and only if the adult wage prevailing in the market is less than W_i; and (ii) adult labour and child labour are perfect substitutes subject to all adult-equivalence correction. Both these assumptions can be relaxed enormously without hurting the conclusions of the model. Let us define $\overline{W} \equiv \underset{i}{\text{Max}}\ W_i$ and $\underline{W} \equiv \underset{i}{\text{min}}\ W_i$.

Suppose that a child's labour is equivalent to γ units of an adult's labour, where $0 < \gamma < 1$. In other words, I am assuming that adult and child labour are perfect substitutes subject to all adult-equivalent scale correction of γ.[22] A more convenient way of thinking of this is as follows. Production depends on the total amount of labour used; and each adult, working all day, produces 1 unit of labour, whereas each child, working all day, produces γ units of labour.

In Figure 18.2, let the vertical axis represent adult wage (that is, the wage paid to an adult for a full day's work). Consider a competitive model in which all agents are price takers. Let AA' be the supply curve of the aggregate adult labour in the economy. For simplicity we show it as perfectly inelastic. Next consider the total amount of 'effective labour' that all the children *can* supply. If there are X children in the economy, this will be equal to γX. Add to the aggregate adult labour supply the effective labour that the children can potentially supply in the economy and draw another line representing this. Let $T'T$ be this new line. Thus $A'T$ is equal to γX, the total amount of labour available from the children in the economy. In other words, *if* the country had a law that everybody would always have to supply labour, *then* the aggregate supply curve of labour in the economy would indeed be $T'T$.

Now it is easy to figure out the actual aggregate supply curve of labour. If the market (adult) wage is below $\underline{W}$, then all children are sent to work; so total labour supply is OT. If the market wage exceeds $\overline{W}$, no child is sent to work; so total labour supply is OA'. As wage rises from $\underline{W}$ to $\overline{W}$ one household after another withdraws its children from the labour force; so the total supply of labour keeps decreasing, as shown by the curve CB. Hence the total supply of *all kinds of* labour (that is, adult plus child) plotted against alternative *adult* wages gives us the curve $ABCT$. Let me call this the 'hybrid supply curve', which should serve as a reminder that it is not quite the standard supply curve.

Not only is this supply curve backward bending but its composition keeps changing as we move along its contour. Along AB it consists of pure adult labour; as we move from B to C it includes more and more child labour; and from C to T it consists of all available labour in the economy.

The possibility of multiple equilibria is now transparent. I shall assume, without loss of generality, that whenever adult wage is W, child wage happens to be γW. Keeping this in mind, suppose the aggregate demand curve for labour in the economy is given by DD'. That is, DD' shows the total effective labour demanded by firms for every possible adult wage W. Then there are three equilibria.[23] Let us ignore the unstable one and focus on the ones depicted by E

and F in Figure 18.2. If an economy is caught at point F, wages will be low (W_{L} for adults and γW_{L} for children) and children will be working. The same economy, however, can be in equilibrium at point E, where wages are high and children do not work.

If the economy is at equilibrium point F, there is scope for an interesting policy intervention, which in Basu and Van's paper is called a 'benign intervention'. Suppose child labour is banned. Then effectively, the supply curve of labour becomes AA'. So if demand conditions are unchanged, the economy will now settle at the only equilibrium, at E. What is interesting is that once the equilibrium settles at E, the law banning child labour is no longer needed (since E was anyway an equilibrium of the original economy). It is in this sense that the intervention is described as benign. After its initial effect, it goes dormant and can actually be removed without loss.[24]

If the demand curve intersects the supply curve only once and on the segment CT, then a ban on child labour may well cause a decline in welfare of the workers, including the child labourers.[25]

If this model were fitted into a Walrasian description of the entire economy, each equilibrium would be Pareto optimal. So between the equilibria depicted by E and F neither Pareto dominates the other. However, working-class households are necessarily better off at E. To see this, consider a point (call it E') where wages are the same as at E but all children work. Clearly worker households are better off at E' than at F, since in both cases everybody works but in the former the wages are higher. Next, since given the wages at E households prefer not to send the children to work, by revealed preference we know that E is superior to E'. Hence, by transitivity, E is preferred to F.

The contestable assumption of this model is the luxury axiom, which takes for granted parental altruism towards the child. In the early nineteenth century, when child labour took some of its worst forms in industrializing Europe, a standard critique of the British elite was that child labour was an outcome of parental callousness (see Nardinelli 1990: 94). There is counter-evidence, however, including from those who themselves worked as child labourers, that the parents sent their children out to work typically when they were compelled to do so by acute poverty (Anderson 1971; Vincent 1981).

Turning to more contemporary evidence, Burra (1995) has reported evidence of parental callousness; and Gupta (2000) has cited sources which support this viewpoint (see also Parsons and Goldin 1989). The much discussed issue of discrimination against the female child in several developing regions, notably in northern India, suggests that the answer may also differ depending on whether we are talking of the male child or the female child.[26] In addition, a study by Basu (1993) of some slums outside New Delhi brings to light another perverse causation between adult wages and child labour. When the wages for female labourers rise, starting from a sufficiently low level, this often prompts the mother to take up work outside the home, which in turn means that she takes the daughter out of school in order to have her do the housework. It is arguable that if the mother's wage rises sufficiently, the daughter would get put back into school with household help now being hired from outside. This suggests an inverted-U relation between adult female wage and child labour, especially the labour of the female child.

A recent empirical test of the luxury axiom, by Ray (forthcoming), suggests that the verdict is mixed. He uses data from Peru's *Living Standards Measurements Survey* 1994, and Pakistan's *Integrated Household Survey* 1991, to check if the luxury axiom is valid. For this test he constructs a dummy variable which takes a value of 1 for households with income below the poverty line and 0 otherwise, and then uses probit and logit models to test the importance of this variable on the household's decision to send its children to work. The estimated coefficients lend support for the luxury axiom in Peru but not in Pakistan. While these tests may be interesting in their own right, they do not really test the luxury axiom, because Ray identifies Wi entirely with the poverty line, whereas nowhere does the axiom suggest that this should be so. What does come out rather interestingly from Ray's paper is, as in Basu (1993), the differential response of child labour to changes in the mother's and the father's wages.

One of the best-crafted empirical studies of child labour is Grootaert's (1998) work on Cote d'Ivoire. It is based on annual data collected for 1600 households over the years 1985 to 1988. Sorting out carefully various definitions, he goes on to use a sequential probit model to find the determinants of child labour. He corroborates that the characteristics of the parents matter and also that who has these characteristics, the father or the mother, matters. It is evident from his study that the very poor households often critically rely on the children's income, and he concludes that, *initially*, interventions should aim to make possible combining light work with schooling, instead of a sudden stoppage of child labour.

This is not the forum to settle this controversy but to pursue the consequences of alternative viewpoints. The extreme case in which parents have no altruism or commitment towards the children but treat them purely as labour-producing machines was modelled in Section 18.5.2. My own preference is for the altruistic model of this section, while admitting that it is best viewed as a polar characterization of reality. For a clearer conclusion we will have to wait for further econometric work.

18.6.2. Norms

With the idea of multiple equilibria in the core, there are several directions that one can purse. Albret Hirschman[27] has rightly argued that the decision to send a child to work is partly a matter of social norm.[28] This may be made more precise by assuming that sending a child to work makes the parents incur a social stigma cost, c; and if many children work, then c is smaller. The latter captures the idea that while making a child work is socially frowned upon, the ferocity of the frown is greater if you live in a society where virtually no one but you sends a child to work. This can yield the result that if all parents send their children to work, it is worthwhile for each parent to send his child to work, and if no one sends their child to work, each parent may find it not worthwhile to send his child to work (because the social stigma would be too high). The argument here is analogous to the one used by Lindbeck et al. (1999)[29] to show how the number of people who are unemployed and live off social welfare can settle at very different values depending on which of the possible multiple equilibria is realized.

This is a simple point analytically but is probably of considerable practical importance in the context of child labour. Also this is an idea that can, potentially, be developed much more and used to address questions of policy.

18.6.3. Distribution and Unemployment

In the model of Section 18.6.1, workers are assumed to be *ex ante* identical, and in the equilibrium that occurs they turn out to be *ex post* identical. A consequence of this is that the model is completely silent on questions of income distribution and unemployment. The literature has relatively little to offer on these topics. The distribution question is raised in a short theoretical paper by Swinnerton and Rogers (forthcoming); there is little that is available on this empirically. On the other hand, the relation between adult unemployment and child labour has been the basis of some empirical investigation (see Goldin 1979; Horan and Hargis 1991; Bonnet 1993; Chandrasekhar 1997); the hiatus here is in the theory. Modelling the relation theoretically is a large and interesting topic, but some initial steps towards it are easy to take using the model of Section 18.6.1 above.[30] Before doing so, I want to briefly recount Swinnerton and Rogers' argument.

Their paper begins with the observation that if a parent's decision to send the children to work depends on (among other things) the parent's income, then we should look at not just the parent's wage but also any profits that may accrue to the parents. So they move away from the polar assumption of Basu and Van's model by supposing that the firms are owned by a fraction λ of the workers. So for workers in this category, income equals wages plus a share of profits, while the remaining workers earn only wages. They then show that, if in an economy there exists a good equilibrium, then there does not exist an equilibrium in which the dividend-earning workers send their children to work. This directs the policy discussion to matters of distribution. Giving workers a share in profits turns out to be a method of curbing child labour. This is a valid argument, though the feasibility of such policy changes may be restricted for reasons of politics.

Turning to the subject of adult unemployment, let us suppose that there are N worker households and each household has one adult and m children. As before, child non-work is a luxury good and, in particular, for each household i there is a critical adult wage W_i such that if the adult wage rises above W_i, the household withdraws its children from working. Adults, on the other hand, always prefer to work, no matter what the wage. This immediately gives us the aggregate labour supply curve as in Figure 18.2.

As before, let us assume that one child manages to produce the equivalent of

γ units of adult labour. Hence, if the prevailing market child wage, W_c happens to be equal to γW, where W is the prevailing market adult wage, then firms will be indifferent between employing adults and children. Let us focus on the case where $\gamma W = W_c$. I should clarify that I am not assuming W_c to be exogenously fixed. Rather I am trying to isolate an equilibrium in which W_c *happens to be* equal to γW.

Within the confines of this case, we can think of the total effective demand for labour to be a function of W. Let us denote such an aggregate demand function by $d(W)$. Let us assume that this is downward sloping and take DD' in Figure 18.2 as representing such a demand curve.

To study the impact of adult unemployment on child labour, we first need a model in which there can exist adult unemployment. The best way to develop such a model is to use a structure that can endogenously explain wage rigidities. I shall, however, for reasons of simplicity, stay away from such complications[31] and simply assume that adult wage is exogenously fixed at W^*, where W^* is such that $d(W^*) < N$. In other words, we are focusing on cases above point E in Figure 18.2. The questions are: How many adults will find employment? Will children be working and, if so what will be the incidence of child labour?

In answering these questions I shall consider the case where $\gamma m < 1$ and $d(W^*) - \gamma m N > 0$. This is merely a sufficient condition for the existence of an equilibrium in which $\gamma W^* = W_c$. A fuller model will have to go beyond this and consider other cases as well, but the *logic* of the relation between child labour and adult unemployment comes out clearly even in this limited model.

Let us use E to denote the number of adults that will find employment. Since the total demand for labour is $d(W^*)$, it follows that $d(W^*) - E$ will be the amount of labour demanded from children. In other words, the number of children demanded by the firms will be $[d(W^*) - E]/\gamma$. Since child wages are not rigid, demand for child labour must be equal to supply of child labour. So what remains to be done is to determine the supply of child labour. Note that if only E adults find employment, $N - E$ households will be earning zero income from the adults. So these will be the households that will send the children out to work. Hence, if E adults find work, the supply of child labour will be given by $m(N - E)$. In other words, E is equilibrium adult employment if:

$$m(N - E) = [d(W^*) - E]/\gamma.$$

To remind ourselves that the value of E depends on W^*, let us write the solution of this equation as $E(W^*)$. Evidently,

$$E(W^*) = [d(W^*) - \gamma m N]/(1 - \gamma m).$$

Since $d(\cdot)$ is a downward-sloping function, it follows that as W^* rises, adult employment, $E(W^*)$, will fall.

If we use $C(W^*)$ to denote the number of children who find employment when adult wage is fixed at W^*, then we have:

$$C(W^*) = m[N - E(W^*)] = m[N - d(W^*)]/(1 - \gamma m).$$

Given that we are considering the case where $\gamma m < 1$, it follows that $C(W^*) > 0$. Further, as W^* rises, $C(W^*)$ rises. Since a rise in W^* increases adult unemployment, a rise in adult unemployment is associated with an increased incidence of child labour.

This confirms intuition and empirical findings but also cautions us about the right policy intervention.[32] If market wages rise, we have good reason to believe that child labour will decline, but that does not mean that this impact on child labour can always be replicated by raising adult wages by fiat. If the adult labour market has oligopsonistic elements, a rise in the legal minimum wage can boost adult employment and cause a decline in child labour, but in competitive labour markets the consequence of raising the minimum wage can be ambiguous.

18.6.4. Dynamics

One big caveat in the large literature on child labour is the treatment of dynamics. Yet the dynamic consequences of child labour are likely to be large, since an increase in child labour frequently causes a decline in the acquisition of human capital. If a child is employed all through the day, it is likely that the child will remain uneducated and have low productivity as an adult.

While the analysis of the long-run consequences of child labour is almost totally ignored in the literature (Baland and Robinson 1998 being an exception), one can draw on some papers on human-capital acquisition and its long-run consequences, a la Galor and Zeira (1993), Banerjee and Newman (1993), and Ljungqvist (1993) to derive some hints for modelling the dynamics of child labour.[33] This is what I attempt here and in the process develop the idea of a 'child labour trap'. I use some strong assumptions to develop my argument but it should be possible to relax these.

Since my aim is to explain multiple equilibria in the long run, it cannot be criticized if I make an assumption that tilts the description of the single-period model away from multiple equilibria. Note that in Figure 18.2, if the demand curve is sufficiently elastic, there will exist only one equilibrium in the single-period model. To ensure that this is the case, I shall assume that the demand for labour is perfectly elastic.

Consider an overlapping-generations model in which each person lives for two periods, first as a child and then as an adult; and at the start of the second period gives birth to a child. As a child, a person can either work or go to school (that is, acquire human capital). So if we denote a full day by 1 and a child works for a fraction e of the day, then the amount of human capital acquired by the child is $1 - e \equiv h$.

The productivity of an adult depends on the amount of human capital, h, he acquired as a child. If we think of L as the number of labour units produced by one adult, then what we are assuming is that

(18.4) $L_t = L(h_{t-1}),\ L' > 0,\ L'' < 0.$[34]

Let us make the normalization assumption that $L(0) = 1$. In other words, the amount of labour produced by an unskilled adult is defined to be 1. That there is an inverse relation between child labour and the child's productivity in later life is also assumed by Parsons and Goldin (1989), though they do not pursue the long-run consequence of this assumption.

Let us use $\overline{V}$ denote the wage of one unit of labour. If labour demand is perfectly elastic, this will be constant and so we take the wage rate to be fixed at $\overline{V}$. Hence, in period t, an adult who as a child, that is, in period $t-1$, had worked e_{t-1} amount, will have an income of

(18.5) $\overline{V}L(1 - e_{t-1}) = W_t$.

As in the model of sub-section 18.6.1, we assume that it is the parent who decides whether to send a child to work. Let us assume that there is a wage $\underline{W}$ such that, if adult income is below $\underline{W}$, the parent sends the child to work full-time, that is $e = 1$. Let us also assume that there is a wage $\overline{W} > \underline{W}$ such that, if adult income exceeds $\overline{W}$, he does not send his child to work at all, that is $e = 0$. Unlike in the model of sub-section 18.6.1, we take all adults to be identical and assume that the child labour is not a $0 - 1$ decision but monotonically varies with the parent's income. This may be summed up by assuming that the amount of work that a child is made to do in period t is a function of the parent's wage in period t:

(18.6) $e_t = e(W_t)$,

such that $e(\underline{W}) = 1$, for all $W \leq \underline{W}$; $e(W) = 0$ for all $W \geq \overline{W}$; and $e'(W) < 0$, for all $W \in (\underline{W}, \overline{W})$.

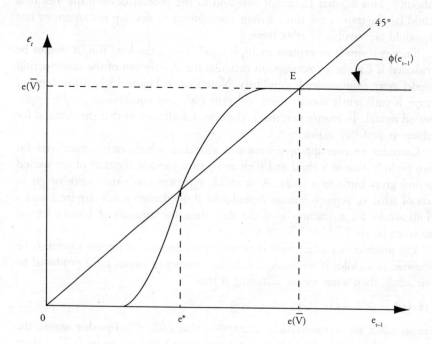

Figure 18.3

From (18.5) and (18.6) we get

(18.7) $e_t \equiv e(\bar{V}L(1 - e_{t-1}))$

which may be described in brief as

(18.8) $e_t \equiv \Phi(e_{t-1})$

From the assumptions made above we know that Φ is upward sloping and bounded above at $e(\bar{V}L(0)) = e(\bar{V})$. In order to focus on the interesting case we consider an Φ which intersects the 45° line more than once. In the case illustrated in Figure 18.3, there are three steady-state equilibria, of which two are stable. These are depicted by points 0 and E. At E, a poor parent makes the child work full-time. The child acquires no skills and so as an adult earns very little and has to send his child, in turn, to work full-time. This equilibrium depicts what may be called a 'child-labour trap'.[35] On the other hand, 0 depicts an equilibrium where a child goes to school, earns adequately as an adult, and so can and does send his child to school. It is a virtuous cycle.[36]

There is scope for fruitful intervention by government. If an economy is caught in a child labour trap, what is needed is a large effort to educate one generation, and this can get the economy rolling towards the virtuous equilibrium without need for further action. Chaudhri (1997) has discussed several versions of 'virtuous spirals' and instances of how child labour tends to decline rapidly once a 'tipping point' is reached.

As is shown by Parsons and Goldin (1989), the sub-optimality of investment in education is closely related to the availability of efficient capital markets (see also, Jacoby and Skoufias 1997). There is also evidence from the field that the availability of credit on decent terms can rescue many from the perils of child labour, since in developing countries, such as India, a typical reason for a child to drop out of school is not chronic poverty but a temporary mishap for the household, such as the father losing a job or a sibling needing medical support.

The credit question comes up starkly in the model of Baland and Robinson (1998). Theirs is a two-period model of child labour in which inefficiency occurs despite parental altruism, because parents may run out of resources needed to educate the child. The only option then is to borrow against the child's future income, and this is typically not possible. This shows that to solve the problem of child labour one has to go beyond providing perfect capital markets. What is needed is the enforcement of inter-generational contracts, whereby what i borrows for i's child's education is paid back by the child when she grows up, by when i may be dead. But it is not clear that creating institutions for enforcing such contracts is desirable, since it will be open to the moral hazard of 'inverse bequests', whereby a person borrows funds in the name of the child's education and leaves the child with a repayment burden.

Another related feature, which I do not model here but is important, is the fertility decision. We have in this chapter treated the number of children as exogenously given. In reality, the number of children a family has is partly volitional, and the decision may well depend on whether children can find work (Cain 1977; Rosenzweig and Evenson 1977; Eswaran 1996; Bardhan and

Udry 1999). Cain's study of Bangladesh shows that not only do children contribute to household incomes, but a boy becomes a net producer by the age of 12 years, and after the age of 15 years his cumulative contribution exceeds their cumulative consumption. Plainly, these are features that a proper dynamic model should be able to incorporate. There is need for such a model and the above outline should be viewed as motivation towards it.

18.7. SEXUAL HARASSMENT AND CHILD LABOUR

Corporal punishment and sexual exploitation have, at several stages of history, been closely associated with child labour. Commenting on Britain during the industrial revolution, Nardinelli (1982: 294) has observed how the use of violence was common against child labourers, though 'by the middle of the 19th century it was seldom used for older workers'.[37] In a model on the use of violence with special reference to child labour, Chwe (1990) has tried to explain this asymmetric treatment of adults and children in terms of the lower reservation utility of the latter. Evidence of violence also cropped up repeatedly during the interviews conducted by the British parliamentary committee investigating child labour in 1832. For instance, a cotton spinner, Thomas Daniel, admitted that the child labourers 'are always in terror; and ... the reason of their being in a state of terror and fear is, that we are obliged to have our work done, and we are compelled to use the strap.' (British Parliamentary Papers 1968: 325).

In what follows I want to raise a different theoretical question concerning violence and sexual harassment. Consider first the case of adult labour. Is there a case for banning violence and sexual harassment when these occur as a consequence of voluntary contracting? I will argue that the answer is a conditional yes, and then try to show that the claim may be carried over to the context of child labour to construct a novel argument for banning child labour in certain situations. Though the theoretical claim applies to all kinds of violence, I illustrate it here with respect to sexual harassment. This argument goes to the core of the philosophical debate concerning the state's right to ban voluntary transactions between consenting individuals, such as the signing of self-enslavement contracts or trade in human organs or a child's decision to sell his labour. The best of the existing arguments are quite tenuous[38] and so this is a matter that deserves closer scrutiny.

Economists usually take the line that a voluntary contract between two agents that does not have negative externalities on uninvolved outsiders ought not to be banned. Let me call this the 'principle of free contract'. If we accept this principle, then it is not clear why sexual harassment in the workplace should always be banned. Consider one kind of harassment which is *ex ante* voluntary. Suppose an entrepreneur advertises for workers, openly saying that he will pay a wage above the market rate but he reserves the right to sexually harass his employees. Therefore, if a worker joins this firm, it must be that she finds that the benefit outweighs the cost.

If we accept the principle of free contract, it now seems difficult to justify banning open sexual harassment of the kind just described. But I believe there is an argument that can be constructed which respects the principle of free contract, and yet may justify a ban.

Note that under normal assumptions the following is true: If harassment is allowed, then those workers who are especially strongly averse to harassment will be worse off because the market wage that they will be able to command will be lower than what it would be if no harassment were allowed by law. I call this the 'harassment lemma', and begin by proving it.

Suppose that we have a market with two kinds of workers, with type-1 workers having a stronger aversion to sexual harassment than type-2 workers. For reasons of algebraic ease, let us assume that type-1's distaste for harassment is infinite (so they would rather be unemployed than face harassment), while type-2's distaste is zero. If the wage rate is W and there is no harassment, the aggregate supply of labour by type-i workers is $f_i(W)$. As usual, $f_i'(W) > 0$.

This is a competitive model; so workers and employers are wage-takers. Let me, for simplicity, assume that there is only one employer and he gets a satisfaction of $\theta(>0)$ from harassing each worker. The production function of the employer is given by $x = x(n)$, where $x' > 0$, $x'' < 0$, n is the number of workers and x the total output.

Let W_H be the wage for those who sign the with-harassment contract and W_N for those who sign the no-harassment contract. If the employer hires n_H workers under the H-contract and n_N workers under the N-contract, his total profit is $x(n_H + n_N) - n_H W_H - n_N W_N + \theta n_H$. The first-order conditions from maximizing this can be rearranged and written as follows:

(18.9) $$x'(n_H + n_N) = W_N$$

(18.10) $$W_H = W_N + \theta$$

Clearly, type-1 workers will sign N-contracts and type-2 workers will sign H-contracts. Hence, the total supply of workers for N-contracts will be $f_1(W_N)$ and the total supply for H-contracts will be $f_2(W_H)$. Therefore, using (9) and (10), we can say that W_N^* is an equilibrium if

$$x'(f_1(W_N^*) + f_2(W_N^* + \theta)) = W_N^*.$$

Consider now a legal regime where harassment is never allowed. Hence, there is only one wage in the market, W. The employer maximizes $x(n) - nW$. The total supply of labour is given by $f_1(W) + f_2(W)$. W^* is an equilibrium wage if $x'(f_1(W^*) + f_2(W^*)) = W^*$.

Since $f_2' > 0$ and $x'' < 0$, it follows that $W_N^* < W^*$. This completes the proof.

What the harassment lemma establishes is this. If we adhere to the principle of free contract, then even though we may have no reason for stopping finite pairs of individuals (an employer and an employee) from getting into harassment contracts, there may be good reason for adopting the *rule* that no harassment contracts should be allowed in the workplace. This is made possible by the fact that, in competition, the aggregate is not simply the sum of all atomistic acts.

Note that the harassment lemma does not provide sufficient reason for banning harassment, but simply shows that allowing contractual harassment cannot be justified on grounds of the principle of free contract, since allowing harassment typically has a negative externality on uninvolved individuals. Clearly, a negative externality cannot be a sufficient reason for disallowing any action. Otherwise we would have to say that no one should be allowed to work on days when there is a cricket match because those who like watching cricket will be adversely affected.

To establish a sufficiency criterion, we need to go beyond economics and identify human preferences which are 'fundamental' in the sense that no one should have to pay a price for having such a preference. This may be a controversial list but very few people will deny that there are such 'fundamental preferences', and also that not all preferences qualify as fundamental. In most societies the preference not to be sexually harassed would be considered fundamental. No one should have to pay a penalty for having such a preference. On the other hand, the preference for missing work when a cricket match is on would not be considered fundamental by most of us. You may of course have such a preference but you should be prepared to pay some price for it.

It is the harassment lemma coupled with the recognition that the preference not to be sexually harassed is fundamental that clinches the case for an outright ban on sexual harassment.

It is easy to see that the harassment lemma, as an abstract idea, carries over from the domain of sexual harassment to child labour, by assuming that households have different degrees of aversion to sending their children to work. For concreteness turn to the model of Section 18.6.1 and assume that there are two types of households, 1 and 2, where a type-i household is one which would send its children out to work if and only if adult wage drops to below w_i. Let us assume that $w_1 = -\infty$ (that is, type-1 households never send their children to work), whereas $w_2 = \infty$ (that is, type-2 households always send their children to work).

By using a diagrammatic technique similar to the one used in Figure 18.2, it is immediately obvious that the market wage rises if a ban on child labour is imposed. Conversely, if a ban on child labour is removed, wages must fall; and so type-1 households become worse off. This establishes the counterpart of the harassment lemma.

Therefore, not having a ban on child labour penalizes households that have a stronger preference not to send their children to work. Following the claims of the above sub-section, this leads to a case for a ban on child labour if we consider a household's preference not to send its children to work to be a fundamental preference. To my mind this is not unambiguously fundamental or non-fundamental. It is plainly *more* fundamental than a person's preference for missing work during cricket matches and probably less so than a preference for not submitting to harassment. So, while the case is not automatic, this is a possible avenue for justifying legal action against child labour.

18.8. INTERNATIONAL LABOUR STANDARDS

A topic closely related to the subject of child labour is that of 'international labour standards' and the use of 'social clauses' as a prerequisite for trade. For many years, overtly or covertly, people have argued the need to enforce some minimal standards of labour concerning working conditions, duration of work, the level of wages, and so on.[39]

Labourers have often had to work in appalling conditions for meager wages. So a part of the agitation for minimal international labour standards is indeed inspired by a genuine concern for the well-being of workers. But, as is only to be expected in such situations, forces of protection and lobbies with their own interest in mind have taken up positions behind this banner. The presence of international organizations makes it now possible, what earlier would be infeasible, to bring multinational pressure to individual nations to comply with some minimal labour standards. In fora, such as the ILO, the General Agreement on Tariffs and Trade (GATT) and now the WTO, the subject of labour standards or social clauses has been a live one (Bhagwati 1995). Some industrialized nations have campaigned for the inclusion of social clauses in the WTO which would either deny nations that do not fulfil minimal labour standards membership in the WTO, or enable other nations to place a trade embargo on any nation that violates the standards.

One major area for setting international labour standards concerns child labour (see Fields 1995; Bloom and Noor 1996; Maskus and Holman 1996; Golub 1997; Brown 1998). As an ultimate objective everybody agrees that children should not work, just as adults should not overwork and get underpaid. Given these objectives, what is the right policy response? Here answers have differed widely. One answer is that since one country's acquiescence to lower labour standards gives it trading advantages in labour-intensive goods, there should be multilateral sanctions against such a country; and social clauses should be used to deter such 'illegitimate advantages' (see, for instance, Collingsworth et al. 1994; and Wilkinson 1994).

At the other end of the spectrum is the argument that countries trade on the basis of their relative advantages, and for some countries the advantage lies in their cheap labour. To try to level these out through the use of multilateral threats is to practice protectionism, which is likely to hurt not just workers in the Third World but consumers in the developed nations as well. In particular, several economists have argued that a social clause in the WTO is not the right response to child labour and other problems of labour standards (Bhagwati 1995; Srinivasan 1996). Instead, Bhagwati (1995: 757) argues for 'methods of suasion' and for the ILO to be the main international agency to strive towards better standards.

A variety of positions have also been taken *between* the two described above.

Rodrik (1996), for instance, argues that, while one has to be aware that the 'upward harmonization' of labour standards, can rob poor nations of their comparative advantage in labour-intensive goods, it may be all right to use trade restrictions against nations that violate a widely held moral code in the importing country so as to safeguard domestic labour standards. He calls this a 'social safeguard clause', and suggests (i) institutional mechanisms for ensuring that these are not misused by one nation against another and (ii) a scheme for providing compensation (under certain circumstances) to developing countries that lose out as a consequence of such sanctions.[40]

To check on the impact of imposing international labour standards on developing nations (and to deduce which ones are worthwhile), it is important to have a suitable theoretical model. My interest here is in *child* labour standards. The theoretical modelling of labour standards is still in its nascency (see Bloom and Noor 1996; Maskus and Holman 1996; Srinivasan 1996). Of these, Maskus and Holman are most directly concerned with child labour standards. Their model is based on introducing the 'demand for child-labour standards' as an argument in the representative agent's Cobb-Douglas utility function. This makes some of the conclusions, such as the need for child labour standards, too direct a consequence of the assumptions of the model; and it also leaves no margin for the fact that people's attitude to child labour may embody a misunderstanding of the implications of child labour for child welfare.

It seems to me more valuable to analyse policy starting from a standard utility function, instead of one chosen specially for the occasion. In what follows we derive lessons for labour standards from a model which (i) does not introduce 'labour standards' as a direct argument in the utility function and (ii) recognizes the interdependence of decisions between nations.

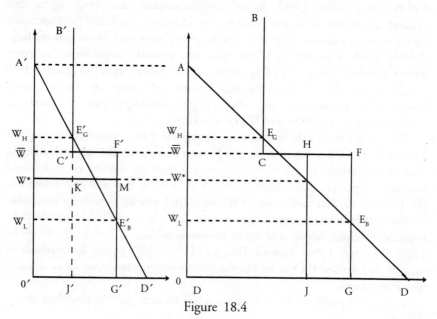

Figure 18.4

Consider the model of Section 18.6.1. Let us simplify it a little by supposing that all households are identical and at adult wage $\overline{W}$ they draw their children out of the labour force. Let us also assume $\gamma = 1$. On the other hand, we complicate the model a little by assuming that while the aggregate demand for labour is given by AD in Figure 18.4 and aggregate supply by $BCFG$ (its strange shape is natural and was explained in Section 18.6.1), the demand and supply are evenly distributed over t regions, R_1, ..., R_t, of the economy. In other words, if there are aggregates of N consumers and n firms, each region has N/t consumers and n/t firms.

In other words, the demand curve AD is a horizontal summation of the demand of n identical firms and also the horizontal summation of the demand curves in the t regions.

While we can think of R_1, ..., R_t as different regions of a country, we can also think of these as t countries belonging to a global economy. We could think of these together as belonging to a 'region' of the world. I shall assume that the world price of the good produced by this region is one and, thanks to free trade, nothing that happens in the region can change this price. Labour, on the other hand, is region specific. Workers cannot migrate from one country to another.

What we shall do is to study the impact of child-labour laws on welfare with and without capital mobility. In this model, I interpret capital mobility entirely in terms of the mobility of firms. In other words we shall consider two alternative scenarios: one where firms can freely move between the t countries (or regions), and another in which the firms are entirely country specific.

Suppose the economy is at the bad equilibrium, E_B. Wage is W_L; the total employment is OG. The left-hand panel of Figure 18.4 depicts what happens in each region. In each region employment is equal to $O'G' = (OG)/t$. The figure is drawn as if $t = 2$.

Consider first the case where firms are region specific. If a ban is imposed on child labour in only one country (the one shown in the left panel of Figure 18.4), then, for reasons given in Section 18.6.1, equilibrium will drift from E'_B to E'_G (in the left panel of Figure 18.4). In the case illustrated in Figure 18.4, workers in this region will be better off by the ban.

Now suppose firms are fully mobile. Once again consider a ban on child labour imposed only in one country (depicted in the left panel of Figure 18.4). This will imply that the total labour supply in these t countries will be $BCHJ$, where $HF = CF/t$, since child labour from one country is no longer available.[41] Hence equilibrium wage rises to W^*.

Let us see what the equilibrium looks like for each individual nation. Clearly, the nation that imposes the ban will be at a point like K, where wage is W^* and total employment is $O'J'$ (that is, only adults are employed). All other nations are at a point such as M. This is caused by the flight of capital (in this case, firms) from the nation imposing the ban.

In this new equilibrium, the country imposing the ban will have to incur large costs monitoring the ban because it is not in the self-interest of workers and employers to comply with the ban. In addition, the workers of this nation are likely to be worse off with the ban. This will be especially true if t is large (which will imply that W^* will be close to W_L).

Now suppose that through an international labour standards agreement all nations agree to impose a ban on child labour. There is now no flight of capital since one nation is as good as another. So the aggregate equilibrium shifts to E_G and each nation shifts from E'_B to E'_G. All workers are better off and the ban does not need to be monitored since in this new equilibrium wage is so high (at W_H) that parents do not *want* to send their children to work.

It is true that we get this extreme result by focusing on the case where the aggregate demand curve AD intersects the aggregate supply curve more than once. Nevertheless, what it illustrates is an important implication of the model of Section 18.6.1 for international labour standards.

There are contexts where, even though labour standards are undesirable for each nation behaving atomistically, they are worthwhile if the standards are co-ordinated across a large number of nations. Indeed, once this is achieved it may be in the self-interest of everybody to live by the standards.

One must add some notes of caution to the above proposition. First, the proposition must not be taken to detract from the claim that labour standards are often a front for protectionism. The proposition claims that it is *possible* for co-ordinated effort to benefit all. It does not say that this will always be the case. What the proposition highlights is the fact that co-ordinated effort is *better* than individual effort. Second, it is conceivable that once we allow for the heterogeneity of nations, the case will be (when there is a case at all) for labour standards which *vary* across nations. Third, if we worked with a demand curve that was sufficiently low so that it intersects the aggregate supply curve of labour once and on the segment FG, we would find that even co-ordinated labour standards imposed on all nations will need monitoring (compliance being not in the self-interest of all individuals), though it will continue to be the case that it is better to have a co-ordinated effort rather than one imposed idiosyncratically on some nations.

18.9. CONCLUSION

The literature on child labour is an illustration of abundance and anarchy. Theoretical writings on the subject are relatively few, though one finds theoretical insights in many unexpected papers and books which may be otherwise purely empirical or descriptive. The empirical writings on child labour are numerous but they are usually not founded on any theory. By bringing together the main theoretical ideas, this survey hopes to encourage not just further theoretical research but empirical work which is analytically better founded.

Also evident from this survey is the fact that there is no unique prescription. Should child labour be banned outright? Should the WTO be given the responsibility of enforcing restrictions on child labour through the use of trade sanctions? Should there be a legal minimum wage for adults so as to make it unnecessary for parents to send their children to work? The answer depends on the context.

It was argued in this chapter that there is much that can and ought to be done, but the precise policy to be followed depends on the economic milieu for which the prescription is being sought. The main policy divide is between legal interventions and what may be called collaborative interventions, that is, public action which alters the economic environment such that parents of their own accord prefer to withdraw the children from the labour force. The availability of good schools, the provision of free meals, and efforts to bolster adult wages are examples of collaborative interventions. I have discussed examples and given arguments to show that such interventions are, in general, a desirable way of curbing child labour. However, many of these actions may not be feasible. There may not be money enough in the government's coffers to run better schools or to improve the infrastructure, which would result in higher adult wages.

In such circumstances, should government resort to legal action to restrict child labour? These seems to be some agreement that some minimal restrictions, such as children being prevented from working in hazardous occupations or under bonded-labour conditions, are worth enforcing legally. It is true that one can always think of *some* circumstance where even such a minimal law will work to the detriment of the child. But, by and large, children being made to work in hazardous conditions is either an act of child abuse or ignorance on the part of the parents and the child, and so, in general, it is better to declare such action as illegal.

But what, about a more general ban on child labour *per se?* The evidence and the theory that we studied in this chapter suggest that there is no unconditional answer to this. There are circumstances where, even if such a total ban were feasible and costless to implement, it ought not to be implemented. To understand this, one must realize that there are worse things that can happen to children than having to work. In very poor regions, the alternative to work may be to suffer acute hunger or starvation. Indeed, when child labour occurs as a mass phenomenon, it is likely that the alternative to work is very harsh, because even poor parents do not in general like to send their children to work if they can help it.

Curiously enough, despite this, there are circumstances where a total ban *may* be desirable from the point of view of the well-being of the children. This is because, whereas a single parent withdrawing the child from work cannot influence equilibrium wages, a large-scale withdrawal of child labour can cause adult wages to rise so much that the working-class household is better off. It was argued in this chapter that this is unlikely to be true for very poor economies but may be valid for relatively better-off countries. Even so, one would need to do detailed empirical work to decide whether such a total bring is worthwhile. The interesting insight that theory gives us here is to tell us that it may be so and to give some hints about the type of economy where this is likely.

Another thing that we know is that, if a ban is deemed desirable, a good way to implement it is by making schooling compulsory. This is because a child's presence in school is easier to monitor than a child's abstention from work. It is true that schooling is compatible with a certain amount of work, since children can work before and after school; but it is a good way to prevent *full-time* work and of course is desirable in itself. It has, in fact, been argued by some that, in very poor countries, we should make it possible for children to combine school with work, instead of thinking of these as mutually exclusive activities.

The case for a ban on child labour in the export-goods sector alone, which would be a natural concomitant of effort in industrialized nations to boycott the import of goods made with child labour, is weaker, since this could result in children being diverted to less-desirable or more hazardous work. In general, it is better to take economy-wide measures against child labour and, if there is to be a sector-specific ban, this should be based on the working conditions of that sector, rather than the destination of the goods.

This reservation carries over to certain kinds of international action, such as the imposition of minimal labour standards as a prerequisite for trade, since this results in the maintenance of standards only in the exports sector. In addition, international labour standards can cause trade distortions by failing to recognize the comparative advantages of different nations. The chapter used some of the models of child labour to investigate the impact of international standards. It was found that one beneficial effect of such standards could be the help that they can provide to developing nations to make a co-ordinated improvement in their working conditions, without causing a flight of capital. The idea of international labour standards as an instrument of collusion among developing countries suggests new ways to think about this problem. The discussion here was brief and preliminary and simply points to directions for future research.

NOTES

1. See, for instance, Anderson (1971); Goldin (1979); Vincent (1981); Cunningham (1990); Nardinelli (1990); Moehling (1995); Horrell and Humphries (1995a, 1995b); Cunningham and Viazzo (1996a); and Galbi (1997).

2. While this is so under 'normal circumstances', Convention 138 does specify some special cases. Thus for 'light work' the age limit is 13 years, and for 'hazardous work' it is 18 years (ILO 1996). See UNICEF (1994) for a discussion of Convention 138 and for alternative conceptions of what constitutes child labour (see also Knutsson 1997).

3. The ILO often distinguishes between 'child work' and 'child labour', the latter being used to describe the more pejorative part of 'child work' whereas 'child work' in itself could include doing light household chores and can actually have some learning value (ILO 1995: 1). I shall, however, here use 'work' and 'labour' interchangeably, while referring to what the ILO calls 'child labour'.

4. This point is reinforced at the all-India level by Weiner (1996: 3007) who argues that 'most of the 90 million children not in school are working children'. See also Labenne (1995) for alternative definitions of child labour and how different vari-

ables affect them in India. Some economists adopt the convention of distinguishing between 'work' and 'home care', classifying children who do not attend school and are not formally employed as 'home care labourers' (Cartwright and Patrinos 1998).

5. One has to be careful not to read too much into these macro statistics. Most of the data are constructed by extrapolating from a few small-scale detailed studies. Even in the US, where a considerable amount of money and effort goes into collecting labour data, the amount of child labour is prone to be under-reported (Kruse and Mahoney 1998). The problem must be that much more acute for developing countries, especially ones where state control makes it difficult for independent researchers to collect and verify data.

6. Going by the census, child labour in England and Wales peaked in 1861 for boys; and in 1871 for girls. The participation rates dropped off rapidly after 1871 (see Cunningham 1996).

7. For a general discussion of inter-country experience in the last century see Weiner (1991) and Cunningham and Viazzo (1996a).

8. I am grateful to Jean Dreze, who was part of this team, for a very valuable discussion on this.

9. For a lucid summary account, see Cunningham and Viazzo (1996b).

10. Quoted in Cunningham (1990: 120).

11. By the time the child labour debate picked up steam in the United States in the late nineteenth century, child labour was viewed as it is today; as an unmitigated evil. The reasons given against the institution of child labour are also rather like the ones given today, the important exception being the argument of 'race degeneracy'. Child labour, it was reasoned, should be ended in the South because that would help 'the preservation of its Anglo-Saxon stock' (McKelway 1906: 261). Similar sentiment was expressed repeatedly by several authors in the March 1906 issue of *The Annals of the American Academy of Political and Social Science*.

12. The children's Act of 1992 prohibits children of age 13 years or less from doing any work as employed labourers. The Labour Act of 1992 places restrictions on the kind of labour that children can do in 'enterprises' that employ ten or more persons (ILO 1995).

13. Subsequently, the text of the bill (version of 17 April 1997) has changed further and this time in the right direction. It now tends to isolate child labour performed 'under circumstances tantamount to involuntary servitude' or 'under exposure to toxic substances or working conditions otherwise posing serious health hazards' as the kind against which the import restriction in the US will principally apply.

14. For instance, Jensen and Nielsen (1997), Grootaert (1998), and Psacharopoulos (1997).

15. A similar point has been made by Bachman (1995: 3), who observed that attempts to bar children from working in the manufacturing sector in Bangladesh have pushed some of them over to prostitution.

16. Empirical investigations cast doubt on whether average wages did fall during this period. However, in certain sectors, such as the handloom, this was certainly the case (Lyons 1989).

17. On the matter of policy, Marx was against a total ban on child labour for the Europe of his time. He favoured restrictions on working hours and compulsory education (Marx 1875 [1938]).

18. These studies, therefore, exclude the case of 'street children' who live on their own and belong to no household as such. The present paper also does not address the problem of homeless children. This is, however, not a negligible category (see Myers 1988).

19. See, for instance, Manser and Brown (1980); McElroy and Horney (1981); Folbre (1986); Sen (1990); Browning et al. (1994); Grootaert and Kanbur (1995); Udry (1996); and Agarwal (1997).

20. It is worth stressing that the important special case of this model is where each person is concerned about his own welfare, and the final household consumption and labour supply are entirely consequences of the power of different individuals.

21. In this model the household allocation is always Pareto efficient. The empirical validity of this is not uncontested (see Udry 1996).
    Many take y to be i's unearned income. I prefer not to do this for reasons explained below.

22. Admittedly this is a simplifying assumption. What is really needed is the assumption that adults *can* do what children do. This is contrary to the pervasive 'nimble fingers' belief—that for some activities, such as carpet-weaving, children are essential. There is however, very little empirical support for this belief (ILO 1996a). One of the most careful examinations of this occurs in the study of India's carpet industry by Levison et al. (forthcoming). By collecting information on actual productivity—for instance, square inches knotted per hour—they reach the conclusion that for no activity are children essential. Adults can always replace them. This is not to deny that such substitution may cause costs to rise, since adult wages are typically higher.

23. An important exception is a sufficiently open, small economy, where wage would be determined by world prices, and so the demand curve would be horizontal, thereby destroying the multiple equilibria result (Dixit 1998). Even in this case, however, there may be multiple equilibria in a dynamic sense as shown in Section 18.6.4.

24. The model also is suggestive of the link between technology and child labour. If technology changes so that children become relatively less productive than adults (perhaps because of the rise of the use of the computer), then we could think of γ as falling. From Figure 18.2 it is clear that this would result in T moving left and the inferior equilibrium, where children work, vanishing.

25. Arguing from a different perspective, Jacoby and Skoufias (1997: 331) reach a similar conclusion: 'Our results suggest that efforts to expand educational opportunities for the poor ... without an understanding of the economic risks and constraints they face may be met with only limited success. Moreover, compulsory schooling laws or laws against child labour, to the extent that they can be enforced in rural areas, could substantially lower household welfare'.

26. The source of this discrimination need not be the household. If job opportunities for females are limited, it may be a rational response of the household to first educate the boys before turning to the girls. In the context of adults, the more puzzling possibility of gender discrimination in the labour market originating from within the household is modelled elegantly by Francois (1998).

27. Personal communication to the author dated 15 February 1995.

28. 'Social norm' has many interpretations (Basu 1998; Dasgupta 1993). I use it here as a social influence that changes our preference. The relation between child labour and

cultural norms has been discussed in the book by Rodgers and Standing (1981), especially in Chapter 1.

29. For the use of similar assumptions, see Granovetter (1978), and Besley and Coate (1992).

30. A different model linking adult unemployment with child labour occurs in Gupta (1997).

31. For a model of child labour and efficiency wage, see Genicot (1998).

32. The model also allows us to derive some theoretically puzzling results, such as how the abolition of a legal minimum wage can cause wages to rise. To see this, start from a minimum wage, W^*, below point E in Figure 18.2 and derive the equilibrium as done above.

33. For an overlapping-generations model of parental schooling decisions, with implications for child labour, see Glomm (1997).

34. So we are assuming that if a child works more, his productivity as an adult falls. We justify this by assuming that a child's non-working time is spent on studying. Even without this assumption one can argue that child labour diminishes adult productivity. As Pigou (1962: 751) had noted: 'Many forms of unskilled labor at present open to boys not merely fail to train, but positively un-train, their victims'. Swaminathan's (1997) study of child labour in Gujarat, India, weakly confirms this. She found that, for boys, entering the labour force as a child lowered productivity when they became adults, though for girls there was no significant effect one way or the other. It is, however, noteworthy that in some special cases this relation tends to go the other way. The English cotton mills of the last century may be a case in point. Galbi (1997) has argued that the share of child labour in the mills fell during the early nineteenth century precisely because the earlier rise in child labour meant that, as these children grew up, there would be a cohort of more productive adult workers.

35. A different kind of trap has been modelled by Eswaran (1996). In his framework the existence of the institution of child labour biases parents towards having more uneducated children rather than a few educated children. And this choice in turn perpetuates the institution of child labour.

36. It is possible to argue that in addition to the fact that an educated parent is able to educate her child, the very fact of growing up in a household in which the adults are educated confers knowledge and, therefore, increased productivity on a child. This could render the better equilibrium even more dynamic than suggested by this model. For a discussion of the externalities of literacy within a household, see Basu and Foster (1998).

37. Nardinelli argued that the use of violence was a mechanism for raising productivity, a claim that has not gone unchallenged (see Mackinnon and Johnson 1984, and Nardinelli 1984). For some contemporary accounts of coerced child labour, see Silvers (1996).

38. For useful discussions of this debate see Ellerman (1992: ch. 9) and Trebilcock (1993: ch. 4). For an outline of the debate on what constitutes sexual harassment, see Hadfield (1995).

39. See Charnovitz (1987) and Srinivasan (1996) for discussion of the roots of the labour-standards movement. For a discussion of alternative interpretations of 'labour standards' see Sengenberger and Campbell (1994).

40. The idea of compensating developing nations for adopting higher labour standards was originally contained in Ehrenberg (1994). See Krueger (1997) for discussion.
41. Note also that JG must be equal to $J'G'$.

REFERENCES

Addison, T., S. Bhalotra, F. Coulter, and C. Heady. 1997. 'Child labour in Pakistan and Ghana: A Comparative Study'. University of Warwick. Mimeo.

Agarwal, B. 1997. 'Bargaining and Gender Relations: Within and Beyond the Household'. *Feminist Economis* 3(1): 1–51.

Anderson, M. 1971. *Family Structure in Nineteenth Century Lancashire.* Cambridge: Cambridge University Press.

Angrist, J. and A. Krueger. 1991. 'Does Compulsory School Attendance Affect Schooling and Attendance?'. *Quarterly Journal of Economics* 106 (4): 979–1014.

Ashagrie, K. 1993. 'Statistics on Child Labour'. *Bulletin of Labour Statistics* 3. International Labour Organization (ILO). Geneva.

—— 1998. 'Statistics on Child Labor and Hazardous Child Labor in Brief'. Bureau of Labour Statistics, ILO. Geneva. Mimeo.

Bachman, S.L. 1995. 'Children at Work'. *Commentary, San Jose Mercury News.* 16 July.

Baland, J. and J. Robinson. 1998. 'A Model of Child Labour'. University of Namur, Belgium. Mimeo.

Banerjee, A. and A. Newman. 1993. 'Occupational Choice and the Process of Development'. *Journal of Political Economy* 101 (2): 274–98.

Bardhan, P. and C. Udry. 1999. *Development Microeconomies.* Oxford: Oxford University Press.

Basu, A. 1993. 'Family Size and Child Welfare in an Urban Slum: Some Disadvantages of Being Poor but Modern'. In Cynthia B. Lloyd ed. *Fertility, Family Size and Structure.* Population Council, New York.

Basu, K. 1994. 'The Poor Need Child Labour'. *New York Times*, 29 November.

—— 1998. 'Social Norms and the Law'. In Peter Newman ed. *The New Palgrave Dictionary of Economics and the Law.* London: Macmillan.

Basu, K. and J. Foster. 1998. 'On Measuring Literacy'. *Economic Journal* 108 (451): 1733–49.

Basu, K. and P.H. Van. 1998. 'The Economics of Child Labour'. *American Economic Review* 88 (3): 412–27.

Becker, G.S. 1964. *Human Capital.* New York: Columbia University Press.

Besley, T. and S. Coate. 1992. 'Understanding Welfare Stigma: Taxpayer Resentment and Statistical Discrimination'. *Journal of Public Economics* 48 (2): 165–83.

Bhagwati, J. 1995. 'Trade Liberalization and 'Fair Trade' Demands: Addressing the Environment and Labor Standards Issues'. *World Economy* 18 (6): 745–59.

Bhatty, K. et al. 1997. 'Class Struggle'. *India Today.* 13 October: 69–73.

Bloom, D. and W. Noor. 1996. 'Labor Standards and the Emerging World Economy'. Harvard University. Mimeo.

Bolin-Hort, P. 1989. *Work, Family, and the State: Child Labor and the Organization of Production in the British Cotton Industry, 1780–1920.* Lund: Lund University Press.

Bonnet, M. 1993. 'Child Labor in Africa'. *International Labour Review* 132 (3): 371–89.

Bourguignon, F. and P. Chiappori. 1994. 'The Collective Approach to Household

Behaviour'. In R. Blundell, I. Preston, and I. Walker, eds. *The Measurement of Household Welfare*. Cambridge: Cambridge University Press.

British Parliamentary Papers. 1968. 'Report from the Select Committee [1831–32] on the Bill to Regulate the Labour of Children in the Mills and Factories of the United Kingdom'. *Industrial Revolution: Children's Employment,* vol. 2. Shannon: Irish University Press.

Brown, D. 1998. 'A Transactions Cost Politics Analysis of International Child Labor Standards'. Tufts University. Mimeo.

Brown, M., J. Christiansen, and P. Philips. 1992. 'The Decline of Child Labor in the US Fruit and Vegetable Canning Industry: Law or Economics'. *Business History Review* 66 (4): 723–70.

Browning, M., F. Bourguignon, P. Chiappori, and V. Lechene. 1994. 'Income and Outcomes: A Structural Model of Intrahousehold Allocation'. *Journal of Political Economy* 102 (6): 1067–96.

Burra, N. 1995. *Born to Work: Child Labor in India.* Delhi: Oxford University Press.

Cain, M. T. 1977. 'The Economic Activities of Children in a Village in Bangladesh'. *Population Development Review* 3 (3): 201–27.

Cartwright, K. and H.A. Patrinos. 1998. 'Child Labor in Urban Bolivia'. In C. Grootaert and H.A. Patrinos, eds. *The Policy Analysis of Child Labor: A Comparative Study.* Manuscript. World Bank.

Chandrasekhar, C.P. 1997. 'The Economic Consequences of the Abolition of Child Labor'. *Journal of Peasant Studies* 24 (3): 137–79.

Charnovitz, S. 1987. 'The Influence of International Labour Standards on the World Trading Regime: A Historical Review', *International Labour Review* 126 (5): 565–84.

Chaudhri, D. P. 1997. 'A Policy Perspective on Child Labour in India with Pervasive Gender and Urban Bias in School Education'. *Indian Journal of Labour Economics* 40 (4): 789–808.

Chwe, M.S. 1990. 'Why Were Workers Whipped? Pain in a Principal-Agent Model', *Economics Journal* 100 (403): 1109–21.

Collingsworth, T., W. J. Goold, and P.J. Harvey. 1994. 'Time for a New Global Deal'. *Foreign Affairs.* 73 (1) 8–13.

Cunningham, H. 1990. 'The Employment and Unemployment of Children in England c. 1680–1851'. *Past and Present* 126: 115–50.

—— 1996a. 'Combating Child Labor: The British Experience'. In Cunningham and Viazzo. 1996.

Cunningham, H. and P.P. Viazzo, eds. 1996a. *Child Labor in Historical Perspective, 1800–1985: Case Studies from Europe, Japan and Colombia.* Florence: UNICEF.

—— 1996b. 'Some Issues in the Historical Study of Child Labor'. In H. Cunningham and P.P. Viazzo, eds. *Child Labor in Historical Perspective, 1800–1985: Case Studies from Europe, Japan and Colombia.* Florence: UNICEF.

Dasgupta, P. 1993. *An Inquiry into Well-Being and Destitution.* Oxford: Oxford University Press.

De Herdt, R. 1996. 'Child Labor in Belgium, 1800–1914'. In H. Cunningham and P.P. Viazzo, eds. *Child Labor in Historical Perspective, 1800–1985: Case Studies from Europe, Japan and Colombia.* Florance: UNICEF.

Dixit, A. 1998. 'Discussion of a Transactions Cost Politics Analysis of International Child Labor Standards'. Princeton University. Mimeo.

Dreze, J. and H. Gazdar. 1996. 'Uttar Pradesh: The Burden of Inertia', In J. Dreze and A.K. Sen, eds. *Indian Development: Selected Regional Perspectives.* Oxford: Oxford University Press.

Ehrenberg, R.G. 1994. *Labor Markets and Integrating National Economies.* Washington, DC: Brookings Institution.

Ellerman, D. 1992. *Property and Contract in Economics.* Cambridge, MA: Blackwell.

Eswaran, M. 1996. 'Fertility, Literacy and the Institution of Child Labor'. University of British Columbia, Vancouver. Mimeo.

Fields, G.S. 1995. 'Labor Standards and International Trade'. OECD, Paris. Mimeo,

Folbre, N. 1986. 'Hearts and Spades: Paradigms of Household Economics'. *World Development* 14 (2): 245–55.

Francois, P. 1998. 'Gender Discrimination Without Gender Difference: Theory and Policy Responses'. *Journal of Public Economics* 68 (1) 1–32.

Galbi, D.A. 1997. 'Child Labor and the Division of Labor in the Early English Cotton Mills'. *Journal of Population Economics* 10 (4): 357–75.

Galor, O. and J. Zeira. 1993. 'Income Distribution and Macroeconomics'. *Review of Economic Studies.* 60 (1): 35–52.

Genicot, G. 1998. 'An Efficiency Wage Theory of Child Labor: Exploring the Implications of Some Ideas of Leibenstein and Marx'. Economics Department Working Paper #463, Cornell University.

Glomm, G. 1997. 'Parental Choice of Human Capital Investment'. *Journal of Development Economics* 53 (1): 99–114.

Goldin, C.D. 1979. 'Household and Market Production of Families in a Late Nineteenth Century American Town'. *Explorations in Economic History* 16 (2): 111–31.

Golub, S.S. 1997. 'Are International Labor Standards Needed to Prevent Social Dumping?' *Finance Development* 34 (4): 20–5.

Granovetter, M. 1978. 'Threshold Models of Collective Behavior'. *American Journal Society* 83 (6): 1420–43.

Grootaert, C. 1998. 'Child Labor in Cote d'Ivoire: Incidence and Determinants'. In C. Grootaert and H. Patrinos, eds. *The Policy Analysis of Child Labor: A Comparative Study.* Manuscript. World Bank, Washington.

Grootaert, C. and R. Kanbur. 1995. 'Child Labour: An Economic Perspective'. *International Labour Review* 134 (2): 187–203.

Gupta, M.R. 1997. 'Unemployment of Adult Labor and the Supply of Child Labor: A Theoretical Analysis'. Jadavpur University, Calcutta. Mimeo.

—— 2000. 'Wage Determination of a Child Worker: A Theoretical Analysis'. *Review of Development Economics* 4.

Hadfield, G.K. 1995. 'Rational Women: A Test for Sex-Based Harassment'. *California Law Review* 83 (October): 1151–89.

Harkin, Sen T. 1994. 'Now Act to Ban the Products of Child Labor', Letter to the editor. *New York Times.* 5 December.

Horan, P.M. and P.G. Hargis. 1991. 'Children's Work and Schooling in the Late Nineteenth Century Family Economy'. *American Society Review* 56 (5): 583–96.

Horrell, S. and J. Humphries. 1995a. 'The Exploitation of Little Children: Child Labor and the Family Economy in the Industrial Revolution'. *Explorations in Economic History* 32 (4): 485–516.

—— 1995b. 'Women's Labor Force Participation and the Transition to the Male-Breadwinner Family, 1790–1865'. *Economic History Review* 48 (1): 89–117.

Hutchins, B.L. and A. Harrison. 1903. *A History of Factory Legislation*. London: P.S. King and Son [References to 1966 ed. by London: Cass.].

ILO. 1995. *Child Labor in Nepal: An Overview and a Proposed Plan of Action*. Geneva. ILO.

—— 1996a. *Child Labor: Targeting the Intolerable*. Geneva. ILO.

—— 1996b. *Economically Active Populations: Estimates and Projections*. 1950–2010. Geneva. ILO.

Jacoby, H.G. and E. Skoufias. 1997. 'Risk, Financial Markets, and Human Capital in a Developing Country'. *Review of Economic Studies* 64 (3): 311–35.

Jayaraj, D. and S. Subramanian. 1997. 'Child Labor in Tamilnadu: A Preliminary Account of its Nature, Extent and Distribution'. WP 151, Madras Institute of Development Studies, Chennai.

Jensen, P. and H.S. Nielsen. 1997. 'Child Labor or School Attendance? Evidence from Zambia'. *Journal of Population Economics* 10 (4): 407–24.

Knutsson, K.E. 1997. *Children: Noble Causes or Worthy Citizens?* Aldershot, UK: Ashgate Publishing.

Kothari, S. 1983. 'There's Blood on those Matchsticks: Child Labor in Sivakasi'. *Economic and Political Weekly* 18 (27): 1191–202.

Krueger, A. 1997. 'International Labor standards and Trade'. in *Proceedings Annual World Bank Conference on Development Economics 1996*. Washington: World Bank.

Kruse, D. and D. Mahoney. 1998. 'Illegal Child Labor in the United States: Prevalence and Characteristics'. NBER, WP 6479.

Kulkarni, M. 1983. 'Matchmaking Children of Sivakasi'. *Economic and Political Weekly* 18 (43): 1855–6.

Labenne, S. 1995. 'Determinants of Child Labor in India'. University Namur, Belgium. Mimeo.

Levison, D. et al. Forthcoming. 'Is Child Labor Really Necessary in India's Carpet Industry?' In R. Anker et al., eds. *Economics of Child Labor in Selected Industries of India*. New Delhi: Hindustan Publishers.

Levy, V. 1985. 'Cropping Pattern, Mechanization, Child Labor, and Fertility Behavior in a Farming Economy: Rural Egypt'. *Economic Development and Cultural Change* 33 (4): 777–91.

Lindbeck, A., S. Nyberg, and J. Weibull. 1999. 'Social Norms and Economic Incentives in the Welfare State'. *Quarterly Journal of Economics* 114 (1): 1–35.

Ljungqvist, L. 1993, 'Economic Underdevelopment: The Case of a Missing Market for Human Capital'. *Journal of Development Economics* 40 (2): 219–39.

Lyons, J. 1989. 'Family Response to Economic Decline: Handloom Weavers in Early Nineteenth-Century Lancashire'. *Review of Economic History* 12: 45–91.

Mackinnon, M. and Paul J. 1984. 'The Case Against Productive Whipping'. *Explorations in Economic History* 21 (2): 218–23.

Maharatna, A. 1997. 'Children's Work Activities, Surplus Labor and Fertility: Case Study of Six Villages in Birbhum'. *Economic and Political Weekly* 32 (7): 363–69.

Manser, M. and M. Brown. 1980. 'Marriage and Household Decision-Making: A Bargaining Analysis'. *International Economics Review* 21 (1): 31–44.

Margo, R.A. and T.A. Finegan. 1996. 'Compulsory Schooling Legislation and School Attendance in Turn of the Century America'. *Economics Letters* 53 (1): 103–10.

Marshall, A. 1920. *Principles of Economics*. 8th edn. London: Macmillan [Original pub. 1890].

Marx, K. 1954. *Capital: A Critique of Political Economy.* Moscow: Progress Publishers [Original pub. 1867].

—— 1875. *Critique of the Gotha Programme.* [References to 1938 English translation in Marx and F. Engels, *Selected Works,* vol. II, NY: International Publishers.]

Maskus, Keith E and Jill A. Holman. 1996. 'The Economics of Child Labor Standards'. Economics Department, University of Colorado Boulder. Mimeo.

McElroy, M. and M. J. Horney. 1981. 'Nash-Bargained Household Decision: Towards a Generalization of the Theory of Demand'. *International Economics Review* 22 (2): 333–49.

McKelway, A.J. 1906. 'Child Labor in the Southern Cotton Mills'. *Annals, of American Academy of Political and Social Science* 27 (2): 1–11.

Mill, J. S. 1970. *Principles of Political Economy.* Harmodsworth, UK: Penguin [Original pub. 1848].

Moehling, C. M. 1995. 'The Intrahousehold Allocation of Resources and the Participation of Children in Household Decision-Making: Evidence from Early Twentieth Century America'. Northwestern University. Mimeo.

—— 1998. 'State Child Labor Laws and the Decline of Child Labor'. Ohio State University. Mimeo.

Myers, W. 1988. 'Alternative Services for Street Children: The Brazilian Approach'. In A. Bequele and J. Boyden, eds. *Combating Child Labour.* Geneva: ILO.

Nardinelli, C. 1982, 'Corporal Punishment and Children's Wages in Nineteenth-Century Britain'. *Explorations in Economic History* 19 (3): 283–95.

—— 1984. 'The Productivity of Corporal Punishment: A Reply to Mackinnon and Johnson'. *Explorations in Economic History* 21 (2): 224–8.

—— 1990. *Child Labor and the Industrial Revolution.* Bloomington: Indian University Press.

Parsons, D. O. and C. Goldin. 1989. 'Parental Altruism and Self-Interest: Child Labor Among Late Nineteenth-Century American Families'. *Economic Inquiry* 27 (4): 637–59.

Patrinos, H. A. and G. Psacharopoulos. 1997. 'Family Size, Schooling and Child Labor in Peru'. *Journal of Population Economics* 10 (4): 387–405.

Pigou, A.C. 1962. *The Economics of Welfare.* London: Macmillan. [Original pub. 1920].

Psacharopoulos, G. 1997. 'Child Labor Versus Educational Attainment: Some Evidence from Latin America'. *Journal of Population Economics* 10 (4): 377–86.

Ray R. Forthcoming. 'Analysis of Child Labor in Peru and Pakistan: A Comparative Study'. *Journal of Population Economics.*

Riley, N.E. 1997. 'Gender, Power and Population Change'. *Population Bulletin* 52 (1): 2–48.

Rodgers, G. and G. Standing, eds. 1981. *Child Work, Poverty, and Underdevelopment,* Geneva: ILO.

Rodrik, D. 1996. 'Labour Standards in International Trade: Do They Matter and What Do We Do about Them?' Policy Essay No. 20. Overseas Development Council, Washington, DC.

—— 1997. *Has Globalization Gone Too Far?* Washington, DC: Institute for International Economics.

Rosenzweig, M.R. and R. Evenson. 1977. 'Fertility, Schooling and the Economic Contribution of Children in Rural India: An Econometric Analysis'. *Econometrica* 45 (5): 1065–79.

Saito, O. 1996. 'Children's Work, Industrialization and the Family Economy in Japan. 1872–1926'. In H. Cunningham and P.P. Viazzo, eds. *Child Labor in Historical Perspective, 1800–1985: Case Studies from Europe, Japan and Colombia*. Florence: UNICEF.

Scholliers, P. 1995. 'Grown-ups, Boys and Girls in the Ghent Cotton Industry: The Voortman Mills. 1835–1914'. *Social History*. 20 (2): 201–18.

Sen. A. K. 1990. 'Gender and Cooperative Conflict'. In I. Tinker, ed. *Persistent Inequalities*. New York: Oxford University Press.

Sengenberger, W. and D. Campbell, eds. 1994. *International Labor Standards and Economic Interdependence*. Geneva: International Institute for Labor Studies.

Silvers, J. 1996. 'Child Labor in Pakistan'. *The Atlantic Monthly*, February: 79–92.

Srinivasan, T.N. 1996. 'International Trade and Labor Standards from an Economic Perspective'. In P. van Dijck and G. Faber, eds. *Challenges to the New World Trade Organization*. The Hague: Kluwer Law International.

Strauss, J. and D. Thomas. 1995. 'Human Resources: Empirical Modeling of Household and Family Decisions'. In J. Behrman and T.N. Srinivasan, eds. *Handbook of Development Economics*. Vol. IIIA. Amsterdam: Elsevier.

Swaminathan. M. 1997. 'Do Child Workers Acquire Specialized Skills? A Case Study of Teenage Workers in Bhavnagar'. *Indian Journal of Labour Economics* 40 (4): 829–39.

Swinnerton, K. and C.A. Rogers. Forthcoming. 'The Economics of Child Labor: Comment'. *American Economic Review*.

Thomas. D. 1990. 'Intra-Household Resource Allocation: An Inferential Approach'. *Journal of Human Resources* 25 (4): 635–64.

Trebilcock. M. 1993. *The Limits of Freedom of Contract*. Cambridge, MA: Harvard University Press.

Udry, C. 1996. 'Gender, Agricultural Production and the Theory of the Household'. *Journal of Political Economy* 104 (5): 1010–46.

UNICEF. 1994. *Children at Work*, Bangkok: UNICEF East Asia and Pacific Regional Office.

US Department of Labor. 1993. *Foreign Labor Trends: International Child Labor Problems*. Washington, DC: Bureau of International Labor Affairs.

Vincent. D. 1981. *Bread, Knowledge and Freedom: A Study of Nineteenth-Century Working Class Autobiography*. London: Europa Publications.

Weiner. M. 1991. *The Child and the State in India: Child Labor and Education Policy in Comparative Perspective*. Princeton: Princeton University Press.

—— 1996. 'Child Labor in India: Putting Compulsory Primary Education on the Political Agenda'. *Economics and Political Weekly* 31 (45–46): 3007–14.

Wilkinson, F. 1994. 'Equality, Efficiency and Economic Progress: The Case for Universally Applied Equitable Standards for Wages and Conditions of Work'. In W. Sengenberger and D. Campbell, eds. *International Labor Standards and Economic Interdependence*. Geneva: International Institute for Labour Studies.

Index

INDEX ■ 313

Bangladesh, child labour and contribution
to household income 294
Bardhan, P.K. 107, 108, 123, 128, 137,
160, 293
bargaining models, of child labour, extra-
household 283–4
intra-household 280–3
Basu, Alaka 4, 53, 287, 288
Basu, K. 16, 24, 29, 54, 58, 72, 74, 75,
95, 107, 125, 142, 143, 151, 153,
163, 168, 178, 187, 192, 203, 214,
215, 217, 218, 246, 247, 252, 253,
255, 256, 257, 260, 264, 268, 276,
285, 287, 289
Becker, G.S. 268, 280
behavioural Nash equilibrium 31
Belgium, child labour in 274
Bell, Clive 6, 158
Bhaduri, A. 74
Bhagwati, J. 28, 213, 297
Bhagwati, J.N. 256
Bhardwaj, K. 147
Bhatty, K. 273
Biswanger, H. 178
Blackwell 2
Blau, P.M. 81
Bliss, C. 149, 178
Bliss, C.J. 128
Bloom, D. 297, 298
Bolin-Hort, P. 274
Bonanno, G. 159
bonded labour 200
Bonnet, M. 255
Borooah, V. 74
Bose, S.R. 135
Bottomley, A. 74
Bourguignon, F. 281
Bowman, W.S. 143, 147, 151
Brandolini, A. 16
Braverman, A. 72, 75, 142, 143, 151,
168
Breman, J. 204
'bribes' 81
Brown, D. 214, 246, 297
Brown, M. 274
Bulow, J.I. 159, 167
Burra, N. 287
business, betrayal and, co-operation in
115–16

Bytheway, W.R. 61

C-equilibrium 68, 70, 72
Cain, M. 135
Cain, M.T. 293, 294
Capital 278
'capitation fees', discriminatory fees in
schools 95
Caplow, T. 65
Card, D. 256
Carlisle, Lord 22
caste, complying with caste rules in 67
equilibrium, Akerlof's notion of 66,
67
and literacy 46
triadic model of relations in 66
casual labour market 180–4
wage and productivity in 178, 180
caucus, around the king, and coalition
69–71
Census of India 1981, on literacy 43
Charnovitz, S. 213
Chau, N.H. 218
Chaudhuri, B.B. 128
Chaudhuri, D.P. 293
Chiappori, P. 281
child labour 7–9, 28, 228, 273
adult minimum wage and 255–65,
283
aggregate and distribution of 269
in Asian and sub-Saharan Africa 215–
16
basic model of 230–6
cause, consequence and cure for 267–
302
and child abuse 227
'child work' and 302n
demand for, and supply of 235, 262,
264, 290
dynamics of 291–4
economics of 226–43
effect of partial ban on 240–2
a general model of 236–8
government intervention in 227–8,
238–42
incidence of 290, 291
international labour standards and
209
legislation in the United States 213

household consumption, and child
    labour/leisure 236
household utility functions, and labour
    247–8, 259–60, 280
human conflict, logic of 111–12
'human development' 13, 22
Humphries, J. 227
Hutchins, B.L. 273

illiteracy/ illiterates 23–4
    isolated 37, 43–5
    proximate 36–8
income, distribution and unemployment
    289–91
    'gap' measure 55
    profile of a country 17–18
India, aging population in 58–61
    land sales in 7
    literacy in 43–6
Indian Social Institute 273
industrialized nations, child labour in
    273
    protectionism policy of 28
industrial organization 6
industrial revolution, child labour during
    273
influence, concept of 79
    'men of' 79–82
informal sector, child work in 257
institutions 4–6
    and norms and power 63
    see also international organizations
interest rates, usurious, in rural areas
    142–55
interim transactions model, of market for
    land 129–34, 137, 138
interlinkage, between landlord
    moneylender and labourers 145–8,
    154–5, 168
    models of 143
    in rural markets 7, 142
    standard theorem on 146
International Labour Organization (ILO)
    211, 213, 215, 226, 267, 268, 276,
    297
    Convention 138 on child labour 269
    estimate on child work 256
international labour standards 7–9, 28–
    32, 297–300

and child labour 209, 267–302
intrahousehold externalities, in evaluating
    literacy 44, 45, 47, 48
international organizations, restructuring
    219–22
investments, adverse selection and sub-
    optimal, in rural economies 122–6
Isenman, P. 17
Ishikawa, S. 204

Jacoby, H.G. 293
Jafarey, S. 217, 246
Japan, aging population in 58–61
Jayaraj, D. 269
Johnson, D.G. 121

Kakwani, N. 54
Kaldor, N. 134
Kanbur, R. 218, 228, 229, 238, 270, 279
Kao, C.H.C. 188
Kautilya 14
Kelley, F. 213
Klemperer, P.D. 159, 170
Kothari, S. 273
Kotwal, A. 123, 193, 200
Krueger, A. 256, 274, 276
Kulkarni, M. 273
Kuroda, T. 53, 60

labour/labourer, demand for adult and
    child 237–8
    efficiency units of 179
    heterogeneity 151–3, 155
    interlinkage with credit market 15
    landlords and, see landlords
    market 72–3
        agents in 73–4
        equilibrium 233
        intervention 9
        as near-competitive 93, 94
    reaction function of 75
    standards 256–7
        codification of 213–14
        compacts, convention and codes
            for higher 211–22
        'core' 214
        recommendations for 217–18
    -tying contracts, in agriculture 137–8
    utility level of 77, 82